Tradition and
innovation

The International Library of Phenomenology and Moral Sciences

Editor: John O'Neill, *York University, Toronto*

The Library will publish original and translated works guided by an analytical interest in the foundations of human culture and the moral sciences. It is intended to foster phenomenological, hermeneutical and ethnomethodological studies in the social sciences, art and literature.

Tradition and innovation

The idea of civilization as culture and its significance

H. T. WILSON

Professor of Administrative Studies and Law
and Fellow of McLaughlin College,
York University, Toronto

Routledge & Kegan Paul

London, Boston, Melbourne and Henley

For my parents

Who showed me by their experience
the significance of familiarity and
strangeness, tradition and innovation

First published in 1984
by Routledge & Kegan Paul plc

14 Leicester Square, London WC2H 7PH, England

9 Park Street, Boston, Mass. 02108, USA

464 St Kilda Road, Melbourne,
Victoria 3004, Australia and

Broadway House, Newtown Road,
Henley-on-Thames, Oxon RG9 1EN, England

Printed in Great Britain
by Billing & Sons Ltd, Worcester

Library of Congress Cataloging in Publication Data

Wilson, H.T.

Tradition and innovation.
(The International library of phenomenology and moral
sciences)
Bibliography: p.
Includes index.
1. Progress. 2. Social institutions. 3. New, The.
4. Diffusion of innovations. 5. Tradition (Philosophy)
I. Title. II. Series.
HM101.W475 1984   303.4'4   84-3458

ISBN 0-7102-0009-9

CONTENTS

PREFACE

A book with the title 'Tradition and Innovation' implies a
strong link between the two concepts, to say the least.   One
may even be tempted to treat the distinction between tradition
and innovation as a dichotomy, rather than merely a statement
of contrast or difference.   The point about dichotomies, however, is that one side presupposes the other, and is sensible
only by reference to it.   Put another way, one side of a
dichotomy is incomplete without the other, even if each term
appears to possess a clear meaning independent of its opposite.
This interdependence is perhaps most graphically illustrated by
the fact that we think in terms of 'sides' and 'opposites' when
formulating and discussing dichotomies.   It is the notion of
the whole standing behind and rendering sensible such reference which serves to underscore the real functions of dichotomies in thought, speech, and language.   And it is the very
human tendency to empiricize dichotomies which allows them to
stand as descriptions of rather than approaches to reality.

While these points appear reasonable as far as they go, they
fail to capture the specific sense that stands behind, and perhaps helps justify, bringing tradition and innovation together
like this.   There is, after all, nothing which demands or requires that they be together beyond the writer's commitment to
generating a range of possible topics available in the title.
In fact, it is precisely my view in what follows that I am *not*
dealing in this case with what is conventionally understood as
a dichotomy at all.   I want to argue that 'innovation' as it is
used and understood today simply cannot stand with tradition,
however much we may wish to relegate tradition to the dustbin
of the past.   Far from functioning as one 'side' in a dichotomy
where its implied opposite is reason and the rational, tradition
must count for more than the non-rational and sentimental,
with all that this designation has come to mean.   A similar
point can be made with respect to tradition's presumed reference to the past.   Here tradition is equated with pre-modern
(pre-urban, pre-secular, pre-capitalist, pre-industrial) forms
of collective life.

Both assumptions favour a unilinear conception of progress
from technique and technology, where rationality is defined
by reference to human agents and resulting effects, while history is the humanly produced panorama in space and time

standing against 'nature' which results. The assumption that rationality, history and progress have superseded tradition, and the allied idea that tradition is an impediment to change, lie at the heart of the claim that tradition stultifies innovation and stupefies creativity. It is largely as a consequence of such thinking that forms of collective life which we label 'traditional' are thought of as 'primitive' 'natural' 'cultures' characterized by a fundamental absence of and aversion to innovation. In what follows I shall paint a rather different picture of the relationship between tradition and innovation in advanced industrial societies. What justifies bringing these concepts together for me is neither the assumption of their mutual exclusivity nor the derived view, underwritten by commitment to the doctrine of progress, that innovation constitutes an unqualified advance on tradition.

Instead I shall argue that our civilization is best comprehended as a culture with a set of traditions embodied in and expressed through this very commitment to rationality, history and progress. In the event, innovation and innovativeness function as contemporary code words designating this commitment as it is seen to take shape in present-day organizations, methods and protocols in these societies. Terms like discovery, invention, and innovation thus bear a clear 'family resemblance' as siblings of more global and parental concepts like rationality, history and progress. As rationality in particular is increasingly seen to repose in collective structures and processes rather than in individuals, it becomes harder and harder to distinguish them from the sort of traditional patterns of behaviour which we so often ascribe to the denizens of 'other cultures'. The very devotion of bureaucratic structures, and the societal division of labour as a whole, to organization, method and process therefore needs to be understood as a central manifestation of a culture or 'form of life' with clear traditional properties rather than an argument against this claim.

I want to suggest further that we urgently need to examine our commitment to disciplined observation and to the impartial spectator as the pre-eminent basis for gaining knowledge and improving practice. This to the end of addressing ourselves and significant cultural 'others' to the limits of this approach to knowing and doing. Central to our form of life is the assumption that there are independent facts of life which make it possible for us to describe, explain, interpret, predict and intervene. It is to disciplined observation and the idealized role model of the impartial spectator that we turn when we require facts of life for whatever purpose. Such a protocol on its own can no longer be presumed to exhibit the sort of self-evident superiority that is virtually given in our commitment to rationality, history and progress.

It is the progressive disembodiment of disciplined observation from practice and reflection which is beginning to have
such grave consequences for both.   The fact that our cultural authority is increasingly global, with so many peoples determined to accept (or unable to avoid) our values, conventions,
and institutions, makes this sort of collective self-assessment
absolutely imperative.   Any effort to address the possible
limits of these undeniably cultural properties will require us
to mobilize them, using the perspective of the outsider.   At
the same time, I shall attempt to show the insufficiency of
disciplined observation on the grounds that in its presently
disembodied and unhinged form it is not objective enough.

A major contention of this study, largely implicit in what
has been said thus far, is that innovation is a culturally specific expression and embodiment of a tradition that reaches
back to the roots of modern Western civilization itself.   From
a Weberian (and Nietzscheian) perspective, it is to be hoped
that it does not signal a culmination of this tradition as well.
At the very least, we must realize that the values, institutions
and actions that innovation stands for and embodies express,
rather than contradict, the common human pattern so central
to the thinking of sources as diverse as Vico, Tarde, Collingwood, Wittgenstein, Kroeber, and Barnett.   It is the presumptions we make about already understanding ourselves
which are, in the final analysis, a key factor in any effort to
address the limits of disciplined observation.   That our understanding of the life experience of 'other cultures' is unavoidably strained through *our own* categories and concepts, with
their roots in *our own* (usually unarticulated) daily life experiences and commonsense understandings rather than theirs,
serves to underscore the need for the sort of antidote proposed here and attempted in the text.

A final point.   The argument that civilization is a culture is
thoroughly compatible as it stands with the position of social
evolutionists like Spencer, Sumner, and Frazer, who believed
that the West was more advanced than the rest of humankind
in an *evolutionary*, rather than simply a technological, sense.
It will be obvious in what follows that I do not subscribe to
any view which extrapolates from technological pre-eminence,
however indisputable, to evolutionary superiority as they did.
Technical mastery, as Weber and Wittgenstein both pointed out,
is rather a core value, an archetypal cultural property, a central element in our collective conscience, not something standing in irretrievable opposition to this conscience, as Durkheim
claimed.

ACKNOWLEDGMENTS

This work was greatly assisted by a sabbatical from York University, Toronto, and a leave fellowship grant by the Social Sciences and Humanities Research Council of Canada. Special thanks go to Mrs Kirsten Semple for superb manuscript typing, Mrs Donna Armborst for careful corrections and revisions to the final draft, and to Trinity College, Dublin, and the Institute of Public Administration of Ireland in particular for research and related kinds of assistance.

What stand should one take? Has 'progress' as such a recognizable meaning that goes beyond the technical, so that to
serve it is a meaningful vocation? The question must be
raised. But this is no longer merely the question of man's
calling *for* science, hence, the problem of what science as a
vocation means to its devoted disciples. To raise this question is to ask for the vocation of science within the total life
of humanity. What is the value of science?

Weber

Simple though it may sound, we can express the difference
between science and magic if we say that in science there is
progress but not in magic. There is nothing in magic to
show the direction of any development.

Wittgenstein

Savages are no more exempt from human folly than civilized
men, and are no doubt equally liable to the error of thinking
that they, or the persons they regard as their superiors, can
do what in fact cannot be done. But this error is not the
essence of magic. It is a perversion of magic. And we
should be careful how we attribute it to the people we call
savages, who will one day rise up and testify against us.

Collingwood

The scientific rationalities are neither stable features nor sanctionable ideals of daily routines, and any attempt to stabilize
these properties or to enforce conformity to them in the conduct of everyday affairs will magnify the senseless character
of a person's behavioural environment and multiply the disor-
ganized features of the system of interaction.

Garfinkel

A whole mythology is deposited in our language.

Wittgenstein

CHAPTER 1

Reconaissance

INTRODUCTION

My inspiration for undertaking the inquiry which follows is
well-captured in the following statement, attributed to
Wittgenstein:

> Our civilization is characterized by the word progress.
> Progress is its form: it is not one of its properties that it
> progresses. It is typical of it that it is building, con-
> structing. Its activity is one of constructing more and
> more complex structures. And even clarity serves this
> end, and is not sought on its own account. For me on
> the other hand clarity, lucidity, is the goal-sought. (1)

What will become readily apparent once into the main body of
the text is my ambivalent attitude to this statement. On the
argument that 'progress' is its form rather than one of the
properties of modern Western civilization I would agree, and
suggest that 'innovation' could readily be substituted for progress in the first sentence. In a sense innovation and innovativeness constitute the tail end of the modern ideology of
progress, conceptually speaking, and perhaps indicate some
small amount of the contemporary disillusionment with all that
this effort and commitment has entailed.

As for the claim that even clarity serves goals external to
it, whilst for philosophy proper clarity is none other than the
goal itself, I am less certain. To be sure, clarity in the
field of knowledge (or knowledge-claims) often does serve the
interests of building and constructing more and more complex
structures. Indeed, clarity frequently justifies the presence
of complex 'structures' in thought as well as in life by providing the 'means' for reducing such structures to their
apparent constituent parts. Wittgenstein had provided off-
hand support for this claim in 'Tractatus Logico-Philosophicus',
with its doctrine of logical atomism and the so called picture-
theory of language, some fifteen years before making the
statement cited. At the same time, it must be clear that for
Wittgenstein the goal of clarity and lucidity as its own justification was intended to function as a *constraint* on the tendency to generate such complex structures in the field of
philosophy. His assertion to the effect that 'anything that

1

can be said can be said clearly', coupled with his logical
atomism and consequent view of 'the world' as a physical,
natural realm, would argue for simplicity (clarity and lucidity)
in thought as a necessary reflection of his view of the world
as well as a corrective applicable to the thinking of others.

This reflection is a direct copy like a 'picture' or photo-
graph however, rather than being mediated by the subject
who for Wittgenstein constitutes not a part of the world but a
limit to it. (2)   Thus the world so understood is itself reducible to its constituent 'atoms', and the goal of clarity and
lucidity expresses the simplicity achieved (or achievable) by
such a reduction when it functions as its own justification
rather than a means to some object outside and beyond it,
whether 'progress', innovation or something else.   In effect,
the world can be ex-plained simply and clearly because of the
fact that a far greater (and far more important) part of life is
inexplicable.   'The world' is nothing more than that small
fraction of life and living which 'is all that is [or can be] the
case.' (3)   What is abstracted out of life in this fashion is
defined not simply by reference to quantity as something that
is simple, at least in its constituents, thus capable of being
described (therefore ex-plained) clearly and lucidly.   This
'world' is what in a sense might be said to remain after life
had been thoroughly de-enchanted and demystified. (4)

Such a tack might be one way of addressing the fact that
Wittgenstein, like Weber before him, could only speak to
values, ethics, aesthetics, religion and the mystical if he had
already stepped out of life and had succeeded in reaching
some Archimedean point from whence it would be possible to
(in Nietzsche's sense) valorize values.   But this could only
mean that this detached and disciplined observer had transvalued value, thereby providing the basis for bringing the
unsayable and unutterable into the world as 'values', etc.
themselves. (5)   Wittgenstein understood this ultimate paradox of 'Tractatus Logico-Philosophicus' when he admitted in
his penultimate remark that 'My propositions serve as elucida-
tions in the following way: anyone who understands me eventually recognizes them as nonsensical....' (6)   It is precisely
the lack of clarity and lucidity present in attempts to address
these allegedly unsayable matters, then, which 'reflects' the
fact that they are terribly complex, utterly unsimple, therefore beyond description and explanation.

My difficulty with Wittgenstein's conception of philosophy
would employ his own idea of limit to ask how one can arbitrarily bifurcate the sayable from the unsayable in this
fashion, taking no cognizance of man's essential nature as both
a cultural and historical animal, and go on to effectively say
what cannot be said.   What makes the 'Tractatus' 'nonsensical'

is the fact that it has no choice but to transgress its own conception of limit in order to posit its reality as the boundary separating facts from values, or rather (following Schopenhauer) representation from will. What is stated to be the limit is only a boundary because one would have to be on both sides of it to 'know' it as limit, yet the result of this very achievement could only contradict the idea of limit itself in favour of boundary. None the less, it must be admitted that Wittgenstein's view of the subject as a limit may effectively transcend the distinction between 'inner' and 'outer' altogether. This would render sensible the following question posed in 'Tractatus Logico-Philosophicus': 'Where in the world is a metaphysical subject to be found?' (7)

A more central complaint directly relevant to my topic would begin by arguing that 'the world' of 'Tractatus' is too circumscribed to include any of the problems which I, no less than Wittgenstein, consider to be paramount in human life. For me, this particular world achieves its simplicity, thereby compelling clear and lucid descriptions and explanations, at a price which is thoroughly unacceptable. It is precisely because of their 'complexity' that these problems are simultaneously accorded the highest significance and alleged to be unspeakable even though they are clearly thinkable. This point poses difficulties for Wittgenstein given his earlier claim in 'Tractatus' that: 'What is thinkable is possible too' where 'A thought is a proposition with a sense.' (8) One is reminded of Max Weber's plight, given the consequences of such an acultural and ahistorical posture for a civilization which all too often by this particular reckoning seems to 'value' facts more than values. I would submit that it is precisely their 'complexity' which demands that we address them the best way we can in the interests of life, even if this means that we fail to meet criteria of clarity and lucidity appropriate to 'the world' as a narrowly defined aggregation of simple (and logically reducible) constituents which we 'picture' to ourselves.

This does not mean that I am any the less committed to an ideal of clarity and lucidity than Wittgenstein in what follows. I only argue that there is a point beyond which the individual (in contrast to the collectivity of individuals) cannot go in his commitment to this self-justifying goal. Indeed I would submit that the lack of clarity which may be argued to characterize parts of what follows is often a function of what is being attempted where issues of great moment are being addressed. To the extent that I insist that such matters properly constitute a part of reality, rather than something totally distinct from it, the very achievement of clarity and lucidity could be seen as a way of avoiding reality. Far from constituting a 'mirror' or 'picture' of reality, then, such clarity and lucidity would be 'unreal' in the extreme, because it would relegate all matters placed under the heading of values, or the ethical, aesthetic, religious, or mystical to the unsayable, even though they are both thinkable and speakable. In light of the foregoing it is hardly surprising that the remarks of both Weber and Wittgenstein pertaining to these matters were so often misinterpreted, even to the point of suggesting that the primacy of the factual and describable over the unsayable and transcendent was a central feature of their respective arguments.

'Innovation', like 'progress', is a concept which expresses our reality as a culturally and historically specific form of life. To say that it expresses our reality is to point to the difference between naming and describing. Here it is the different nature of the knowledge and knowing present in naming and describing which is at issue in addressing the phenomenon of innovation. We can describe *an* innovation, but efforts to get beyond particular examples in pursuit of the phenomenon that stands behind and allows us to know these examples lead invariably to definitions. Thus innovations can be seen in retrospect to possess the sort of novelty that results from a restructuring and recombining of already existing properties and activities. Innovation as such is therefore qualitatively new only in the sense that it is more than an addition of parts which yields mere quantitative variation. (9)

This only serves to underscore the universalistic character of concepts. Concepts address realities which are beyond the capacity of either descriptions or formal definitions to capture. Even formal definitions like the one provided of innovation only point to the common properties and activities that particular already-described instances are seen to exhibit. It may seem paradoxical to argue, as I do in this chapter, that concepts are more than the definitions that seek to capture the reality they address yet incapable of grasping and absorbing their objects. Nevertheless, it is through precisely this realization that we are able to reconcile the power and limits of thought relative to life. The concept shows its power by addressing its limits, and it is in this address that we understand why thought cannot rest content with any programme like that proposed in 'Tractatus Logico-Philosophicus' which would restrict that which can be known to what can be described and formally defined.

Both these claims demand that certain key dichotomies be taken to correspond to reality, something which I direct my critical attention to in the text. In particular, I refuse to honour the distinction between thought and action on which practically all idealist philosophy, even Wittgenstein's, is based. It must be clear that a major way of acknowledging

just such a distinction is to restrict the sayable so that what
is thought to be unsayable will be held as 'values', etc. and
directed to action in life which reflects a decision of the willing subject who limits the world. The author believes that
it was one of Wittgenstein's great disappointments to have to
give up the possibility that ethical action might take the place
of ethical talk in life. This because of the way that such
talk regularly functioned as a substitute for ethical
action. (10) Unwillingness to acknowledge man's character
as a cultural and historical animal acted as a further support
for Wittgenstein's tendency to treat life as a whole whose
reality was given in the rigid bifurcation between thought and
action. Though the interpretation of the term 'nonsensical'
formulated by the logical positivists may be said to have
missed the point of the 'Tractatus', the rigid distinction
between thought and action does serve to support the view
that men possess something like an innate ethical sense which
is transcultural and transhistorical. The further fact that
reason and rationality are restricted to activities which are
sayable argues for decisionism in the ethical sphere for both
Weber and Wittgenstein.

From what has been said thus far, it must be apparent that
I am at least as concerned about 'tradition' as I am about
'innovation' in the title of this study. It is precisely because
I see no way of addressing 'innovation' as a cultural concept
and form without engaging in thought and theorizing, as distinct from both life, and the disciplined observation of life,
that the 'traditional' properties of innovation per se will figure
prominently in what follows. I do not begin with the idea
that 'innovation' can be brought into the world as a phenomenon which is nameable and describable (or definable) at the
outset, not because this is impossible but because if I do it I
will find it virtually impossible to address topics that any sensitivity to the phenomenon which the concept is addressing
seems to cry out for. Of equal importance is the point that,
had I taken this tack, I would have once again succeeded in
fetishizing Western development, and Western values - including 'progress' and 'innovation'. I want neither to impose
such a version, nor to accomplish its other side, namely, the
argument that innovativeness is non-problematic because, after
all, it is (and has been) everywhere, that is, all 'cultures',
past and present, exhibit it.

I want instead to mobilize the concept of innovation in order
to address the scope and limits of what *it* can speak to as a
code word. Not only what values it bespeaks or embodies,
then, but how I can address its limits by showing the problems given in the commitment to it in operation. As a cultural concept, unawareness of this fact poses unique difficulties for a civilization in which, while not necessarily equally

distributed, it is nevertheless in principle 'available' as a
resource to those socially produced 'individuals' whose very
innovativeness is seen to constitute evidence of the *success*
of this socialization effort rather than speak to its limits.
This is one way in which it makes clear and unambiguous
sense to speak of innovation as a cultural form rather than
simply a property of a culture which characterizes itself as a
'civilization', where this distinction is seen to reflect the developmental superiority of the latter to the former. (11)   In
what follows, I try to transcend the present tendency to
either fetishize 'development', given its instantiation of a
technical bias and an unhinged observation function, or to
treat innovation as a non-problematic property readily available in all cultures, past and present, thus needing only
adequate description by the observer.

'Innovation' is therefore both my origin and my goal.   It is
an occasion for thought and thinking in the interests of practice given its central ideological and solidaristic function in
the advanced societies.   No attempt to employ it to speak to
the limits of societies which have installed it can ignore
what is alleged to be 'other' to it.   And the fact that it
stands somewhere between the sayable and unsayable makes it
more, not less, important as a cultural concept.

CRISIS AS OPPORTUNITY

The Chinese, I am told, have two symbols for crisis, the first
denoting danger and the second opportunity.   In what follows
I view a focus on innovation as an opportunity precipitated by
a 'crisis'.   In pointing to crisis in this way, I do not thereby
endorse the authority of the term as something which 'corresponds' to objective reality.   I only signify acceptance of
the idea of crisis as an important tool in Western bourgeois
thinking.   It 'makes sense' of a situation that significant elements of the articulate population, including many 'intellectuals', believe they are experiencing.   To me, a crisis suggests or presupposes two things.   First, the potential for
development within a given social formation has shown itself
in and through this very process to possess some unanticipated and unexpected aspects which appear to challenge or even
negate the preferred features of this development.   But
second, these events, though acknowledged to be one manifestation of a development process beneficent in most of its
aspects rather than something external to this process, are
not seen to be irreversible or incontrovertible.   Indeed, few
things in bourgeois thought as a whole are more significantly
paradoxical for an understanding of development as a process
than the uneasy equipoise its advocates achieve between the
apparent determinism and materialism of the first presupposi-

tion and the idealism and commitment to 'free will' of the second. I have tried elsewhere to show how and why this paradox is so central, even necessary, to idealistic thinking in particular. (12)

When I view a focus on innovation as an opportunity I am not therefore endorsing anything beyond the fact that this alleged crisis of advanced industrial societies is very closely related to my concern (and that of others) with innovation. One could go further than this and argue that the clear concern for all aspects of innovation and innovativeness at the present time is a direct response to the alleged crisis itself. It is nothing less than a central mode of response to the allegation of crisis by key individuals, groups and institutions in the advanced societies. The language of crisis becomes virtually synonymous in certain settings with the view that we are experiencing a crisis in innovation, invention, discovery, creativity, and leadership. This is the way the crisis is understood, and it is also the way that it may be overcome: innovation, broadly speaking, or more (or different kinds of) innovation. John Gardner, for example, sees society as a mechanistic aggregation of individuals who have to be renewed as individuals in order for the 'innovative society' to emerge. Gardner feels that this required renewal is only comprehensible as *self-renewal*, and that, paradoxically, the only possible way to realize the desired result given his (bourgeois) commitment to individualism is for the society to provide a 'hospitable environment', and 'produce men and women with the capacity for self-renewal'. He points to the 'discoveries' of social and psychological research in order to justify his claim that people can continue to achieve self-renewal long beyond the time when they normally 'fall into a stupor of mind and spirit'. (13)

This kind of thinking is something which I am determined to address critically in what follows. Innovation, or rather 'innovation', is therefore an 'opportunity' for me in a sense quite different from what might be expected. I want to try to show the scope and limits of the idea of innovation, in order to see how much it can hold of what I (and others) want to say. It thus constitutes an opportunity not to address a crisis with its solution, where the only problem is to be discovered in finding the technically correct 'means' to the desired objective (innovation), and where this objective is itself a means to social, economic, cultural and political 'ends'. Innovation is as much a problem because of the way its contemporary understanding conceives of 'problem' as it is a way of speaking simultaneously to the problem and its solution. Indeed, one could make a strong case for the claim that the latter way of conceptualizing the problem is false inasmuch as it assumes that the problem must be formulated in

ways which effectively *presuppose* its solution.   Only by formulating the problem in a way which does not presuppose
resolution would the problem itself be conceivable as a 'real'
problem.   Otherwise, the availability of its solution in the
very definition of the problem qua problem (crisis;   innovation) suggests that the solution itself, as well as the problem,
is false because it can be achieved without surpassing or
overcoming the problem.   Solution is achieved by reconcep-
tualizing the problem as a crisis, where by crisis is meant a
problem with a solution given in (rather than rendered impossible by) the very structure of thinking which both acknowledges determinism and sees it adequately dealt with by 'free
will'.

ADDRESSING /DESCRIBING

I have distinguished between innovation and 'innovation' not
to be obtuse, but rather in order to contrast the prevailing
problem-solving orientation with my approach.   In the first
case it is assumed that we already have the phenomenon in
hand as a nameable and describable state of affairs discoverable in 'the world'.   Thus we talk about innovation, on the
assumption that knowledge-claims can only be made if we can
assert precisely what it constitutes as a state of affairs.
Here knowledge and knowing are comprehended by reference
to a set of metaphors appropriate to the polar dichotomies of
scarcity and surplus.   Operative analogies regarding knowledge act as if it were a tangible commodity to be grasped,
appropriated, accumulated, even reproduced and renewed like
the harvest of nature.   To know about innovation is to be
able to describe what it is and ex-plain how one finds/gener-
ates it.   In addition, however, the emphasis on accumulation
in particular points not to general acquisitiveness as an
alleged 'innate' characteristic of the human animal, but to
capitalism as an historically specific form of acquisitiveness
premised on surplus creation through saving and investment
as well as through labour and effort.   Knowledge can be
stored up, but it is increasingly necessary to condition this
point with a proviso which stresses not only accumulation
rather than easy spending once grasped or appropriated, but
renewal.   The crisis and its solution given in innovation as
the scarce commodity requires that we produce or generate it
on the assumption that it is in ever shorter supply, in part
because of our need for it but also because we have spent the
surplus of it we once (potentially) had. (14)

The determination to produce innovation or innovative individuals presumes that the problem of description on which explanation depends is really no problem at all, while I would
argue that, properly put, the problem is a central one for

our culture as a form of life.   I agree that description is
absolutely necessary as a precondition but submit that the
reason that innovation is a problem is that it is a code word
for something we think we need, put in contemporary par-
lance, but something we cannot in fact comprehend in and
through the activity of describing particular innovations at
all.   The question then becomes whether we can say anything
about it once we admit to the fact that the problem of innovation is really our inability to capture in descriptions of it
what we can in one sense know by name. (15)   Wittgenstein
would argue, at least in 'Tractatus', that our inability to
'really' describe it would preclude our knowing it by
name. (16)   On the other hand, the Wittgenstein of the
'Philosophical Investigations' would contradict his earlier work
by arguing against the claim that the limits of logic are the
limits of knowledge.   'If you are surprised that one can know
something and not be able to say [*viz.* describe it], you are
perhaps thinking of a case like the first.   Certainly not of
one like the third.'   The first case, 'how many feet high
Mont Blanc is', is to be contrasted to the third, 'how a clari-
net sounds'. (17)   My point is that prevailing conceptions of
knowledge and knowing equate innovation with the first case,
whereas I would claim it to be far closer to the third.

To thus say that things can be known by being named even
though they cannot be understood through descriptions and
formal definitions is to shift the burden of the exercise away
from description/explanation/intervention/anticipation/produc-
tion toward an effort to address the phenomenon qua phenomenon.   Initially it seemed sensible to argue that in consequence of this difficulty regarding comprehension, I would
have to say that we can know things that do not exist, where
by existence was meant the capacity to be *both* named and
described.   But such a formulation simply served to show the
serious limits of a non (or anti)-dialectical understanding.
The issue should rather have been put this way: one moment
of the whole requires us to define existence narrowly, e.g.
physically so that 'the world' is limited to the nameable and
describable as in 'Tractatus'.   Only by contrasting the world
and the whole in this fashion would it be reasonable to say
that we cannot know things that don't exist.   However, in
the other moment of this whole it and the world become one
and the same.   In this case the world is not understood as
that which exists for the observer outside and apart from
him;   it clearly comprehends him in its proper conception.
What makes this latter conception so significant is the fact
that it is both the 'other side' of the empiricist view dependent on correspondence requirements and the moment that
renders both sides dialectically momentous. (18)

Seen in this light we are not only authorized to say that we

can know what we cannot describe but can only name, but
also that if 'existence' is to make sense given these points
then what we know must be included in what exists.   Any
narrower conception of existence is too restrictive and can
only be justified where a reflexive understanding is being
sacrificed to strategic and interventionist concerns.   One
might be better advised, however, to say *immediate* strategic
and interventionist concerns in this case, if only because I
would argue that successful interventions probably depend at
least as much on the imperative need for greater reflection as
on the demand for piecemeal or incremental approaches such
as Popper has recommended. (19)   Indeed, it is precisely
Popper's significant shift away from a strict correspondence
conception of reality, and knowledge about it, in his earlier
work, toward the view of a 'third world' (World three) con-
sisting of the products of the human mind, which helps us
see one way that we could know things that either didn't exist
or that existed in a way which did not depend on their description.   True, Popper totally abjures a dialectical understanding in his commitment to simply adding a third category
to the two which have been provided for modernity by Cartesian rationalism: physical objects (World one) and mental attributes (World two).   Popper's conception of World three is
plainly reminiscent of Hegel's notion of 'alienation of mental
property to totality' discussed in one of the early sections
(nos 43-6) of 'The Philosophy of Right', a point of considerable significance given Popper's uncontrolled outburst against
Hegel in 'The Open Society and Its Enemies'.

Popper's argument regarding 'the objectivity and autonomy
of world three' is concerned to establish the difference
between mental states and 'the structure of the products' of
thought. (20)   In a way it is compatible with earlier claims
which he made in support of the role of theories and concepts
in his attack on induction.   His argument is particularly
effective when addressed to the relationship between a reader
and a book.   A two-world view would hold that what we have
here is simply a reader (mental states) and a physical object
with print, etc.   But Popper disagrees: the book 'contains
objective knowledge, true or false, useful or useless;   and
whether anybody ever reads it and really grasps its contents
is almost accidental.' (21)   Another supporting instance might
be provided by the situation in which several centuries from
now, someone discovers a 'time-capsule' which contains a book.
While Popper admits that his argument for World three requires
that there be at least one person in principle capable of deci-
phering and understanding the book, this in no wise justifies
a view which treats the book as a mere physical object in the
absence of an interpreter.   Popper's notion of World three
comprehends all products of the human mind, whether ideas,
concepts, theories, problems, 'knowledge', etc. or tangible
artifacts constructed by men.

Perhaps the most important feature of World three for our
purposes, however, is its alleged autonomy, the fact that even
though its 'objects' come about as the result of human activity,
planned or unplanned, conscious or otherwise, 'it creates in
its turn, as do other animal products, its own *domain of
autonomy*.' (22)   It acquires a life of its own for men, and the
signal difference between human and non-human products is
that the products of the human mind include ideas, theories,
etc.   Popper's further point about the role of language and
the uniquely human concerns expressed in language's 'higher
functions', namely the descriptive and the argumentative,
simply serves to underscore the unfinished character of both
efforts.   Without descriptive languages there can be no
objects for discussion; thus the descriptive function is a
prerequisite for the argumentative one which Popper believes
to lie at the root of man's problem-solving orientation-
criticism. (23)   My differences with Popper on this score
would include my unwillingness to view description itself as
something which the presence of what he calls descriptive
language resolves.   What the insuperable problem of description leads to, however, is not stupefaction but rather the
view that we can know things in ways that are beyond the
capacity of descriptions to capture, and therefore that do not
exist in the narrow sense of the term.   Innovation as a phenomenon to be addressed slips right through our fingers when
we try to capture or grasp it as a describable state of affairs
discoverable under correspondence rules in some empirical
world of causes, effects, and ex-planations. (24)   But this
does not thereby render innovation so understood 'irrational',
nor should it justify invoking science as the paragon case as
Popper does.

REFERENTIAL AND CONDENSATION SYMBOLS

The idea of an empirical world made up of nameable and describable states of affairs whose relationship to one another as
parts of a whole can be 'ex-plained' in terms of causes and
effects trades heavily on the distinction first formulated by
Sapir between referential and condensation symbols.   The
first is intended to inform, the second to generate an emotion-
al response in the listener, and both are looked at as key
functions of human language. (25)   One aspect of the contemporary crisis voiced in terms of the issue of innovation
would compel me to argue that 'innovation' has become far too
important for its emotive effect precisely because attempts to
point to referents lead at best to descriptions.   But surely
this downplays or ignores the way that certain terms and concepts become 'buzz words' whose function is neither descriptive nor hortatory, but rather solidaristic or group (class,
occupation, etc.) binding.   Usage itself is a signal of either

'membership' or some related notion of awareness performing a
similar, if less specific, function.   This would seem to be
what has really happened to innovation as a concept once intended to hold knowledge as well as represent a dilemma.   It
is precisely this problem of referential content which has led
its users to employ it in a two-faced way.   Its real function,
what Merton might have called its 'latent' function, is to help
bind individuals into groups by acting as a code word indicating insider status, while its alleged or 'manifest' function is
to convey information of a descriptive kind. (26)

   I want to preserve the term as a concept because I believe
it could convey relevant meaning, but only if examined reflex-
ively.   It is therefore problematic that the only options open
to such terms in a world which has empiricized dichotomies
emerging out of the man/nature and mind/body distinctions
(e.g. subject/object, ends/means, and, most significantly,
values and facts) is to function either referentially in the
narrow sense cited earlier (facts, states of affairs) or conden-
sationally (values).   If all that remains after an empirical
(nameable/describable) world has been formulated is values,
emotions, etc., then the distinction between mind and body,
thus of mental and physical states, becomes the basis of the
subject/object distinction.   Here the subject's mind is equated
with value, emotion and unreason while objective reality is
understood to be coterminous with physical objects and their
relationships as describable states of affairs.   Furthermore,
wherever it goes, reason, though acknowledged in weak
moments to be the property of the subject, increasingly seems
to harbour itself outside the individual in allegedly objective
'structures' standing apart from him.   Reason is gradually
reformulated as rationality by social science as disciplined
observation, with the result that reason becomes synonymous
with 'rational' organization, structure and process 'outside'
him. (27)   Popper's notion of World three is of great value in
addressing the clear insufficiency of such dichotomies, even
though he only adds a third world rather than challenging the
idea of empiricizing dichotomies by once again rendering them
dialectically momentous as topics.

   It is difficult nowadays to take issue with the claim that
there increasingly appears to be an inverse relation between
use of the term 'innovation' and the presence of the phenomenon the term is supposed to correspond to.   It is not unlike
the university situation in which periodic requirements of updated curriculum vitae from professors come to impede the
work which the CV is intended to record, particularly when
one considers the organizational requirement as one which
demands a continuing written inventory (and the requisite
state of mind) of exactly what one is doing.   The term innovation is *intended* to address an incomprehensible phenomenon,

and movement either in the direction of reduction to a describable state of affairs or to 'buzz-word' status will not deal
with the problem. In the first case, it is by such a reduction that the notion of innovation as a describable state of
affairs is created. This commitment to description, in turn,
is understood to be a precondition to any effort to generate
or produce innovativeness. The whole is viewed as an
abstract concatenation of concrete particulars in the form of
events, whose status as facts derives from their ex-planation
in terms of causes and effects. It is precisely explanation,
and particularly causal explanation, which provides the basic
model for production and generation, since it must be external
to its effect, or at least treated as external to its effect given
a narrow notion of the world as empirically observable. (28)

As for the idea of innovation as a code word, the problem
with the above dichotomy is precisely the fact that this idea
has no place to go but under the category of condensation
symbol. This notion is itself a 'symbol' for all forms of
activity and feeling which fail to satisfy narrow logical criteria
setting the standard for what can reasonably be said to be
'part of' the world. If the first understanding wants to
place it in World one - the world of physical objects - this
one seeks to 'reduce' innovation (and related terms) in the
opposite direction - in the direction of World two - the world
of mental states. I would want to include such terms in a
broader understanding of World three, accepting Popper's
proviso that there must be at least one other individual
besides the speaker who could in principle know what it
means. The idea of innovation, to be sure, starts out as a
mental notion which is seen to correspond to something in the
world, but it becomes autonomous and independent at precisely the point at which it is no longer anchored exclusively in
such an understanding. Thus the fact that it has been reduced in the two directions indicated should not serve to support the claim that innovation cannot possibly be viewed as a
product of the mind. Indeed, what makes innovation and related terms so significant is precisely the fact that they constitute a product of the mind addressed to products of the
mind. Such terms show the limits of description by showing
what is lost when a phenomenon is described, and by pointing
to what happens to what is left once description has been
achieved.

Another way of looking at this would be to contrast the
initial dependence of innovation on innovations where an empirical world is in control of the proceedings, with the situation in which the term can stand on its own. Here 'innovation' can hold distinct innovations, innovativeness, innovative
behaviour, etc.; it is a substantive denoting process and
function, individual and collective behaviour, past, present

and (contemplated) future activities.   The term holds all
this plus a genuine 'value' commitment to innovation as
opposed to its 'other'.   This means that the issue of values
or the normative, whether implied or made explicit in the way
the term is employed, may conceivably be discovered within
its various uses, but in no wise is one warranted in categor-
izing it as a 'condensation' symbol as a consequence.   Distinctions built upon such dichotomies draw their strength
from an empirical conception of reality where the parts are
real (viz. 'concrete') and the whole which is (or can be) concatenated out of this aggregation abstract.   To bring innovation into 'the world' so understood means describing what innovation is, or, rather, employing language in its descriptive
dimension.   I would argue for bursting the bounds of such
false (e.g. empiricized) dichotomies because these distinctions
simply are incapable of holding all that 'innovation' really
stands for. (29)

Thus it is not the pragmatic problem of seizing upon some
'operational' definition as a prelude to conducting a search for
the phenomenon now tentatively described.   The illusion of
an instrumental approach like this depends heavily upon the
preliminary power of the operational (or related) definition,
for this latter convention conveniently masquerades as a description for all respectable (re)search purposes but can be
thrown in the bin virtually at will.   Few things more clearly
point to the impotence of the social sciences and related disciplines than their inability to really stand against society by
challenging these variations on Max Weber's 'rationalistic bias',
expressed in and through his reliance on 'ideal types' for purposes of 'methodological convenience.' (30)   Operational definitions are perhaps the most convenient techniques of all for
giving vent to this allegedly 'objective' rationalistic bias in
the social sciences.   Here the real (if not avowed) purpose
of these formal definitions is to self-destruct on the completion of the study in question.   There is a premium placed on
the practice of individual customizing in such cases, for the
object is to come up with a new formulation rather than to
work through established notions.   Far from arguing for
clarity and development in dealing with the problem of description, this practice attests to the way that formal prelimi-
naries can be used to avoid (or sabotage) the problem altogether.   The possibility of description is not only no longer
problematic;   the definition itself provides what is alleged to
be a tentative, perhaps even a conclusive, description on its
own. (31)

NOMINAL AND REAL DEFINITIONS

A final point needs to be mentioned before I turn to a discussion of the concept, one hinted at in what I just said. The distinction between nominal and real definitions provides what is perhaps the clearest instance of a contrast which proceeds out of the idea of 'the world' as a nameable and describable state of affairs whose empirical character ordains that the parts be concrete and the whole abstract. Indeed, it is the preliminary view, shared by all empiricists, that definitions appertain to concepts and descriptions to phenomena in the world which I need to look at carefully in what follows. I shall try to show further on how this arbitrary delineation of the world, which honours only descriptions under a correspondence requirement, and banishes concepts to the observer's mental apparatus where they must be reduced to definitions, is at the root of the confusion. Before doing this, however, I need to sketch out the essentials of Bierstedt's argument, directed as it is to the difference between nominal and real definitions and the consequences of this difference for sociological theory. (32)

After contrasting two sets of antagonists, one contemporary, one ancient, on the matter of the arbitrariness or tentativity of definitions and their correspondence to phenomena or events in the 'real' world, Bierstedt attempts to mediate their respective claims. What he does is to both agree and disagree with each side, saying that advocates of the arbitrariness/tentativity position are correct if they are talking about 'nominal' definitions, while those who believe that definitions are not mere research protocols but correspond to what they address, or 'mean what they say' are correct if they have in mind 'real' definitions. Bierstedt effectively endorses an empiricist view of the world as an 'other' to be 'found out', that is, as something that could be (and is) 'all that is (or could be) the case'. The bias in this distinction clearly favours real definitions because of (1) what 'real' must mean relative to its opposite and (2) the way that nominal definitions, however sensible at the time for all socially sanctionable research purposes, necessarily 'function' vis à vis the desired outcome. Bierstedt is unabashedly a proponent of the interventionist approach, thus the view which supports 'theory' only in the form of testable/falsifiable hypotheses, however much he criticizes the 'rather odd emphasis that would make theory subordinate to research'. To this possible problem, Bierstedt simply offers us another dichotomy: between metasociological and sociological, or methodological and substantive, theory. (33)

The point here is that 'real' (e.g. valuable, productive) theory is once again equated with the 'sociological' and 'substantive', while their respective complements are looked at in the first case as the real thing with a speculative modifier ('meta'), and in the second as mere procedure or technology relative to what it is able to effect ('methodological').   Who could doubt the consequences, if not the intentions, of such distinctions, when one version of theory is referred to as 'substantive'?   Regardless of what Bierstedt intends by such a classificatory scheme, it is quite clear that his attempt to be 'fair-minded', and provide a 'balanced' view, only serves to underscore the points made earlier regarding the empiricist bias, with its commitment to the concrete particular (part-as-fact-as-event) and the abstract whole (collectives; relations; structures) allegedly concatenated out of these particulars. His notion of intervention necessarily depends on this set of presuppositions because for him it is the only thing which really justifies theoretical work in the social sciences, his protestations to the contrary notwithstanding.   As evidence in support of this claim, simply reflect on the distinctions as he has chosen to formulate them.   What sanctions 'nominal' definitions is precisely their possible, and hoped for, pro-ducts: they are ideally a *means* to real definitions.   Their necessity is accepted retrospectively in the light of what they promise: a set of probabilistic generalizations whose explana-tory character has carried the so-called definition to (and per-haps even beyond) what any social scientist would prefer to call a tentative *description* of phenomena as events in 'the world'. (34)

Bierstedt is committed to the idea that reality is coterminous with the real definitions which are generated out of research protocols that in turn depend on nominal definitions.   These real definitions are alleged to correspond to what they address, and therefore depend on precisely the distinction between life and the world that Wittgenstein implies in the 'Tractatus' when he states that the subject is not a part of the world but a limit to it.   It is the very presence of the disciplined observer as a subject who produces 'facts of life' from outside all worlds that makes the idea of intervention as such comprehensible to us as the basis for change.   Only by formulating a notion of knowledge and knowing as the privi-leged grasp of an impartial spectator who produces descrip-tions from outside all worlds is it possible to justify a view of change as the result of his intervention.   In the event, it is the idea of departure and return which is problematic in all of this.

The 'real' definition of innovation cited in chapter 1 (35) clearly accords with the procedure noted here, since this defi-nition is the result of isolating common properties and activi-ties thought to be present in the particular instances of inno-vation which have been described.   For Bierstedt, it is the

initial productive or generative function of nominal definitions
which justifies them. They are not then a mere protocol but
all too often constitute a necessary preliminary. What
Bierstedt ignores is precisely the underlying assumptions
which make his distinction between the nominal and real, the
methodological and substantive, the metasociological and sociological, sensible to us as members of a culture that honour
facts of life and the privileged position of the disciplined
observer as their producer and generator. In addition there
is the central role accorded to causal attribution and cause
and effect reasoning here. Models of human action and
agency in life are treated by the impartial spectator as instances of causation, given the dependence of this mode of reasoning on the idea of an abstract whole comprised of concrete
empirical particulars available for the production and generation of describable states of affairs (facts of life;
worlds). (36)

To say that nominal definitions help make real definitions
possible is not, however, to see them as productive or generative in and of themselves. It is rather to their role as sur-
rogates, 'deviations', incomplete versions of the real thing,
that we must turn in order to see them as a vehicle through
which social science researchers, going about their tasks in
urban industrial societies, themselves produce or generate new
knowledge, however tentative because probabilistic or statistical in its generalizability this knowledge is alleged to be.
Bierstedt makes this clear enough when he defines the two
types of definitions cited, basing his definitions on Ralph
Eaton's 'General Logic'.

A nominal definition (sometimes called a verbal definition) is
a declaration of intention to use a certain word or phrase as
a substitute for another word or phrase. The word or
phrase with which we begin is called the *definiens*; the
word or phrase we substitute is the *definiendum*. A nominal definition has three important properties: (1) the meaning of the *definiendum* is dependent upon that of the
definiens; that is, the expression or concept defined has
literally no other meaning than that given arbitrarily to it;
(2) the definition has no truth claims; that is, it can
neither be true nor false, it is not a proposition; and
therefore (3) it cannot serve as a premise in inference. (37)

Bierstedt goes on to point out that, 'only propositions can
serve as premises in inference and a nominal definition, being
neither true nor false, is not a proposition.' He then proceeds to contrast real and nominal definitions in the following
way:

A real definition differs from a nominal definition in that it operates not only on the symbolic or linguistic level but also on the referential level. It may be defined as follows: a real definition is a proposition announcing the conventional intention of a concept. In more technical language, a real definition is a proposition predicating a distributed intention of its subject term. A real definition also has three important properties, as follows: (1) a real definition states that two expressions, *each of which has an independent meaning*, are equivalent to each other; (2) it has truth claims ie., it is a proposition; and (3) it can therefore serve as a premise in inference. (38)

This sounds very much like Wittgenstein's distinction in 'Tractatus' between sense and non-sense, propositions about nameable/describable worlds and mere names, handy perhaps for logical argumentation, but having no truth value because not 'corresponding' to any external reality in an agreed upon way.   Wittgenstein, however, anchored his 'truth tables' in that logic which he then believed to 'scaffold' the world, which is to say that the grounds for propositions themselves had to be in some generic sense 'logical'.   This is evident from the statement in 'Tractatus' which says that it is impossible to think illogically. (39)   Regardless of what Wittgenstein subsequently jettisoned of his early thought, it must be clear that the distinction between nominal and real falls back behind the 'Tractatus' in some respects precisely because it ignores its very dependence on the preconditions for human thinking.   Emphasis on truth claims and the possibility of inference only cloud the issue further, because inference from one or more 'propositions' to new ones assumes that so-called nominal definitions stand apart from and do not depend upon earlier 'knowledge' in the form of real definitions.   Indeed, we can really only make sense of this distinction if we equate real definitions with descriptions which (necessarily) include an explanatory (causal or related) aspect, and nominal definitions with concepts.   To be sure, these concepts have been reduced to fit the functional or operational requirements given in the commitment to knowledge as something produced and generated, thus to a considerable extent dependent on the state of the (methodological; technological) art.   Sociologically speaking, concepts are a nuisance until reduced to nominal (read operational) definitions, where they can thereafter function as the light infantry in the production of real definitions.

The view which ascribes truth value to terms which are alleged to possess meaning 'independent' of arbitrary and idiosyncratic assignment, apart from ignoring the ongoing interdependence between real and nominal definitions, is nowhere near so free of dependence on agreement concerning conventional usage as might be supposed.   Far too much is made, for example, of the arbitrariness given in positing nominal definitions as mere 'declarations of intention' than experience and culture, even in science, would seem to warrant. One might go even further along the lines already suggested and argue that nominal definitions constitute a theoretical dilemma for thought because of the reductivist conception of meaning given in such truncated concepts. This is only underscored by an interventionist approach to social change which treats nominal definitions mainly as vehicles for the production and generation of real definitions. Even their arbitrariness is seen to be a lesser evil when one considers what may be gained by 'going along' with someone's arbitrary (nominal) definition in order to see what they are really saying, if anything. Far from criticizing this approach, I simply argue against any view which sees this posture as self-sufficient relative to the more expansive role of concepts as substantive universals. Bierstedt makes a strong case for 'four important functions' of nominal definitions. They 'introduce new words into a language', 'indicate the special importance of certain concepts in scientific schemata', 'permit us to economize space, time and attention', and 'permit us to substitute new concepts for the familiar words of ordinary speech'. (40)

All this has an important bearing on 'innovation'. We can arbitrarily assign to a particular outcome or activity the status of *an* innovation, and can retrospectively agree that such and such was truly an innovation, or an example of innovative behaviour. But does this get us what we're after? Will the process of employing innovation in the first sense, that is, nominally, help us produce an understanding of innovation in the sense that the activity itself can be isolated and pointed to as something in the world. I doubt it. Innovation is something we know which we cannot, however, comprehend in and through description. (41) It is neither reducible to what it 'really' is in the absence of such reduction, nor is it merely non-sense and/or a 'condensation' symbol on its own. These dichotomies cannot hold what it must be for us to know it in precisely the way we do. The struggle to address innovation as I intend doing here hardly warrants cynicism or long faces. The following statement in 'Tractatus' is entirely appropriate to my concerns and preoccupations in the study which follows. Speaking of 'the relative position of logic and mechanics', Wittgenstein states:

The possibility of describing a picture like the one mentioned above [that provided by Newtonian mechanics] with a net of a given form tells us *nothing* about the picture. (For that is true of all such pictures.) But what *does* characterize the picture is that it can be described *completely* by a particular net with a *particular* size of mesh.

Similarly the possibility of describing the world by means
of Newtonian mechanics tells us nothing about the world:
but what does tell us something about it is the precise *way*
in which it is possible to describe it by these means.   We
are also told something about the world by the fact that it
can be described more simply with one system of mechanics
than with another. (42)

Finally, there is no point in criticizing our language for
possessing concepts like 'innovation' which cannot be adequately comprehended either nominally or in 'real' terms.
They point to the past as well as the future, and suggest the
possibility of 'worlds' other than (and to) the ones we can
produce or generate methodically and reductively in the
present.

CONCEPTS AS UNIVERSALS

Instead of viewing concepts as potential nominal definitions
awaiting reduction in line with the interventionist bias of an
empiricist world view, they should be understood as universals
or substantives signifying far more than what they can be
formally defined to mean.   The universalistic and substantive
nature of concepts is evident from the very notion of what we
mean by either 'definition' or 'concept' when we use these
terms.   'Definition', for example, is a concept of definition,
not a definition.   As for the definition of concept, no effort
to define it can ever justify confusing the definition of concept with particular concepts.   To say that concepts are universals and substantives underscores what is lost when they
are rendered 'functional' or 'operational' by being reduced to
the literal meanings found in nominal definitions.   Even
Blumer, however much he appears committed to criticizing
positivistic research methodology in the social sciences, shows
his real support for the empirical bias and a correspondence
conception of truth when he argues for the 'role' of concepts
qua concepts in research, however 'vague' they may be relative to 'empirical observation'.   Vagueness and ambiguity
here testify to a view of the parts as concretely real and the
whole as abstract, whether this whole is alleged to be 'more
than the sum of its parts' or merely their concatenation. (43)

It is the analytic separation of thought, then speech, from
action, and the subsequent empiricization of this and related
dichotomies which provides the central clue to the problem
here.   Speech, thus distended from activity as a key feature
of the 'real' world, can only rehabilitate itself if it assists in
making its occasion justified by reference to its own proper
'function' in an appropriative quest for knowledge.   Speech
becomes language and language 'communication', thereby effec-

tively bowing to the reductivist agenda in the same way that
theory is obliged to do when it permits, and even assists in,
its structural decomposition into testable/falsifiable hypotheses. (44) What I am really addressing here is the notion of
meaning, in particular the idea that what a concept means is
synonymous with its formal (nominal or real) definition. A
functionalist or operationalist conception of meaning reformu-
lates the concept as a word in need of a proper definition.
Whether we are talking about nominal or real definitions here
is moot, because what is at stake is the absorption of the
concept into a literalist conception of meaning. Speech must
be efficient and effective, which is to say that functional or
operational usage demands that one be understood to convey
all that he means when he speaks, where his speech is treated
atomistically as statements which can be analysed word by
word. Such an analysis, far from missing much of the point
of speech, is seen to provide a near sufficient criterion for
understanding the speaker's meaning.

This, of course, is speech in the written tradition, speech
subject to criteria of meaning wholly dependent on Biblical
literalism and its distinct secular equivalents like double
ledger bookkeeping and bureaucratic rules, files and records.
The idea in the case of 'operational' usage is to factor as
much 'ambiguity' and 'noise' out of language as possible.
After all, it is a tool for communicating, and, like all tools,
it must be kept sharp.   There is a clear ring of 'time is
money' in such thinking, inasmuch as the ideal speech situation would be one in which there was no ambiguity whatsoever, thus one which would show its mettle by generating
silence rather than talk. (45)   Bacon's attack against speculation that 'talks and talks and gets nowhere' can faintly be
heard in the distance as well. (46)   My point is that such a
view of the ideal speech situation, both from the standpoint
of the participants (silence) and the disciplined observer as
analyst (complete analysis), takes no cognizance of the real
role of concepts in human thinking.   Only an interventionist
bias could see talk like this proceeding under the assumption
of actual (or potential) universal intelligibility as mere dis-
traction and time-wasting.   It is as if the sole purpose of
speech were itself purely instrumental, a means for grasping
and appropriating 'knowledge' of one kind or another in a
piecemeal and incremental way appropriate to logical atomism.
This raises what is perhaps my central point in attacking
functionalist or operationalist canons of meaning in speech
understood as language.

I have already noted how such requirements demand that
the thing said be identified with its 'function' in the observable world.   More to the point is the refusal to treat nouns
in speech as real substantives having universality at the same

time that they are understood to be concrete, rather than
abstract, like the whole which they simultaneously speak from
and address. The reason for dwelling on this point, one in
express opposition to operational usage, can be readily seen
if we think about the way individuals actually speak, talk and
discuss various matters with one another. The theoretical
potential in speech is evident in a whole host of situations
where functionalist canons only serve to point up the poverty
of linguistic analysis as a 'tool' whose very utilization only
underscores the impossibility of capture. There is a sense
in which a term like innovation speaks to possible as well as
past realities in a way which can be glimpsed perhaps, but
never grasped (Hegel), made manifest but never actually said
(Wittgenstein). Words or terms are the real vehicles of
speech, and often poor vehicles given their aggregate inability
to really capture the sense of what the subject wants to say.
What is said in speech is merely a part of what is spoken, the
more so where the recipient is firmly committed to reducing
the terms to words with clear definitions in pursuit of the
speaker's meaning. (47)

   This is not presented as a permanent stumbling block to
intelligibility in discourse, but neither does it intend to downplay the shortsighted character of the reductivist viewpoint.
Indeed, I would argue that the latter approach, often in the
name of intervention for its own sake, achieves at best a
patina of the intended meaning in its haste to meet efficiency
and effectiveness criteria. The less time-consuming way is
likely to be generative - increasingly as a centre (rather than
a side) effect - of the sort of confusion all too evident in the
activity of individuals who may only appear to be 'using'
language 'responsibly' as a set of referential symbols or a tool
for achieving real definitions. There is also the distinction
between science and life at stake here, because the requirements of clarity in the first case, far from precluding or
rendering inapplicable my point about concepts as substantives, underscore this point by the very way in which scientific theories reach the world. In the case of the social sciences, we have a more recent set of developments which
threaten to annihilate many (or most) commonsense conceptions
and usages in the name of literalism and the written tradition
as these biases are expressed in and through key institutions
of urban industrial societies, among them capitalism, legalism
and bureaucracy. What the social sciences do to the concept
and to theory in their own bailiwick, following Popper's model
of the social sciences as social technologies, they also do to
the latent and possible (as well as actual) expressions of conceptualization and thinking in a commonsense realm increasingly subject to disciplined observation, role-taking, the 'rehearsal in imagination' and those other appurtenances which indicate the clear primacy of the so-called 'secondary' group in
these societies. (48)

The only thing that can be said for operational canons of functional usage is that they do provide a solid basis for civil rather than real talk, where the prototype is either the market, the firm, the bureau or the courts. These institutions are (in)famous for the way they exhibit various forms of 'social' rationality in action, yet the key characteristic of the 'legal-rational' speech which they formally require is its pursuit of anonymity, another version of silence. (49)   Anonymity is virtually preordained by their operation to the extent that the purpose of the sort of reductivism and the corollary commitment to atomistic clarity and piecemeal aggregation which they demand cannot help but reduce or annihilate 'individual differences' between individuals as speakers whose speech is a deed rather than an alternative to (or escape from) it. Hannah Arendt made this point with great force in 'The Human Condition' when she argued that social scientific emphasis on means, modes and medians associated with the law of large numbers could not help but threaten real individuation as *display*. She was only addressing the 'other side' of bureaucracy - the social sciences - taking her cue from Weber, with his fear of the consequences for individualism of the *social* levelling accomplished by bureaucratization. What the social sciences support from the standpoint of 'legitimate' conceptualization and theory is, after all, little different from what organizational bureaucracies demand of their employees as well as their clients: anonymous speech as the inverted mirror image of conformist behaviour and function. (50)

My reference to Weber and Arendt is not intended to indicate their support for concepts as universals, however.   Both ultimately honour an empiricist vision of reality and a correspondence conception of truth which has little choice but to stand by while the concept (like theory) is reduced in line with operational requirements.   Both endorse pessimism and resignation regarding the possibilities for men inhabiting an 'iron cage' (Weber) or an 'artificial realm' (Arendt).   What Herbert Marcuse said of Kant holds for all such idealistic thinking when it laments a reality which, it is alleged, can only get worse, and thereafter attempts to acquiesce in such a fate.

Defining its concepts in terms of potentialities which are of an essentially different order of thought and existence, the philosophic critique finds itself blocked by the reality from which it dissociates itself, and proceeds to construct a realm of reason purged from empirical contingency.   The two dimensions of thought - that of the essential and that of the apparent truths - no longer interfere with each other, and their concrete dialectical relation becomes an abstract epistemological relation. (51)

The resulting dissociation of mind from the world, and its
resultant flight into a self-made 'iron cage' in which subjectivity is enshrined *because of* its encirclement by the realm of
technical, economic and political reality, is at best a gesture
of futility.   Idealism is clearly the inverted mirror image of
positivism, the 'conscience' that gives one pause (like 'ethics')
but never really stops him from doing what he 'must' do (will).
My endorsement of the concept as a universal and substantive
is thus not put forward in defense of the sort of collective
self-abnegation readily discoverable in idealistic thinking.
Idealism is, after all, philosophy 'in its place' under the economic regime of capitalism and the intellectual regime of positivism in its many guises.

What I would argue is absolutely central to any effort to
think through and make sense of social, economic and political
phenomena and events is precisely what Popper and his sup-
porters believe to be anathema to the 'open society', namely
resuscitation of the whole as concrete and the 'parts' as
abstract because necessarily abstracted from a whole which
must 'be' even if it is ungraspable in its wholeness. (52)
From this follows both the idea of the concept as a substantive universal which is always more than the terms to which it
is reduced in efforts to define it, and the notion of theory as
more than the cannon fodder of hypotheses which are themselves the light infantry of an appropriative and accumulative
conception of knowledge premised on the mastery and domination of 'nature'.   At the same time, the commitment here to
the concreteness of the whole is not an effort to reify this
whole, but rather constitutes recognition of the fact that the
whole and its parts are in a dialectical relationship as moments
whose reality may be known but never comprehended as such
through the acts of naming and describing.   After all, 'the
world' that their successful description would locate them in is
itself a dialectically related aspect of the concrete totality.
Finally, what is also at stake in this critique of false concreteness is the necessary incompleteness and insufficiency of concepts and theories relative to the objects to which they are
addressed.   This point also holds for the idea that speech is
or ought to be self-sufficient and complete unto itself.   Such
a notion is at best a 'methodological convenience' and at worst
a fiction whose very arbitrariness serves to underscore the
limits of intervention vis à vis both theory and practice in
collective life. (53)

CONCEPTS AND OBJECTS

My commitment to the view that concepts mean more than their
formally reduced definitions can possibly say in no wise justifies a position which fails to acknowledge the priority of

objects to the concepts which try to grasp and absorb them.
Indeed, it is precisely the universalistic character of concepts
which requires them simultaneously to speak to and exhibit
their kinship with a whole which includes them even as they
address it. It is clearly this aspect of objects vis à vis concepts which demands their preponderance and makes dialectics
materialistic, rather than simply a standpoint or a method of
cognition. Adorno put the matter this way:

> The name of dialectics says no more, to begin with, than
> that objects do not go into their concepts without leaving a
> remainder, that they come to contradict the traditional norm
> of adequacy. Contradiction is not what Hegel's absolute
> idealism was bound to transfigure it into: it is not of the
> essence in a Heraclitean sense. It indicates the untruth of
> identity, the fact that the concept does not exhaust the
> thing conceived. (54)

Adorno goes on to point out how inherent in thought and
language the presumption of identity is. To even dispute
the emphasis on graspability given in description, for instance,
I must of necessity act as if my critique itself grasped the
ungraspable. A good example here would be the concept of
an object in the notion that concepts 'really' cannot grasp and
suborn their objects. Here by object I mean 'its physical
side', that aspect of it which results from my making it an
'object' of cognition. It is this concept of an object whose
reduced status permits it to be given a definition of sorts,
and it is by reference to this narrow and undialectical notion
of an object that I am able to generate the subject/object
distinction. In this form, 'object' truly loses its objectivity.
Extrapolated from the distinction between mind and body, it
comes to represent, and even to describe, empirical states of
affairs to which it is seen to correspond. True objectivity
would comprehend the dialectically momentous character of
parts which comprise the whole even as they draw their meaning and significance from its very concreteness. Only a
frozen and one-dimensional notion of the whole and its parts
could sanction the idea of a world where, in Wittgenstein's
words, the subject is a limit to rather than a part of it. (55)
Furthermore, only in such a world could the concept of object,
and objectivity, be so denatured that its meaning could be
seen to be captured in terms like objects (things) or objectives (goals). These notions are incomprehensible in the
absence of an empiricist bias, with its support for correspondence and reduction, and a technically rational commitment to
mastery and productivity. What makes something an object,
given one-dimensional thinking, is, after all, the view that it
is mere potentiality awaiting its real destiny in the form of
human definition, appropriation, and/or transformation.

One seemingly related conception often confused with what I have just said is provided by Max Weber's 'ideal types'. The key to seeing through what may appear superficially to be similarities between Weber's 'heuristic devices' for 'methodological convenience' and what I have in mind by concepts as more than their formally reduced definitions but less than their objects is Weber's conception of reality itself. At one point Weber refers to his ideal types as composite representations of a reality far too complex to be described. In doing so, Weber in effect accedes to the empirical bias already mentioned, because he sees these types as abstracting aspects of the whole that are more central than others out of the indescribable complexity that is the world. (56) The fact that this complex whole is an extrapolated version of Wittgenstein's world rather than a dialectical whole must be evident from the way Weber discusses the impossibility of its capture. It is beyond the grasp of the social scientist because of its abstractness and complexity relative to the concrete particulars, only a limited number of which can be grasped. It is the endless 'complexity', of the empirical world itself, then, which speaks to the limits of disciplined observation, not the dialectical nature of reality as a concrete totality which includes or comprehends this world in its physical or apparent aspect.

Weber, one could argue, definitely speaks to the priority of life over its individual and aggregated disciplined observations here. At the same time, he does this from the perspective of a disciplined observation which acknowledges all the (now empiricized) dichotomies and distinctions so central to empiricism: values and facts, ends and means, subject and object, mind and body. In true idealist fashion, Weber treats his own reflexivity and criticalness as an instance of bias and subjectivity, stating that, after all, 'substantive rationality' is itself but a formal concept in sociology's conceptual armoury. (57) Thus, instead of a posture like mine which puts life or practice before theory and theory before disciplined observation, Weber's 'world' contains only tradition and science, broadly conceived, with affect and principle as individual properties occasionally mobilizing themselves around the periphery. Indeed, one of the more tragic aspects of Weber's sociological work is precisely the way his determination to stand in support of principles he was personally opposed to led him to treat his own 'substantive rationality' as a 'deviation'. In honouring the split between work and life, thought and action, Weber has no choice but to point to himself as an instance of failed rationality, thereby impugning reason itself by identifying it overmuch with the process of rationalization and resulting world de-enchantment. (58) This leads him to refuse to distinguish between reflexivity and disciplined observation in sociology, and consequently to banish the first to the realm of bias, subjectivity, values and principles given his commitment to science as a distant (but ultimately unemulatable) model for sociological inquiry.

Weber's pessimism and resignation signify not so much the defeat of hope as of thought itself.   After all, it is Weber who, though occasionally questioning the claim that Western institutional modes of rationality (capitalism, science, technology, bureaucracy, legalism) really do constitute or express 'reason', gradually came to see the two as synonymous.   As a result he often appears tempted to turn away from reason altogether because he sees reason expressed and embodied in these institutional modes.   Similarly with thought or theorizing: its claim to stand apart from disciplined observation is really intolerable to Weber, for Weber, regardless of his apparent hesitation, really wants social knowledge to be productive. This means reduced concepts and structurally decomposed theories, thus formal definitions and testable/falsifiable hypotheses respectively.   Even Weber's demand for an individualizing method in the face of sociology's generalizing objective is posed as much so that sociology can do its job right as it is to stop it from doing it at all. (59)   Finally, the ideal type itself, which Weber claims (unlike the word 'ideal') to have no normative or 'value-laden' content given in its sociologically necessary 'rationalistic bias', is only to be tolerated if it issues in probabilistic generalizations possessing explanatory value.   Weber lamented the extent to which the composite 'representations' themselves were functioning as generalizations and explanations for others, but it is probably correct to say that they occasionally did the same thing in his own work. Thus even these 'devices' are means or instruments in support of a sociology whose empiricism, reductivism and commitment to a correspondence conception of truth have their inevitable complement in incrementalism, and an ultimately interventionist bias.

A final point on Weber relates to the direction and source of inspiration for the act of typification.   What gives the 'concept' its value for Weber in every case remains its empirical content.   Even its composite character is a necessary bow to the complexity of a world which he lamented had become totally 'knowable in principle'. (60)   In addition to his support for empirical content rather than universality and substance in the concept is the direction these recurrent acts of 'methodological convenience' cannot help but take the sociologist in.   They are not, in other words, 'really' for heuristic purposes after all, but have as their hidden, and occasionally explicit, objective the realization of an ideal (Western) society modelled on social function and performance norms.   It is not that Weber 'intended' that this should be the case, simply that sociology's commitment to objectivity in the apparent absence

of the object shows what objects or objectives it really favours
once the object of its false objectivity has been unmasked. (61)
What would be the purpose of all the effort that Weber makes
it plain is involved in sociological research if it were not to
harness productivity in support of some end?   The fact that
Weber elsewhere states that in science the problem is precisely
the way its demands make it impossible for it to ever come to
an end only suggests the fictive character of the subject/
object and ends/means (and value/fact) distinctions themselves
as dichotomous concepts incapable of really capturing the
whole. (62)   Weber, in effect, tells sociologists to partake in
what he personally believes to be an absurd enterprise, science defined broadly, because it is after all their damned duty
to stay at their posts 'in spite of all'.   In short, Weber
cannot stand in support of reflexivity and thought because he
is convinced that reason really does inhere in the institutional
structures of modern Western societies.

This is precisely what critical and dialectical thought abjures,
and, along with it, pessimism and resignation.   When it
accepts the notion that things either can be known that cannot
be described, or cannot be comprehended even in the face of
descriptions, it does not, as a consequence of this, follow
Wittgenstein into either mysticism or a preoccupation with
language usage and cultural functions. (63)   Neither does it
accept or endorse the view that this is but a temporary confusion which 'research' can and will repair in due course.
Thus the problem is not one which requires us to stake out a
nominal (operational) definition, formulate hypotheses, and
convert this 'effort energy' into real definitions, along with
generalizations and explanations containing them.   This would
provide the illusion of completeness, but at the cost of the
phenomenon itself, as Herbert Blumer suggests in the case of
the concept of 'intelligence'.

This procedure may be illustrated by the current view held
by some students that 'intelligence' is what intelligence tests
measure.   The argument is that intelligence tests do catch
something that is stable, and in place of declaring that one
does not know what is this stable content that is caught,
one calls it 'intelligence', and assigns it numerical value.
Some points should be noted about this interesting means of
escaping the problem.   First, the stable content that is
isolated has no nature;   that is to say that the operation by
means of which one arrives at that content does nothing
more than indicate that there is something that is stable.
The operation as such cannot analyze or characterize that
'something';   confined to such operations, that 'something'
neither has a nature nor could it ever secure a nature.
Thus, to illustrate, 'intelligence' becomes merely a numerical
value.   Second, not having a nature, the conceptualized

item cannot be studied - it gets its significance only through
being related to other items. These other items (if one remains inside of the framework of this kind of operational
procedure) would be other 'somethings', also without a
nature - presumably in the form of other numerical values.
The relations between the items could be only in the form of
quantified correlations. (64)

These and related observations are central features of
Blumer's criticism of narrow positivistic research methods in
the social sciences. While the excerpt catches key aspects of
problems that I have already alluded to regarding 'innovation',
it is Blumer's belief that this deplorable state of affairs can be
repaired by paying more attention to 'actor's' intended meanings, instead of concentrating on observed behaviour.
Blumer's objectives are thus Weberian, like his research programme, to the extent that neither one is really capable of
bearing fruit. There is, as Fallding has observed, only one
sociology, and the more efficiently and productively it appro-
priates, accumulates (and invests) the better. (65) Like
Weber, Blumer endorses science as a model, but goes on to
argue that it is the 'subject matter' of the social sciences that
requires them to go about the business of being rigorous and
scientific in a radically different way from what we allegedly
see happening in the 'natural' sciences. And, like Weber,
there is no quarrel about the ultimate nature and constituents
of reality, the concrete and abstract, and the correspondence
theory of truth. Both see the sociological task as a necessary one, albeit one which is necessary in Weber's case
because of the fated character of the world that Western
civilization has built. It is only the refractory or 'complex'
nature of the 'subject matter' - human beings - that renders
a strictly linear and mathematical scientism in the social sciences ultimately unproductive and ineffective even as it provides a patina of competence, performance and accomplishment.
Instead of seeing sociology as a creature of society whose
objective and value-neutral study of it reveals its true object
or objectives (where society is an historically and culturally
specific *form* of collective life rather than a synonym for collective life itself), Weber and Blumer abjure such reflexivity,
with all that this implies, in favour of endorsing disciplined
observation as a central task in these societies.

A CASE IN POINT

Let me conclude this section by attempting briefly to illustrate
what I mean when I speak of the need for a dialectical
approach to and appreciation of concepts. The case in point,
highly appropriate to the task of thinking about innovation,
concerns the relationship between and respective influence of

ideas and social structure on the development of novel attitudes, techniques and practices. Instead of pointing to the
insufficiency of a distinction like this, which so clearly proceeds out of more basic dichotomies (e.g., man/nature, mind/
body, subject/object, thought/action, etc.), in order to encourage operational reduction and 'empirical research', I shall
show how for me the consequences of this distinction's inability
to hold very much of the problem of innovation leads to a reflexive attitude toward the world, the whole, and the nature
of reality. Such an exercise points unavoidably toward the
universal character of concepts and the way in which such
universality speaks to the concept's insufficiency vis à vis its
objects rather than to its completeness. Clearly this reference to identitarian thinking, unavoidable in all cases where
we want to say something, can only make sense of its insufficiency by using the occasion of its speech to try to address
it. Again, however, such an address as often as not re-
affirms the concreteness of the whole by crashing up against
the limits of the world that it comprehends in and through the
language of dichotomization.

It has been a commonplace of Western thinking since at least
the mid-seventeenth century that culture and collective life
exercise a significant, if not a determining, influence upon
the ideas and thinking that emerge from culture and collective
life. Yet apart from more specific empirical claims asserting
a cause-and-effect relationship, the assertion has a mildly
tautological ring about it. It seems, in other words, to
simply be 'the case' by definition: it has to be true and
could not conceivably be otherwise. Apart from raising the
very serious issue of the possibility of a tautological circum-
scription of most, if not all, 'empirical' claims on 'the world',
it suggests that such a framework, following Wittgenstein, tells
us nothing about the world but the fact that the world can
hold such speech within it. In recognizing this, Wittgenstein
had gone as far as he could without invoking an explicitly
dialectical sensitivity and understanding in the 'Tractatus'. (66)
What I shall try to show in what follows is how dialectics and a
reflexive posture cannot help but emerge from the question I
have no choice but to ask. After all, empirical research can
only proceed once concepts have been operationalized and
theories structurally decomposed into testable/falsifiable hypotheses. This is the way in which 'the world' is simultaneously
defined and made the relevant externality for such efforts at
sociological (and scientific) 'research'.

There are several variations on this general theme, from the
invocation of a dialectical and materialistic understanding like
that of Marx to the manifestly undialectical one-way determinism of sociology of knowledge, with its unreflexive commitment
to the 'mode of production' as something which is responsible

in a *causal* sense for ideas, attitudes, values, etc. I have tried elsewhere to point out how thoroughly un- (or anti-) Marxian such a linear and one-dimensional view is. It turns out to be one of the central presumptions underlying what might be termed the 'American ideology'. As an intellectual enterprise and school of thought, sociology of knowledge, which achieved its highest notoriety in the work of Karl Mannheim, exhibits that commitment already noted for those with an empiricist view of the world (parts and wholes) and a correspondence theory of truth: the commitment to reductivism. Mannheim's 'technique' required him to (attempt to) reduce every idea, theory, concept, etc. to interest, position or class in society in the search for an explanation of why people hold and express certain views and how one 'accounts' for these views. In common with Marx's critique of the so-called 'objective' historians for a similar reductivism, I reiterate an earlier point. Such a one-dimensional understanding, which reduces in order to avoid reflexivity and a consequent acknowledgment of the contradictory character of any unfinished whole, constitutes the sort of false objectivity given in the subject/object distinction. Like Kant and the idealists, Mannheim is too ready to acknowledge the supremacy of the practical side *in the abstract*. (67)

On the other side of the issue, there is the claim, which I also support in general terms, that 'practical' or 'technical' innovations are necessarily preceded by innovations in thought and thinking. New ways of doing things are preceded by new ways of conceptualizing the world, and these latter probably include counter-imitation (Tarde), the displacement of concepts by analogy (Hesse; Schon), or the generally related phenomenon of bisociative thinking (Koestler). (68) As we shall see in the next chapter, this view can be either exclusivist where it acknowledges post hoc only special discoveries, creations and inventions as 'innovations', or it can be 'distributed' in the sense that innovativeness is seen to be a *human* faculty possessed by all of us. Thus the new thinking that precedes practical innovations may be understood to be the preserve of intellectuals, scientists, artists and/or especially 'intelligent' people, or it can be understood to be virtually given to men by dint of their sociality and dependence upon collective life itself. In this instance we are told something very significant about the way we have conceptualized and formulated the problem by the fact that the matter of truth or falsehood seems to depend overmuch on our initial definition of what constitutes an innovation.

Indeed, I would go further and argue that a theory of innovation which was compelled to distinguish in this fashion between innovation or innovativeness as an activity or process and innovations as specific outcomes would be an alienated

understanding too dependent upon the unreflexive dichotomy
between thought and action to really be taken seriously.
Popper's more expansive notion of an object in his theory of
World three, while in some ways an improvement on Wittgenstein's more restricted physicalist conception in 'Tractatus',
can only be useful to us in what follows if we allow it to
generate a reflexive and dialectical understanding.   Then we
are able to see how the products of the human mind could be
comprehensible neither from an idealist perspective nor from
an empirically materialistic one, but rather as 'things' standing on their own apart from their physical attributes while
nevertheless implying the possibility of human interpretation.
Popper, following Hegel, has in effect exploded the limits of
the mind/body dichotomy as a tool for holding our problems
and pointing the way to the things we want to say, but refuses to carry his understanding further to what I think
ought to be its end-point in recognition of the concreteness
of the whole.   Instead, as noted, he simply adds a third
category of 'world' to the world of ideas, etc. on the one
hand and that of physical externalities on the other.

What draws attention to both the scope and the limits of
this sort of thinking is precisely the fact that both assertions
appear to make sense, and do make sense.   So long as we
do not allow recognition of the influencing character of structure to become too deterministic in its ambit (or tautological),
it clearly makes sense to argue that ideas, attitudes, etc.
are influenced by collective life, that is, its organized, hierarchical, coercive, traditional, etc. character.   If we go too
far in one direction with this claim, however, we have determinism (e.g. ideas are *the result of* social structure;   social
structure *determines* ideas).   If we go too far in the other
direction we also lose the sense by reducing the universal
(concept) to a definition and the theory to testable/falsifiable
hypotheses as a prelude to 'empirical research'.   It is the
dubious distinction of Mannheim's sociology of knowledge that
it sought to combine both these excesses in its research programme.   One of the best efforts to hold the contradictory
character of both claims in its speech, without acceding to
either 'side', can still be found in Marx and Engels, 'The
German Ideology'.   One excerpt is worth quoting at length,
because it constitutes recognition of both the societal/cultural
influences claim and the conceptual priority claim.   Human
consciousness as a result is effectively located in history but
is not allowed to become coterminous with it.

The production of ideas, of conceptions, of consciousness is
at first directly interwoven with the material activity and
the material intercourse of men, the language of real life.
Conceiving, thinking, the mental intercourse of men appear
at this stage as the direct efflux of their material behaviour.

The same applies to mental production as expressed in the
language of the politics, laws, morality, religion, metaphysics of a people.   Men are the producers of their conceptions, ideas, etc. - real, active men, as they are conditioned by a definite development of their productive forces
and of the intercourse corresponding to these, up to its
furthest forms.   Consciousness can never be anything else
but conscious existence, and the existence of men is their
actual life process. (69)

If we remember that Marx and Engels are committed to the
principle of universal intelligibility, and that therefore innovativeness must be understood as a socially distributed capacity
as well as the expression of special abilities of an exclusive
minority, then we are well on our way to seeing how the two
claims can be reconciled.   At the same time, the distinctively
critical aspect of Marxian thought insists upon seeing the
problem of innovativeness as part of the larger problem of
human development.   Under the ideologies and realities of
capitalism and science, innovativeness is likely to be construed
overmuch in terms of profit maximization, or some less immediate form of 'comparative advantage'.   Here the argument
would focus on the fact that technology's development as knowledge and process is not an 'objective' one in the truest sense
of this term.   Apart from the conditions under which 'know-
how' is generated and recognized as such is the lack of automatic articulation between technology as knowledge and its
'conversion' into productive, etc. processes.   The crucial
intermediary here, of course, is capital allocation decisions,
and it serves as the basis for determining what 'basic' and
applied research will be carried out in research and development settings, whether it will be permitted to continue, and
whether the 'know-how' generated by applied research will be
'developed' or considered too much of a threat to existing
work and labour processes from the standpoint of profitability. (70)   What makes it necessary, empirically speaking,
to countenance the distinction between man and nature in the
advanced societies is precisely the fact that the productive
relations of men are alien to their real humanity, thus not
yet in accordance with their real 'nature'.   In addition, an
exclusive conception of innovation may be 'correct' in the
advanced societies precisely *because* of the unfinished and
alienating character of the present structure.

A final remark would draw attention to the way that a
dialectical understanding is virtually preordained by the simultaneous dependence of ideas on social structure and the fact
that the claim itself is how we 'know' the limits of the sphere
of consciousness.   It makes sense to say both things then,
but only so long as they contain the tension of contradictori-
ness and momentousness rather than abjuring it in favour of

either tautology or reductivism.   To really think about innovation, I have argued that it is necessary to address it as a
phenomenon.   Any effort to describe it and thereby bring it
into the world as a state of affairs that can be known empirically rather than simply by name must keep clearly in mind
the universal character of the concept and how this universality speaks to the priority of objects over concepts rather
than the reverse.   In what follows I necessarily fall into the
trap, from time to time, of acting as if I know what innovation
'is', when it is precisely the purpose of my inquiry to address
the sense of this very claim.   Only a commitment to the
whole as dialectically momentous can remind us of the shaky
ground we are on when we claim to have achieved comprehension through description and definition.

CHAPTER 2

Availability/bias

Having contrasted addressing the phenomenon of innovation
with attempting to define and describe it by reference to
'concrete' examples, I can now reiterate what this exercise
tells us about the relation between concepts, their objects and
collective life in advanced industrial society.   Concepts are
substantive universals and as such are not reducible to definitions.   They speak to or address more than can be captured
in and through reduction to 'concrete' operations of the sort
employed by the social sciences.   At the same time concepts
cannot absorb the objects or phenomena to which they are
addressed.   Indeed, they are rather in a dialectical relation
to the whole which they address because they are simultaneously within and without it.   The fact that concepts are substantive universals underscores the central role of ideas in
innovation, while their inability to absorb their objects speaks
to a general social determination.   The relationship between
each of these two parallel assertions only appears paradoxical,
as the excerpt from 'The German Ideology' helped us realize.
Only dialectics, materialistically conceived, can comprehend the
precise way that the non-reducibility of concepts in the face
of their inability to absorb the objects to which they are
addressed is expressed in the priority of ideas in innovation
in the face of an overall social determination.

A PRELIMINARY DISTINCTION

At the outset, it is necessary to contrast the ordinary and
extraordinary views of innovation.   In the latter case, innovation focusses on end-products - innovations - and this in
turn favours an emphasis on inventions.   Historically, our
culture-as-civilization has generated a very powerful ideology
of individualism based on the 'great man' as inventor out of
such a focus on end-products.   To be sure, this has taken
place mainly in areas where inventiveness was seen to contri-
bute to technical and technological progress.   The inventor
was a solitary individual whose success was supposed to be an
object lesson to others, especially children.   This focus was
given further support by the fact that normally this inventor
was not scientifically trained, but rather was seen to combine
commonsense capacities with effort, determination, and self-
confidence, even in the face of temporary setbacks.   Indeed,

technical progress exhibited very little dependence on scientific knowledge from the time of the origin of modern experimental science in the seventeenth century to the close of the nine-
teenth.   Even where there was some articulation and interdependence, it was rarely consistent and continuous. (1)

In contrast to the extraordinary view stands an approach to
innovation which argues that its occurrence is relatively well
distributed in practice and relatively 'available' in theory.
Here the emphasis, not surprisingly, tends to be less on end-
products and more on behaviour or activity.   Proponents of
this position often point to the doctrine of universal human
intelligibility in support of their claim.   It is in this sense
that innovation is seen to be a relatively ordinary property of
all cultures.   The fact that our culture-as-civilization seems
more open to an ordinary (distributed, available) view than
was the case in the past will be discussed in ensuing sections.
It constitutes a highly significant shift in our collective thinking and attitudes, and is related in a very central way to the
progressive organization and rationalization of all spheres of
collective life in advanced industrial societies.   It also suggests the limited validity of a rigid distinction between tradition and reason, given the way reason has ceased to be the
property of the individual and is instead seen to repose in
objective 'rational' structures.   As these structures develop
institutional, as opposed to merely organizational, properties,
it becomes harder and harder to make a case for the core distinction between culture (them) and civilization (us). (2)

To the extent that innovation is defined as a human capabil-
ity which is exhibited in practice, it ceases to function as an
ethical or moral ideal which is seen to fly in the face of the
facts.   This is highly significant, for it turns our attention
to training and socialization as cultural properties of advanced
industrial societies.   Here it is the belief that we have an
innovative, or potentially innovative, society which serves to
overcome the apparent tension between morality and reality. (3)
Nevertheless, we continue to tacitly resist any view which
argues for innovation as a humanly distributed capacity,
following as it does from the fact that people are rational *by
dint of being human* rather than as a consequence of specific
modes of training and certification.   Indeed, as we shall see,
this view becomes a positive hindrance to the compromise
position which has been reached in modern managerial, bureaucratic, and social-scientific thinking on the matter.   It is the
determination to preserve the culturally specific attitude of
superiority, while redefining innovation as innovativeness
rather than the diffusion of inventions, which marks our contemporary understanding. (4)

What has transpired in the realization of this compromise

between the extraordinary and ordinary views is that innovation has largely taken on a life of its own relative to invention. At the same time, it is understood more in terms of
behaviour and activity than end-products, even in the face
of the dependence of economic organizations on applied science
and already existing science-based technology as the basis
for technical advance. (5) 'Research and development' co-
opts the end-product focus formerly ascribed to the solitary
pre-scientific inventor, while innovation as innovativeness
comes to be understood in managerial and organizational terms.
Both R & D and innovation are viewed as collective processes
and activities, albeit ones which allow those that have been
properly socialized to exhibit their individualism in the act of
making their contribution to the group, team, or organization. (6) By 'properly socialized' is to be understood not
simply 'primary socialization' in the family, play group, school
and neighbourhood, but the subsequent acquisition of training
and the resulting degrees and certificates attesting to it
(MBA; PhD).

What makes the emerging reformulation a compromise is precisely the way it preserves cultural superiority while increasing the life-chances of certain individuals being innovative, if
not necessarily inventive in the process. At the same time it
also preserves the formalized meritocratic commitment by requiring training and certification of one form or another in its
gatekeeping role as a control on the context-specific opportunity to display innovativeness in the form of innovative behaviour. (7) Thus it is possible to simultaneously overcome the
tension clearly present in the gap between morality and reality
while preserving both idiosyncrasy in the form of superiority
and what is nothing less than a meritocratic caste structure in
the advanced societies themselves. All of this bears impor-
tantly on the cultural anthropologist's attempts to help us
appreciate the central role of innovation in all cultures, past
and present. In effect we exhibit the very properties ascribed by Barnett and others to 'primitive' peoples when we produce compromises of the sort just outlined, for such compromises are precisely the way that a culture attempts to preserve
its institutions in the face of change. (8)

This is not to ignore or play down the arguments made by
proponents of team or group process in scientific and technological R & D. In this case a team or group focus and the
consequent redefinition of individualism away from the solitary
inventor is deemed necessary on 'objective' grounds. There
is, they claim, simply too much knowledge and too many complex processes, techniques and systems already in existence
for an updated version of the solitary inventor to be taken
seriously, even for those with the most advanced training and
knowledge. To be sure, it may be precisely the lack of

applicability of such thinking to entrepreneurial activity which serves to delineate significant societal parameters within which innovation in *our* culture *must* take place. (9)   Managerial and organizational thinking often trades on the status and legitimacy available to those who participate in and supervise corporate and state-run R & D activities, but is far less capable of sustaining the appeal to objective knowledge as a basis for decision.   Though science is required to compromise itself before the public and its representatives by pointing to the technological outcomes generated by its theoretical and mathematical, as well as its experimental, work, management and bureaucracy have no such recourse.

Indeed, these occupations are only able to hitchhike on the largely self-congratulatory schema available to science because they ignore the role of capital allocation decisions in mediating the relation between scientific research and technological outcomes.   This may seem ironic until it is remembered how little like capitalists and entrepreneurs these public and private bureaucrats really are.   Thus it is organizational managers and their social-scientific apologists, rather than either pure or applied scientists or engineers, who encourage what is clearly technocratic thinking on these matters.   Such thinking favours the assumption that we live in a post-industrial (and therefore a post-capitalist) society where science and technology are directly tied to one another rather than mediated by capital allocation decisions, whatever their source. In the event, it is the attempt to tie their decision and policy processes to the sort of objective knowledge claims which Weber had made for now-conventional bureaucratic administration at the turn of the century which is the central element in contemporary technocratic ideology. (10)

Innovation as a key code word legitimizing the power position of these new managers, bureaucrats and technocrats thus functions to what are clearly solitary and in-group ends. Because it combines greater availability, and an emphasis on behaviour and activity rather than outcomes, with controls on the contexts within which this behaviour may be exhibited, it is a peculiarly organizational, and increasingly institutional, conception of novelty and change.   It is because collective life as a whole is increasingly subject to organizational and managerial values and predefinitions that this conception of innovation has begun to acquire society-wide legitimation. No longer restricted to the market or the office, these values now threaten to overturn what remains of the so-called traditional values of the family and allied institutional groupings. Managerial, bureaucratic and technocratic work settings function as the model contexts for the display of innovative behaviour in a society in which there is little if any effective resistance to such pre-emption and co-optation.   This is what

Weber meant by the rationalization and consequent de-enchantment of contemporary life, and it bears poignant testimony to
the capacity of the compromise cited to attempt simultaneously
to preserve established assumptions and accommodate to the
perceived internal and external problems facing our culture-
as-civilization.

INDIVIDUALISM AND DIVISION OF LABOUR

My focus on cultural adaptation and accommodation constitutes
what is, at the very least, a necessary counterweight to unilinear notions of development, with their manifest technical
and technological bias. The shift in emphasis in prevailing
conceptions of innovation clearly reflects a process of adaptation and accommodation of the sort outlined above. This is
highly significant for any attempt to see contemporary Western
civilization as a culture in the ways indicated. Another illus-
tration of this process is provided by the fate of the concept
of 'individualism' over the past century or so in Western
Europe and North America. Initially the term functioned as
a code word expressing a tension between the individual and
society as a collective structure with behavioural rules and
normative expectations. A clear parallel to the 'solitary inventor' is evident in this case, because here the individual
must express his individuality by seeking to *overcome* residues
of tradition and convention hostile, or at best indifferent, to
entrepreneurial or scientific motives and interests. This is
why it makes sense to cite early industrial capitalism's
struggle with these mercantile and pre-modern values and
habits as a key element in the success of this undertaking,
which success is all too readily subject to one-sidedly deterministic explanations and presuppositions. (11)

This leads to another point supportive of the suggested
parallel. In both instances, we are faced with an exclusivist
conception, whether of innovation or of individualism, because
in both cases the relevant phenomenon is not seen to be particularly well distributed. One only needs to think of what
is meant by 'bourgeois negative individualism' to appreciate
how much it was presumed that one's behaviour must approach
a zero-sum game with society if he were to be so classified
and categorized. In addition, of course, there is the joint
emphasis on outcomes rather than behaviour, that is, upon
tangible inventions, marketable ideas, or successful capital
accumulation and investment. (12) Exclusivity thus appears
to go hand in hand with a concentration on outcomes of a
tangible, or at least a 'practical', sort, rather than on behaviour or activity per se. This in turn points to something I
shall address in the next two chapters, namely, the question
of whether there is a theoretical basis for perceived innovative

practices, and how the so-called 'problem of rationality' figures in all this.   It is in the tension between intent to be rational and effort to achieve desired outcomes on the one hand, and the 'objective consequences' (e.g. success) of the behaviour in question on the other, that a clear parallel between the above matters and those germane to studying the phenomenon of innovation and individuation presents itself.

This matter of exclusivity v. availability in the analysis of 'individualism' can be made more explicit by remembering that one of Durkheim's signal contributions was to make individualism far more 'available' than more negative, zero-sum notions appropriate to early industrial capitalism had been.   In an effort to provide a realistic 'middle path' between Social Darwinism's defence of 'rugged (negative) individualism' and Marxism's apparent commitment to revolutionary overturn, Durkheim had argued for a reformist posture which would endeavour to cure the ills of society from within by repairing the abnormalities which attended the experience of Western European industrialization. (13)   The key element in his commitment to 'normalization' involved expanding the idea of individualism so that it could be made 'functional' for societal development rather than being seen to stand against it. Durkheim, after all, had viewed negative individualism, with its emphasis on the priority of exchange and contract to solidarity, as a central feature of the 'abnormal' division of labour. (14)   Thus his concern for radically revising this core notion so that it might be made more readily 'available' to the majority of denizens in industrial societies.

It is on work and labour contexts that Durkheim focusses in his efforts to 'generalize' the norm of individualism so that it becomes more available, thus a relatively ordinary (potential) accomplishment.   The prescience of Durkheim's analysis, in light of the subsequent 'democratization' of both individualism and innovation fifty years afterward, is truly striking, particularly when seen against the backdrop of the organization of capitalism over the past sixty or seventy years.   Here individualism was seen to be synonymous with the efficient and effective (e.g. 'functional') performance of specified occupational activities or less specific occupational roles. Ideally, Durkheim argued, one's occupation ought to be chosen voluntarily.   Indeed the difference between coercion and voluntary initial choice was central to his distinction between the abnormal and the normal(ized) division of labour in industrial societies.   That this voluntarism is only conditional is evident from the way Durkheim distinguishes initial choice from the subsequent societal obligations which follow fast on one's decisions.   Thus:

once our resolution has ceased to be internal and has been

externally translated by social consequences, we are tied down. Duties are imposed upon us that we have not expressly desired. It is, however, through a voluntary act that this has taken place. (15)

It should come as no surprise to discover that Durkheim's radically revised notion of individualism, what has often been called 'positive' individualism, goes hand in hand with a view of innovation as virtually synonymous with the progress of the social division of labour. This is a point of view with which I shall take more extended issue in subsequent chapters, largely on the grounds that any sensible understanding of innovation in our culture-as-civilization must have room in it for ideas, discoveries, techniques and inventions which cut across some existing division of labour and imperil it by rendering many of its established ways of doing things obsolete. (16) This only serves to underscore the issue of capital already cited, by pointing once again to the threat such innovative ideas could conceivably pose to corporate sunk costs and to future profits, growth and control of given markets. It is *because* Durkheim sees the division of labour itself, albeit a normalized division of labour, as the key to innovation rather than a threat to it, that his democratization or generalization of individualism implies a similar fate for innovation as a phenomenon.

Thus to say that individualism becomes more available is to argue the same thing for innovation. Instead of challenging established structures and ways of doing things in one fashion or another, Durkheim equates his new individual with the person who carries out largely predefined tasks or generally defined roles in a society whose occupational structure is essentially or, at the very least, increasingly, given. For Durkheim, abnormality or pathology is to be discovered in the *tension* between the individual and society, in competition and competitiveness, in short in 'negative individualism'. Rationality comes to inhere in the environing structure of a society characterized by a normal(izing) division of labour precisely to the extent that the 'positive' individuals he wants to produce no longer experience anomie or 'normlessness', but are now acknowledged to be creatures in need of secure moorings which only an overhaul of the system from within it can guarantee. Society becomes fetishized as the only 'available' collective in response to the greater availability of individualism through performance of socially defined and enforced occupational functions, as the following excerpts make clear.

The division of labour does not present individuals to one another, but social functions. And society is interested in the play of the latter; insofar as they regularly concur, or do not concur, it will be healthy or ill. Its existence thus

depends upon them, and the more they are divided the
greater its dependence. That is why it cannot leave them
in a state of indetermination.

Among lower peoples, the proper duty of man is to
resemble his companions, to realize in himself all the traits
of the collective type which are then confounded, much more
than today, with the human types. But, in more advanced
societies, his nature is, in large part, to be an organ of
society, and his proper duty, consequently, is to play his
role as an organ. (17)

It is important to see in this opening out of the concept and
category of individualism a way of liberating this new positive
individual from collective controls of a traditional and conventional (pre-industrial) sort not as an end in itself, but rather
in order to bind him ever more closely to the emerging apparatus of a 'normalizing' society. This point is clear first of all
from Durkheim's view of the individual as mainly a non-rational
and sentimental creature in need of the solidaristic bonds discovered in customs, conventions and established ways of doing
things. Such a position would incline him to view 'liberation'
in the negative sense of a tension with society as 'dysfunctional' in virtually all of its aspects save as a *means* to new controls. Second, there is Durkheim's belief that the atrophy or
'enfeeblement' of a pre-industrial 'collective conscience' characterized by similarities, likenesses and shared values and attitudes was not to be counted in and of itself an 'abnormal'
phenomenon. Far from being the 'cause' of the abnormalities
he observed, Durkheim viewed such enfeeblement as a normal
and natural outcome of development per se. (18) The choice
for Western industrial societies was between continuing in the
present 'abnormal' situation, and repairing and reforming this
situation *from within* through the concerted joint action of
occupational groups in pursuit of the new solidarity, and
sociology, with its commitment to a new moral code authorizing
intervention to ameliorate the anomie or normlessness. (19)

This meant that the real problem was not atrophy but the
failure of a new basis for solidarity to emerge and fill the
vacuum left by the collapsing collective conscience. Durkheim's effort at normalization centres about the new individual
as a legal *and social* 'person'. and on the new individualism as
a concept or notion which simultaneously opposes these pre-
industrial traditional norms and standards while constituting
their last vestige in industrial, or industrializing, societies.
For Durkheim, 'negative individualism' would ideally constitute
little more than a brief interlude in the 'general movement'
from one system of collective organization based on pre-industrial norms and attitudes to one characterized by an individualism now rendered functional for an emerging division of

labour whose normality was seen to inhere in its success in
overcoming the tension between the individual and society.
It should be easy to see how such an integrationist position,
with its emphasis on sentimental individuals and functional
(or dysfunctional) structures, would tend to support a far
more available notion of innovation (and individualism) than
one which viewed individuals as free of, rather than essentially produced by, society as a culturally and historically
specific form of collective life. (20)

To be sure, the argument for a parallel between the greater
'availability' of innovation relative to invention and the new
(positive) individualism relative to bourgeois negative individualism only serves to underscore the transmogrification of
reason itself in the advanced societies. Thus reason in its
newly pre-eminent form - 'rationality' - is seen to be less
the possession of the subject, particularly as he has been
portrayed in idealist thinking, but in established legal and
positivist understandings as well, and more the property of
those formally organized structures which collectively perform
the functions of 'secondary socialization'. It is by reference
to these structures, including but certainly not exhausted by
work, labour and occupational settings (e.g. schools, higher
education, media) that we now understand what it means to be
both innovative and an individual. It is the collective, continuous, and long-term character of these processes that
speaks to a societal agenda, where by society we understand
a culturally and historically specific form of collective life,
rather than the only kind of collective life 'available', or
desirable.

Durkheim's position is of the greatest significance to this
study because it constitutes the basis for one of two central
approaches to innovation, development, and social change.
Durkheim refused to accept the view of his predecessors, who
argued that there were 'objective' limits beyond which the
division of labour could not be pressed without 'becoming a
source of disintegration'. Durkheim asserted that the problem was rather a matter of reforming the abnormalities of a
society which was fundamentally satisfactory *from within this
society*. The division of labour, though not automatically
'moral', could be rendered moral with the help of sociology as
a 'moral science' committed to a new solidarity. Thus 'the
remedy for the evil' was 'not to seek to resuscitate traditions
and practices which, no longer responding to present conditions of society, can only live an artificial false existence.' (21) This probably constitutes the most sophisticated
defence of a 'science of society' committed to ameliorative interventionism and piecemeal reform ever written. At the same
time, of course, it plainly and unambiguously points to the
fact that sociology's pose of 'neutrality', like the initial

voluntary choice of the workman, is conditional. Sociology
stands in support of *society* as an historically and culturally
specific collective to the extent that the 'moral code' it is
obliged to help draft has at its vital centre the commitment
to distinguish those 'social facts' conducive to the new solidarity from those inimical to it, and thereafter to seek to
realize the first and defeat the second. (22)

THE OBSERVER AND 'BEHAVIOUR'

Durkheim's emphasis on the need for a 'moral science' committed to realizing the new solidarity in the face of industrial
unrest and disorganization marks a central event in the development of industrial societies. It now becomes clear, albeit
not for the first time, that, left to itself, this new form of
collective life may not be capable of weathering the difficulties
attending economic growth, urbanization and the consequent
concentration of populations, and dislocation generally.   Even
the presence of economics as simultaneously the disciplinary
mirror of industrial society as a system of values and purposes, and the ideological lynchpin of this society given its
basic presuppositions about human nature, is no longer seen
to be sufficient to assuring the long-term survival of capitalist industrial society in the West. (23)   Sociology, and thereafter the behavioural and administrative/managerial 'sciences',
are now perceived to be absolutely necessary if the economic
gains made thus far are to be consolidated and preserved.
Durkheim's tack was essentially to try to reconcile the commitment to work and labour in the interests of productivity and
growth with the need for a new form of solidarity given the
unavoidable 'enfeeblement' of the collective conscience following upon economic and industrial development.   And it was
his reformulation of the prevailing conception of individualism
to make it far more available, even ordinary, *given effort*,
which is the key to understanding how he wanted at one and
the same time to stand against the collective conscience
('development') while preserving its last vestige in industrial
societies ('solidarity' *through* division of labour). (24)

This ideal of synthesis is important because of what it
implies about the insufficiency of both theory and practice in
urban industrial societies.   To the extent that a general commitment to the disciplined observation of collective life is seen
to be central to Durkheim's 'normalization' project, the observer role will also come to figure more prominently in the reformulation and reconceptualization of the idea of innovation
and innovativeness.   A shift away from past events and tangible outcomes, and emphasis thereafter on activities and
behaviour, portends a view of the present as something potentially or actually observable rather than simply lived experi-

ence.   It also suggests a principal role for social structure in producing both the relevant social spaces where innovation (and individualism) might occur, while simultaneously generating the properly socialized individuals able to 'function' properly in these spaces.   This in turn presupposes a view of the 'future' as a potential and actual extrapolation out of a present which is effectively controlled in terms of its main lines of development.   No such conception of the future would be conceivable in the absence of the disciplined observer as potential or actual intervenor.   In the case of innovation as both a perceived problem ('crisis') and its effective solution, I am addressing the idea of the disciplined observer, understood as an individual committed to trying to increase the amount and frequency of innovation by trying to find out what it is so he can attempt to produce or generate, at the very least, the conditions required to 'make it happen'. (25)

Once it is thought both possible and desirable to determine 'the future' through such disciplined observation, with its commitment to intervention and reform, it is almost axiomatic that the shift noted away from an exclusivist conception of innovation toward a more available and ordinary one would occur.   Indeed, it is suggested here that this 'generalization' or democratization of *the idea* of innovation goes hand in hand with the more available view of individualism as a *societal resource* located in properly socialized individuals performing socially (and organizationally) sanctioned occupational tasks and roles. (26)   With a bit of the sort of effort which *reflects* proper socialization, the new individual can become an innovator, the more so where innovation *means* the spirited performance of largely predefined and predetermined activities. This is the real significance of the notion of *behaviour* so central to the social-scientific enterprise: it cannot be seen to occur at all in the absence of a disciplined observer.   To the extent that this observer becomes coterminous with the actor or practitioner himself, one is warranted in speaking of a sociological society characterized by a hierarchy of reciprocal observers and role-takers where the 'stranger' is the norm rather than the exception.   Practice is essentially recast as a consequence of the impact of this new discipline at the same time that theory in the form of reflexive and dialectical thinking about society and culture is threatened with annihilation, either on grounds of its sterility (Bacon) or its danger (Popper). (27)

What I am therefore pointing to here is the possibility that a key feature of advanced industrial societies may well be precisely the merger of positive individualism and disciplined observation.   The more available individualism is perceived to be in these societies, the more its 'conversion' into innovative activities requires the internalization of behavioural norms

understood as ways in which an observer might readily iden-
tify an instance of the phenomenon of innovation itself.   Innovation as innovative behaviour is increasingly treated as if
it could be learned, at least in general terms, in advance.
This squares with my earlier point about the observer's concern to produce or generate innovation by treating the future
as an extrapolation out of a present which is comprehended
observationally and (thus) in terms of ameliorative intervention
and reform.   If innovation is learned behaviour, or if the
conditions for its occurrence can be learned, then it must be
presumed possible to produce or generate the desired behaviours.   An innovative individual is thus someone who, in the
emerging equation, reflects his normative socialization by producing the learned behaviours, or expected ones, in the
appropriate occupational and organizational circumstances.
He achieves this only because he has internalized the normative commitment to self and other disciplined observations
which is absolutely indispensable to the success of the undertaking.   Only in this way can he be seen to be an 'innovative individual'. (28)

    Durkheim's view that conflict between the individual and
society was dysfunctional and dangerous to social stability
reflected his belief that where such a tension existed the
individual, as a 'social' product', was not being correctly produced.   Such an attitude could nowadays be more directly
tied to an anti-innovative position than might perhaps have
been true when Durkheim was writing (e.g. 1893 to 1902).   It
is precisely because the emerging industrial division of labour,
however abnormal, possessed features at variance with traditional divisions of function based upon ascription that it might
readily have constituted a 'lesser evil' for the individual
labourer.   He might, to use Durkheim's own words, have felt
less 'hemmed in' by the collapse of the collective conscience
than he had in a pre-industrial 'traditional' setting in which it
was pre-eminent.   Durkheim may well have overdrawn the
problem of anomie for his own purposes as an observer favouring intervention and reform, and it may be a point of view
which we today and in retrospect are perhaps too ready to
support when we discuss the development of industrial societies in the West.   We should instead be viewing any division
of labour more as the result of prior innovations in theory and
practice than as the guarantor of future ones.   It is Durkheim's overestimation of the causative role of the division of
labour in *producing* innovation which led him to deny the need
for social and group *conflict* in its interests, something of
central importance in taking account of the subsequent work
of Elton Mayo, among others. (29)   The conformity and normative adjustment required of properly socialized individuals
had the same effect on innovation that it had on individuation.
Once again, however, we need to keep the essential *novelty*

of the emerging industrial division of labour in mind when assessing Durkheim's motives and addressing his concerns.

On the other side of such a caveat is Durkheim's position, already noted, regarding the central role of sociology as the science of society committed to producing the new solidarity through disciplined observation and ameliorative intervention in the service of piecemeal reforms.   Here I must give greater weight to Durkheim's subsequent impact precisely because it seems to square so closely with his motives and interests at the time.   The limits of innovation, conceived as innovative behaviour, can be readily seen in the fact that the merger between the new (positive) individual and the disciplined observation subsequently 'generalized' from academic sociologists outward to encompass the entire middle-class socialization experience, favoured specialization and conformity to largely preordained occupational functions.   By allowing the idea of division of labour to acquire 'objective' status, following on the deification (and reification) of 'society' as the only 'available' form of collective life, Durkheim had effectively fetishized functions whose functionality was contingent upon unacknowledged *economic* criteria rather than objectively given.   In addition, of course, was the matter of observational disciplines having as their specific goal the realization of a particular form of collective life. This collective was characterized in turn by a particular kind of solidarity based on the spirited performance of occupational functions in an industrial society whose manifestly capitalistic (as opposed to 'industrial') aspects stand virtually unquestioned by Durkheim. (30)

A limited and essentially conformist conception of innovation cannot help but be shored up and supported by disciplines so committed to beginning in the limit which is virtually preordained by their stated task, as the following statement by Durkheim makes clear.   It draws attention to the way that the objective of positive individualism has as its upshot a bias in favour of 'positive' innovation - behaviour aimed at completing and perfecting the existing social structure rather than challenging it or addressing it critically in any concerted way. Speaking in 'The Division of Labour in Society', first published in 1893, albeit with a highly significant preface added to the second edition in 1902, Durkheim says:

This book is pre-eminently an attempt to treat the facts of the moral life according to the method of the positive sciences.... We do not wish to extract ethics from science, but to establish the science of ethics, which is quite different. Moral facts are phenomena like others; they consist of rules of action recognizable by certain distinctive characteristics.   It must, then, be possible to observe them,

describe them, classify them, and look for the laws explaining them.   That is what we shall do for certain of them.
Perhaps it will be objected.... However, no one would argue
about the possibility of the physical and natural sciences.
We claim the same right for our science.

Although we set out primarily to study reality, it does not
follow that we do not wish to improve it; we would judge
our researches to have no worth at all if they were to have
only a speculative interest.   If we separate carefully the
theoretical from the practical problems, it is not to the
neglect of the latter; but on the contrary, to be in a
better position to solve them. (31)

If this argument favouring the merger of positive individualism and disciplined observation is accepted, then it has serious implications for any view of innovation which equates it
with relatively ordinary and available behaviour which is well
distributed, at least so far as the expanding middle class is
concerned.   It suggests that the ambit of its applicability is
necessarily restricted to individuals who complete what might
be termed an urban-middle-class socialization experience
through the joint aegis of family, neighbourhood, and school,
and who thereafter take positions in some organized occupational 'order' where innovativeness can be 'produced' as an
outcome of socially learned and sanctioned behavioural rules
and expectations. (32)   Thus does innovativeness as an eminently 'available' phenomenon go hand in hand with positive
individualism.   To be sure, availability is compromised by its
context-boundedness and urban middle-class bias in the sense
that it underwrites and rationalizes the growth of a meritocratic 'elite' in the advanced societies.   The concept is effectively 'democratized', but only because the contexts to which
it is limited in the advanced societies are themselves becoming
more and more 'available' as a result of the impact of education, the media, and the growth of organizational and managerial careers.

IMITATION/COUNTER-IMITATION

The most serious resistance to Durkheim within France at
roughly the time that he was writing came from an older contemporary named Gabriel Tarde. (33)   Tarde believed that
inventive and innovative behaviour (the English translator
actually employs both words, writing in 1903) was extraordinary and that any correct sociology would have to be premised
on the most ordinary human traits.   The most central of these
traits in his opinion was to be discovered in what he considered to be the most ubiquitous of all human 'social' characteristics — universal repetition.   Universal repetition took two

forms, neither of which was to be considered inventive or innovative, the first being imitation and the second its direct
opposite - counter-imitation. Neither imitation nor counter-
imitation was to be confused with non-imitation however.
Here the refusal to imitate or counter-imitate constituted a
form of action rather than inaction which had potential significance for invention and innovation, if only as a fundamental
point of departure away from clearly uninventive and uninno-
vative behaviour patterns. (34)

Tarde emphasized how central imitation and counter-imitation
were to social cohesion and the idea of society as a 'structure'
existing apart from the individual, who, in a certain sense
was its product. At the same time, Tarde never went as far
in endorsing the sui generis character of social facts, thus
society itself, as did Durkheim, but saw his work as a contribution to social psychology. There was also a far greater
willingness on Tarde's part to see social and physical traits
and characteristics as two sides of the same coin. This in
clear contrast to Durkheim, who viewed the social as a distinctive feature clearly set apart from the fact that men were also
physical and biological entities. Durkheim's resort to termin-
ology from medicine and the physical and biological sciences
was, on the whole, essentially analogical and metaphorical,
while for Tarde the study of human collective traits was
understood to be directly connected with these concerns and
disciplines, as well as psychology.

In a certain sense, Tarde's emphasis on ordinariness was
most compatible with the work of those critical of Western
ethnocentrism, while the effect, if not the intent, of Durkheim's work has been quite different, even opposed. While
it is true that Durkheim made the phenomenon of innovation
more 'available' by generalizing the concept of individualism,
the result of this was to make both society and a 'normal'
division of labour the effective basis for its appearance and
exercise. Tarde, on the other hand, saw inventive and innovative behaviour as an unpredictible and unanticipatable
outcome which could not be adequately comprehended in and
through a focus solely on the social division of labour.
Indeed, it is precisely this division of labour which expresses,
in *all* its forms and essential aspects, the reality of collective
life as fundamentally imitative, counter-imitative, and non-
imitative, and from this comes the need to analyse 'universal
repetition' as a bridge between heredity and environment. (35)

At the same time Tarde did believe that there were different
types and classes of invention and innovation, and that any
attempt to address them would have to acknowledge their
potential and actual presence along the entire continuum of
behaviour, from the concertedly rational and goal-oriented

type through to mechanical habits and routines characterized
by unconscious and involuntary activity. (36)   What Tarde
perhaps failed to underscore here was the difference between
the behaviour or outcome which actually takes place and the
recognition, either by the individual or group engaging in it
or by other parties, that what occurred was indeed inventive
or innovative (or an invention or an innovation).   While the
first may indeed occur at any point along a hypothesized
continuum of behaviour and activity, either as an intended
consequence of this behaviour or as a completely unanticipated
outcome of calculation, effort, habit, routine, or the unconscious and involuntary, *recognition*, no matter by whom,
always and necessarily possesses a 'rational' dimension.   I
shall argue in later chapters that this distinction is a central
one in addressing the largely moot issue of whether invention
and innovation are 'rational' or 'non-rational' events or occur-
rences. (37)

   In the excerpt which follows, Tarde makes a distinction
between the ordinary and extraordinary, the available and the
exclusive, which cuts across my earlier discussion of invention
and innovation.   His understanding of the phenomenon sees it
as both distributed and exclusive, not only in terms of tangible outcomes but in terms of practical techniques and processes and even concepts and ideas.

   I might have been ... justly criticized for having over-
   stretched the meaning of the word *invention*.   I have certainly applied this name to all individual *initiatives*, not
   only without considering the extent to which they are self-
   conscious - for the individual often innovates unconsciously,
   and, as a matter of fact, the most imitative man is an innovator on some side or other - but without paying the
   slightest attention in the world to the degree of difficulty
   or merit of the innovation in question.... Some *inventions*
   are so easy to conceive of that we may admit the fact that
   they have arisen of themselves, without borrowing, in almost
   all primitive societies, and that their first accidental appearance here or there has little significance.   Other discoveries, on the contrary, are so difficult that the happy advent
   of the genius who made them may be considered a pre-
   eminently singular and important chance of fortune. (38)

Tarde goes on to note that his characterization of 'the most
simple innovations' as inventions or discoveries is warranted,
if only because the 'easiest are not always the least fruitful
nor the most difficult the least useless.' (39)

   This statement, with its emphasis on the ordinary as something often *more* socially and culturally valuable than the
extraordinary discovery or invention, also addresses the pos-

sibility that social and cultural values emerge as the product
of non-rational, habitual, even unconscious and involuntary,
actions as much as 'rational' ones. This in turn suggests
how dependent such a view is on the idea of social or cultural
value as something which is relative to the society and culture
in question at a particular point in its ongoing evolution or
development. The contrast to the more idiosyncratic understanding evident in Western conceptions, with their scientific,
technical, or economic bias, could not be more clearly drawn.
In this regard, it is disconcerting to note that it is precisely
this latter understanding which leads Western thinkers to
characterize their own pattern of development as 'objective'
and constitutive of real 'progress'. Without going too far in
the opposite direction and hypostasizing particular 'structures'
performing alleged functional requisites necessary to the survival of any culture, I can nevertheless note the difficulties
attendant upon commitment to such presuppositions and
biases. (40)

   Tarde's notion of availability turns out to be far more 'universal' than Durkheim's, because Tarde focusses upon traits
and characteristics much less hostaged to Western understandings.   Indeed, Durkheim's concern for division of labour is
far more idiosyncratic in the sense cited than Tarde's emphasis on repetition in the form of imitation and counter-imitation
because Durkheim's central analytical concept reflects the bias
cited at its core.   Durkheim's available individual, and available innovator, as noted, are no less confined to Western (or
Westernizing) contexts than more exclusivist views concentrating on tangible outcomes were in the past.   Durkheim is no
less inclined to generate a congratulatory schema derived from
looking backward than many of those whom he opposed, something readily in evidence in his discussion of the 'general
movement', with its commitment to progress through the
achievement of a new solidarity which would simultaneously
preserve what had been economically and productively attained.
Durkheim's conception is confined to Western industrial societies, whereas Tarde's position is far more sensible in any
effort at comparative research.

   Durkheim's schema in 'The Division of Labour in Society'
views resemblances, likenesses, and similarities as a basis for
a traditional ('mechanical') solidarity which Western industrial
societies are allegedly beyond.   His insistence that there
could be no return to earlier pre-industrial forms, but only
the choice as to whether to continue the abnormal present, or
repair and normalize it from within with the help of a 'moral'
science of society, underscores his view of mechanical solidarity, with its collective conscience based upon likenesses, as a
more primitive form of collective life than either the abnormal
division of labour under nascent industrialism or the hoped-for

normal division of labour premised on solidarity in and through
his 'new' individuals. Durkheim's developmental schema thus
treats imitation and counter-imitation as low-level human traits
at best, traits which more aptly characterize the less-devel-
oped human types referred to in an earlier statement from the
text. (41)   Tarde is arguing not only that his position is
more relevant for comparative purposes, but also that these
same traits remain central to any effort to study industrial
societies in the West.

What is so significant about this claim is the way it points
up the extent to which my earlier argument must be seen to
hold for Durkheim.   It is precisely Durkheim's failure to
escape the biases cited which makes itself evident in the fact
that his sociology is unavoidably in the service of *society*.
An 'objective' conception of division of labour, undergirded
by the alleged ideal of 'functional interdependence', with its
effective fetishization of 'function', serves to *underscore* the
fact that he treats society as the only 'available' form of collective life rather than a culturally and historically produced
'type' of it. (42)   This is not to say, however, that Tarde
was entirely innocent of such preconceptions, for it is highly
doubtful whether anyone writing from a particular cultural and
historical perspective can escape these biases to a very great
extent.   Nevertheless, there can be little doubt that Tarde's
schema has much greater applicability to comparative research,
then if not now, than Durkheim's ever possibly could.   It is
also clear that Tarde's motives, unlike Durkheim's, did not
include a commitment to muffling critical thinking about the
reality of a capitalist industrial society with an emerging
stratification order all its own, in favour of disciplined observation in the service of completing this very order in the
name of a new solidarity.

A CROSS-CULTURAL APPROACH?

What has been said thus far suggests that innovation must be
counted a *human* characteristic which appears in all cultures
and societies, and in one way or another in all individuals
from time to time.   Innovation as a social and cultural phenomenon is relative precisely because of this reference, and
efforts to understand it must necessarily take account of
cross-cultural and historical comparisons wherever possible. (43)   This point is made not in order to undercut the
contemporary concern in industrial societies of all types with
the phenomenon of innovation, but rather because no adequate
comprehension is possible where this cross-cultural and historical reference is absent.   If it makes sense to speak of
innovation as a human phenomenon, a characteristic of human
collective life at the very least, then an effort to address it

based solely or mainly on an idiosyncratic approach hostaged
to Western conceptions of (technical) progress, development
and value is bound to be unsatisfactory. (44) Even the concern to produce or generate such innovation, or to search
after it by conceptualizing particular outcomes or processes in
this fashion, presupposes the need to make such an effort.

This effort is not to be confused with the sort of 'comparative' research which concentrates solely on comparing different industrial societies (or organizations) along national-state
lines, however. Indeed, it is one of the major claims of this
study that comparisons on these matters which are not cross-
cultural, and possibly even historical as well, are not really
meeting the crisis which the so-called problem of innovation
should be speaking to at all. Perhaps, as noted already, this
difficulty is endemic rather than incidental to the very way in
which the problem is formulated as a crisis. In common with
science's oft-noted refusal to question its own limits, the idea
of problem here often appears to have been formulated in such
a way as to guarantee resolution without challenging fundamental assumptions and auspices. The 'other side' of this argument may be more compelling, drawing our attention as it does
to the possibility that 'resolution', so understood, may appear
to be effectively precluded where an effort is made to engage
in cross-cultural comparisons because this in fact constitutes a
'going-outside' of the unit of focus or analysis - the industrial
society. (45) It is suggested here that such a preliminary
attitude or protocol is problematic because it encourages an
overly restrictive approach which presumes the likelihood, if
not the certainty, that we can know or understand 'our own'
culture far better than others, or cannot understand these
latter cultures at all. This presumes that we can have a
more secure hold on one context than another, yet it is the
very limits of knowledge itself which would dispute such collective self-limitation in the field of social and cultural research. (46)

This is not intended to deny the idea of 'difference' as a
salient point of departure in such researches, but is rather
directed to the contingent character of *all* knowledge which
claims empirical status as a description and/or explanation of
any nameable and describable world. (47) In *all* cases I am
either directly or obliquely addressing the scope and limits of
the observer role, not only in terms of the notion of 'strange'
foci or units of analysis (non-Western cultures; historical
structures), but in terms of the difference between this posture and that of the lived experience of inhabitants. I would
submit that this 'difference' is in the final reckoning *more* significant than one which is based on the notion of culturally
different units of analysis. Again, I am not disputing the
idea of difference here, just pointing to the auspices which

make such a posture culturally and intellectually possible, sanctionable, respectable. Concentration on the differences between various units of analysis thus obscures a more significant difference by presuming that the distinction between disciplined observation and lived experience counts for less in advanced industrial societies than it does when denizens of these societies observe 'other' cultures.

What kind of 'grasp' of one's own culture or way of life is presupposed by such a commitment? Lived experience is mobilized, albeit perhaps latently, by the disciplined observer in order to justify his right to compare 'his own' culture to 'others', while it is effectively played down as a vehicle for self-understanding by the individuals and groups who are the 'objects' of his investigation. A privileged position with respect to this 'other' culture simultaneously plays down the importance of lived experience *there* while mobilizing this very lived experience as a resource and a basis for legitimating disciplined observations in and on these 'other' cultures. Social and cultural matters of this sort would thus appear to be premised on a conception of difference quite at variance with one appropriate to mathematics, perhaps even philosophy. In the former case alone, so it appears, difference is the more seriously argued for, and acknowledged, where it can be shown to contrast the familiar with the strange, the alien, the 'other'. The grasp that must be presupposed of the familiar, and the resulting conception of otherness, are in clear contrast to a concerted effort to reflect on our own cultural presuppositions as evidenced by the very presence of disciplined observation and the observer role themselves.

Reflection on 'our own' auspices would include reflection on the very concepts and frameworks employed by disciplined observers when they study *any* society or culture, whether 'our own' or 'an-other'. Reflection in the sense alluded to here would acknowledge how much more we are told about 'our own' culture by the way we go about studying 'an-other' than about that 'other'. Reflection would also draw attention to how much more we 'begin with' than we think, and would suggest how much more consequential what we begin with is than what we usually end up with. It would also, as a consequence of this, point up how central what we begin with is for what we end up with. (48) Parameters for conceptual and intellectual innovation are such that room for manoeuvre 'inside' given concepts and frameworks with respect to this possibility is strictly limited. It is probably precisely this realization that leads to, and helps justify, the view that flexibility and openness is to be discovered in the willingness to apply established concepts and frames of reference to 'different' externalities in the person of 'other' cultures. Reflection, I submit, can only display itself by addressing *its own* limits when it speaks to the limits of any and all forms, types and manifestations of 'disciplined observation'.

An excellent example of a wide-ranging and comprehensive effort to study innovation as a cross-cultural and historical phenomenon is provided by H. Barnett's 'Innovation: The Basis of Cultural Change'. Here innovation is defined as 'any thought, behaviour, or thing that is new because it is qualitatively different from existing forms.' (49) Barnett's definition quite understandably fails to allude to the dichotomy between the individual and society which is a cornerstone of Durkheim's analysis. This because for Barnett innovation is in truth a collective cultural phenomenon first and an individual performance only secondarily. Nothing is clearer from Barnett's study than the fact that for him innovation is a device not only for advancement but for adaptation and survival. In the latter instance, it makes sense to characterize innovation as those individual performances whose concatenated net effect, or relatively isolated effect in sub-groups of the culture, is often to preserve a given cultural collective by accommodating to those changes which cannot be controlled or effectively influenced. This understanding simultaneously makes sense of the individual/society distinction *as a topic* and at the same time draws attention to the fact that change can be dealt with both by controlling or effectively influencing its causes, or by accommodation and adaptation to its effects where such control or influence is not possible.

Anyone familiar with the speciality within the social, behavioural and administrative/managerial disciplines known as organization theory or organization analysis will be struck by the contrast between Barnett's view of cultural change and the 'systems' approach in the latter disciplines, with its emphasis on domain and environment. Interestingly enough, such frameworks can be shown to follow the pattern of actual organizational behaviour rather than leading it. Thus, for example, the gradual shift away from the closed system approach, with the idea of the external environment as *constraint*, towards a reformulation of this environment as a potentially exploitable domain for organized action. Such a shift expresses an affirmative attitude to organizational growth and the extension of organizational rationality to more and more sectors of collective life in the advanced societies. (50) This point of view reached its high-water mark in the middle and late 1960s and was effectively terminated by the onset of the oil crisis and military and political disillusionment in the United States in the early 1970s.

It now appears that Barnett's view of innovation as an ordinary phenomenon addressed to individual performances in collective cultural settings where adaptation, accommodation and survival are central is increasingly applicable to theory and practice *in the advanced societies themselves* rather than simply to the 'Third World', or to historic or eccentric contemporary groups in the West. One way of explaining the emergence of a view of innovation as ordinary, available, and distributed, like Durkheimian individualism (and the significantly revised concerns of organization analysis since the mid 1970s), is as a *reaction* to the realization that advanced industrial societies are now faced with external elements in their environments which they can only respond to by accommodation and adjustment rather than by domination and control. (51) Again the oil crisis would appear to be the principal example, but this must be extended to encompass the dependence of the advanced societies on a vast range of natural resources which they either lack, or which have never been exploited in their own countries because it was more economically rational from the standpoint of the interests of capital to 'develop' Third-World resources while keeping their own relatively intact. (52) In addition, I cannot ignore the military, and subsequent political, debacle in Southeast Asia, the success of liberation movements in Africa, and the possibility of a permanent downturn for capitalist economies of all kinds as factors contributing to the need for a reformulation of innovation as a cultural and adaptive/accommodative phenomenon rather than solely a technical and progressive/developmental one. (53)

Barnett gives very little attention in his book to the 'landmarks of technological progress', on grounds that such a focus places too much emphasis on tangible things or objects and not enough on ideational processes and activities of thought.   In addition, as I noted earlier, such an emphasis makes innovation too much an extraordinary activity carried out by special individuals. (54) I would add to this an element not stressed by Barnett, namely, the culturally idiosyncratic and retrospectively congratulatory bias of such a focus. Barnett would encourage advanced industrial societies to shelve their pejorative conception of 'culture' vis à vis civilization and recognize that they too are 'cultures' in the best anthropological sense of the term. The present organizational and managerial emphasis in North America and Western Europe on innovation as relatively ordinary, given correct socialization and training, points not only to the realization of Durkheim's organically solidary society, with its 'normal'(ized) division of labour, but also to an increasing, and consequential, inability to control certain political, economic and socio-cultural elements in the 'environment' of their respective societies. It must be clear that only the presence of the state socialist societies in the Soviet Union and China stand between this social and political reality and Western attempts to 'persuade' the Third-World countries considered 'responsible' for the present situation. (55)

Barnett's emphasis on *all* innovations as ordinary, 'even important ones', addresses the difference between innovation as an activity and phenomenon on the one hand, and innovations as tangible end products on the other. More important, however, it points to the collective aspect, particularly in respect of the question of the 'acceptance or rejection' of innovations. The adaptive or accommodative is stressed in his cross-cultural study, in clear contrast to the attitude in advanced industrial societies. In this latter case, the question of acceptance or rejection is mainly concerned with the issue of whether technological innovations will realize the sort of capital allocation support which will allow such 'know-how' to be sedimented in actual processes and structures in these societies (and organizations). Acceptance or rejection as a cultural and collective phenomenon draws attention to the question whether change is to be construed (and accounted for) *in terms of adaptation or development*. The more narrowly technical the conception of rationality, the more likely that change (thus innovation) will be endorsed by, and measured against, a unilinear and developmental conception, and valued to the extent that it is seen to approach this standard. (56) The more broadly cultural this norm of rationality is thought to be, the more likely that change will be valued where it approximates some adaptive and accommodative standard consonant with survival and persistence in the face of change.

The idea of innovation as efforts and outcomes directed to *technical* domination and mastery begins to seem far more 'culture-bound' than the more enduring and longer-term view which sees 'nature' as a partner rather than mere raw material awaiting human transformation and consequent definition. Levy puts my point precisely when he states that:

It is one of the conceits of most people in highly modernized contexts that somehow what we do, if not proper and good, is at least normal, reasonable and easily intelligible. The nonmodernized parts of human experience tend to be regarded as dubiously rational and above all as exotic and bizarre. Yet from all the evidence at our disposal, in terms of the total experience of human-kind, it is the patterns of the highly modernized that are the most exotic and the most bizarre, and - innate optimism to the contrary notwithstanding - we have yet to learn whether such patterns are even viable. Even if life may be sustained on this basis, many may question whether they will care to live so. We, the modernized, are the true queers of history. (57)

The problem here is only accentuated by the fact that capitalism is incompatible with a no-growth, steady-state condition. This means that the commitment to growth, 'development' and

'progress', conceived economistically and in terms of science
and technology, is virtually *built-in* to the dynamic of this
system, not optional for it.   Thus, even in the face of clear
signs announcing limits to these dynamic processes from both
the natural and cultural 'environment', the system grinds on.
The only limits it is willing to acknowledge, it turns out, are
limits of a political and military kind imposed upon this system
from outside it.

   It is this notion of limit that should encourage us to address
critically the present infatuation with innovation in the advanced societies, because its emphasis on behaviour and process
is more than made up for by its continuing concern for technical and technological outcomes, especially when this is
coupled with its gatekeeping role.   As I shall argue in the
next section, and off and on throughout the book, such a
shift still favours the idiosyncratic, and often ethnocentric,
view of Western development.   It is simply that conditions
have changed sufficiently in advanced industrial societies to
question the way we go about expressing our persistent technical bias.   The emergence of a managed economy comprised
of organized corporate structures in the primary and secondary sectors, underwritten by the state as permanent receiver,
has led those convinced that R & D establishments and 'sub-
systems' are the real generators of innovation to argue for a
more organized and planned approach to the 'production' of
this phenomenon in these contexts. (58)   As it turns out,
this constitutes an approach which exemplifies many of the
points made by Barnett, since it argues for a shift in thinking
in order to *preserve* the idiosyncratic and ethnocentric technical bias rather than subjecting it to critical analysis by direct-
ing attention to cross-cultural comparative research and discussion.   This is what I meant earlier when I pointed to the
fact that the real problem in the advanced societies is the way
that 'problem' is conceived in terms of crisis, where the solution is innovation of a technological kind, or more (or better)
such innovation.   It is the very way that 'problem' is formulated, then, which effectively guarantees that it can (and will)
be resolved, thereby leaving the real problem of innovation in
Barnett's sense not only intact, but fundamentally misunder-
stood.

   Barnett overcomes aspects of the ideal/material distinction
when he insists that innovation be defined as 'any thought,
behaviour, or thing that is new because it is qualitatively different from existing forms'.   While the source of all innovations must be 'an idea or a constellation of ideas', some innovations by their nature must remain mental organizations only,
whereas others may be given overt and tangible expression.
Thus: 'Innovation is ... a comprehensive term covering all
kinds of mental constructs, whether they can be given sensible

representation or not.' (59)   This suggests that a focus on innovation as a phenomenon must jointly address psychological activities and processes and collective attitudes in the form of stimuli and support relevant, among other things, to the issue of acceptance or rejection.   Barnett, following Tarde, appears to merge an emphasis on the qualitative aspect of distinctiveness with the view that innovation is an ordinary, available and distributed phenomenon.   In effect, he wants this notion of difference to be treated as *a part of the* ongoing cultural continuity of collective life, rather than understood as a threat to such continuity. (60)   Ordinary and extraordinary are to a great extent reconciled by being transcended in such a position, one which forces us to reflect on the difference between our own cultural bias, based as it is on the domination of nature and a concomitant commitment to economic growth and development on the global scale, and a more adaptive and accommodative focus which should be as central to studies of the advanced societies as it is, or once was, to the Third World.

Indeed, the continued view of non-Western cultures as potential resource centres and markets for the advanced societies speaks to the persistence of our own determination to extend our values in spite of the emerging evidence of clear limits to such a domination and accumulation-oriented worldview.   It is the persistence of this dynamic of growth and development in the face of increasing recognition by governments, international organizations, even large multinational corporations in the advanced societies, of these limits and constraints which serves to underscore the Western (and Japanese) dilemma.   An emphasis on innovation which addresses it as a *human* phenomenon and experience, one given as much in the past as in the present to all forms of collective life, focusses on such novelty as dependent on materials from 'the cultural inventory that is available to the innovator' as well as those components of experience which exist 'independently of human ingenuity and control'.   Here Barnett would likely accept Popper's distinction between World three ('cultural inventory') and Worlds one and two, the worlds of physical objects and mental attitudes respectively. (61)   In his effort to link the ordinary (innovative acts) and extraordinary (innovations which are culturally accepted), Barnett draws attention to a culturally specific version of what I have already referred to as capital allocation decisions in the context of advanced industrial societies.   These decisions serve to underscore the contrast between discovery and invention per se, and its actual sedimentation in ongoing processes and structures.

Barnett is making a point not dissimilar to the one I made in the first chapter, where I acknowledged that it made sense to assert *both* conceptual priority (innovative acts) and social determination (cultural, or organizational, influence and acceptance). He wants the notion of novelty or newness central to the idea of innovation to be understood in a way which speaks to the limits of the (largely Western) distinction between the individual and society rather than underwriting it. This is evident in the following statement, which merges ordinary and extraordinary aspects.

In defining an innovation as something that is qualitatively new, emphasis is placed upon reorganization rather than upon quantitative variation as the criterion of a novelty. Innovation does not result from the addition or subtraction of parts. It takes place only when there is a recombination of them. Psychologically this is a process of substitution, not one of addition or subtraction, although the product, the novelty, may be described as having a greater or lesser number of parts than some antecedent form. The essence of change, however, lies in the restructuring of the parts so that a new pattern results, a pattern the distinctness of which cannot be characterized merely in terms of an increase or decrease in the number of its component elements. This limitation clearly excludes from the category of innovations the many instances of change that consist solely of a multiplication or an extension of the dimensions of an existing thing. The manipulation of parts that can be treated as mathematical units produces an entirely different result from that which occurs when incommensurable variables are added, dropped or interchanged. (62)

LIMITS OF THE TECHNICAL BIAS

One way of addressing the idea that a technical bias in innovation has clear social and environmental limits is to contrast a culture in which adaptation and accommodation occur mainly through changes arising *outside* the culture in question, and one where the aspect of change has become virtually synonymous with a technical bias underwritten by economic/political and scientific developments ('progress') generated *from within*. Indeed, in the latter case I am really talking about a set of values whose realization entails the gradual acceptance of change not just as a 'response', even to these internal developments, but of change as an essential *objective* of any culture committed to a concept of progress which equates it with progress in technique and technology. In effect, then, the changes both given in and caused by technical progress become evidence that given cultural norms are in proper order, not that they are being sabotaged or threatened. (63) This point is especially significant when considering the contemporary dilemma faced by Third-World countries no longer able to ignore the conflict between relative cultural autonomy, and economic and technological development initiated largely, if not completely, from the outside.

Looked at from another angle, however, our attention is drawn not to external pressures to 'modernize', complemented, to be sure, by self-interested indigenous elites, but rather to the tension which increasingly is to be found in advanced industrial societies themselves. One way of pointing to this problem is to note that these latter societies, as 'cultures', have both a continuing commitment to the technical bias, albeit in the face of a relatively 'available' conception of invention as innovation, *and* an increasing realization that it is precisely this core value which is largely responsible for present problems which speak to the real limits of the bias itself. (64) It is thus the difference between changes and problems generated internally given this bias as a core value, and the emergence of real external constraints in their respective 'environments', which leads to frustration because of the very *dependence* of these societies on the resources (material and human) and markets (potential or actual) of the Third World as a prerequisite to completing the Western project of development. The lack of effective control by the West over relevant policy processes and decisions in the Third World, as already noted, is mainly a function of the presence of the Soviet Bloc and China as permanent and highly influential forces (and models) in world politics. (65)

Yet acknowledging the central role of this technical bias in the advanced societies cannot justify efforts to treat it as an 'independent variable' responsible *on its own* for development and for the recent problems arising out of development. Though I shall be making use of certain parts of Jacques Ellul's thesis in 'The Technological Society' and elsewhere a bit further on, his argument regarding the unhinged and increasingly autonomous, monistic, automatic, self-augmenting and universal character of technique and technology, understood as a 'technical phenomenon', constitutes for me an example of unjustified reification on his part. (66) Even as knowledge, technique and technology in the advanced societies only *approaches* objective status relative to other (competing) values in such a culture. It does this in the main by becoming virtually pre-eminent, in one guise or another, to be sure. But the perceived ubiquitousness of the technical bias is no argument in support of its objective status as a reified phenomenon functioning from outside and acting upon us. Indeed, the only way to make sense of the idea of technique as a phenomenon would be to investigate first the conditions under which, and the reasons for which, such knowledge was and is desired, encouraged, and supported, and thereafter, how such knowledge in the form of 'know-how' was and is sedimented (or *not* sedimented) in societal and organizational structures, processes and practices. (67)

It is precisely an approach like this which compels us to admit to the central role not only of science and technology as knowledge, but of economic and political interests expressed through non-military capital allocation decisions embodying, embedding, and sedimenting technological outcomes. A focus on 'R & D', whether carried out by elements in the broadly economic or governmental/political sectors of the advanced societies, would carry this to its conclusion by pointing to sedimentation and the role of economic and political interests as ultimately determinative. These interests are increasingly central to the actual production of science-based technological knowledge, which depends on the presence of the complex, massive and highly expensive facilities that only these interests can sponsor. (68) Thus there is no automatic 'conversion' of technology as 'know-how' into sedimented structures, processes and practices, even in the face of corporate or state sponsorship of R & D. However rational or irrational such decisions are seen to be when judged in terms of either process or outcome, it is through the aegis of capital allocation decisions and determinations of military effectiveness that economic and political interests in these societies give content to their respective concerns for 'comparative advantage'. While these decisions may arguably be said to be influenced by a technical bias, as noted, this in no way justifies the view that such a bias constitutes a real interest whose realization is the objective of individual and group efforts, or even the outcome of such efforts in a sense independent of them. (69)

Let me return to the tension between the Third World and the internal dynamic expressing a technical bias in the advanced societies, reserving more detailed discussion of the relation between capital, science and technology for later chapters. Applied to the Third World, the distinction already noted between internally generated changes based upon an ethos favouring the equation of technical progress with real development found in the advanced societies, and changes which arise external to given (Third-World) cultures in the form of pressures to change, is especially important. This is because it can be shown that these contemporary pressures on Third-World countries and cultures almost uniformly favour 'modernization' and the technical bias over values more in tune with indigenous traditions and customs. This is not to argue that this technical bias, and numerous institutional settings arising out of its central role, have not in a way become part of the 'traditional' or 'conventional' ballast of the advanced societies; far from it. Indeed, it is precisely this fact that justifies our referring to these societies as 'cultures'. (70) But it does suggest that in this case we are faced with a conflict of cultures, where one culture points to the distinction between culture and civilization itself in order to argue that it is, after all, not really a 'culture' in any meaningful sense. In this conflict, the real dilemma is now to be discovered in the reasons behind the decision of certain non-Western countries to become a problematic element in the environment of the advanced societies on matters like energy, other raw materials and natural resources, and rights of access, co-operation and reciprocity generally.

While there is no attempt here to play down the role of political and ethnic, religious, and tribal motives as reasons on their own, it must be quite clear that development itself is a major reason for such behaviour by non-Western countries in international affairs. The so-called technical bias favouring modernization and development is therefore a fact having *global* significance because it is often as central a factor dictating or influencing the policies of the Third World toward the West as it is in the advanced societies themselves. This is increasingly the pattern that political and ethnic, religious and tribal nationalism is taking, one based on the view that a viable nationalism increasingly requires a modernized, industrialized nation-state if it is to be taken seriously in international affairs. (71) Perhaps the most significant predictable upshot of such an attitude would be reflected in the paradox of a country whose natural resources will be increasingly necessary for *its own* internal development. In effect, the proverbial lines on the graph can be expected to cross, because it was the very export of this natural resource which provided the financing and capital on which infrastructural economic and technological development could first be based. This holds with most force, to be sure, in the case of the oil-exporting countries, but it is a consideration for any non-Western nation attempting to modernize and develop through the sale of its natural resources to the developed world, not to mention its unavoidable subsequent investment in the economies of these latter countries. (72)

The question which suggests itself here is how long it would take key Third-World countries to generate a sufficient industrial infrastructure, including at least the rudiments of organized invention and innovation in the form of 'research and development', for them to become a force substantially independent of *all* advanced countries while providing political and economic support for other Third-World countries wishing to industrialize. This would require the gradual transfer and utilization of the natural resources initially used to finance industrial development from the advanced countries back to the developing Third-World countries in question, at least to some extent. This would appear to be the *only* way key Third-World countries can *both* industrialize and avoid the near-total dependence syndrome which is seen to occur when a given country rich in natural resources finds that it needs more of what it is exporting in order to industrialize itself when these exports were what made development initially possible.

Even were this to take place, however, the dialectic of development suggests that the key Third-World countries which had industrialized, even with this end partly in mind, would likely lose too much common ground with their less (or un-) developed brethren to maintain links of real solidarity, forged as they were in large part out of what was originally their common economic status vis à vis the Western countries, Japan, and the Soviet Bloc. Here I am simply addressing the essentially local, tribal, or at best national basis of particular Third-World cultures as the real bedrock. Intercultural relations between them, employing as its major vehicle the nation-state created largely out of the colonial/imperial domination, would of necessity be 'superstructural' relative to these cultural factors and the desire to preserve them even in the face of development as a general phenomenon. Even were the possibility of generating such an 'independent' infrastructure conceivable given the minimum time frame required for doing so, then, the upshot would likely include a situation in which, over time, the developing Third-World country would have progressively *more and more* in common with other industrialized countries, both in terms of a superficial interest in commodities and processes associated with them, and in terms of an industrial ethos which would simultaneously underwrite and be responsible for this emerging common ground.

At this point, a comparison between non-Western cultures in the contemporary world, and Western Europe in the pre-modern period, might be useful. The purpose of this brief sketch is to underscore the difference between the present tension in world politics, based increasingly on the central role of the technical bias *almost everywhere*, and the conditions in which economic growth and technical development first became conceivable and possible, as well as desirable. The tension, present in both instances, was radically different in the pre-modern West from the present situation. Both constraints and possibilities were mainly internal factors in the later Middle Ages, not external and cross-cultural as in the contemporary world. While it is no doubt true, as noted, that an internal tension within many non-Western countries is in the process of emerging as a response to the view that equates a viable nationalism with a modern industrial nation-state, this has not gone far enough at the present time to justify an attempt to play down the role of tensions between external elements favouring development, and indigenous cultural forces determined to preserve pre-modern mores and values, whether to the exclusion of the new attitudes or in an effort to achieve an equipoise with them. Add to this the undeniable dynamic of multinational corporate capitalism, buttressed by international funding and financing agencies, and the continuing role of these elements as mainly external factors cannot be seriously disputed.

This distinction between a situation where pressures for development are internal, both initially and over the long pull, and one where such pressures are mainly external to a given cultural configuration, may in fact simply point to the unique status of the pre-modern 'unit of analysis' in the West vis à vis the contemporary non-Western nation-state, the latter created in the main out of nineteenth-century colonialism and imperialism. The idea that Western Europe as a whole was once at least as comprehensible as a single cultural configuration as it is as twelve or thirteen national-state units may appear to be straining credibility, yet the presence of a common religion, common methods (and modes) of work and labour, common agricultural techniques, common forms of political rule, and common enemies certainly provide support for such a claim. In particular, it is to the tension between the guilds, religiously influenced corporate bodies in charge of determining the pace and character of work and labour activities in the towns and cities, and the (then) *subversive* interest in an unhinged technical invention and innovation, supported by secular undercurrents in the areas of commerce, politics, and science, that we must turn in order to appreciate the way in which invention and innovation, broadly conceived, functioned as internal *threats* to the hegemonic reality of (late) medieval collective life. (73).

I would therefore take substantial exception to Ellul, and argue that it is only in a situation like this, where the desire for an unhinged technical interest in invention and innovation *stands against* the culture in question, that you have the possibility of a technical phenomenon. For in this case it is the presence of a vast reservoir of value, interest and commitment which is present below the surface in latent or unrealized form which is truly expressive of such a phenomenon, not a situation in which the technical bias is pre-eminent, and increasingly global in its reach as well as its aspirations. In this latter instance, far from having the conditions which would justify such a description and explanation of contemporary affairs - not only in the advanced societies but to a certain extent in the Third World as well - the reality and ubiquity of the technical bias itself is what necessitates and justifies a focus like mine on actual decisions, processes, structures and practices. This is en route to underscoring the *contingent*, rather than the autonomous, monistic, automatic, self-augmenting, and universal character of technique. Far from constituting a factor on its own, it only becomes compre-

hensible as a world-view or attitude characterized by these
features to the extent that it is contingently sedimented in
the ways suggested above. (74)   This is related to my earlier
claim that technology only approaches objective status as
knowledge, for it is in the pre-modern West in particular that
such knowledge could exist subversively in a latent or unrealized form because it could not, under the prevailing
norms, be sedimented in new (or existing) processes, structures or practices.   Technique is comprehensible as a phenomenon, I would argue, precisely to the extent that the desire
and interest is present, for whatever reason, while the possibility for actualizing this knowledge by realizing its potential
is minimal or altogether non-existent.

   Guild controls on invention and innovation were directed,
among other things, to governing technical changes so that no
change would take place which would challenge the primary
role of the individual vis à vis his tools.   His tools were to
remain in an instrumental relation to him as an extension of
his person, and any apparent development which threatened
this arrangement was not permitted.   Such controls were
often claimed to be necessary not because invention and innovation themselves were frowned on, only *technical* inventions
and innovations whose net effect might lead to a situation in
which the craftsman would become an extension or instrument
of his tools rather than the reverse.   Indeed, our understanding of a craftsman even today is an individual whose
craft requires that his tools remain in an instrumental relation
to him as an extension of his productive knowledge and
powers.   Admittedly, the crafts are as a general rule confined to those areas of fabrication where the nature of the raw
materials to be transformed acts as a real (present) limit to
the development of technical instrumentalities which would
reverse the individual's role vis à vis technology. (75)   In
the guild situation, in contrast, I am talking about a policy or
rule of action which opposed all such developments almost unequivocally, regardless of what could be done, if the craftsman's priority appeared to be threatened.

   It is really only by pointing to the difference between such
inventions and innovations, and ones which were permitted,
that we can understand how it was that improvisation came to
be viewed as a type of behaviour or activity clearly and unambiguously in opposition to inventiveness and innovativeness
expressing a technical bias.   I would submit that what we
have here is a distinction between new patterns of behaviour
in the crafts compatible with the culture in question (improvisation), and those which were perceived to threaten what was
thought to be its 'common core' of shared values (technical
invention and innovation).   In this case, the guild, in effect,
argued that such and such an invention or innovation should

be forbidden because it would deny the craftsman the opportunity to improvise, that is, to make the most 'inventive' and
'innovative' use of the tools *to which he was confined.*
Improvisation was threatened by an unhinged inventiveness
and innovativeness expressing a technical bias precisely to
the extent that it would make improvisation impossible (or
less possible), by transferring the power of decision and
action away from the individual craftsman into the hands of
those in charge of the (now) independent instrumentalities
themselves.   This is not to argue that the individual craftsman was a 'free agent' under these obvious constraints.   It
rather points to the lack of freedom under a modern, or
modernizing, order in the interest of making useful comparisons. (76)

This leads me to make the following claim: it was the very
unhinging of invention and innovation favouring this technical
bias from guild (and ecclesiastical) controls, where improvements were confined to human techniques given the presence
of instruments functioning as extensions of the craftsman,
that helped generate, and supported, an oscillating asymmetry
between prices, wages, thus of capital and labour, central to
the growth and development of what we today call an 'economy'. (77)   That this oscillation has, as a consistent rule,
favoured capital over labour does not detract from my point,
but rather underscores once again the contingent nature of
technological advance vis à vis allocation decisions, and the
difference between a technical bias and real (economic/political)
interests.   Seen in this light, the possibility that technological advance across a wide range of human activity could
occasionally (or frequently or continually) be construed as a
threat to the perceived comparative advantage of established
economic structures and interests should come as no surprise
at all.   It is the difference noted by numerous economic historians between the radical and unconventional values of the
new urban and commercial classes standing in support of an
unhinged technical bias and against established institutions,
and the later-to-emerge situation in which traditional attitudes
are in retreat in the face of the bourgeois ascendancy following upon Western industrialization under capitalist auspices,
which is relevant here.   Only in the latter development do
we have the makings of the kind of contradiction (as well as
irony) which Marx had in mind when he alluded to the unavoidable emphasis on the *control* of technological invention
and discovery which would attend the increasing concentration
of capital in all sectors of the capitalist economy. (78)

One of the more intriguing consequences of this technical bias
in operation, however mediated by economic and political interests it may be, is the way that invention and innovation increasingly come into demand as ways of dealing with prior inventions

and innovations which have arisen *internal* to the culture in
question. While this has always been true to a limited
extent, such a need is now effectively built-in, therefore
central rather than peripheral, to advanced industrial societies
with few pre-modern 'traditions' left to oppose further 'progress'. In point of fact, a major factor directly opposing
such development turns out on close scrutiny to be *organized
corporate capitalism itself*. (79) Apart from this, however,
there is the impact of technological change, institutionalized
and underwritten by economic and political interests, not only
on residual elements of tradition, but on those individuals and
groups in society who claim to be in general agreement with
such values. The issues of 'resistance to change', and
thereafter of 'future shock', are all-too-often ways of conceptualizing problems of adaptation, accommodation and adjustment
to the effects of technological development for denizens of the
advanced societies rather than for recent immigrants or individuals in the Third World. An indication of the gravity of
the present situation is that authors like Toffler argue against
virtually *all* conventional adaptive behaviours as dysfunctional
ways of 'coping'. It now seems that the only effective
method of coping in the face of these changes and their
effects, short of pathology, involves a wholesale reaction
against the values of the system, whether this response be
conscious or otherwise. When this pattern of group and individual behaviour is combined with the increasing corporate
stranglehold on 'research and development', particularly in
the secondary sector, the human limits to certain features of
the 'innovative society' can be dimly perceived. (80)

From a situation in which patterns of adaptation were
already available, or could be built up as a response to
changes in an individual's life space, we now discover ourselves on the verge of claiming that no such piecemeal approaches can any longer be expected to 'work'. Even two generations ago there were substantial areas of collective life that
produced and supported values and attitudes hostile, or
clearly indifferent, to technological progress and the technical
bias generally. That this often took place among persons
supportive of capitalism, even industrial (as well as commercial) capitalism, only serves to draw attention to the difference
between the ascendant bourgeoisie and their heirs, and the
new middle class of managers, professionals, and bureaucrats
so central to the emergence of the employee society. It is
the threat posed to the ideology of automatic progress held by
this latter group alone which is so central to any attempt to
understand the real problem which the contemporary problem
of innovation in the advanced societies speaks to. It strongly suggests that the piecemeal approach embodied in reformist
and interventionist ideologies could only be successful when it
was able to stand against residual elements opposed in principle

to capital and to the idea that one realizes his true individuality mainly or exclusively through work and labour activities.
In the absence of such resistance and opposition, a strong
case could be made for the claim that this approach is manifestly *incapable* of underwriting the further extension of the
values of urban industrial society. Indeed, Goldthorpe has
noted the trend among prominent British and American main-
line economic and sociological theorists (Parsons, Bell,
Rostow, Kerr, Kahn) toward the sort of holistic and deterministic thinking which should be inimical to Popper's vaunted
open society thesis, with its attack on such 'utopian' conceptions, but really is not. (81)

It is suggested here that one of the most significant limits
to the present ideology of innovation, with its combination of
a continuing commitment to technique and technology, and an
emphasis on behaviour, activity and process in groups, is the
fact that it goes on for the most part inside large organizations whose members have been taught to treat *societal*
effects as factors 'external' to them in their respective 'environments'. Social responsibility and social accounting, while
in one sense clearly an attempt to address this dilemma, seem
already to have failed precisely because they were never intended to challenge long- (or medium-) term comparative advantage, but were a belated response to the changed nature
of competition which occurred after the mid-1950s and the
rise of consumerism and environmentalism. The point about
the organization itself being the relevant 'system' can be made
with even greater force in the case of the giant multinational
firm, where a wide range of opportunities are available for
'end-running' many of the societal, governmental and cultural
controls that operate, however weakly, on domestic enterprises
doing most or all their business in one nation-state. Adaptation as a collective cultural necessity and achievement is inconceivable in what Zijderveld has called the 'abstract' society
because of the many different, ambiguous, even conflicting,
roles 'available' there. It is the fact that one's life is so
fragmented which allows him the luxury of believing that he
can shift problems arising in one role context over into others
without having to face the consequences of such behaviour.
The idea that a social structure could become so 'complex' that
the relevant 'systems' would be organizations *inside* it helps
explain how the external environment of these organizations
could be construed by their members as essentially 'other' to
them in their *central* (occupational) role. (82)

In the absence of significant pre-modern values and traditions in the advanced societies, what were once the 'side
effects' of invention and innovation directed to improving on
prior inventions and innovations can more easily and quickly
aggregate into 'centre effects'. The point here is that the

view of society provided by role theory and analysis becomes
less valid as the opposition posed by traditions and customs
becomes weaker and less effective as a constraint. To be
sure, the view of society as a whole broken into separate
compartments where effects in one area could be hermetically
sealed off from others had ceased to be a very accurate picture even before Henderson and Mannheim attacked it. (83)
Ellul's way of dealing with this aggregation of side-effects
into centre effects is to point to the 'technical phenomenon' in
contemporary industrial societies as the result of a conspicuous excess of means over ends. Indeed, only in the case of
technical invention and innovation is it conceivable that we
could have this sort of excess in the first place. It is in
and through the act of splitting ends and means in this
fashion that we put ourselves in the position of anticipating,
rather than simply responding to, problems. This effort to
anticipate is in a very real sense 'unnatural' inasmuch as it is
based upon the idea that one must *invent* presently unreal
problems which might pose contingencies in some 'environment'
in the future. This attempt to have extra 'solutions' on hand
backfires when it is discovered that this extensive supply of
'means' has become its own justification, thus a part of, if not
central to, the real problem (or crisis) itself. (84) Since
'solutions' in advance are by definition non-adaptive, they
often tend to be more problematic than doing nothing at all.
The 'functional' response to the crisis in the form of the
problem of innovation and its 'solution' thus becomes an essential feature of the crisis itself.

This chapter has tried to draw attention to the significance
of invention and innovation as terms denoting phenomena,
events, processes and behaviour which have changed in important ways over the past century. Parallels between polar
conceptions of innovation and individualism were noted, and a
brief effort was made to cite Gabriel Tarde's work as more
helpful than Durkheim's for my purposes. Then I singled
out H. Barnett's brilliant and comprehensive study, 'Innovation: The Basis of Cultural Change', in order to further
underscore my view of innovation as *both* ordinary and extraordinary, following Tarde. Finally I turned to the issue of
technical bias as a core value in Western thinking about invention and innovation, and attempted to show the limits of such
a bias in the advanced societies, in support of an emphasis
like Tarde's and Barnett's. My argument is that Western
societies must become conscious of themselves as *cultures*, and
must as a consequence give more attention to adaptation than
to change, more attention to learning from 'other cultures'
than is provided for by the present internal dynamic of the
advanced societies, which all too often sees the rest of the
world as an 'obstacle' to further progress and development,
when not the 'raw material' of such progress and development
itself. (85)

If I have posed more questions than answers, more problems than solutions, that is because I am suspicious of such a facile rendering of 'the problem', one which is soluble, so it would seem, without fundamentally challenging the auspices increasingly responsible for the real problem. Put another way, it is the fact that questions are often posed *because* they have ready (or available) answers on these matters which concerns me. (86) None of the foregoing, to be sure, presumes that *I* have the concept of innovation 'under control', as it were. It is rather my determination to address it as a phenomenon expressed conceptually which is the essence of the analysis offered here. Furthermore, it is the likelihood that it is simultaneously ordinary and extraordinary in the senses indicated which points to this distinction itself as one incapable of holding the phenomenon. I would argue that this distinction between an ordinary and an extraordinary conception of 'innovation' can only address 'innovation' topically if it is used to speak to the limits of dichotomies themselves.

CHAPTER 3

Practice/theory

The way that the technical bias exhibits its clear limits is
only underscored, rather than disputed, by the fact that it is
a necessary feature of development and modernization which
now threatens to displace traditional views of innovation as
adaptation in parts of the Third World itself. Technical bias
implies a basis for valuing particular inventions and innovations, without, however, presuming that this bias functions
as its own justification. One can rate or evaluate particular
types of inventions and innovations by reference to such a
bias, then, only if one accepts that technical interests are
ultimately surrogate in character relative to whatever real
interests (status, power, remuneration) are sought by the
commitment to this bias. In the case of the modern domination of nature, even the broadly instrumental interests of
science in transformation remained isolated relative to a strict
technical bias until after the profit-maximizing concerns of
industrialization under capitalist auspices had generated an
industrial system in which it was desirable, whether for economic, political, or military reasons, to secure an articulation
between them. Scientific theories clearly do relate to technological outcomes through the aegis of applied science, but this
mediating function or activity is only comprehensible if the
real interests motivating and supporting such an intervention
aimed at bringing science and technology together are properly
understood and appreciated. (1)

THE CONCEPT OF PRACTICE

At the outset I must acknowledge a serious difficulty inherent
in talking about 'practice'. The term appears to have
acquired a number of different, and in some cases conflicting,
meanings. There is first of all the view of practice as the
kind of 'traditional' behaviour which is at one and the same
time routinized and expressive of a foundational commonsense
rationality. This latter takes the form of improvisations when
tried and tested 'recipes' based on the experience of 'daily
life' fail or are found wanting. The idea of including both
routinized and commonsensically rational behaviour in the
designation suggests that even the basic pattern of improvisations undertaken in response to difficulties, as well as the
routines themselves, lie within the familiar terrain of a given

society, culture, or group for the individuals concerned.
This means that the phenomenon of improvisation, in line with
the contrast already cited between it and innovation during
the later medieval period, is seen to be essentially adaptive.
It is a response to the limits of applicability of given 'recipes'
from daily life, but in the interests of securing, rather than
undermining, the status of these recipes as *the* fundamental
reality of daily life. Thus 'practical' often is understood to
refer to one's competence in responding to sudden or unpredictable problems, albeit problems which, by the very way in
which they are formulated, essentially affirm rather than subvert the value of the society, culture, or group in question.
Perrow's distinction between an 'exception' for which a search
rule or method is available, and one which is truly exceptional
because no such rule or method exists, is germane to my
point here. (2)

A second conception of practice uses it almost as a synonym
for praxis, a term from the Greek meaning theoretically informed practice, practice based on reflection rather than activity
engaged in routinely or even commonsensically. The idea
that practice could be theoretically informed presupposes both
universal intelligibility as a possibility and theoretical capacity
as a resource. But a problem arises for any view which endorses the ideal of praxis because of its ambiguity on the
question of the priority of collective versus individual change.
Marxists tend, on the whole, to favour the priority of collective to individual change, whilst idealists, particularly of the
Kantian stamp, put the individual first and argue that a sort
of prior rational agreement is required in order for collective
transformation to proceed. Recent work by Jürgen Habermas
has attempted to reconcile these two views and thereby achieve
a conceptualization which is largely beyond the individual/
society dichotomy itself. In both cases it is the commitment
to an ideal whose attainment depends either on 'objective conditions' which are not thought to be forthcoming, or on
rational debate and discussion leading up to agreement, which
defines the contours of such 'utopian' postures. (3)

A third version of practice is neither presentist like the
first nor futurist and utopian like the second, but points to
the classical tradition because it sees practice and the practical as action in the world *necessarily* infused with an ethical
or political dimension. Here the clear contrast between the
practical and the technical is even more in evidence than in
the first and second understandings. It is this distinction
which is so central to Aristotle's discussion of forms of knowledge and knowing. Aristotle contrasts theoretical, practical
and productive knowledge, the last virtually synonymous with
what we call instrumental reason or the technical interest
today. In the contemporary context of the advanced societies,

the distinction between the *practical*, understood (with Aristotle) as that form of activity unavoidably infused with an ethical and/or political dimension, and the *productive*, instrumental or technical, is clearly central to Hannah Arendt's distinction between work and labour on the one hand, and 'action', 'power' or politics on the other. It is Arendt's staunch resistance to the idea that political action requires an explicitly theoretical grounding which links her to a view of politics and the political which Plato had effectively turned away from in his determination to generate a blueprint for statecraft and political rule. (4)

There are, however, important similarities between Plato and Aristotle which are worth noting here, inasmuch as they address Plato's preoccupations in 'The Republic', 'The Statesman', and 'The Laws' with the role of both theoretical and productive knowledge in ethics and politics. The role of the productive is evident from the emphasis in the above writings on the *technique* of statecraft and the notion of a blueprint for the ideal state. The role of the theoretical is evident from the very way in which Plato reconceptualizes contemplation, drawing it out of practice as a form of knowledge which is no longer presumed to be automatically relevant to practical interests. It is as if he felt it necessary, having done this, to formally assert a link between the two in order to establish what could no longer be presumed to hold, namely, that all knowledge was aimed necessarily at the improvement of practice, understood in both daily life terms and in its ethical and political aspects. (5)   Only theory's assertion of a difference between it and practice, and the claim of distinctiveness based upon it, would lead the theorist to point to a specific type of knowledge different from both theory and practice which could promise to value, and thereafter be oriented to, the practical from 'outside' it. Theory would have to distinguish itself in fundamental ways from the practice that made it possible, in other words, in order for the problem of linkage in the form of an apparent need for knowledge possessed of 'practical' concerns to arise at all. How could a need for such knowledge possibly make itself felt in the absence of the fundamental distinction between theory and practice produced by the theorist himself?   This, I shall argue further on, is the real basis in thought for the notion of a *disciplined* observation independent of both theory and practice. (6)

Marcuse's observations of classical philosophy on this score, while helpful, therefore miss my point:

The doctrine that all human knowledge is oriented toward practice belonged to the nucleus of ancient philosophy. It was Aristotle's view that the truths arrived at through knowledge should direct practice in daily life as in the arts

and sciences.   In their struggle for existence, men need
the effort of knowledge, the search for truth, because what
is good, beneficial and right for them *is not immediately
self-evident* (emphasis mine). (7)

Marcuse goes on to criticize the Aristotelian notion inasmuch
as the hierarchy of knowledge forms it ordains rigidly bifur-
cates theory and practice by the formal introduction of 'productive' (e.g. instrumental) knowledge as a type standing
between them.   Marcuse thus cites Aristotle's concern as
one which shows an appreciation for the problem, but fails to
realize how the very classificatory scheme Aristotle promoted
cannot help but deny his real commitment to unity.   It is an
incomplete, but none the less correct, rendering to notice that
Aristotle did indeed criticize the idea of a purposeless theory
which, in Bacon's words, 'occurs only for its own sake and to
afford men felicity'.   But Aristotle's tripartite distinction provides a tacit defence of such a split because it could not have
been conceptualized at all had this split between theory and
practice *not already occurred*.   Aristotle is at the point in
his own thinking on these matters where it is necessary to try
to put everything back together because he believes that it
makes sense to speak of *three types* of knowledge.   This is
the real origin of Max Weber's vaunted 'ideal type', for Aristotle is using this hierarchy of typologies as 'heuristic devices'
without accepting responsibility for the real commitment that
such usage entails. (8)

   In this instance, practice would appear to be denuded of the
ethical and political content which I have cited as a central
aspect of Aristotle's understanding of practice.   What has
really happened in this case must, however, be clear: practice and the practical, conceived in terms of this content, has
been so conceived precisely because of the bifurcation between
theory and practice, underscored by the presence of productive, or technical, knowledge, as the middle term establishing
the boundary and the difference between them.   Thus there
is really no conflict between the idea of an ethical and political content to practice, and the view that such a notion
affirms, rather than disputes, the difference.   It is only by
acknowledging such a bifurcation that the *need* for asserting
an ethical or political content to practice arises at all.   This
content is a way of responding to the (alleged) reality of the
split itself, not a way of opposing or overturning it.   The
central role of productive, or instrumental, knowledge, seen
in this light, must also be clear as a consequence.   It *says*
that theory and practice are henceforth irretrievably split,
and it *justifies* this claim by pointing to the presence (or
'availability') of productive knowledge.   This means that some
forms of knowledge need not be oriented toward practice, and
affirms for the first time the idea that what is rated as a

'higher' form is *ipso facto* less useful. Only productive
knowledge, it would appear, can act as a substitute, however
pale, for both theory and practice. With this, the basis for
an independent observation function is born.

My attitude, in clear contrast, refuses to deny the practical
possibilities of theory, and thereby refuses to acknowledge
the tripartite split itself. Thus I recognize that the idea of
practice as a 'traditional', or at best a commonsensically
rational, activity constitutes the end point in the 'de-naturing'
of practice which Plato and Aristotle inaugurated. In effect,
Aristotle responded to the split, with its explicit acknowledgment of productive knowledge as a new (and middle) type, by
asserting the ethical and political character of practice. Why
else would such an assurance have been necessary, unless
practice was in danger of being construed in precisely the
way it later came to be construed, as thoroughly nonreflective
activity virtually synonymous with *behaviour*, thus activity
which presupposes a disciplined observer actively exercising a
relatively unhinged observation function? The idea of an
ethical or political element, first suggested by Aristotle, could
only *later* be admitted without cavil because such an element
had, by this time, and in consequence of the modern domination of nature, been construed as tantamount to a recognition
of the individual's subjectivity in a hostile world where he
alone was a valuing subject concerned with ultimate ends.
Phenomenology's further reduction of practice to the conventional and traditional simply bespeaks the extent to which this
element, originally in the possession of the negative bourgeois
individual standing against a hostile order, could now be presumed to be the property of society itself, with its 'individuals' now the socially produced 'subjects' of its socializing
agenda. (9)

I therefore acknowledge in what follows the idea of practice
and the practical as a category of human action which promises possibility as well as actuality, action as well as behaviour. At the same time, practice does constitute a code word
functioning as an observer's view of the way 'significant
others' live their daily lives. Thus it is important not to
ignore the fact that *any* concept of practice, however utopian,
must comprehend a clear empirical moment in its understanding. What this means, among other things, is that any
utopian or idealized picture of practice and the practical must
be informed by empirical work, particularly empirical work of
the cross-cultural and comparative variety. Theory has an
obligation to practise precisely because *all* knowledge is
necessarily a form of practice, today no less than in the past,
rather than being superfluous (e.g. an end in itself; its own
justification, etc.) in certain of its aspects. But saying this
hardly justifies ignoring empirical research of the sort cited.

Indeed, the reason it makes sense to address this work in our commitment to any conceivable utopian posture is precisely because theory needs to take account of this activity today if it is to overcome the flattened out, one-dimensional conception of practice such work often espouses. Such a conception grants the individuals concerned their subjectivity only on condition that they cede their reason to the now-sedimented structures of organizational and technical rationality functioning in the service of accumulation, domination and transformation. (10)

Only in such a way would it be possible, through theoretical reflection, to address the limits of the observer role itself, in particular the phenomenon of disciplined observation which points to a relatively unhinged and free-floating observation function alleged to be independent of both theory and practice in any of its guises. The very fact, as noted, that practice is an observer's way of conceptualizing life speaks to my claim that observation is increasingly unhinged and free-floating relative to *both* theory and practice. It is unhinged from theory because it sees no reason to articulate any reflexive posture whatsoever, confining theory to the scientistic demand for testable, falsifiable hypotheses. In this case it often goes further, suggesting that reflection, far from being sterile, is a highly dangerous intellectual activity. (11) The observer role's pre-eminence is effectively underwritten by the claim that the 'success' of social research can only be judged by the effects of interventions in ongoing social life based upon its findings and recommendations. The observer role is unhinged from practice because the upshot of all this activity, in line with the real mission of the social sciences - the completion of society as *an historically and culturally specific form of collective life* - is to reconstitute practice in the image of the disciplined observer himself. It is almost axiomatic that in this effort the thoroughly dressed-down conception of practice as tradition, convention, or 'daily life' will be of far greater use (and support) than the idea of practice as either a utopian praxis or an ethically and politically infused activity, and will as a consequence be preferred by the social sciences. (12)

This clear preference suggests the tie between a pre-eminent observer role unhinged from both theory and practice, and the commitment of the social sciences which honour such a posture to the view that the individual's status as a subject can only be purchased by his tacit or explicit acknowledgment that rationality is to be discovered in the institutionalized socialization processes of the advanced countries (society) rather than in the individuals who emerge from and effectively 'reflect' these processes. Socialization *creates* the individual as a 'subject' just as Durkheim had insisted it must if the new

solidarity was to be realized, but it does this in order to
effectively reduce his real options to the choice of being a
disciplined observer eschewing both theory and practice, or a
'subject-as-object' of this very enterprise.   To the extent
that these interdependent postures are discovered in the *same*
person in the form of what sociologists euphemistically call
role conflict (or conflict within particular role sets), we see
the consequences of the societal 'capture' of the idea of individualism itself.   The observer role, thus unhinged and increasingly autonomous, can only show its limits if it is employed in a way which allows it to maximize this very possibility. (13)   In effect, it is inconceivable that we could
revise our technical bias in thinking about invention and innovation in the absence of a concerted effort to address conceptions of innovation which challenge the commitment to disciplined observation undergirding this bias.   While the need
for such an 'innovation' in thinking points to the general
phenomenon of social determination, the *possibility* of such a
change asserts once more the dialectic between such a truth
and the central role of knowledge in achieving and/or recognizing it.

An excellent testimonial to the disciplined observer's limitations is provided by Pierre Bourdieu in 'Outline of a Theory
of Practice'.   Bourdieu stresses in particular the observer's
need to fill in the 'abstract space', which he has by dint of
his lack of practical knowledge, with formal rules, and 'communications' which require decoding making use of these rules.
There is also the observer's unavoidable habit of flattening
out the lived experience of observed (cultural) 'others',
thereby achieving a false 'totalization' of these experiences by
thoroughly *de-temporalizing* them.   This occurs not only
because the time factor, so central in lived experience, thus
for *making sense* of lived experience, is ignored in the interpretation or report of a single transaction.   It also occurs
because this allegedly 'single' transaction itself is a 'fragment'
whose integrity and meaningfulness is to be discovered not
just in its inner significance for the actors engaged in it at
the time they are engaged in it, but also because it is one
element in an ongoing stream of collective consciousness called
culture which has no real beginning and no real end. (14)
The problem which the observer faces in these matters is
nicely captured in Bourdieu's discussion of the giving and receiving of gifts amongst the Kabyles, which I have taken the
liberty of citing at length.

In every society it may be observed that, if it is not to
constitute an insult, the counter-gift must be *deferred* and
different, because the immediate return of an exactly identical object clearly amounts to a refusal (i.e., the return of
the same object).   Thus gift exchange is opposed on the

one hand to *swapping*, which, like the theoretical model of
the cycle of reciprocity, telescopes gift and countergift into
the same instant, and, on the other hand, to *lending*, in
which the return of the loan is explicitly guaranteed by a
juridical act and is thus *already accomplished* at the very
moment of the drawing up of a contract capable of ensuring
that the acts it prescribes are predictable and calculable.
The difference and delay which the monothetic model oblit-
erates must be brought into the model not, as Lévi-Strauss
suggests, out of a 'phenomenological' desire to restore the
subjective experience of the practice of the exchange, but
because the operation of gift exchange pre-supposes (individual and collective) misrecognition (*méconnaissance*) of the
reality of the objective 'mechanism' of the exchange, a
reality which an immediate response brutally exposes: the
interval between gift and counter-gift is what allows a pattern of exchange that is always liable to strike the observer
and also the participants as *reversible* i.e., both forced and
interested, to be experienced as irreversible.... If the
system is to work, the agents must not be entirely unaware
of the truth of their exchanges, which is made explicit in
the anthropologist's model, while at the same time they must
refuse to know and above all to recognize it.   In short,
everything takes place as if agents' practice, and in particular their manipulation of *time*, were organized exclusively
with a view to concealing from themselves and from others
the truth of their practice, which the anthropologist and his
models bring to light simply by substituting the timeless
model for a scheme which works itself out only in and
through time. (15)

Bourdieu's critique of the 'normal' anthropological observer
is highly germane to my concerns here.   In a sense it shows
us what has happened to our own collective self-understanding
of practice in the advanced societies by criticizing the way we
have looked elsewhere.   In so doing it draws our attention
to the reasons why the disciplined observer often annihilates
practice in the effort to (re) constitute it from 'outside' it.
It also suggests the incipient dangers to be discovered in a
collective situation in which the stranger as observer and outsider is coming to constitute the pre-eminent model for 'practice' in advanced industrial societies.   This fact would only
be underscored by the way in which he reconstructs the lived
experience of others, collapsing the temporal aspect no less
than the gestural and expressive features of speech and language, all too often reduced to 'communications' requiring 'decoding' in 'normal' sociology and anthropology.   In the case
cited, it is obvious that any attempt to classify the gift/
counter-gift practice exclusively as an *exchange* would be
thoroughly wrongheaded, manifesting both detemporalization
and the desymbolization of speech and language.   Openness

to 'other cultures' should not therefore be construed as a
self-sufficient guarantee, if only because it is precisely the
clear (and increasing) autonomy of the observer function
which both makes this concern conceivable as a project, and
at the same time guarantees its failure wherever it is not held
in check by theory in the interests of practice. (16)

It is reflection, theory in the dialectical sense, then, that
is necessary if we are to make the proper (because limited
and circumscribed) use of disciplined observation as a device
for revealing its own possibilities (thus limits) relative to
practice as lived experience. Bourdieu is addressing the
fact that the problem which is built into the very strengths
of disciplined observation as its 'other side' requires a commitment to thought and theorizing which does not view its authority as one subordinate to and dependent upon the scientistic
impulse, with its requirement of structural decomposition into
testable, falsifiable hypotheses. (17) Indeed, only a reflexive moment or aspect makes it possible to remember the difference between practice and (its) disciplined observation, and
to go on from there to show this difference in the interests of
a concern for reality as it is culturally conceived and collectively constituted. Once again, the significant parallels
between the technical bias in invention and innovation and
disciplined observation suggest their interdependence as central components of the still-prevalent world-view in the advanced societies, a world-view whose ethnocentricity is of signal
importance precisely because of its 'global reach'.

THE TECHNICIZATION OF PRACTICE

Before proceeding to a discussion of the observation function
as it relates to the problem of innovation in particular, I need
to look more carefully at the relationship between the increasing pre-eminence of disciplined observation vis à vis both
theory and practice, and the gradual technicization of practice
in the advanced societies. To say of practice that it has
become progressively more susceptible to technique is to point
to an environing value whose alleged neutrality, given instrumental reason as the base-line standard for judging the rationality of conduct, is precisely what explains its apparently un-
challengeable pre-eminence, according to Ellul. (18) At the
same time my focus on the technicization of *practice*, by presuming that practice exists in the world relatively independent
of technique prior to the emergence of this process or situation, is anxious to retain the individual moment rather than
allow such action to be absorbed by a reified phenomenon.
My reason for wanting to do this is not simply that such a reduction is to be preferred on objective grounds, but rather
because it is no less worthy of consideration as a starting

point (conceptual and ideological), and is in fact probably
more useful for this purpose. In neither case, however, is
it to be confused with a dialectical analysis whose commitment
to objectivity requires it to render these polar bases for
social theory and explanation momentous as topics, rather than
allow them to be empiricized, thereby becoming components of
states of affairs in *any* nameable/describable world. (19)

Practice, particularly of the 'daily life' variety, but in its
guise as ethically and politically significant activity as well,
becomes technicized to the extent that a plurality of different,
often competing and conflicting, values is gradually subordinated to one value whose power, as noted, lies in its claim to be
beyond value, hence 'objective'. Once again, however, it
makes little sense to make such an assertion if we are not
willing to see values as 'means of support' serving objectives
or goals whose prior determination as objects of desire does
not detract from their deferred status as 'ends'. It would be
like endorsing the view that specialization speaks to values
which underwrite ends that are given in the values themselves,
when it is clear that such a commitment on its own is 'rudder-
less', and only makes sense when it is seen to be serving or
realizing ends 'outside' it. This point is perhaps most clearly in evidence when the notion of 'interest' is raised, for the
idea of a technical interest for its own sake would strike me
as a way of avoiding the issue of the real interests being
served rather than a way of speaking to them. What happens
to practice when it becomes 'technicized' happens to it because
practice, in its pre-technicized form, is seen to be less and
less 'functional' for the emerging order, and so must be displaced by new, different, and conflicting socialization processes more committed to the 'individual' as a repository for
socially produced and sanctioned 'norms of rationality'. These
appear at one and the same time to be his own possession and
the product of society as a collective and historically specific
structure with an increasingly clear agenda. (20)

I have already remarked on the way that Max Weber raised
this issue in his discussion of the doctrine of progress so
central to modern Western civilization. Though too pessimistic to see in Western development the possibility that completed
processes just might produce their opposites, his tripartite
distinction in what follows is of signal importance to my objectives here.

There is a recurrence here of the widespread confusion of
the three following meanings of the term 'progress': (1)
merely 'progressive' differentiation; (2) progress of *technical* rationality in the utilization of means; and finally (3)
increase in value. A *subjectively* 'rational' action is not
identical with a rationally 'correct' action, i.e., one which

uses the objectively correct means in accord with scientific
knowledge. Rather, it means only that the *subjective*
intention of the individual is planfully directed to the means
which are *regarded* as correct for a given end. Thus a
progressive subjective rationalization of conduct is not
necessarily the same as progress in the direction of rationally or technically 'correct' behaviour. (21)

In this excerpt we see an important parallel between the
notion of value and that of practice. Just as the notion of
'practice' points to what it cannot grasp or capture given its
basis in the observer role, so also does the idea of 'value' as
something 'valuable' address an unhinged observation function
precisely because the speaker must have transvalued value in
order to recognize it as such. (22) Weber goes on to equate
'technique' 'in its broadest sense', with 'rational action in
general', thereby acceding to the very ground rules for conceptualizing 'the world' which were supposed to be so foreign
to him.

What we really learn from a careful reading of Weber is how
dependent his puerile criticism of Western values and institutions is on its 'other side'. Weber's entire criticism is based
on a prior 'empiricization' of the individual - society dichotomy.
It is the fact that such an enterprise requires him to simultaneously concretize the individual as a bourgeois exemplar
standing against the collective, and to fetishize society as the
only conceivable kind of collective life rather than a culturally
and historically produced form of it, which effectively fuels
his pessimistic rationalization/de-enchantment thesis. What
Bendix called a cumulative linear eschatology proceeding *downwards* simply maintains the dominant metaphor and essential
format of the Enlightenment vision of 'progress', confining its
criticism to arguing that what the Enlightenment produces
could be construed as an inversion of what it claims to have
realized in and through development itself. Weber stands
almost unequivocally with the concrete part-as-fact-as-event
(the bourgeois individual) and the abstract totality (society)
when he refuses to leave his post in the rationalization process to argue against the authority of such a model of human
existence under capitalism. Even the individual as an intending and valuing substantively rational 'actor' is put in front
of this process of rationalization and de-enchantment so that
his opposition might be made all the more poignant by his
annihilation. It is here, to be sure, that Weber is most
undeniably biographical. (23)

Weber's determination to produce an equally deterministic
eschatology to that provided by Enlightenment thinking shows
his commitment to its values, and his rage at the way these
values miscarried as goals or objectives which would produce

a truly human social order.   The limited analytic capacity of
this tendency to construct the world in dichotomous terms,
whether in its original or inverted form, suggests a difficulty
inherent in the notion of a technicized practice.   On the one
hand it is as close to the reality which the concept practice
addresses in *any* of its forms, since in *all* cases what is required is an observer who steps 'outside' of life to comprehend discrete aspects of it.   This points to a technicized
practice as no less 'real' than one based more securely on
pre-modern 'traditional' conceptions, whether or not they
comprehend an ethical or political element.   On the other, of
course, we have in a technicized practice the argument that
what has displaced 'practice' is a substantially different set of
requirements for engaging in 'daily life'.   In place of several
sets of values we now have one.   Weber's very constriction
of the problem in this way underscores his own loyalty to the
idealized (bourgeois) conception of capitalism, which he insists
on preserving from the critique that would show how it produces its apparent opposite by adherence to its ground rules.
Weber will deposit the blame for this miscarriage with any
other phenomenon he can find, whether it be technique,
bureaucracy, legal-rational authority or rationalization and de-
enchantment themselves. (24)

He will do anything to preserve what is in fact a thoroughly
self-serving view of early bourgeois capitalism as 'pluralistic'
and committed to an unqualified 'antagonism of values' in the
social and political sphere. (25)   One only needs to be reminded that the history of the modern social (and economic)
order in the West is uniformly a middle-class (re)construction
(or 'enterprise') to have the beginnings of a critique of such
a 'rationalization'.   It is not dissimilar to the more pervasive,
and equally legitimate, claim that history is written by 'win-
ners' rather than losers.   Weber's view is manifestly undialectical, and therefore seriously deficient, precisely because it
sees social and cultural development as a process that culmi-
nates in the total annihilation of what has allegedly been completely rationalized, rather than in the generation of its opposite.   In point of fact, Weber has no theory of social-structural *change* at all, since all that is 'available' to him as a
disillusioned product of the Enlightenment is a vantage point
(allegedly) beyond the values he needs to isolate, where he
can *watch* the impending immolation and at the same time be
included within it.   In place of change, Weber posits termi-
nus, end, conclusion; in place of social transformation, he
posits collective cultural, moral, and spiritual self-annihilation.
From the standpoint of any conceivable theory (or concept) of
innovation as a cultural and adaptive enterprise, such a position shows the essentially affirmative nature of non-critical
criticism in Weber, because it presupposes the validity of the
empirical phenomena or events, and confines itself to simply

offering another 'interpretation' of what has allegedly
happened.

There is no apparent reason why the technical bias already
discussed would necessarily have to lead to the technicization
of practice, understood as a different way of carrying on
daily life from the way it was carried on before technicization
occurred.   Even the claim that such a modification of practice has in fact taken place cannot be allowed to imply that
practice, and the practical, no longer exists.   This would
mean that human beings could no longer be counted on to
constitute a resource of potential for new ideas, attitudes and
practices, very much on the order of Max Weber.   I would
therefore submit that the concept of innovation would be a
notion far more alien to Weber than to Marx.   Rationalization
is, after all, a one-way street whose claims can either be
accepted as they stand, or can be treated as a mere 'vision'
or 'view' held by a particular valuing, intendedly rational,
subject, in this case Max Weber.   In either case it underscores the conceptual impoverishment of such a manifestly undialectical exposition, dependent as it is on the empiricization
of dichotomies whose frozen one-dimensional status as concrete
parts-as-facts in an abstract whole encourages that either/or
attitude to reality so central to such thinking.   In this case,
it is the distinction between facts and values discovered in
the work of Weber himself which one sees presented as the
alternatives 'available' to one attempting to interpret the
rationalization thesis.

The upshot of this analysis is that Ellul and Weber differ
only within a more fundamental set of similarities, Weber
stressing the need to reduce reified concepts, then *using* this
isolated emphasis as a way of justifying reifications whose
effects are little different from those put forward less ambiguously by Ellul.   Though 'technique' for Ellul is problematic
as a phenomenon because it is characterized by a number of
secondary features whose net effect is to underwrite the idea
of its reification as an entity outside and beyond effective
human agency and control, rationalization for Weber only pur-
chases the idea of *process* from the priority in his thinking of
the concrete (negative) individual as 'actor', combined with
his view of history as properly the study of the unique and
non-recurrent acts of individuals which turn out to be 'responsible' for human social and cultural development. (26)
Apparent here is an attitude to history which provides an
interesting parallel to the exclusivist view of innovation as innovations of a technical kind discussed in Chapter 2, since
for Weber individual acts and decisions are the key isolates in
the study of history.   It is only the modern *crisis* fore-
ordained by the Reformation as the basis of an ethic that
gives aid and comfort to a 'spirit' of capitalism which generates

an industrial civilization whose leading institutions offer less and less opportunity for the concrete individual to affect the course of what for Weber is clearly a unilinear and cumulative eschatology *downwards* culminating in a 'dead mechanism' - total rationalization and its corollary, total de-enchantment. (27) No approach to innovation as a genuine, rather than a specious, problematic, should content itself with the alternative of either the superficial contemporary affirmations which abound today, or the anti-dialectical and anti-materialist exercises in pessimism and determinism like those of Weber.

Perhaps the best point from which to begin an analysis of the technical bias as a Western cultural bias would be with Herbert Marcuse's conception of the 'technological a priori'. Marcuse sees technique as a monolithic standard of value whose very 'success' as such is to be explained by the fact that it operates on behalf of real interests which are effectively concealed by it. This does not mean that the nature of technique and technology has not changed, only that the changes we notice are at least as dependent upon science, particularly applied science, as science in all its forms is on technology. This point is only underscored by the way that corporate and state decisions and policies allocating capital to research and development activities make a mockery of the alleged distinction between public and private spheres or sectors. Marcuse calls what he sees standing behind this activity and these values a 'technological a priori' because here for the first time men see 'nature' *exclusively* as other to and absent from them. The fact that such an attitude has probably always been central to man in his active dimension toward human and non-human externalities only serves to emphasize how different is the modern understanding. Science's broadly instrumental commitment to man in the world encourages a habit of mind in which men consistently and continually view 'nature' not only as alien or other, but in terms of what might be *following* human transformation rather than what it 'is'. (28)

To be sure, it is almost impossible to separate the view of 'nature' as other from the technological a priori, if only because the latter appears on close examination to be a logical outcome of the former. Once men view nature as an object realm in the narrow sense, and claim that a knowledge of nature so conceived is different and distinct from any conceivable knowledge of man as a social and cultural being, the stage is set for an orientation to this externality which defines it in alienated human terms as pure potential, raw material awaiting human definition. (29) Instead of a forest, cut lumber and land where tract housing can be built upon it making use of the lumber. The technological a priori is clearly a mode of orientation which must become sedimented as

a form of practice, or a basis for its modification, if it is to
be spoken of as a habit of thinking. And it must, as a consequence of being sedimented and becoming an accepted habit
of thinking 'given' to a particular culture, constitute a consistent and continuing basis for comprehending 'nature', not an
intermittent and relatively infrequent one. The question
which suggests itself to me at this point, however, asks
whether this provides us with the sense intended by the idea
of the technological a priori. I have suggested that this
notion is a useful way of conceptualizing one factor central to
the genesis of modern Western civilization, and one of its most
important world-views and habits of thinking. But does this
tell us *why* practice has been effectively reconstituted in a
technicized form?

Again, I would submit that neither at the individual nor at
the collective level does it make sense to argue that such an
a priori became so pre-eminent because of a narrow technical
interest, or even science's broader instrumental concerns.
To the extent that men have technical interests, these are
constructive human traits, variously encouraged or suppressed, over the brief period of human history on the planet.
In *every* culture and collective, not just 'our own', is it the
case that these interests are engaged in only rarely and in
the most aesthetic sense 'for their own sake'. In contemporary urban and industrial societies this interest functions at
least as much as an ideology deflecting public consciousness
away from the real interests being served as anything else.
If we try to focus on technology as the 'party responsible',
we find ourselves forced either to condemn ourselves for
possessing this capacity by dint of being human, or compelled
to acknowledge that its historical appearance in a particular
culture (or 'civilization') at a particular time must be attributed to other factors and, as a consequence, to other 'interests'. To be sure, the false needs that are generated as a
consequence of the economic-cum-social system of capitalism
in operation rely on a technical *intent* which has always been
an important attribute of human beings in the world. But
this is not to say that such an intent is a sufficient (rather
than a minimal) condition for such developments in the form of
an autonomous interest, or that it must inevitably generate
false needs on its own. Above the basic, and recurrent,
need for food, shelter, security and freedom from pain and
suffering, we find motives and interests like power, status and
desire for wealth, whose transcultural presence suggests the
transparency of the claim of a technical or instrumental interest as anything more than an expression of the very cultural
bias it should be attempting to explain, and often claims to be
explaining.

Thus when I speak of the technicization of practice I am

aware that the apparent security of the observer as an alleged
stranger or outsider is illusory.   Such a concept, no less
than technical bias, technical interest, or technological
a priori, is a part of the collective under examination, not a
neutral description of it from 'outside' it.   To argue that
some factor is central, for whatever reasons, is to make this
observation a part of the whole being subjected to analysis.
Thus the fate of 'practice' as a counter-concept to more conformist patterns exhibiting proper socialization when such
patterns are unsatisfactory to the observer.   Thus also action
v. behaviour in Max Weber, where the real contenders are
negative (read 'real') individuals and industrial fellaheen,
given the demise of practice and its transformation into 'traditional behaviour'. (30)   Or finally the concept of 'value'
itself, with its presupposition of an Archimedean point which
the observer in question has finally achieved by constituting
himself as the direct and total opposite of that which he allegedly wishes to protect and preserve.   To honour value and
principle, Weber will have to isolate it from life, then show its
essential difference from life en route to producing himself as
the near-perfect disciplined observer who has 'in fact' transvalued value.   What he has created he must destroy in order
to make his point.   He can only make his point by denying
himself life in order to 'stand up' for life.   The technicization of practice and the commitment to disciplined observation
must in consequence become increasingly interdependent with
one another in the emerging equation.

I would submit that our technical bias in invention and innovation is a more specific manifestation of the technological
a priori where the crucial phenomenon providing the explanation I said we needed is in fact disciplined observation.   Like
technique itself, or what is today called a technical interest,
men have always exhibited the capacity to interpret their sur-
roundings as social and cultural beings, thus as observers.
What I am after, though, is neither the presence of a technical capacity or interest nor the propensity to observe, interpret and reflect.   It must be quite clear, as stated earlier,
that the idea that men can reflect, analyse and engage in dialectical thinking is incomprehensible in the absence of the
capacity, indeed propensity, to observe and interpret.   When
I argue for the need for reflection in the advanced societies
today, I am neither denying the fact that reflection depends
on life and that life includes an observation function, nor
suggesting that through the aegis of development or evolution
we are somehow beyond the initial and recurring dependence
of reflection on observation and of both on life.   On the contrary.   In the present circumstances the service that reflection and dialectic can perform requires it to speak to the limits
of disciplined observation and an unhinged observation function
in the interests of returning such activity (and with it the

technical bias) to its place in the human hierarchy of *activi-ties*. The observer role, unhinged from its responsibilities to practice, turns on both practice and theory, constituting itself as the sole basis for interventions aimed at reforming structures and processes presumed valid in their essential outlines. (31)

Technique becomes a factor central to the reformulation of practice in urban industrial societies when it reflects the triumph of the stranger as *the insider*, the 'norm'. Techni-cization is inconceivable in the absence of motives and inter-ests which value the outcomes achieved by disciplined obser-vation, whether in the market-place, the courts, bureaucracy, the firm, or the laboratory. It is only because disciplined observation as the vital centre of a technicized practice helps realize these outcomes in the form of needs above subsistence concerns that technique itself can participate as an alleged 'value', 'bias' or 'interest' in such achievements. The mes-sage of this section must therefore be that there can be no real broadside aimed at addressing the limits of our technical bias in invention and innovation in the absence of fundamental changes in our attitude toward thought and thinking. Since it is theoretical reflection which is required, in concert with real-life experience, to bring the pre-eminence of disciplined observation relative to both theory and practice to light as the real basis of the present technicization of practice, no attempt to extrapolate present dispositions and preferences for modes of thinking predicated on the assumption of this pre-eminence can meet the real problem. This would only achieve a resolution of the *false* problem posited by the present understanding of a 'crisis' as something both comprehensible in terms of and soluble by reference to a conception of inven-tion and innovation still in the grip of a Western cultural bias, however well-distributed, organizationally speaking, it is alleged to be. (32)

DUALISMS AND DICHOTOMIES

It is an unhinged observation function which has forgotten its interdependence with both practice and theory then, which is the sine qua non without which a frozen and one-dimensional conception of practice such as that criticized by Bourdieu would be impossible. Technicization means only superficially a technical bias which is focussed on desired outcomes. It is far more important to see in such a bias regarding outcomes the impact of disciplined observation as *a technique* which ex-hibits this unhinged observation function in a way far more central to my argument than a bias which simply reflects this prior commitment. That a major consequence of this commit-ment would take us beyond the mere utilization of dualisms

and dichotomies as vehicles in thought and thinking to sanction their unreflective, and thoroughly one-dimensional,
'empiricization' must be clear.   Indeed this is the most
obvious form which the reduction of speech and language to
'communications' requiring 'decoding', and the phenomenon of
detemporalization cited by Bourdieu, take.   Once empiricized,
the continued tendency to allow these dichotomies and distinctions to breed and underwrite others, with no effective control on such an enterprise by either practice or theory, has
become more responsible for the perception of a reified technique circumscribing a one-dimensional social and cultural
reality than anything else.

What is needed in any analysis of dichotomies and dualisms
addressed to the problem of their empiricization is a clear
idea of what I have in mind by the term 'empirical'.   This
because I am not, after all, either addressing dichotomization
itself as a problem, or am I underrating its importance as
something essentially given in the human situation, before as
now, in non-Western as well as Western cultures.   Whether
exhaustive historical and cross-cultural research on the subject would yield anything more than suppositions regarding an
alleged *human* tendency to dichotomize which is both transhistorical and transcultural is not at issue here.   At the same
time, I suspect that such a tendency is present, and point to
the problem of empiricization in order to highlight what
appears to me to be the *real* problematic *given* given this
tendency or likelihood.   My animus in doing this is doubtless
the fact that I can offer a remedy for this difficulty which
takes the form of topicalizing such dichotomies by rendering
them dialectically momentous.   While obviously not offered as
a cure-all for problems attendant on the way Western peoples
in particular often conceptualize 'the world', such a suggestion
does point to theoretical reflection about collective life as a
more important requirement for improvements in practice than
the truncated notion of practicality based on the present pre-
eminence of disciplined observation would acknowledge. (33)

My view of 'practice' as a term referring to lived experience
which it can never hope to capture from its observer's position 'outside' what it claims to be conceptualizing and/or describing is one which underscores the limits of an unhinged
observation function.   Such a concept, no matter how well-
intentioned and well-informed by theory and immersion in the
culture or collective under examination, can never hope to
achieve in and through description the reconstitution of the
totality in question.   This problem, to be sure, holds to
almost the same extent when Western social scientists observe
and report on 'their own' societies and cultures, something
which even Bourdieu, Winch, Horton and Beattie, interested
as they are in 'other' cultures, often forget or downplay. (34)

While I readily admit that 'membership' in the society or culture being observed *may* improve the accuracy and overall
performance of the observation function, the problem which I
speak to is one which afflicts the phenomenon of disciplined
observation to some extent in all its forms and guises.   The
improvement to which I allude, to be sure, has to do even in
the case of a study of the member's 'own' culture with the
role his participation, and resultant lived experiences, play
as influences (thus effective limits) on the observer role.
Accuracy and corollary virtues associated with the observer
function in this case, if present at all, are, I would argue,
present precisely because it is here that both practice and
theory can exert the most influence over the tendency of this
function to unhinge itself from their respective requirements
and constraints.

There is thus no warrant for presuming that either 'own'
culture or 'other' culture studies confirm the need for disciplined observation as an unhinged and free-floating observation function which demands an initial effort at forgetfulness
requisite to achieving proper 'distance' and 'objectivity'.   In
a sense what I am arguing is that an unhinged observation
function is *not 'objective' enough precisely because* it tends to
freeze dichotomies into a rigid one-dimensional mode which simultaneously de-temporalizes and 'empiricizes' them.   Objectivity in such an enterprise would have to have at its vital
centre the reflexive realization that dichotomies and dualisms
are ways of producing 'the world', thus topics rather than
potential or actual descriptions. (35)   Dialectical momentousness is synonymous with a *partial* reflexivity in the sense
that for me *neither moment* - the empirical/observational or the
reflexive/theoretical - can be allowed to cancel out the other.
In the first case the result is an unhinged observation function and a corollary technicization of practice, while in the
second we generate a total reflection in which man's status as
both a social and an historical animal is effectively denied by
pointing to a frozen 'Being' standing against a 'mere' world of
appearance.   It is commitment to partial reflexivity which requires me to take reports about 'external worlds' seriously as
embodiments of a function whose real contribution to the human
condition requires its interdependence with both theory and
practice in the ways suggested. (36)

Empiricism might therefore be best understood as a convention which presumes the observer's ability to reproduce 'the
world' as it is, either directly or by dint of some sort of per-
ceptual screening or interpretation.   Indeed, Wittgenstein's
point in 'Tractatus Logico-Philosophicus', however limited it
was to the physical realm of 'nature', saw any viable concept
of 'the world' as something which effectively presupposed the
operation of this very convention.   Central to the proper

operation of this convention is the idea that what we see 'corresponds' to what is there, or rather that the accuracy of what we say we see *should* correspond to what is there. This means that someone uses 'what is there' as a standard for judging what we say we see. In science this requires replication of what operations were performed if the resulting claims appear significantly anomalous rather than normal, ordinary, and 'legal', since this enterprise in such situations goes to the trouble of *not* presuming that 'the world' at stake in the description or (re)conceptualization proffered is mistaken because in some disagreement with the one heretofore taken for granted. Such a corrective, not being generally available in the social and behavioural sciences at all, is rarely used as a 'distant model' for these disciplinary practices, with the result that different world-views, perspectives, points of emphasis, etc. tend to coexist until such time as social conditions themselves lead to changes in the hierarchy of conceptual and theoretical 'structures'. (37)

I have noted how the observation function tends to trade on its interdependence with *both* theory and practice without acknowledging this interdependence, at the same time that it appears to be trying to suppress the reflexive element in thought en route to reconstituting practice in its own image. It does this in particular in 'own' culture studies where the stranger is increasingly becoming the 'insider' rather than the marginal, but also in Third-World and related researches where an unquestioned bias favouring an unhinged observation function in the form of disciplined observation underscores the latent presumption of superiority of the 'developed' to the 'underdeveloped'. (38) Without the proper and continuing interdependence between practice and theory, there is no way that such an enterprise can possibly avoid the one-dimensional empiricization of dichotomies whose reductive and de-temporalizing effects reveal the real (latent) commitment of such studies - strategic intervention in the interests of completing society as an historically produced 'culture' supporting advanced industrial capitalism in its unceasing commitment to 'global reach'. (39) The fact that individual social scientists follow practitioners of the natural sciences in being largely unaware of a social division of labour which all too often demands that even their ordinary, normal researches be made potentially utilizable for these purposes constitutes no refutation of the claim being made at all. (40)

Indeed what we need to remember in any discussion of the observation function is first the fact that it is a property, in one form or another, of all human cultures, not just ours, but that it is only in our particular culture that it has been successful in so completely unhinging itself from both theory and practice as to be able to accept the benefits of this interdependence without acknowledging the limits, ethical and epistemological, posed by it. In a sense it is the commitment to specificity embodied in the false concreteness of both technical rationality and specialization as allegedly 'objective' phenomena which underwrites the problems inherent in such allegations of autonomy. (41)   Indeed, false concreteness, whether in this form or in others, signifies that an observation function unrestrained by either theory or practice is effectively in control.   It is only as a result of the operation of this function, unhinged and (apparently) autonomous, that the standard for describing what would constitute reason could proceed from technical rationality and specialization at all.   Ignorance, premised on a thoroughgoing rejection of reflexivity as inappropriate, sterile or dangerous for the study of man in his historical and collective dimension, guarantees that these allegedly 'concrete' types of activity will be put forward as *the* standard. (42)   They are, if you will, the 'natural' outcome of the operation of an unhinged observation function in the advanced societies.   Their dismissal of reflexivity in favour of empiricized dichotomies and distinctions attests to the effects of the prior denial of theory's (therefore the observation function's) dependence upon practice as I understand it.   More to the point is the way such a distancing operation *reveals* its auspices (in terms of both origins and objectives) in the very effort to hide them. (43)

Nature cannot be dehumanized without reason being effectively denatured.   When men install the man/nature dichotomy by simultaneously allowing it to underwrite the modern empirical convention and at the same time be the most prominent example of this convention as an already presupposed reality, they guarantee that their strategic 'exit' from the whole, however untrue on reflection it can be shown to be, will have the effect of denuding their capacity to think and reason of its real and ultimate animus, now as before.   Marx knew that the long-term effects of men acting out such an exit, with its requisite demands for distance, objectivity and neutrality, would be to express their interest in knowing themselves at the root. (44)   This because central to man's concern to know himself was his determination to ferret out the secrets of 'external nature'.   Indeed, external nature, so conceived, only achieved man's exclusion at the cost of turning away from the fact that, thus understood, 'nature' expresses man's objective need to know himself as an object, thus objectively. Again we encounter the distinct possibility that an unhinged observation function, with its derived technicization of practice and denial of reflexivity, is problematic not because it aims at objectivity as a means, but rather because it is not objective enough in terms of its true animus (origins and objectives).   The fact that natural science, oriented to its key concept 'nature', is today one of the more subtle ways in which man attempts to comprehend himself as an object, can readily be seen from a quick inventory of those dichotomies and distinctions which in both the conceptual (possible *in res natura*) and the historical/cultural sense derive from the distinction between man and nature. (45)

Pointing to the authority of this latter dichotomy in order to justify the way that these derived distinctions are themselves empiricized, they give credence to the 'naturalness' of such one-dimensionalization by confusing this historically and culturally contingent development with the possible naturalness of the human tendency to dichotomize itself. A partial list of the central exemplars in this lineage would have to include the following distinctions: mind/body; subject/object; ends/means; values/facts. My point is that the difference between the human tendency to dichotomize and the modern Western tendency to empiricize certain key distinctions constitutes the basis for contrasting that which appertains to man as a concept-forming being (conceptual priority) and that which points to man as a being both contingently and ultimately defined by less general historical/cultural possibilities and developments (social determination). (46) The confusion alluded to above (and earlier) between what may be 'natural', that is, common to all peoples past and present, Western and non-Western, northern and southern, namely dichotomization, and that which is a reflection of certain developments expressing man's historical and social character, in this case the tendency to empiricize dichotomies, *reflects* the clear difference between common conceptual capabilities and parochial factors which point to social determination. Thus the capacity to conceptualize would include the capacity both to observe and to dichotomize, while the tendency to step out of life by empiricizing the resulting dichotomies as a prelude to strategic re-entry as a disciplined observer/intervenor would reflect the presence of a particular form of social determination generated by capitalism and modern laboratory science as culturally specific kinds of human industry or activity. (47) The derived dichotomies cited are either directly relevant to worldviews supporting accumulation and the mastery of nature, conceived of as 'externality', or provide props compatible with these interests in other areas of human life.

Another way of looking at the problems posed by the tendency to detopicalize dichotomies and distinctions by empiricizing (thereby one-dimensionalizing) them would be to see *both* elements proceeding out of the unsayable with Wittgenstein. (48) This 'unsayable-which-is-spoken' would be life, and the point here would be to draw attention first to the fact that 'practice' remains an observer's category, an expression of the observation function, even though the effect of contrasting it to life does the same thing to the latter notion. Secondly, however, I would argue that these considerations are an indispensable element in any effort to challenge the idea that precedence is central rather than peripheral to the issues under discussion.   Thus it would not only be a question of whether practice or theory is historically/socially/culturally prior in our understanding of the real significance of that particular dichotomy.   Though it may be poignant to reflect on the way that this dichotomy seems to demand recognition of the priority of practice over theory, as noted earlier, I am no less concerned with the common human tendency to dichotomize as it is reflected in the mutual dependence of each 'side' (or moment) on *its* 'other' for its meaning.   An unhinged observer role is probably *less* perplexed with the matter of precedence alluded to here (where it is even willing to touch upon such matters) because the issue of priority at least promises some sort of 'resolution' consonant with causilinear thinking.   This resolution will serve to overcome the negative in true dialectics in favour of treating dialectics, with Gonseth, as solely a mode of thinking or reasoning about 'the world'.   The point, of course, is that dialectics only *appears* to resolve itself into such an understanding because it is a (mediated) reflection of the world as a concrete totality. (49)

When I cite the mutual dependence within a given distinction between each of its sides-as-moments for its meaning, I am only pointing to life as the source of: (1) dichotomization;   (2) the development of subsequent dichotomies from earlier ones;   (3) where this generation indicates not only the presence of the tendency as a key feature of human thinking (conceptual priority);   (4) but also the capacity of earlier distinctions to generate subsequent ones in particular historical/ social/cultural settings (social determination) given this human tendency.   None of this, to be sure, acts as a sanction for empiricization.   It rather endeavours to ex-plain this practice by pointing to the role of observation vis à vis both theory and practice in the advanced societies, and the corollary effects produced by or indicative of this development like the attack on reflexivity and the technicization of practice.   In talking about the human tendency to dichotomize, and contrasting it with the more culturally specific tendency to empiricize key distinctions thus produced, I am not trying to argue for a rigid bifurcation between that which appears to be a common human tendency and that which is a product of specific cultures in particular historical periods.   Indeed, it is to the idea of dialectics as a glimpse rather than a grasp that I turn when I point to the phenomenon of derivation as something which underscores the historical/social/cultural character of conceptualization even as it appears to build upon and give particularistic expression to this common tendency.   Thus successive dichotomizations out of the man/nature distinction would simultaneously point to this common tendency as something which is necessarily expressed in particular ways.

In the case of modern Western Civilization, the man/nature distinction in science is neatly paralleled by the mind/body distinction in (Cartesian) philosophy, and both are 'responsible' for subsequent dichotomies like the ones cited in the sense that what is produced as part of the common tendency to dichotomize is given specific content in the effort at derivation itself. In this effort to generate successive dichotomies, it must be clear that it is only by effectively empiricizing the prior distinction that one can say of subsequent distinctions that they are produced out of 'one side' of an earlier one. Thus to say that the distinction between the individual and society is derived from the distinctions between man and nature and mind and body is not simply to point to the historical/social/cultural locus as a way of *placing* the common human tendency to dichotomize. It is not, in other words, simply an 'example'. Such an understanding, I would submit, is both unreflexive and undialectical because it presumes an *abstract* totality comprised of concrete parts-as-facts-as-events under what is clearly an empirical convention. (50) In order to make real sense of such a claim, we would have to realize how earlier dichotomies had been sedimented in commonsense, as well as theoretical, understandings of the world so that now they functioned both as a support for the empirical convention and as its foremost exemplars. The presence of sedimentation at the commonsense level *on its own* might tend to shore up and provide support for the view that successive dichotomies are historically relevant only because they indicate how and where the common human tendency asserts itself. Yet it is precisely this view of specifics as 'examples' which dehumanizes history by turning its back on men as uniquely historical animals, just as it denies man's status as a social and cultural animal by treating 'society' and 'culture' as given existents rather than notions expressing the tension in Western thought between possibility and reality. It is reflexivity, the theoretical mode, then, which shows the untruth of what appears to be indisputably true.

To carry the example cited a bit further, we would need to see in the dichotomy between the individual and society evidence of a prior empiricization of the man/nature and mind/body distinctions. This would be reflected in the way in which one 'side' of the earlier distinction became a basis for the generation of a subsequent dichotomy. This latter distinction would have to presuppose the empirical validity of the man/nature distinction (and the mind/body distinction) as something which corresponds to observable/sensible *differences* in the world as an externally perceivable 'natural' realm. By 'individual' would be meant mainly man as an 'unnatural' being whose uniqueness lies in his status as a rational subject (mind; consciousness), and by 'society' would be understood an equally unnatural aggregation, whether it was seen to

be more than or the same as the 'sum of its parts'. Man
would have to have *already* exited the whole, now reconstituted as nature ('the world'), in order for the distinction
between the individual and society to make any sense, or
indeed be possible, at all. Efforts to resist this claim by
pointing to those who see 'society' as 'second nature' entirely
miss the point, for here nature, in the form of second nature,
affirms rather than disputes the man/nature distinction by
attempting to establish a correspondence on return between it
and society, conceived as second nature. As for the mind/
body distinction, it is central inasmuch as man acquires his
claim to uniqueness as a rational subject (mind; consciousness) only by ceding his body to 'nature', already absent of
man as he conceptualizes himself and his life. (51) We can
also see evidence of the problem of objectivity already alluded
to here, since man's status as a subject requires him to hypostasize external nature as the central 'object' of his concern to
know. The distinction between values and facts quickly
follows suit as a further expression signifying the subject's
essence (values) and the natural realm as concrete parts-as-
facts-as-events under the empirical convention. (52)

To return to the difference between practice and life, conceptualizing life and the world suggests that dialectics, so
understood, simultaneously says what is unsayable for Wittgenstein but in the process *shows* how unsayable what is said is
by trying to say it. 'Life', in contrast to 'practice', addresses the unsayable by saying what cannot be said, what is
beyond having its 'other', by showing that when something is
said that cannot be said, the result is simply a form of unavoidable conceptual regression. Pointing to 'life' may put
'practice' into bold relief as an observer's concept, but life,
thus spoken, cannot escape a similar fate. Dichotomies are a
way of making speech as a saying possible, but fail inasmuch
as what is brought into speech as language in this manner can
only enter 'the world' by *losing* its holistic character as an
expression of concrete totality, dialectically conceived, and by
acquiring an 'other' in consequence. This indicates that an
empirical moment in the form of the observation function is
present, reflecting the common human tendency to conceptualize, thus dichotomize, but is not synonymous with what I
have called empiricization. Empiricization is the repudiation
of reflexivity and the technicization of practice, and reflects
the relative autonomy of the observation function in the form
of disciplined observation. This is different from the claim
that there exists a legitimate (and necessary) empirical moment
expressive of the presence of an observation function found in
men along with theory and practice. This latter is present
whenever men think, conceptualize, and express themselves in
dichotomies and distinctions in and through speech and language.

Dialectics encounters this as the necessary contradiction between 'knowing' that concepts cannot grasp their objects without leaving something behind as a remainder, but nevertheless being committed to attempting to do just this thing, not in the sense of claiming to have done it (correspondence rules; empirical convention), but by showing that it cannot be done (dialectics). It is at this point in the discussion that the essential complementarity and interdependence between Marx and Wittgenstein becomes readily apparent. Marx shows this by trying to address life and the world dialectically as a concrete totality while Wittgenstein pushes the empirical convention and correspondence requirements to their limits from *inside* this tradition by showing how absurd *real* philosophy has to make itself in order to do its job - saying the unsayable. The identity that is achieved as a consequence of asserting a 'grasp' of another in the form of knowledge and knowing needs otherness in order to render sensible its idea of knowledge and knowing as something useful, valuable, necessary, indeed even *possible*. (53) Correspondence rules reflect our commitment to an observation function which becomes problematic only if we allow this function the sort of free reign which refuses to reflect upon its technical bias in the name of practice, or life. Instead it hypostasizes the empirical moment, thereby denying the true object of conceptualizations addressed to otherness - man himself - in favour of empiricizing dichotomies so central to conceptualization as a common human tendency.

INNOVATION IN THEORY AND PRACTICE

At this point it might be appropriate to ask whether the concept of innovation has an 'other' which may be related to it both precedentially and in terms of reciprocal dependence for its meaning. On the one hand the claim, made in Chapter 1, to the effect that 'innovation' addressed a phenomenon which was beyond capture in and through descriptions seems to speak to the whole as a concrete totality. On the other, however, the fact that this is indeed the case rather expresses the price to be paid for bringing any phenomenon into 'the world' by attempting to grasp it. In the case of innovation, I am employing language, speech and an empirical moment in order to point back toward the whole which it simultaneously comes from and expresses, thus to the difference between the legitimate phenomenon of dichotomization as the essence of conceptualization and human thinking, and the more culturally specific tendency to hypostasize the observation function by allowing the resulting dichotomies to freeze, be one-dimensionalized, in line with the repudiation of reflexivity and the technicization of practice. The question would therefore not be whether 'innovation' has an 'other' which is required to

explain it (precedence) and make it sensible (reciprocal meaning dependence), but whether this other is maintained in a
momentous or topical relation with innovation, or whether the
dichotomy itself - thus both 'sides' - are effectively empiricized and made synonymous with an actual description in/of
the world.

In Chapter 2 I alluded to one candidate which might fit the
bill in this regard - imitation and the corollary notion of
counter-imitation discussed by Gabriel Tarde. (54)   Here the
idea was to show how such practices, built into any conceivable culture, must be distinguished from innovation, but at
the same time to suggest the possibility that such a distinction could exist alongside the view of innovation as less than
extraordinary.   One might be able, in other words, to validly
distinguish innovation from imitation and counter-imitation
without subscribing to the position that innovation is extraordinary from the standpoint of a given culture.   In point of
fact, such a claim would be difficult to sustain, as Barnett
had argued, inasmuch as it would require us to see the extraordinary as something which quite literally comes from outside
the social and cultural milieu in which it is found.   Even
were we to accept such an understanding and apply it to
present-day relations between the advanced societies and
Third-World cultures, it would only serve to underscore the
claim of societal and cultural reference rather than disputing
it.   This because in such a case our only conceivable base
point for judging whether something was an innovation would
be the societal and cultural milieu that had actually spawned
it.   And this would be true no matter where its author had
brought it about because in this case his heredity and prior
environment would be a more significant factor than the place
where it occurred or had relevance.   While no doubt there
are occasional examples where subsequent sedimentation has
led to some development which reflected the unique status of
its author as a person of two (or more) cultures, the large
majority would seem to fall under my generalization without
cavil.

Tarde had argued that innovations often begin in simple
non-imitation - the refusal either to imitate or counter-imitate
- and had to be considered more available than the technical
bias, with its emphasis on exclusivity and discontinuity, would
suggest.   Both he and Barnett had drawn our attention to
the need to focus less on outcomes expressive of 'progress' as
it is defined under this bias, and more on behaviour and process, thereby pointing to adaptation rather than mastery and
domination, and to culture rather than economy and technique. (55)   My determination to carry this further, and to
see the advanced societies, and their key institutional supports and embodiments - science, science-based technology,

capitalism, bureaucracy, meritocracy and the rule of law - as evidence of a particular *culture*, owed a great deal to Alfred Kroeber, particularly his 'Configurations of Culture Growth'. (56) In insisting upon this emphasis, I was not addressing the narrow, and very judgmental, notion of culture (*Kultur*) as it was found in the pessimistic analyses of Nietzsche, Spengler or Alfred Weber, concerned as they were with the 'decline of the West' attendant upon the rise of 'civilization'. Mine was an anthropological understanding which sought to embrace as 'culture' not just the old and established (Europe), but what they understood as 'civilization' itself (America; Western Europe since 1960). 'Civilization' for them meant societies characterized *solely and exclusively* by the modern Western institutions listed above. Thus could Alfred Weber in a mean moment argue vociferously that the Americans had no culture. (57)

My effort to turn a more anthropological conception of culture back on itself in light of the past century of anthropological research on Third-World 'cultures', by seeing the advanced societies themselves as cultures, sought to contrast the adaptive and dominative modes. (58) This in order to discuss the present challenges posed to the West, Japan, even the Soviet Union and its allies, by Third-World countries in possession of a common religion or attitude to complement their possession of petroleum and other raw materials necessary to industrialized economies, and, increasingly to their own development as well. The idea, suggested by Levy, among others, that we were reaching both the economic/political and ecological/environmental limits of developmental possibility on this planet seemed to find support from an analysis of the ways in which the Third World was exercising its recently acquired prerogatives. (59) Their equation of national-state prestige with economic development and the possession of an industrial infrastructure, combined with the dim outlook for Third-World countries and cultures which lacked vital resources or preferred not to participate, suggested that the technical bias, and the interests which stand behind and support it in the name of specific values and ideals, needed to be understood and addressed as *a culture* with global objectives and pretensions rather than an alternative to culture in the form of 'civilization'. (60)

What this strongly suggests to me in my search for the 'other' relevant to innovation is that this other really can be nothing else but 'tradition'. Again, however, we need to keep in mind the points already made and restated, namely, that we cannot permit tradition, with Max Weber, to be understood in a way which denies the component of rationality (thus innovativeness) to commonsense practices. Weber, as noted, effectively stupefies tradition and daily life by treating them as borderline manifestations of rational behaviour *at best*, thereby evidencing the problem I have addressed on several occasions elsewhere. (61)   Here I have in mind his enigmatic effort to criticize key Western institutions without really going 'outside' the rationality norms these institutions honour, in particular, his determination to 'stay at his post' inside the so-called rationalization process and defend standards like technical rationality, and the technical bias itself, when these standards were clearly not his own as a valuing subject.   I argued that tradition needed to be seen in its adaptive aspects as something far more dynamic than such an understanding could possibly promote. (62)   This, to be sure, would be a way of addressing the idea of the advanced societies as 'cultures' from the other side, as it were.   In doing so I effectively challenge the idea that tradition and innovation are co-eval 'sides' of a dichotomy, in favour of treating the distinction as an expression of the technical bias and an unhinged observation function, with their joint repudiation of reflexivity and support for a technicized practice.

It is the rigid empiricization of this particular dichotomy which is at issue here, since by such an act of one-dimension-alization we are persuaded to view the two moments undialectically as 'sides' which stand for the West (innovation) and the Third World (tradition) respectively.   In point of fact such detopicalization obscures and denies the extent to which the dichotomy between innovation and tradition actually expresses modal possibilities *within the advanced societies themselves*. (63)   Now we can see how and why an unhinged observation function in support of the technical bias would prefer to address the issue of precedence where dichotomies and distinctions are involved rather than the issue of reciprocal dependence for meaning and significance.   In the first case, precedence promises a resolution compatible with technical rationality and causilinear thinking in the sense that innovation is seen as evidence of an historical and societal progress based on temporal dissociation and consequent difference. (64)   Tradition *means* the past and/or the un(or less) developed 'other', whilst innovation stands for the West, and for those countries loyal to its fundamental values and institutions.   Reciprocal interdependence for meaning and significance, on the other hand, hints strongly at the need to reflect on the social (or 'cultural') roots from which this distinction (and others) itself springs, as well as the biases, processes and developments underwriting and rendering sensible its empiricization.

The limits of innovation are therefore to be discovered not in its need for an 'other', or even in the particular other that is chosen, but in the empiricization which appears to both ordain and support the collective and historical process by

which given ideas and concepts become sedimented in public
as well as intellectual consciousness as adequate *descriptions*
of the world for all 'practical' purposes given an unhinged (or
increasingly unhinged) observation function.   My commitment
to 'innovation' and 'tradition' as modal possibilities in the advanced societies is perfectly in keeping with my critique of
the technical bias, and my effort to treat it as expressive of
a particular culture. (65)   For in this tension we discover
that the rigid bifurcation suggested by the phenomenon of
empiricization in the person of an unhinged observation function is part of the 'American' (or Western) ideology itself
rather than a description of some state of affairs separate and
distinct from it.   Reflected upon, and thereby rendered
momentous (e.g. topical) in the interests of practice (or life),
the disfinction between innovation and tradition points to their
interpenetration rather than their mutual exclusivity, and suggests that where such an understanding is frustrated or made
impossible in practice, the result will be problematic because
both the innovative aspects of 'tradition', and the extent to
which innovation has become (like 'rationality') a *tradition* in
the advanced societies, will be downplayed, ignored, or
lost. (66)   Innovation will be understood to be extra-cultural,
while tradition will be treated as synonymous with culture,
and accordingly relegated to secondary status in a society
which appears to value 'civilization' over culture, whether this
latter takes the form of tradition, convention, or 'superstruc-
ture'.

At this point my contrast between innovation as *outcomes*
expressive of a technical bias and improvisation becomes germane.   To submit that innovation ought to comprehend an
emphasis on behaviour and process as well as (or instead of)
outcomes is not only to take issue with the empiricized bifurcation so central to 'instrumental rationality', with its split
between ends and means. (67)   This emphasis on adaptation
also suggests, as noted, that there exists a partial parallel
between the pre-modern West and the present-day Third World
on the matter of the relation between adaptation and mastery.
Reasons for labelling it a partial parallel would have to include
the difference between relatively (or purely) indigenous factors in the first case and predominantly external factors in
the second.   I would submit, none the less, that this parallel
is important because it underscores the problem of internal,
cultural adaptation in both instances.   In other words, the
problem of adaptation is not one limited to the Third World,
especially now that the very rationale for the capitalist, industrial and modernizing/developmental ethic has been called into
question.   Problems of adaptation to such a 'culture' have
never ceased to be severely problematic for Western man, as
Freud was fond of pointing out near the end of his life. (68)
While it is no doubt true that the present tendency to assoc-

iate having 'arrived' with the existence of an industrial infrastructure in key Third World countries does serve to point to
the limits of this cultural dynamic, it does so from only one
side, as it were.

Ignored, or played down, since the 'oil crisis' of the early
1970s and the formation of the Oil Producing and Exporting
Countries (OPEC) is the fact that students of development,
economics and ecology have *already* pointed to the limits of
this dynamic. In addition, of course, there was Hegel's
prescient analysis of the concept of 'need', given the dependence of industrial production on an expanding middle class,
in 'The Philosophy of Right', originally published in 1821. (69)
Hegel's brilliant analysis was subsequently complemented by
economic and technological studies of the limits of these modes
of rationality, particularly the presumption that technological
advance could be presumed to be conducive in almost every
case to capital formation in the advanced countries and elsewhere. As early as the 1850s Marx was making a similar
point, and it is likely on any estimate that a fundamental res-
triction on the operation of an (allegedly) unhinged and autonomous technique has *always* been a central feature of capitalist
industrialization. (70)   Only during the period prior to the
discovery of steam power, and therefore prior to the emergence of a clear capitalist interest in producing commodities as
well as simply exchanging objects produced by guild and related methods, could one make any case for a relatively clear-
cut support by capitalism for technique as an objective and
autonomous basis for 'development'. Indeed, it was precisely
its later interference in this process of development which
Marx feared would prolong the capitalist epoch. I already
suggested that this initial support on the capitalist's part was
to some extent a function of the presence and residual power
of pre-bourgeois landed elements standing against accumulation, coupled with the emergence of capital as the central
factor of production.

Once the innovation/tradition distinction is seen as a frozen
and one-dimensional dichotomy emerging out of the maturing
of urban industrial societies, rather than an empirical claim
contrasting such societies with those less (or un) developed in
the Third World, the reciprocal interdependence and lack of
exclusivity between each 'side' understood dialectically as
moments addressing the whole as origin and object becomes
obvious. Like the self (and other) characterization of the
advanced societies as legal-rational and meritocratic, innovation can be seen as part of a 'tradition' of thinking expressive of a world-view and value commitment appropriate to
these societies given their technical bias and unhinged observation function, along with the consequences already cited.
In a sense even Max Weber's gloomy outlook for collectives

characterized by this commitment to 'rationality' can be put in
perspective by remembering Hume's persistent claim: we may
reason though we do *not* do so 'rationally', but rather by reference to custom, convention and tradition. (71)   Similarly
with the embeddedness of what might be called truly innovative activities, processes and outcomes, in contrast to those
manifesting imitation, counter-imitation, even perhaps non-
imitation as well.   Bourdieu captures something of my point
when he addresses 'generative schemes and practical logic'
exhibited by the Kabyles in their everyday life as an example
of 'invention within limits'. (72)   The argument put forward
here is not unlike what I said earlier about improvisation as a
cultural artifact in late medieval collective life, given the
subordination of fabrication and production to the guilds and
the guilds to the church.

It also points to what we have in common with the Third
World regarding even what passes for innovation in the advanced societies today, once these societies are comprehended
as cultures which exhibit problems of adaptation within their
boundaries complementing those which they produce in 'other
cultures' increasingly subject to their values, interests and
imperatives.   My insistence here on the applicability of the
term 'culture', far from alluding to the possible exclusion of
the activities, outcomes and institutions which are alleged to
collectively constitute such societies as 'civilizations' rather
than cultures, only intends to put such aspects in perspective by pointing to those elements of collective life which we
have in common with the rest of humankind, however submer-
ged or subject to denial and repudiation they may be in the
contemporary context.   Tarde believed imitation to be the
central concept for developing a social psychology having
trans-cultural significance and relevance, and Bourdieu
appears to back this up when he cites 'reinterpretation' of
customs and conventions as a key point of departure for the
exercise of innovative activities and behaviour.   In effect,
he points to non-imitation, and thereafter limited invention in
the form of improvisation, as evidence of the way in which
any culture permits its denizens to see the world in novel
ways, thereby displaying their uniqueness, albeit as social
and cultural animals, 'within limits'. (73)   I would submit
that such an understanding exemplifies what I had in mind
when I spoke of the need for an antidote to the dangers of an
unhinged observation function whose repudiation of reflexivity
virtually guarantees that 'practice' as the observer's concept of
experience will be effectively technicized. in the ways indicated.   Again, however, this is neither a denial of the necessity of the observation function as an element in human knowledge and knowing, nor a suggestion that we are beyond its
unavoidable constraints when we address the 'other', whether
in 'our own' or 'other' cultures.

This brings me to an important claim which is suggested by the foregoing as well as by what I discussed earlier, namely, that the technical bias, with its ideology of innovation as extraordinary, simultaneously and in consequence, is disposed to assert the fundamental discontinuity of innovation relative to tradition, however atrophied the latter is thought to be. I had suggested in Chapter 2 that it was possible/conceivable to view innovation under the technical bias in a way which did not necessarily presuppose the rigid distinction between extraordinary and ordinary, exclusivity and availability. I did this by addressing the 'socialization' of individualism as it is manifested in Durkheim's work, particularly 'The Division of Labour in Society'. At the same time I suggested that Durkheim's solution to the problem of conflict, anomie, and bourgeois negative individualism generally really did not get us very far when it came to taking account of our own culture, with its joint commitment to rationality and innovation. My point is that the present tendency to focus on innovation as fundamentally discontinuous is an expression of a technically biased conception, whether concerned about outcomes, as in the phase of early capitalist industrialization, or with process and behaviour as well, as has tended to be the case in the period since 1950 in the West. Yet it is precisely this understanding which is increasingly non-adaptive, not only in 'external' relations with the Third World, but even internally in the advanced societies themselves. But there is an even more serious difficulty which this bias in its present form manifests, and it has more to do with our prevailing conception of technique and technology than anything else.

It is the clear continuity which our present culture exhibits on the matter of technique and technology which suggests the limits of the technical bias in its present guise. We have tended to associate this bias in our commitment to innovation almost exclusively with outcomes, and have as a consequence treated it as a discontinuous exercise in mastery and domination at a time when it has clearly become the reflection of successful socialization processes whose impact would be incomprehensible in the absence of *continuity* rather than discontinuity. Without agreeing with Ellul's effective reification of technique and technology as a 'phenomenon' whose autonomy, universalism, automaticity, monism and self-augmentation underscores its objective and thoroughly unhinged and determinative character as an interest in its own right, we can nevertheless see in this point of view recognition of the danger of a technical bias. (74) This danger resides, it would appear, in the way it has become both externally and culturally maladaptive in the absence of practical and theoretical controls and concerns. In effect, I am addressing the limits of its adaptive capacity at the point in time at which the technical bias has become embedded in the value system of the

advanced societies as an ideology outside and beyond the constraints of practice and reflexivity.

Like most ideologies, it lags behind reality to the extent
that the values associated with an extraordinary and exclusivist conception of innovation under this bias continue to fuel
the goals and objectives of these societies, even while the
actual centre effects of its impact and overreach argue instead
for full recognition of the essential *continuity* which is being
underwritten by organized corporate and state structures committed to generating the individuals and groups that they
believe they need. (75)   Residual loyalty to the individualistic ideal of early capitalist development, what I called 'negative individualism', continues to function as a support for
institutions and structures determined to produce not only
innovative individuals, but also an 'innovative society' comprised of individuals who *believe* that their society alone constitutes the repository of globally necessary innovation.   In
Chapter 1 I cited John Gardner's 'Self Renewal' as supportive
of this point of view.   Though published in 1963, it continues
to express the lag cited above between ideology and the practical difficulties of the present situation in the advanced societies which no unhinged observation function manifesting a
commitment to autonomous technique seems able to confront. (76)   Even the disorganizing events of the 1970s,
which challenged the internal dynamic of capitalist economic
development in its ongoing efforts at global reach in the Third
World, as well as the threat posed by 'external' elements in
this latter arena in control of key natural resources, could
not be expected to lead to significant changes because of the
unarticulated but deeply sedimented faith in the ideology of
progress.   This ideology continues to be defined mainly or
exclusively in terms of technical invention and innovation.

The distinction in the French language between that which
is brand new and that which is new only to a given individual,
though part of the established situation, may help make my
point here.   Present conceptions of innovation, still hidebound to an emphasis on outcomes and fundamental discontinuity on the matter of the operation of this technical bias in
the advanced societies, treat inventions and discoveries which
it values or esteems as new in the first sense.   They are
presumed to come from 'outside' the society even while the
society is recognized as the exclusive repository of such outcomes.   These in turn are understood to serve more abstract
ideals deeper and more fundamental in nature than 'mere'
technique.   The idea that any conception of innovation still
under the control of this bias could pose serious problems
precisely because it is now more available and less exclusive,
thus more a centre effect than a side effect in 'our culture',
appears ridiculous to most because it challenges the assump-

tion that the observation function can be presumed to be self-policing even as it goes about its quiet task of repudiating reflexivity and reconstituting (technicizing) practice in its own image. Innovation as newness or novelty has ceased to have any clear reference to real progress in the form of greater humanization, mainly as a result of the way in which it is employed to affirm and legitimize the outcomes of largely self-congratulatory institutions, globally as well as 'locally', in the advanced societies. (77)

The ideology of innovation as novelty or newness thus emphasizes the notion of 'brand-newness' rather than newness in the conditional sense intended by the second understanding (e.g. Barnett), and totally misses the point that the continuity ordained by its 'rational' institutions and organizations renders the notion of individualism on which Durkheim's new (organic) solidarity depended at best meaningless and at worst the vital centre of the prevailing ideology itself. (78) The 'availability' or 'ordinariness' of innovation in the recent development of the advanced societies, however restricted it has been to those dependent upon urban middle-class salaried employment in the organized corporate and state sectors of these societies, has not by any means displaced the technical bias, but only superseded its negative and individualistic components through the development of a 'system' which produces 'individuals' who see novelty or newness of the first type in efforts and outcomes which at best yield novelties of the second. (79) What passes for superior innovation in these latter circumstances is to be accounted for not in terms of its innovative power at all, but is better understood as a centre effect resulting from the institutional and structural 'magnification' of its impact as at best a counter-imitative outcome. The auspices of 'rational' social organization are what produce this effect, not the superior innovative capacity of organizations, or individuals and groups within them. Even trivial novelties and changes can therefore account for more significant effects, both 'locally' in the advanced societies and elsewhere, when such a collective and highly organized and interdependent system of institutions and structures is in place to 'make them happen'. (80) It is public and corporate support for an unhinged observation function, which both expresses and supports the technical bias for the reasons outlined above, that is responsible for the contemporary poverty of policy and loss of confidence in these societies today.

CHAPTER 4

The rationality question

The upshot of my attempt to formulate an *idea* of 'practice' in Chapter 3 attempted to resist two tendencies. First, it is important, following Marx in his (legitimate) critique of Kant, *not* to fetishize the practical by developing the idea of its primacy too much in the abstract. (1) Second, however, it was necessary to address the limits of the observer role, unhinged and apparently autonomous, relative to both practice and theory. This latter task could only be accomplished if this function were employed to its full capacity, for only in this case could I be faithful to the notion of *limit* in contradistinction to boundary. For me, 'full capacity' would have to include the willingness to attempt to address 'practice' as the observer's conception of life, as well as the need for reflection given the technical bias and the resulting technicization of practice which an unhinged observation function has helped bring about. It is because I distinguish a legitimate observation function from an unhinged one in the person of disciplined observation that my commitment to reflection is partial rather than total. (2) It involves, as noted, my determination to accept the very human tendency to dichotomize while resisting the more historically and culturally specific tendency to empiricize certain distinctions without subjecting them to reflection as topics, as if they were coterminous with reality rather than constituting a way of addressing it. Without disputing the fact that it is impossible to speak and think at all without resort to dichotomization as a central aspect of concept formation, (3) I drew attention to the need to reflect on reality as a dialectically momentous whole or totality which is 'reflected' in our capacity to render frozen and rigid bifurcations once again topical. Thus it is only because this very momentousness *is* the 'nature' of reality itself that I comprehend reality as a concrete, rather than an abstract, totality. (4)

In so doing, I use the observation function to speak to the limits of theory relative to practice, and in the process display the limits of this very function relative to both theory and practice. At the same time, the 'regression' I pointed to in speaking of practice as the observer's way of conceptualizing life, because it affects *all* concepts brought into the world (thus 'life' to some extent as well), points to that which is truly beyond the capacity to be addressed at all as synony-

mous with limit.   Notice that I have said unaddressable rather
than inexplicable.   Apart from the one-dimensional character
of 'ex-planation', my choice of this term is intended to distinguish between acknowledging Wittgenstein's conception of
limit in 'Tractatus Logico-Philosophicus' and elsewhere as
something which makes sense to me, and disputing his largely
disregarded distinction between what can and cannot be
said. (5)   In the latter case what is at stake is my unwillingness to accept the view that things that can be thought, even
spoken, cannot be said.   As for 'clarity', this is another
rule or requirement altogether.   Indeed, it is a collective
cultural and historical task which can only be carried out if
we try to say what we can, do, and have thought as individuals.   The idea that dialectical thinking of the sort I have
counselled here (in concert with practice and observation)
belongs in the 'spoken but not sayable' category only makes
sense where the distinction is seen to proceed from a *norm* of
clarity which has itself been fetishized and hypostasized.
Seen in this light, Wittgenstein's notion of limit would appear
to have an arbitrary element of boundedness about it, if only
because we *need* to speak what we can think.   And the function of clarity in this endeavour, contrary to Wittgenstein,
must be that of an indispensable element which is not in the
final analysis an 'end in itself'.   This is an important point
for anyone attempting to understand the differences between
the Marxian and Wittgensteinian conception of 'philosophy'. (6)

REASON AND RATIONALITY

If any term were calculated to bring heat rather than light
into a discussion of innovation and innovativeness, it would
appear to be 'rationality', and the allied 'problem of rationality'.   In a sense this problem, which I have reformulated
(and somewhat deflated) here as the rationality *question*,
indicates a certain uneasiness about the so-called 'modern
project' that is contemporary Western civilization.   The
malaise alluded to is to some extent reflected in the presence
of collective self-doubt which is leading an increasing number
of individuals in a great many walks of life to question their
own (Western) values and institutions.   A recent review perhaps put my point best when it stated: 'During the past
decade or so, the West has had to accept company in the
world: people who do not recognize themselves as Orientals,
say, or primitives - purely imperial categories - but as human
beings who have needs, take up room.' (7)   I shall be concerned with this theme in more detail in a subsequent section.
Any question as to whether the auspices of a particular activity or enterprise are 'rational' at one and the same time reflects our confinement within particular culturally defined concepts and problematics and suggests that there exists some

likely (but indescribable) limit beyond which such concepts
and frameworks cannot go. In the case of the problem of
rationality, I shall try to show these limits by using the concept to its greatest analytical capacity. The rationality
question, like all issues allegedly directed to the Third World
or 'primitive' *other*, tells us a great deal more about the
culture-as-civilization which is the source of these formula-
tions than it does about those cultures which are alleged to
be the 'subject-as-objects' of disciplined observation. (8)

Perhaps I should begin by trying to set out some distinctions which have proved to be of either immediate or indirect
relevance to those trying to answer the question whether innovation is indeed rational. It must be apparent that here,
as in all other cases where terms are alleged to make reference to actual states of affairs in the world, it is the 'other
side' of reason and rationality that must figure prominently in
any effort to define or describe what is meant. Such conceptual deflation is readily understandable in the case of terms
like reason and rationality, for they have played a central
role in legitimizing values and institutions of the West by reference to either explicit or latent comparisons with non-
Western cultures. Max Weber perhaps more clearly exemplifies this point than any other modern thinker of note, especially when he is engaged in attacking institutions like science,
bureaucracy and 'rationalization' generally. Indeed, it is
Weber's ambiguous version of the 'other side' of reason in the
person of both traditional and 'affective' behaviour which
highlights the difference between tradition as *non*-rational and
affectivity as *ir*rational, whether in the form of emotion at
the one extreme or involuntary reflexes at the other. The
fact that Weber completed his inventory of key analytical concepts in sociology by contrasting instrumental (*zweckrational*)
with principled or 'value-rational' (*wertrational*) action suggests
one of his most central concerns as both a proponent and a
critic of Western values and institutions. (9)

No focus on Weber's typology of the four kinds of action or
behaviour would be adequate if it did not begin by noticing
the way this typology presupposes more fundamental matters
regarding the nature of the rational. Weber's very determination to contrast action and behaviour belies his commitment
to the view that ultimately it is the 'individual' rather than
structure or the collective which is the proper focus for such
a study. Indeed, the so-called 'rationalization' process is
pictured throughout Weber's work as an element of the drive
to mastery and domination in the West which is problematic
precisely because of the threat its collective and processual
and structural aspects pose to 'real' (negative) individualism.
Action is contrasted to behaviour for Weber, not unlike
Hannah Arendt later, by pointing to the presence or absence

of the rational component.   Thus instrumental rationality, or
rationality with respect to an ultimate value, are both categorized as *action*, whilst tradition and affectivity are treated as
'behaviour' precisely because in these latter cases the rational
component is at best peripheral and often absent. (10)
Again, it is from the standpoint of the individual, defined as
someone in a 'zero-sum' relation to society, that Weber proceeds when he labels activity either action or behaviour.
Adjustment to structural or collective rationality remained on
the whole a repudiation of reason for Weber, which is to say
that for him the individual was seen to be substantively
rational only if his values and goals *stood against* the rationalization process.   I have elsewhere tried to show how this
posture was subsequently reformulated as a problem with a
social-structural (thus sociological) 'solution' by Karl Mannheim. (11)

One of the most intriguing aspects of Weber's typology, and
the tension between action and behaviour prefigured therein,
is the way he insists upon maintaining that in adhering to
principles or 'ultimate ends', the actor is acting rationally
rather than affectively or emotionally.   Along with the case
of goal-rational or instrumental action devoted to more proximate ends concerned with satisfaction or maximization, this
'type' underscores a central feature of an 'actor'-based,
rather than an observer-based, conception of reason and
rationality.   Emphasis in both cases appears to be on *the
actor's intentions* to behave rationally in pursuit of ends,
whether ultimate or proximate in nature, rather than on the
'objective' consequences of his efforts or commitment.   Weber
attempts as a sociologist to overcome the strict commitment of
the disciplined observer to 'objective consequences' rather
than intent in his definition of rational action.   The observation function is therefore employed, but not allowed to become
unhinged from certain theoretical requirements which emerge
from reflexivity and are committed to practice and the practical. (12)   At the same time, however, Weber nevertheless
compromises aspects of this emphasis on intent when he states
that the individual who acts in a principled fashion exhibits a
diminished capacity for the self-interest which remains at
centre stage whenever the actor acts in a strictly goal-rational
fashion. (13)   In the final analysis, Weber reveals his own
'inner' tension as an individual who feels he must accept sociology's standards even though they are clearly not his own.

He does this by insisting that the actor-based focus on
intention be taken 'seriously' in order to keep the observation
function 'responsible' to reflection in the interests of practice,
but at the same time admits that sociology, as an instrument of
the ubiquitous rationalization process, must *necessarily* prefer
an observer-based to an actor-based conception of reason if it

is to carry out its project and achieve its own goals. It is
as a consequence of this irresistible fact that Weber is forced
to make the following admission midway through his 'Theory of
Social and Economic Organization'. This statement concludes
a section in which he has been discussing those categories
relevant for the sociologist interested in studying 'economic
action', and resolves the tension between the substantive
rationality of the individual actor and the formal rationality
central to capital accounting practices and procedures.

There is no question in this discussion of attempting value
judgments in this field, but only of determining and delimit-
ing what is to be called 'formal.' In this context the concept 'substantive' is itself in a certain sense 'formal', that
is, it is an abstract generic concept. (14)

Weberian pessimism regarding the long-term prospects for the
individual as a repository of rationality could not be better
underscored than in this statement. It cedes even the
reality of resistance to the rationalization process to sociology
and its disciplined observation, saying that the only sense
one can really make of such a category would require one to
see it as an element in the social-scientific armoury.

To the extent that Weber laments the demise of the value-
bearing and principled individual whose principles put him at
loggerheads with the rationalization process, he does so with
the conviction that this is an inevitable and irresistible outcome of these very developments. Sociology as a creature of
this process is obliged to query, and thereafter to undermine,
the very right to exist of the categories of value-rational
action and substantive rationality because they no longer
appear 'rational' by reference to what now must be sociology's
standard - the kind of individual rationality *compatible with*
rather than standing in opposition to this very process of
rationalization. (15) Weber must accede to the reality of
social life as it is defined by the unhinged observer from
sociology precisely because sociology stands in the relation
that it does to the rationalization process. Decline of the
real (negative) individual is synonymous for Weber with the
eclipse of capitalism by bureaucracy and of economic by sociological categories of action. Thus Weber's defence of the
individual as intending actor is virtually inseparable from his
commitment to early bourgeois capitalism over the later-to-come
features of its subsequent development - oligopoly, bureaucracy, managerialism, corporatism, etc. Weber shows us, in
Veblen's words, 'What things have come to' by *using* the tension between reason and rationality to demonstrate why reason
itself, in the person of the rationalization process, must seem
irrational. (16)

It is the very organization of collective life which super-
sedes early bourgeois society and its 'negative' individuals
that turns this latter group from social benefactors into
public threats. That it was the 'conspicuous production' of
these very individuals, along with the values and institutions
that registered their prior ascendancy, which helped guarantee their subsequent eclipse only serves to underscore the
way that capitalism as a world-historical phenomenon not only
creates its opposite in the act of completing itself, but does
so by adherence rather than opposition to its original ground
rules. It is the fact of their eclipse, combined with Weber's
refusal to acknowledge these subsequent developments as
irresistible because of the origin of modern rationalization in
Western capitalism as well as science, which compels him to
try to deal with the matter as a sociologist viewing processes
rather than an 'actor' with a vision, value or view. In
effect Weber puts the stamp of sociological authority on his
observations, but only to provide a patina of 'evidence'
against which the reader must measure Weber's own invest-
ments and 'sunk costs'. This is evident, as noted, from a
close inspection of Weber's discussion of the categories of
value-rational action, suspended between goal-rational action
and affectivity, and substantive rationality itself. This
latter is little more than a residual category within sociology,
which in turn is treated as a disciplinary embodiment of disembodied formal rationality where the theorist hides a critical
commitment of which he is thoroughly ashamed. The theorist,
speaking to and on behalf of practice, effectively superintends
his own annihilation by thus encapsulating these unstated
bases for critique within the formal categories of sociology,
with its unavoidable commitment to formal rationality, and ultimately, the rationalization process itself as desirable because
an objective and (allegedly) irresistible state of affairs.

A final point should conclude this discussion of Weber as the
archetypal sociologist of reason and rationality who simultaneously addresses and exhibits the limits of reason as rationality
in his sociological work. This point is particularly relevant
to the discussion of 'dualism and dichotomies' in Chapter 3.
It draws our attention to the problems which are bound to
arise when reflexivity is controlled and confined in its efforts
to resist the empiricization which goes hand in hand with an
observation function which has become unhinged from both
thought and life. Jameson makes my preliminary point, but
fails to see in Weber's elaborate scheme of dualisms and dichotomies the basis for what I have called empiricization.

Max Weber's thinking offers a privileged object for what
must initially be a purely logical or conceptual analysis,
inasmuch as it is explicitly organized into pairs of binary
oppositions, albeit of a rare complexity. 'When one comes

to try to isolate the main *logical* outline of Weber's analysis,' Talcott Parsons tells us, 'the prominence of the pattern
of dichotomization is striking'....

At the same time, the extraordinary intricacies attained by
combinations between these various terms, particularly in
late Weber ... suggests that to try to read Weber term by
term, to comprehend each semantic phenomenon in isolation,
or even in combination with its conceptual opposite number,
is an agonizing, and in the long run sterile, enterprise. (17)

Jameson goes on to argue for the applicability of A.J. Greimas's
'semantic rectangle'. Greimas suggests that we view Weber's
conceptual structure in terms of the difference between a term,
its contrary, and its simple negative. (18) Since the contrary of a given term has its own simple negative, the rectangle
consists in the case of Weber's four types of 'social action' of
the standard (sociological) - goal-rational or instrumental
action, opposed by its contrary - value-rational or principled
action, and its simple negative - affective or emotive behaviour. Since the simple negative of principled action is traditional behaviour, the rectangle is, it would seem, complete. (19)

The difficulty here is that such a one-dimensional scheme
only serves to play down Weber's efforts (however unsuccessful) to use such categories to speak to the limits of typologies
as mere 'representations' of a reality far too complex to be
captured conceptually. Thus I can agree that: (1) goal-
rational action is *the* standard for Weber the sociologist 'doing
his damned duty': (2) principled action is the contrary *type
of rationality* to goal-rational action: (3) each of these two
types of action has its own simple negative in the person of
affective and traditional behaviour respectively. But
Jameson's claim that affective and traditional behaviour are
residual relative to the 'official analytic system' ignores the
role that these types play first in the tension between goal
and value rationality, and second in the victory of the first
over the second. It is in and through the ultimate triumph
of goal-rationality over principled action that the latter type
of reason is obliged (along with substantive rationality) to
self-destruct. Sociology, far from acknowledging this type,
as Jameson implies, increasingly sees it as a threat to goal-
rationality, and is obliged as a consequence to reformulate it
as affectivity. This is what I meant earlier when I cited
Weber's admission that for any 'formally rational' enterprise
(e.g. sociology), substantive rationality must be subsumed
within its system of categories rather than be allowed to stand
against it as an opposed way of viewing reality, and the
proper role of the individual therein. Thus Jameson is correct to argue that there is, after all, a real *qualitative* difference between goal and value-rational action, but wrong not

to take up this difference in a more straightforward *topical*
way. (20)

Weber, it turns out, has the so-called 'last laugh' on most
of his interpreters, however, even if he has it at the cost of
his own sanity and his own life. Here too the types and
categories are of central importance. While it is true, as I
have argued elsewhere, that Weber is obliged by his fidelity
to sociology to see his own pessimism in the person of rationalization and de-enchantment as nothing more than the vision,
views and 'values' of an acting 'subject', with all that this
designation has come to mean since Kant, the way in which he
annihilates himself in the process of wiping out both value-
rational action and substantive rationality must give the reader
pause. Goal-rational action, with the individual its alleged
repository, is itself wiped out as a real form of action independent of tradition because once the 'individual' has been
taken in hand by society in the ways already indicated,
'rationality' itself becomes the only thing which appears to
possess real continuity in the culture of advanced industrial
societies. The organization of life and the consequent creation of the individual as a social 'type' is nothing less than
the subsumption of *goal* rationality as a legitimate category of
individual action into the rationalization process seen as a
collective endeavour characterized by organization, structure,
and increasing complexity. This is what Weber really has in
mind when he questions the rationality of such a structure as
a valuing, intending subject whose convictions can only be ex-
tirpated at the cost of the standard for evaluating the reason-
ableness of behaviour itself - goal rationality. It is also
directly relevant to the reasons why he refused to see in
bureaucracy a later development out of capitalism, and instead
came to view the two as diametrically opposed institutions of
modern Western civilization. (21)

This exegesis on Weber has attempted to use him as a type
case (in his own words) of ambivalence where the central
analytical focus is reason or rationality. Weber, to be sure,
held himself back from a truly dialectical analysis which would
render his dichotomies topical and resist their one-dimensional
(e.g. untopical) empiricization. This *in spite of* his claim to
have realized and acknowledged the conceptual limits of sociology relative to the society that brought it into being, gave it
its mission, and sustained it in its efforts to create types as
representations of a reality too complex to be grasped conceptually. Though this sounds very much like what I cited in
Chapter 1 as an instance where concepts are recognized as
universals which cannot absorb their objects, Weber's approach
is clearly quite at variance with this. (22) Weber, for all
his emphasis on resistance to rationalization, provides no alternative to a world in which de-enchantment has rendered all

subjects and all cultures 'rational'. His problem is that he is
still inclined to see reason as sufficiently synonymous, or at
least compatible, with the rationalization process that any real
opposition to this state of affairs must take the form of a
value, vision or view of the subject. That Weber can mobilize only nostalgia for an earlier (and departed) state of
affairs - capitalism and the bourgeois ascendancy in the early
industrial period - suggests that there is no real future for
industrial societies, only a past they are reluctant to acknowledge, coupled with a one-dimensional present in which we
must all do our damned duty and stay at our posts. This
present presumably completes itself by generating its absolute
opposite in the person of the thoroughly rationalized bureaucratic and corporate society of industrial fellaheen who, as he
suggests in the concluding pages of 'The Protestant Ethic and
the Spirit of Capitalism', not only build their own 'iron cage'
but do so in the full conviction that they are free individuals
living truly meaningful lives whilst engaged in this project. (23)

The absence of a theory of social change, or even a real
interest in thinking about the constructive possible alternatives
to rationalization and de-enchantment in industrialized societies,
provides evidence that Weber was determined to have 'Götter-
dämmerung' in the West if he was to be denied a permanent
capitalist and bourgeois society. Marcuse made this very
point in arguing that Weber's allegedly 'objective' category of
rationalization, like the dualisms and dichotomies whose effective empiricization helped promote such a pessimistic posture,
was actually an historically specific outcome evidencing the
economic reality of capitalism and the political reality of the
self-satisfied and ambitious national-state. Marcuse was only
pointing out what I alluded to earlier, albeit in a more strident
vein: the fact that technique and technology are *not*, after
all, objective phenomena but events, processes and outcomes
whose 'progress' is heavily dependent first on economic allocation decisions involving the deployment and utilization of capital, and second on political realities which influence even day-
to-day considerations in the area of research and development
in the case of certain industrial and government activities. (24)
In summary, then, Weber's view would have seen very little
hope for real, significant innovation in a society so dominated
by the institutions he had so carefully studied, described, and
ultimately condemned. The rational individuals on which such
developments would depend could do little more than play their
part in helping construct the iron cage. Even if it were
called 'innovation', such progress would only further the
effects of rationalization in the direction of dehumanization.

Weber allowed his central sociological dichotomies - the
subject/object and value/fact distinctions - to almost totally

dictate the encapsulation of the valuing subject. In Weber's
case the only answer, as noted, was to valorize values, but
this meant that in so doing he had to *transvalue* value altogether. Only as an unhinged observer could Weber claim to
have achieved such an objective objective. The fate of
Weber's category of 'charisma' reveals an institutional parallel
to that of intention, principled action and substantive rationality, one which is especially relevant to a discussion of innovation. To the extent that ongoing structures in the advanced societies are able to 'routinize' charisma at the individual
level, it loses its meaning in his typology of authority as a
category denoting a combination of principle and 'the gift of
grace'. Charisma can only stand in opposition to the rationalization process once this latter process is fully in place if it
too is 'reduced' by being denied its value-rational component,
and thereafter reformulated as an anti-institutional force which
must now be counted 'irrational' because it stands against
structures whose very organized character bespeaks the 'progress' of rationalization itself. (25)

Ironically enough, innovation would appear *increasingly*
'available' for Weber only in the political sphere because of
this development. Even here, however, Weber would come to
see the 'ultimate ends' aimed at by the charismatic leader as
truly irrational when seen against the backdrop of what he
called a politics of 'responsibility' standing as the only real
alternative to it. When Weber described this latter form of
political life as 'a slow boring at hard boards' in Politics as a
Vocation, he pointed to it as a lesser evil because what such a
politics would help produce and superintend would be the
worst thing short of charismatic irrationalism in control of
modern organization and technology and in pursuit of some
'ultimate end' - namely, faceless rationalization itself. (26)

IS INNOVATION 'RATIONAL': I?

The fact that such a question can even be asked only underscores our heavy investment in reason and rationality as both
complimentary and pejorative concepts. It also points to the
'rationality question' as a central cultural problematic in Western societies. Clearly, however, my reason for asking the
question has much to do with the possibility of intervening in
some existing state of affairs in order to alter the situation,
hopefully in the direction of more (and/or better) innovation
rather than less. The answer to the question usually presupposes precisely the tension between the individual and the
collective (macro or micro), then goes on (like Durkheim) to
try to work out some basis of reconciliation between the two.
Is the fact that what has thus far been achieved in the advanced societies would be seen by Weber as *evidence* for his

pessimism carry any weight in the day-to-day activities and decisions of governments and large corporations? Optimism, it would seem, is virtually a prerequisite for the successful occupancy of such decision-making positions, as well as for the production of the sort of social-scientific knowledge which directly or indirectly provides support for the social structure where such decision-making activities and requirements are found. (27)

No less significant is the way that the very asking of this question, as a consequence of what has been suggested above, draws attention to the vested interest in human reason and rationality in Western 'culture-as-civilization'. In effect, to ask whether innovation is rational is to ask whether it is really a human product, where by human product is implied: product of man's mind, his reason, that capacity which truly distinguishes him from the rest of animate life. To argue that innovation is not really rational in the sense in which reason and rationality can be securely referenced to some concrete individual actor in space and time is to suggest that it must be almost extra-human. Even an emphasis on convention and tradition can do little to bring us to a recognition of the burden to be borne by those with a real vested interest in what is called the rationalist 'tradition'. Only a residual reference to society and culture is acceptable, but even here it usually leads to an effort to address these collective configurations as themselves 'rational' (or irrational) in some way. Thus the question: Is innovation rational? usually points to our own conception of difference, not only from the rest of animate nature, but from other human beings as well. For me it is therefore *both* the Greek and the Judaeo-Christian conceptions of humanness which prevail here, challenged only tangentially (at best) by non-Western (and non-Northern) conceptions. In both cases it is the insistence on unique characteristics which creates a picture of world peoples in which other 'cultures' are little less 'barbarian' than the rest of animate nature and far closer to the latter (so it would seem) than to the way we see ourselves. (28)

This emphasis on our alleged uniqueness, even now apparently under some siege, has had the same effect in the modern period, then, that the Greeks in particular intended it to have during their ascendancy, and subsequent influence. The idea that only Western man could survive scrutiny under this category-become-norm of 'rationality' is a generalization from the way in which it functioned for the ancient Greeks relative to other peoples - from the Persians to the Macedonians and from there on into their political and military subservience to the Roman Republic and thereafter the Roman Empire. Thus in both cases it operated as a cultural description where the requisites of a real description were yet necessarily lacking.

Surely it is important to suggest with Vico that an emphasis
on *common human capacities* might be at least as necessary
today, in light of present problems and difficulties attending
our insistence on rationality and reason as centrally significant human categories. (29) Even if such an emphasis
served to bring the whole human community into our reckoning at the expense of the rest of 'nature', particularly animate nature, such a development might be deemed desirable.
None the less it must be clear that the rationality question
really probes the limits of modern Western rationalism. If it
can be said to appertain to other cultures and peoples, past
or present, it must be seen to do so precisely to the extent
that these latter peoples are effectively co-opted into this
'tradition', faith, or ideology. This is not to argue that the
pattern of influence has been entirely one way, only to point
to the dominant reality, for better or worse, in the contemporary world.

My point, then, is that an emphasis upon reason and rationality tends, on the whole, to provide aid and comfort to ethnocentrism, and may even be the central intellectual category or
conception in this sort of thinking. Even the author's admitted ethnocentrism, like his commitment to the importance of
'practice', could be said to be problematic, but not for the
reasons which may seem to be implied by what has already
been said. Ethnocentrism, after all, could be expected to be
a property of *any* 'culture' which deserved this appellation, if
only because a culture which did not put itself first in certain
rather specific ways in the minds and traditions of its denizens would be a very hollow affair indeed. It is rather the
peculiar (so it would appear) character of our ethnocentrism
which is significant in any discussion of the points made thus
far. (30) Think, for example, of the central role of what I
have called an unhinged observation function in the second
and third chapters of this book, and my concern for bringing
it more consistently and continually to heel relative to practice
with the help of reflection. I have elsewhere argued in considerable detail for the view that this unhinged observation
function, with its corollary empiricization of dichotomies, and
technicization of practice, is simultaneously annihilating the
commitment to reflection while reconstituting practice in its
own image. The argument here is that the social, behavioural, and administrative/managerial 'sciences', far from being a
neutral, unbiased, and 'objective' way of studying the problems of advanced industrial societies, are a central institutional
force in generating these very problematics, along with their
allegedly independent solutions. (31)

Thus, beyond a certain point, it is reflection which points
to ethnocentrism as a problematic but in no way does it dispel
the difficulty as a consequence. Indeed, I would argue that

what this reinvigoration of the reflexive (and the practical) does is to elevate our present ethnocentrism, still possessing global pretensions, to the level where it can begin to address its own limitations, particularly as they are manifested in the commitment to a reason and rationality counterposed precariously against 'nature'. (32)   That rationalism requires a reflexive capacity and commitment to show it its limits may seem absurd, but my point in saying this is not to suggest that by doing so we can, will, or should somehow consciously endeavour not to be rational.   This was a stillborn (and quite impossible) demand promoted by the now defunct 'counterculture' in the United States and in other urban, industrial societies, and could only have generated hypocrisy.   Rationality is at the core of 'our culture', a grouping different from other human configurations past and present.   To say it is an intellectual *and commonsense* 'tradition' is not therefore to attempt to abrogate the difference between West and non-West, North and South.   It is simply to argue that these differences are the basis for distinguishing aspects of our culture from others, and in addition that reason and rationality are central clues to an understanding of this *cultural* difference where the West is concerned.   The fact that in modern times it is Western peoples who have accompanied their political and economic expansion into other areas of the world with their intellectual and cultural values and interests is, once again, part of this cultural reality, one whose full understanding *as a culture* would require its denizens to reaffirm the role of reflection, and in the process bring the observation function into a more salutary equipoise with practice, tradition and 'nature'. (33)

A final point needs to be made about the rationality issue before trying to answer the question that heads this section. It appertains to the way that unreformed Western ethnocentrism, with its emphasis on reason and rationality, attempts to preserve the rest of animate and inanimate nature from the alleged ravages of humanity as a whole.   While much can be said for the general movement which includes all those concerned about ecology and the environment, one of its most tangible features is precisely the tendency to address certain problems of 'natural balance' in the Third World as dilemmas whose resolution demands that 'nature' be protected against *all* human intervention rather than that of Western (or Northern) man alone.   Thus the emphasis on prohibiting *all* forms of human hunting in vast areas which it is now decided we must cordon off and turn into 'reserves'. (34)   Interestingly enough, it is just this approach and general attitude which underscores the rigid adherence of so many of the environmentally minded to an empiricized man/nature dichotomy rather than disputing it.   Thus the alleged commitment to the reality of man's 'membership' in nature, rather than a status external to it, is effectively confounded when it is claimed that 'nature' can only reassert itself in isolation from all forms of human intervention. Yet it is precisely the need for food on the part of traditional hunting communities which helps guarantee the *limited* killing which will preserve 'nature', in clear contrast to the sport killing and even slaughter of animals that has marked Western (or Northern) man's ascendancy in Africa, and elsewhere. As a part of 'nature', these human beings tend, on the whole, to use their rational capabilities in order to look after their need for food, shelter, etc., not to destroy these areas through unnecessary hunting and killing. (35)

Rationality of the sort that all human beings share (or should share) in common thus is not only compatible with but absolutely instrumental in looking after real human needs. The fact that Western man has generated a consistent social and economic 'surplus' over the past century which appears to be available in some form or other to increasing numbers of persons should not blind us to the effect this development has had in progressively distending our rational capacity *as reasoning animals* from basic needs which only *appear* to be 'automatically' looked after, therefore unproblematic. The 'other side' of this surplus would challenge the Greek notion to the extent that it would take issue with any schema which allows us to get so far away from our basic needs that some of our (allegedly) most sensitive denizens on this matter - the ecologists and environmentalists - can only affirm their commitment to an empiricized man/nature distinction in their effort to defend the idea of a 'nature' absent of human beings against those who need this 'nature' to live and are required to *know* this on a day-to-day basis. The reason for adding this last proviso bears on the present situation: it reminds us of the fact that we too have such continuing dependencies, but often refuse to acknowledge them because such things are looked after by others in our complex economic and social division of labour. Like the man in Max Weber's streetcar, we could find out how the 'system' looks after our primary needs but rarely inquire unless: (1) things go wrong, and 'normal deliveries' fail; (2) it is our job to do so (e.g. economist, bureaucrat, politician, corporation executive or manager). The upshot of my point about the 'game reserves', then, is that the tendency to group all human beings together in the (desired) prohibition against hunting and killing exhibits an unhinged observation function in operation rather than evidence that its ambit is properly confined. This because it refuses to admit that the real line of demarcation, one that shows that we do *not* know how man should be at one with 'nature', would separate 'us' from nature and 'them'. To be sure, we often honour this line of demarcation, but only when it suits us to group the rest of humankind with non-human nature. (36)

It is, after all, a rather two-faced way to bring these 'primitives' into a human community which they have been denied access to for so long in our thinking, and reflects the continuing centrality of our co-optative and absorptive commitment, and the corollary role of 'rationality', in this effort. A technicized practice, characterized by the predominance of an instrumental conception of reason and rationality incorporated into an organized collective framework, is the central characteristic of the economic and social division of labour in urban industrial societies. It is this 'structure' or 'system' which Max Weber rightly took issue with in his commitment to the individual as an intending, value-bearing, and substantively rational actor. At the same time, Weber's individual, though no worse than Durkheim's dutiful functionary (and perhaps better given the contemporary situation) is the *negative* individual of early bourgeois capitalism who survived only the first two or three generations following industrialization under capitalist auspices. Thus the (correct) image of the individual in an unrelenting tension with 'society' as that form of collective life which emerged following the rise of the Third Estate. (37) Further to my point about Weber, and perhaps conclusive of my view of Weber's preference-become-nostalgia for capitalism, is his refusal to see the society which he believed was obliterating his negative individual to be largely the result of his very maximizing activity and enterprise, rather than the result of overcoming such negative individualism in favour of other formative influences. Weber would answer my question by contrasting reason and rationalization, going on to argue that innovation could only really be rational where the individual was pre-eminent as a 'cause without which'. To accord rationality to the system, structure, or collective organization which surrounded and increasingly defined the new individual would be apostasy for him because his real individuals would have to stand in irremediable opposition to such a system. To the extent that they saw themselves in harmony with it they would be automatons, fellaheen, functionaries in a thoroughly rationalized structure which could only claim the mantle of reason so long as such reason was seen to be substantively irrational. Weber thus tries to bring us to the limits of the concept-become-norm of rationality by showing us what it must become once it ceases to be pre-eminently an *individual* possession and expression, and instead comes to constitute the central prop of our society as a 'culture' with this most peculiar 'tradition'. (38)

Generally, it is a different point of emphasis rather than an explicitly different focus which distinguishes schools of thought on the matter of innovation. Those who emphasize *ideas*, and therefore a somewhat more individualistically 'rational' aspect in the study of innovation, are contrasted in much of the literature to those who stress *structure*, circum-

stances, etc. It provides us with something of a parallel to
the now-classic debate in biology, psychology and other
behavioural sciences between those who stressed heredity and
those who stressed environment as central influences in both
physical and psychological development, but in this latter
case points of emphasis quickly became explicit foci as each
side of the distinction was empiricized and seen to be in a
relation of mutual exclusivity to the other. In effect, by
failing to see the topical whole as one characterized by the
necessary interdependence between the two sides, such empiricization was tantamount to an ideological posture, a doctrine
around which 'schools' could be formed. Increasingly, we
now realize that any adequate understanding must *begin* by
recognizing the need to tailor particular emphases between the
two options to specific cases. Thus it is the reciprocal interaction between a given organism and its particular environmental circumstances, where the organism is both a part of its
environment and something which has an effect upon it, that
is significant. (39) Resistance to detopicalization leads to a
more dialectical sense of the whole within which particular
'moments' as topics interact. The whole is no longer residual,
that is, presumed without such presumption being acknowledged, but instead becomes the truly 'concrete' point of
departure and continuing resource for understanding.

In discussions of innovation's alleged rationality or non-
rationality, it is not only the tension between ideas and circumstances which serves to define the contours of debate, but
the parallel distinction between the individual as the rational
'concrete' repository of these ideas, and the collective or
'culture' as the shaping, moulding reality *sui generis* which not
only 'produces' the individual but sets the effective contours
of what is available to him in the form of possible thoughts,
ideas, etc., and thereafter recognizes them as such. Even
'newness' or novelty itself is seen to be circumscribed by such
environing collective and cultural factors. Here again we can
appreciate the need to customize any explanations to specific
cases, even in the face of an emphasis on the whole, the dialectical interpenetration of ideas and structure, and individual
and collective/cultural 'moments'. This sensitivity, to be
sure, speaks to the clear limits of 'explanation' in the ways
noted by Spencer Brown earlier, because it says that concepts
are universals and because of this do not absorb their objects
without leaving a remainder. (40) Knowledge in such matters
ought to be comprehended metaphorically in terms of glimpse
rather than grasp. Where there can be no true grasp, it
has often been determined that there is, after all, no real
knowledge that can be spoken of or pointed to. The example
of Wittgenstein's 'Tractatus' is perhaps the most significant
philosophical document of the twentieth century in this regard.
On the other side of the issue is the commitment, shared by

dialectics, to try to say what allegedly cannot be said because
we can not only think it but speak it.   Lack of clarity,
should not, as Wittgenstein argued, function to shut down
discussion, but should rather be a spur to it.   Clarity is a
goal, but not a goal that should function as a *prerequisite*
for speaking.   Instead, it should operate as the goal of
thought *and speech*, as the later Wittgenstein argued. (41)

What I have been addressing thus far is *the way* in which
rationality is brought into discussions of innovation and innovativeness as a code word for both 'new' activities and processes and 'new' outcomes in the advanced societies.   The
reason for putting it this way is to point out that even those
who deny the label of reason or rationality to innovation as
an activity engaged in, or outcomes 'caused' by, *individuals*,
smuggle this criterion into the discussion by addressing
'structures' as variously good or bad depending upon the
extent to which they seek to organize and plan 'circumstances'
so that a maximum possibility for innovativeness can arise.
Here it is the characterization of given structures as 'rational'
precisely to the extent that they replicate what would be
termed an ideal organized environment.   There is the further
matter of the disciplined observer as designer and facilitator
as well.   Conceptual priority and social determination are
brought together in the tacit (often explicit) commitment to
making facilities and circumstances more 'rational' so that the
individual or group may have a better chance of innovating
than would be the case in less structured, more random, settings. (42)   Thus it would be a mistake not to see the individual as the ultimate repository of innovation in both its
understandings for this school as well as one which lays
greater emphasis on ideas.   It is simply that it deems a focus
on context and circumstances necessary in order to facilitate
desired processes and outcomes by the individual.   Though
the small group has off and on been cited as innovative, this
still appertains to inspiration and stimulus (e.g. prerequisites),
and it has been more recently argued that beyond a certain
point the group becomes a vehicle of conformity rather than
innovativeness.   Thus even 'brainstorming' sessions punctuate
group discussion with individual privacy in the interests of
innovation. (43)

Few things could better underscore the way that reason and
rationality function as central problematics in Western culture-
as-civilization than the way its demands operate even for
schools allegedly opposed to the idea that innovation is
'rational'.   On close scrutiny, it turns out that what these
latter groups are really saying is that more emphasis must be
put on planning and organizing in the interests of de-random-
izing collective settings if the individual is to be given the
maximum opportunity to do what he alone can do. (44)

'Structure' is seen as the answer to the problem of innovation, which is to say that the frequency and quality of innovation can be influenced, if not actually 'produced', by the
explicit efforts of designers and intervenors to make the circumstances more conducive. Not surprisingly, this approach
is almost exclusively relevant to the analysis of work and
labour settings in the advanced societies. (45) Indeed, to
the extent that it becomes a property or requirement of settings outside the 'secondary' sector, a serious threat is posed
to competing customs, traditions, ways of life and world-views
in these societies. I have already addressed this matter as
a real issue in such societies, and have suggested that, far
from resisting such a development, the social sciences and
related disciplines have their own 'vested interest' in increasing the ambit of secondary group norms relative to those of
the so-called 'primary' group. (46) The question which
thereafter arises in work and labour settings addresses not
the need for innovation, however defined, but rather the best
circumstances in which individuals might have the most fruitful (and/or useful) ideas.

What is significant, then, is the tension that cannot help
but arise between the formal organizational setting of large
corporations and bureaucracies, and the more collegial, less
hierarchical, emphasis on the coincidence of authority and
specialized knowledge which should ideally characterize 'research and development' settings. Though those interested
in producing or generating innovation readily admit that this
sort of innovation needs different 'structures' from other elements of the organization, it is difficult to avoid the reality of
economic factors and constraints, particularly in the so-called
'private sector'. Thus there is a real dilemma for proponents
of this view in the opposed requirements of profitability and/or
growth on the one hand, and non-hierarchical flexibility based
on a collegial model of authority and characterized by discussion and thought, on the other. This latter anti-system of
unstructured structure can only be carried so far, however,
whether in R & D settings, or elsewhere where innovation is
desired or thought necessary, before pressure will be brought
to bear by those in authority to make decisions based on economic, rather than strictly scientific/technological considerations favouring deliberation and contemplation. This dilemma
is also evidenced by the amount of leeway allowed in following
up particular ideas, given the requirements of capital allocation and the problem of 'sunk costs'. (47) One is warranted
in arguing that much of the rhetoric surrounding 'production
and generation' in this vein ebbs and flows depending on the
state of the particular industry sector and the economy,
domestic and international, under scrutiny. Thus it is less
likely that 'Theory Y' and a flexible, humanistic approach will
be allowed to prevail in times of austerity like we face in the

West today. Only where there is seen to be a consistent and continuing pay-off from such approaches will they be able to survive in the face of the real goals and objectives of the system and those who direct it.

IS INNOVATION 'RATIONAL': II?

Perhaps one of the clearest statements setting out the problem that should be avoided throughout large organizations, whether in the public or private sector, in the interests of innovation and innovativeness, is to be found in Karl Mannheim's 'Man and Society in An Age of Reconstruction'. Apart from the way in which he reformulated Weber's dilemma as a sociological problem soluble in and through society as an historically and culturally specific form of collective life, this statement addresses the tension between an individualistic emphasis in the analysis of reason and rationality, and one based on structural prerequisites and requirements. It can be seen as a prototype of the problem which I alluded to in my critique of the properly 'sociological' individual in Durkheim's normal division of labour, one who innovates as an expression of his correct socialization rather than in opposition to it.

> Increasing industrialization, to be sure, implies functional rationality i.e., the organization of the activity of the members of society with reference to objective ends. It does not to the same extent promote 'substantial rationality' i.e., the capacity to act intelligently in a given situation on the basis of one's own insight into the interrelation of events. Whoever predicted that the further industrialization of society would raise the average capacity for independent judgment must have learned his mistake from the events of the past few years. The violent shocks of crises and revolutions have uncovered a tendency which has hitherto been working under the surface, namely, the paralysing effect of functional rationalization on the capacity for rational judgment. (48)

Clearly this statement is applicable in the main to elements of innovativeness as a commonsense, or at least a non-scientific and non-technological, feature of life. To the extent that a technical bias favouring tangible outcomes intrudes on, or serves to play down the significance of, such an observation as Mannheim's, it probably exacerbates the very tension which he refers to. This because given in such an observation, as Diesing implied, is an appreciation of the importance first of commonsense rationality as inseparable from good judgment by the 'normal' individual in changing situations, and second of the clear limits of the technical bias in its *internal* operation in the advanced societies. (49)

This was what I meant earlier when I argued that this bias is not simply problematic in its external application but has never been fully understood in its internal consequences for the denizens of the advanced societies themselves. It is another way of alluding to the dilemma posed to any cultural collective committed to organizing and structuring its activities so that more and more elements of it in the form of subsequent activities and outcomes are predictable and anticipatable. M.O'C. Drury, following Wittgenstein, makes the very cogent point that such an effort in no way diminishes the realm of the inexplicable. (50) This is only an illusion which our emphasis on quantification, measurement, and productivity allows us to promote. We think of a fixed configuration of elements, then argue that the more we come to grasp as knowledge, the less that remains that is inexplicable. Even Max Weber fell for this one. Indeed the so-called 'de-enchantment of the world' discussed in his second vocation address means nothing if it is not understood as a response to his belief that modern science and technology actually were demystifying the world as central elements in the process of Western rationalization. (51) Wittgenstein argued that memory, perception, and language could *never* be understood because these were the means or tools which were required to even address problems of understanding. They were code words, in point of fact, for the inexplicable. Thus 'understood', they show us what Wittgenstein really meant when he argued that the subject is not a part of the world but a limit to it. (52) The fact that we can only study our faculties by displaying them, even (and especially) to one another, only affirms this limit. To the extent that innovation is a phenomenon whose comprehension is dependent upon our own vested interest in rationality as the cultural problematic of modern Western civilization, it too operates as a code word for the inexplicable.

In the process of institutionalizing both the idea of innovation as a prerequisite to good social and organizational life, and the idea of crisis as something whose solution is guaranteed by its very formulation as such, we have only provided the illusion of 'availability'. This availability depends upon residual obeisance to the technical bias, combined with the view that an unhinged observation capacity is the best way to realize the desired solution. Theory and practice are both shunted to the side in the 'innovative' society construed as a 'rational social organization', but the result of doing this, far from better distributing an innovative capacity as a quality coincident with 'good judgment', makes judgment increasingly problematic (and precious) as a commonsense possession. (53) Socialization for careers and for secondary group values generally in the 'artificial realm' that is advanced industrial society includes the socialization of judgment as an 'innovative' response to real crises so that it now is defined as something

which the society produces so it can show how well it can
resolve its 'problems'. Weber's point, in contradistinction to
Durkheim, that real rationality (thus innovation) would demand
resistance and opposition to the prevailing order may now
appear far less 'negative' than it originally had seemed.
More significantly, it is the way that the capacity for judgment becomes increasingly affixed to the occupancy of social
and organizational roles in what is euphemistically termed the
'open society' which suggests that this age-old problem, far
from being resolved by advanced industrial societies, has at
best been sidestepped. (54)

Think, for example, of Mannheim's allied claim that only
those who direct the process of functional rationalization
benefit substantially from increases in 'its' (functional) rationality. While it is true that Mannheim's 'substantial' rationality is to be contrasted to Weberian 'substantive' rationality
because of the former's correspondence to goal-rational
rather than value-rational or principled action, Mannheim's
point suggests the hierarchical and highly circumscribed
character of this increasingly scarce commodity in an urban,
secular and industrial milieu. (55) The idea that we might
no longer seriously expect good judgment in the form of an
intelligent assessment of situations exhibiting marked depar-
tures from the 'normal' and routine way of doing things may
be disconcerting. It means, so Mannheim would argue, that
we can no longer count on this substructural resource, but
now must content ourselves if we can discover it anywhere at
all, say in the upper reaches of formally organized structures
amongst the political, technocratic, entrepreneurial and executive 'chiefs' who oversee them in one way or another from
their perch in the increasingly ubiquitous public bureaucracies
and private corporations. Reference to the 'chiefs' was pur-
poseful: it is intended to underscore Mannheim's 'kinship'
with Weber not only on the issue of leadership and power, but
also on the matter of the residual nostalgia of both for the
alleged pluralist society of early bourgeois industrial capitalism, with its market, supply and demand, unadministered
prices, etc. In the very same introductory section from
which the above excerpt was taken, Mannheim sings the
praises of the early capitalist past, speaking of the rough and
ready equipoise between entrepreneurs and 'unattached' intellectuals in this the 'free society'. No less than in Weber's
case is it necessary to bring ourselves back to reality here.
It may, of course, be true that today there is a problem
affecting the 'capacity for independent judgment' amongst the
large majority of the population in the urban and industrial
centres of the advanced societies, but this claim should not
obscure the fact that the dilemma which Mannheim in particular addresses himself to has *never* been resolved at *any* time in
our history as a modern 'culture'. (56)

This difficulty is only compounded if we reflect on the way we claim to have resolved the problem, or at least encountered it, since Mannheim's time, e.g. as a 'crisis'. Making innovation more available by reformulating it as the expression of a properly socialized 'positive' individual only speaks to 'functional rationalization' as a property of the social structure as a whole rather than simply a feature of work and labour contexts therein. Society reveals its true character as an historically specific form of collective life ('culture') rather than the only form of collective life conceivable, possible, or desirable when it shows itself to be coterminous in its completed stages with a 'rational social organization', a functionally rational(ized) organization of the bureaucratic variety writ-large. Corollary to this is the fact that this form of 'availability' is only possible where the positive individuals cum innovators to whom I have referred make themselves 'available' for (upper) middle-class careers in the employee society, usually in large multinational corporations or public bureaucracies. Apart from these contexts, 'innovation' (rather than invention, discovery, inspiration or successful risk-taking) appears meaningless, since it presupposes precisely the sorts of structures, along with the individuals to improve their operation in pursuit of given goals and objectives, that underscore innovation as an activity or outcome unqualifiedly in support of the established social and economic division of labour. Indeed, I have argued elsewhere that a commitment to innovation, particularly of the functionalist variety, but of the intellectualist type as well, tends on the whole to view the division of labour as an objective reality exhibiting a non-controversial and basically beneficent 'functional interdependence' of 'parts'. As a consequence, it is seen to be the repository of present and future ideas of an innovative kind, rather than mainly the result of prior novelties that collectively sundered earlier forms. It is only from the perspective of the latter point of view that I would favour an understanding of 'innovation' which equates it with ameliorative intervention, reformism and incrementalism in the interests of perpetuating the existing division of labour and the social structure constructed 'meritocratically' atop it. (57)

Let me proceed further in this discussion by trying to isolate a type case which will hopefully render sensible the points of significant difference, albeit in brief, between an intellectualist concern with ideas as the stuff of which innovations are made, and the functionalist emphasis on context, setting and circumstance, with its only slightly less obvious 'rationalistic bias'. In my initial discussion of the relation between claims of conceptual priority and social determination in Chapter 1, I tried to show why it would be absurd to treat the issues as zero-sum in character. Of course there is both conceptual priority and social determination. Indeed, if there is one there must be the other. They are themselves interdependent rather than mutually exclusive, as are individual and collective moments in social life. I would isolate two general types of situations, given my view that there must exist some points of entry into the stream of collective consciousness which are less arbitrary than others. First, there is the situation in which someone has an idea about how to *do* some existing activity better, which involves him as much in the act of conceptualization as some idea that is seen to constitute a theoretical rather than a 'practical' innovation. (58) This may precede the actual effort to carry out the (re)conceptualization, or it may take the form of a post hoc realization that an activity which is already completed was or can be innovative in one way or another. This issue of 'lag', whether in one direction or the other, points to an important difference between the act on the one hand and recognition of its significance on the other.

While not completely arbitrary by any means, the retrospective act of recognition appears less process-bound than the more prospective approach which conceptualizes a new way or pattern in the midst of the given activity or a related one, and thereafter attempts to work it out. Two points are relevant to this distinction. First, the matter of the collective element or factor which may possibly account for the fact that often it is someone else who recognizes the significance of a given activity or conceptualizes a new way of doing it once it has been carried out. A second consideration also relates to the collective factor, and draws attention to everything from capital allocation to social mores as possible constraints lying in the path of the unwary innovator. Like 'technology' in its generic sense, innovations rarely exist in unmediated form only as ideas. The effort to 'convert' ideas as knowledge into real processes, activities and tangible outcomes, not surprisingly, encounters numberless obstacles, depending on the innovation. (59) This is not, of course, to argue that as ideas they exist in their completed and objective 'pure' form as innovations: such a claim can be made only for ideas whose conceptualization bespeaks a real theoretical interest of the kind already discussed, and then only under specified conditions. Again, however, it is the collective consciousness in its individual moments and individual consciousness in its collective moments that requires us to acknowledge that even retrospective, as well as subsequent prospective, recognitions are themselves ideas exhibiting the priority and central significance of conceptualization as a common human capacity. Indeed, the difference between the prospective and the retrospective reveals the clear limits of a causilinear time frame analysis. It is a pattern of reasoning and explaining which never really compromises an emphasis on 'progress' as both the basis for and the expression of innovation as well as reason and rationality.

A final point on the question: Is innovation 'rational'? will
require me to look briefly at a study done over fifteen years
ago which directly addressed this issue.   Donald Schon's
'Technology and Change' proceeds out of an earlier book in
which he argued that new ideas were the result of a metaphorical or analogical shift which he labelled the 'displacement of
concepts'. (60)   Schon's approach in 'Technology and
Change' is to try to show that it is precisely because of what
innovation 'is' and the way that it occurs that we can in fact
focus our attention on the circumstances and overall setting
in the hopes of producing innovative individuals, particularly
in work organizations but elsewhere (presumably) as well.
Schon subtitles his essay 'the new Heraclitus' as evidence of
his commitment to change, both as an approach to and view of
'the world'.   Schon's formulation is supremely remindful of
Popper's argument in 'The Open Society and its Enemies' about
Heraclitus as the founder of 'historicism'.   Popper argued
that it was precisely Heraclitus's belief that change was the
'essence' of reality which led him to develop a philosophy committed to governing and controlling change by producing and
generating, or stopping, it through *thought*. (61)   Schon's
argument is very similar to the one ascribed to Heraclitus by
Popper, for in this case the effect and intent of Schon's position is to argue for the 'non-rational' character of innovation
in order to justify intervention and structure.   Schon, however, betrays the latent rationalistic bias which I suggested is
no less applicable to 'functionalists' like himself than to intellectualists (like Popper) when he seeks to compensate for this
alleged lack of rationality *through* 'rational' (social) organization.

Schon creates something of a straw man by redefining as
non-rational the claim of intellectualists that innovation is
rational because characterized by ideas and conceptualization
on the part of the individual.   For Schon this must be construed as evidence of its 'essentially' non-rational character,
even though it may partake of the properties and characteristics assigned it by the intellectualists, precisely because it is,
as a consequence of this very fact, unpredictable and unanticipatable.   Schon's technique is to define the rational as that
which can be anticipated in advance, then to show that since
innovation cannot be so anticipated, it must be non-rational
rather than rational. (62)   The first difficulty here has
already been mentioned, and relates to the way the rationalistic bias creeps in in the form of efforts (following Heraclitus)
to come as close to anticipating, or at least producing with a
fair regularity, this allegedly non-rational phenomenon by
resort to the organization and manipulation of contexts and
settings where innovation is desired.   The second point relates to the complementary and interdependent character of key
dichotomies like the rational and non-rational.   Schon, and

functionalists generally, are forced to formulate the idea of
reason and the rational in a way which almost totally violates
any acceptable Western cultural understanding of the concept.
This is evident in the way the individualistic element, affixed
to the capacity for conceptualization (ideas), is downplayed or
ignored by being denied any significance in the discussion of
reason and rationality.   In addition, note the fact that
Schon's conception of rationality is ultimately an unhinged
observer's category standing (allegedly) apart and distinct
from activities, processes and outcomes of a 'practical' kind,
where practice has already been largely technicized.

Schon's critique of the rational view of innovation creates
its straw man by arguing that such a view presupposes an
almost automatic process by which knowledge is converted into
technology.   Without becoming an uncompromising advocate of
the intellectualist position, it must be quite obvious that this
is precisely what the rational view does *not* presuppose.
Schon's extensive succession of case histories all address
critically the straw man he has created.   Innovation is not
rational in the sense of being consciously goal-oriented
because 'you do not know what you are going to do before
you do it.'   Neither is it an orderly undertaking characterized by linearity and a serial-sequential process from start to
finish.   Finally, it is not, he argues, 'intellectual' because it
does not take the form of a simple application of knowledge to
problems at hand(!).   Instead, he argues, innovation lacks a
clear beginning, often can be observed to be working retrospectively, and appears altogether 'accidental'.   Thus he
argues that: 'It often moves not from a clearly defined goal
to the discovery of technical means but from observation of a
phenomenon to exploration of a use for it.   Often, innovation
consists in exploiting a phenomenon that pops up while someone is trying to do something else.'   This means that innovation often 'consists in carrying techniques from one field to
another', what he had earlier called 'displacement of concepts'. (63)   Now the difficulty with this position is evidenced
in its own tendency toward automaticity, for what is missing in
such a characterization is precisely the key element of the
rational component, namely, the 'good reasons' for focussing
on one part of reality (or set of ideas) rather than another,
and thereafter for 'applying' it (or them) to one context or
set of problems rather than another. (64)   This two-phase
reconstruction of what makes any 'displacement of concepts'
possible/conceivable therefore would suggest that certain
rational characteristics and properties of the activity are at
least as significant to understanding innovation as is conceptual displacement. (65)

From this brief summary of Schon's argument, illustrative of
that of functionalists in general, one feels obliged to suggest

not only that there is a useful distinction which should be made between the issue of the rationality of innovation and that of the rationality of theories about innovation, but that rational theories are probably necessary and best served by *resisting* the sorts of blandishments which tempt the unhinged unreflexive observer in these matters. This holds equally for functionalists and intellectualists: my emphasis on the former 'school' only recognizes its greater influence *given* the clear association of the intellectualist position with both negative individualism and with exclusivity and extraordinariness. Indeed, what is there in Schon's argument that allows us to feel we have a secure grip on the phenomenon of innovation at all? One wonders whether it is not more than a simple muddle when someone ignores the fact that he must 'know' what innovation is in order to be able to justify so many efforts directed to showing *what it isn't*. This raises the issue of innovation as a concept addressing some phenomenon which is virtually inseparable not only from the rationality question but from progress, change and mere novelty or difference. It has often been remarked, of course, that so much of what passes for progress is really only change, and that we have become overly biased in favour of change over stability. But surely such a claim must have its other side. We often become so blasé about what we euphemistically call change that change becomes the order of the day no less than rationality becomes a 'tradition'. Thus to be 'open' to change is to presume not only that it coincides with progress (and is therefore desirable), but that it is valuable in and of itself rather than simply functioning as a code word *within* an ongoing collective reality. More to the point, what makes 'change' easier to handle is precisely its status as a predictable, or already experienced, 'exception' rather than an exceptional one (Perrow).

In order to justify such frenetic activity, in other words, it is necessary to internalize the process of change as a disciplined observer whose thoughts proceed from and return to his observations. The ideal of such practice would likely be 'the describer' found in Jonathan Bennett's essay 'Rationality'. (66) The positive individual achieves this designation precisely to the extent that he is able to avoid thought and thinking, and to substitute a disembodied observation function and the 'empirical convention' for both theory and practice, the latter now thoroughly technicized. Once this 'individual' has internalized openness to change, it functions (*vide* Heraclitus and Schon) as a way of *avoiding* change by taking on the garb of the observer *sine ira et studio*. The lack of objectivity in the trajectory of technological development in the West is precisely what imperils the commitment to openness regarding change, no less than it makes a mockery of any doctrine of 'availability' premised on the notion that successful socialization in the corporate or bureaucratic 'mode of life' is synonymous (*pace* Schon) with reason and rationality. Innovation beyond mere novelty or newness could then coincide with progress only to the extent that we treated it respectfully as a development whose 'seamy side' is either absent or 'necessary'. The final irony would be the way such a posture endorsed what Goldthorpe called liberal historicism in the very act of denying the role of capitalism and the consequent lack of automaticity and objectivity in Western development. (67)

NATURE, TRADITION, AND THE PRIMITIVE

These three terms are the key concepts by which we acknowledge the impact on our thinking of otherness and the other. They are the residual aspect of reality, the 'other side' of dichotomies whose opposite is so 'familiar' to us. Thus the argument would go: nature is the other side of man, tradition of reason and rationality, the primitive of the civilized ('developed') and urbane Western man. There is only one difficulty with this, however. It begins in the presupposition that the observation function is best carried out in a way disembodied from thought and reflection, and goes on from this not only to sanction but virtually to require that dichotomies be rigidly empiricized in line with the commitment to the technical bias and the resulting technicization of practice. Once we render these distinctions again dialectically momentous as 'topics', rather than (alleged) shorthands for describing the world, we realize how false was our characterization of our object as 'other' to us. Reflection suggests that what we conceive as other to us under an empirical convention is really that part of us which is most important (e.g. familiar) *precisely because* it is beyond the grasp of an appropriative conception of knowledge and knowing.

Wittgenstein would say that we are effectively brought to the limit of what can be said from inside that limit when we make such an admission. Thus the subject is not the limit of the world because he either produces it or endows it with meaning and significance. He is the limit of the world because this world can only be conceptualized by reference to faculties and abilities which are themselves beyond understanding. (68) 'Nature' would be synonymous in such a formulation with perception, memory or language: it would address our 'essence' as beings who posit that which is essential to them, but who often forget the priority of the common human pattern and, more broadly, of our 'membership' with 'everything else' as participants in reality. So also with 'tradition' relative to our vested interest in what Max Weber called the 'rationalistic bias', and 'primitivity' relative to

Western man's unending commitment to the 'de-enchantment of
the world'. Once we comprehend that these other sides are
man's way of formulating the taken for granted *in himself* as
his real object (e.g. the familiar), we realize how dependent
the Western project is on empiricization and the empirical convention generally as a way of *avoiding* reflection in favour of
unhinged 'disciplined' observations as a vehicle for appropriating and dominating 'externality'.

No analysis of the meaning and significance of 'nature' has
ever superseded that provided by Karl Marx in his early
writings, particularly as it bears on the development of natural science. (69) In contrast to Hegel, and largely as a reaction to his thinking on the matter, Marx refused to contain
reflexivity by viewing nature as a mere thought determination,
the concept in its non-conceptuality and barrenness, and
instead insisted that nature was the way that man posited
himself as the real object of natural science by addressing the
external world. In this endeavour Marx is in a sense mediating between Hegel at the one extreme and Ludwig Feuerbach,
with his nostalgic view of nature as the whole from which men
originate and in which they dwell. Marx's commitment to
making the man/nature dichotomy momentous requires him to
show *why* an acquiescence in the Hegelian method must lead to
a position at variance with Hegel's conception of nature. (70)
At the same time, however, it is precisely his utilization of
dialectic which leads him to be thoroughly sceptical of the
nostalgic view of nature found in Fichte, Schelling, Schlier-
macher and Novalis. In the event, such utilization reveals
the limits of an idealistic vis à vis a materialistic conception of
dialectics. Marx, as a consequence, accepts that dialectics
is a pattern of thought and thinking, but only because it expresses the mediated character of thought and thinking as a
'reflection' of reality itself. (71)

Let me, however, allow Marx to speak for himself on the
relationship between 'nature', natural science and man's concern with objective knowledge.

Man is the direct object of natural science; for directly
sensuous nature for man is sense-experience (the expressions are identical) in the shape of other men presented to
him in a sensuous way. For it is only through his fellow
man that his sense-experience becomes human for him. But
nature is the direct object of the science of man. Man's
first object - man himself - is nature, sense-experience;
and particular human sensuous faculties are only objectively
realized in natural objects and can only attain to self-know-
ledge in the science of nature in general. The elements of
thought itself, the element of the vital manifestation of
thought, language, is sensuous in character. The social

reality of nature and human natural science or the natural
science of man are identical expressions. (72)

Nature is therefore the central mode of self-reference which
men employ when they address themselves as objects in and
through natural science.   Rendering the man/nature distinction momentous means that nature is man-defined in its forward dimension - that of sense experience - and a whole
which always includes men as this sort of animal in its backward dimension - that of sensuous need.   Marx's commitment
to a dialectics which is materialistic rather than idealistic thus
points to a far broader notion of mastery and domination than
that forwarded by natural science, understood as a 'discipline'
directed by men to external objects.   Just because nature
becomes an 'object' for man, this does not mean that it stands
solely in a relationship of otherness to him.   This is the
major presumption simultaneously asserted by and displayed in
an observation function whose disembodied character is manifested in empiricized dichotomies like the man/nature distinction and others derived from and interdependent with it.

Marx's analysis is premised, significantly, on the refusal to
entertain as true. (rather than empirically 'correct'), the only
distinction as fundamental as the one between man and nature
- the dichotomy between thought and action.   Commitment to
the whole through dialectical materialism demands that we both
reflect and theorize, and thereafter comprehend such reflection as activity, a manifestation of our human being, our
being a human animal.   Similarly with natural science, which
Marx insists on treating as a form of historically specific and
culturally relevant human industry no less than capitalism.
This because both science and capitalism are ways in which
men display the forward and the backward dimension of sense-
experience and sensuous need as beings for themselves.
Marx takes specific issue with Hegel's tendency to treat consciousness and intelligence, as well as perception, memory and
language, as 'unnatural' states and conditions, pointing out
that such states must be comprehended as both vehicles for
and expressions of man's contradictory character as a 'natural'
being whose 'nature' includes his consciousness even as this
very consciousness allows him to 'know' this.   Far from disputing man's membership in the whole as a natural being with
sensuous needs which must both be served and 'known' by
this capacity for consciousness and sense-experience, this
latter capacity underscores such membership and participation.
Thus Marx's understanding of consciousness as *conscious existence* given man's consciousness of his existence in 'The
German Ideology', in contradistinction to Hegel's fetishization
of the subject as its source rather than its 'object'. (73)

Industry is the manifestation of man's active dimension as a

being oriented to 'externalities', and determined to manipulate
and transform them through labour. At the same time,
labour also appertains to man's capacity to conceptualize and
'know' these things as an expression of his industry. Natural science, it turns out, is only able to 'demarcate' itself
from philosophy on the one hand and practice (life) on the
other to the extent that it legitimizes and underwrites a particular conception of the whole as a 'world' absent of men as
uniquely *human* animals. The key concept of natural science
- 'nature' - marks it out as an historically specific form of
human industry committed to maximizing man's active dimension through self-experience, while suppressing the truth of
membership and participation (sensuous need) by discouraging
reflection in favour of an unhinged observation function. (74)
Nature becomes the whole as 'the world', an abstract totality
(allegedly) comprised of empirically concrete parts-as-facts-
as-events which is constitutive of reality itself for natural
science. Natural science only achieves such a conception of
nature by forgetting the truth of self-reference which it turns
away from when it condemns reflection, however. Its commitment to the active dimension of man as an animal who expresses himself in and through his industry thoroughly suppresses
the moment of his consciousness as conscious existence wherein he would see such orientation to external objects as a way
of knowing himself as an object, thus objectively. 'Nature'
is thus simultaneously an outgrowth of man's industry and
intelligence and the whole which man sees himself originating
and dwelling within as an animal whose rational capacity is
seen to be disembodied from his being as a 'natural' animal.
The abstract totality of 'nature' (the whole as 'the world')
which consciousness constructs, allegedly from 'outside' it, as
'the world', is thus permitted to stand as our origin and
dwelling place only if the faculty which knows this is acknowledged to be 'unnatural'.

The man/nature dichotomy in science must obscure what *it*
needs in order to rigidly empiricize the distinction between
consciousness and sensuous need so that the latter is seen to
appertain only to the body, with the mind's disembodied character affirmed in a similarly disembodied observation function.
Science's suppression of the moment of need is an attempt to
underscore its commitment to 'nature' as an externally observable abstract totality, knowledge of which is categorically distinct from knowledge of man. Thus does man's alleged external object eschew the agent as the real object of natural science, and perpetuate the illusion that the social sciences
ought to look to natural science as their model. Commitment
to the idea of an alleged 'unity of method' suppresses the very
moment of need which would compel us to see natural science
itself as an historically specific production of Western culture
as civilization. (75) The issue of whether natural science

can or cannot be a 'model' for the social sciences beyond their participation in a generalized 'unity of method' therefore misses the point, because it ignores the impact of failing to 'situate' natural science within the 'legitimate' ambit of thought and theorizing in these disciplines. It is precisely the *lack* of reflexivity in the philosophy of science, for example, which firms up science's similarly unreflexive conception of nature, and an empiricized man/nature distinction with it, as an unquestioned starting point for the social sciences as social technologies. 'Theory' in these latter 'disciplines' can only justify its right to exist and be 'taken seriously' where it not only sanctions, but actively participates in, its structural decomposition into testable/falsifiable hypotheses. (76)

Once we realize that natural science is really an inquiry addressed to the question of the 'nature' of man as a species-being who makes himself an object by projecting this concern externally, then the distinction between sense-experience and sensuous need, like that between natural and social science, collapses. Having rendered the man/nature dichotomy dialectically momentous as a *topic*, the scope and limits, and analytical significance, of a number of related and overlapping dichotomies and distinctions fall into their proper place. Man is no longer able to treat the fiction of his own disembodied status as disciplined observer as synonymous with 'objectivity' because his alleged external object is a vehicle for meeting *his own* sensuous needs through the display of sense-experience. Consciousness is comprehended as conscious existence once it is seen to necessarily include man's consciousness of his existence. (77) As the kind of animal who addresses externalities as objects of concern, his historicity is reflected in the way that one of his central cultural institutions - natural science - suppresses the moment of sensuous need in order to point to the products of sense-experience under certain conventions as 'all that is the case'. In this activity, an historically specific form of human industry possessing general and specific cultural sanction is able to persuade itself and others that its results do not themselves constitute a 'form of life', but merely a basis in knowledge for the exercise of such life and living. (78) Empiricized dichotomies which have yielded to the one-dimensional character of man's active moment as a species-being underwrite a technicized practice as the necessary upshot of a disembodied and unhinged observation function. Suppression of the reflexive moment as a vehicle for acknowledging sensuous need guarantees that a truly 'objective' understanding of 'nature' itself will be denied us.

When we turn from nature to 'tradition' we realize at once that we have moved from a central concept of natural science to one vital to the social sciences. Think of the way, noted

in Chapter 3, that we understand notions like tradition, traditional behaviour (or action), traditional authority, and traditional society in the West. Apart from what particular 'other
side' is called up by reference to such apparently residual
categories emptied of purpose and the human dynamic, think
of the 'nature' of behaviour or activity that such a label
ordains. It would seem at the outset that we are told much
more about *ourselves* than about the unfortunates who fall
under such categories as a result of disembodied observation.
This must be evident from the largely stupefying conception
of tradition in the form of traditional action and traditional
authority which continues to be an unspoken-because-taken-
for-granted presumption in the sociological armoury. What
could better display the real auspices, as well as the real
mission, of the social sciences as creatures of society in the
person of rationalization and de-enchantment? Blum puts the
matter particularly poignantly in the case of Max Weber's
understanding of tradition as 'traditional action' in the 'Theory
of Social and Economic Organization' and elsewhere when he
says: 'Is there a better example in the history of thought of
what sociology has done to thinking than Weber's treatment of
tradition. To exempt it by saying that it is a "sociological
treatment" only affirms what is being said.' (79)   I would
readily accept this, and would cite as support the following
statement from the above text, where Weber says:

> In the great majority of cases actual action goes on in a
> state of inarticulate half consciousness or actual unconscious-
> ness of its subjective meaning. The actor is more likely to
> 'be aware' of it in a vague sense than he is to 'know' what
> he is doing or be explicitly self-conscious about it.   In
> most cases, his action is governed by impulse and habit.
> Only occasionally and in the uniform action of large numbers
> only in the case of a few individuals, is the subjective
> meaning of the action, whether rational or irrational,
> brought clearly into consciousness. (80)

Weber's understanding in this statement typifies the 'transvaluation of values' alluded to earlier because here he speaks
up for the individual, allegedly from the standpoint of the
disembodied observer.   At the same time, Weber's attempt to
address the rationality question is freighted with ambiguity.
On the one hand the actor 'acts' without real consciousness;
on the other, the subjective meaning of such 'action' could be
either rational or irrational.   Weber clearly confuses intendedly rational with rationally correct action in the last sentence,
a not too subtle way of addressing the collective and cultural
grounding of 'objective correctness' by this the most individual
centred of social theorists. (81)   Weber's discussion of the
'types of social action' a few pages later only serves to confirm the view that such behaviour could only be 'traditional'
rather than affective, principled or goal-rational.

Strictly traditional behaviour lies very close to the borderline of what can justifiably be called meaningfully oriented
action, and indeed often on the other side. For it is very
often a matter of almost automatic reaction to habitual
stimuli which guide behaviour in a course which has been
repeatedly followed. The great bulk of everyday action to
which people have become habitually accustomed approaches
this type. (82)

Weber goes on to counsel the reader not to treat this type of
behaviour as merely a residual sort, however. Far from
being a 'limiting case', he suggests that 'attachment to habitual forms can be upheld with varying degrees of self-con-
sciousness and in a variety of senses.' Nevertheless this
constitutes an example of what Weber constantly cites in order
to exonerate himself from the accusation of incomplete (or incorrect) descriptions: the mixed case which 'shades over'
into principled action (in this case). (83)

Greimas has noted that for Weber tradition has its contrary
in affectivity and its simple negative in principled action. (84)
At the same time Weber allows to society perhaps too undispu-
ted a mandate when he plays down the collective and cultural
character of tradition alone vis à vis what are clearly far
more individualistic types. Indeed, tradition is the only
collective type in the scheme *because* it is synonymous with
culture. The fact that 'rationality' becomes collectivized and
institutionalized, thereby imperilling both the principled and
the goal-rational action of the individual, tends to be ignored
by Weber in his disastrous attempt to treat tradition as a form
of individual action-cum-behaviour. Weber's treatment is
disastrous because it fails to see in this institutionalization
and 'collectivization' anything else but faceless rationalization
and de-enchantment. While it is no doubt difficult to argue
in an optimistic vein about a societal reality in which 'rationality' (thus progress and innovation) becomes a 'tradition' in
this sense, it does underscore the fact that such a collective
has 'rationality' at its centre as the always-ambiguous centrepiece of its reality as a 'culture'. (85) Weber tends to
stupefy tradition because he reduces it to his self-obsessive
'individual action components', which effectively leaves him
with behaviour where collective sense is *at best* 'meaningless'. Being the only type in his scheme whose sense is
gained almost *in totem* from its collective character, Weber's
parallel suspicion of both societal and sociological (conceptual)
'collectives' leaves him no choice but to treat the collectivization of 'rationality' as rationalization. (86)

Even when scholarly conceptualization gets beyond the individualistic character of Weber's 'rationalistic bias', as for
example, in Lerner's 'classic' discussion 'The Passing of

Traditional Society', (87) we are told almost nothing beyond
our own preoccupations. The other side of 'tradition' is
either rationality, progress or innovation, depending upon
generality and context. In the case of Lerner's discussion,
the problem parallels Weber's to the extent that Weber's self-
contradictory notion of traditional action-cum-behaviour
(and traditional authority) as an individualized (and individualistic) notion reappears in the person of 'traditional society'
as a simple extrapolation of this individualized category.
The question: How can *action* (or authority) be traditional?
is made even more central to a critique of this sort of thinking when it leads one to query: How is it possible for there
to be a 'traditional society'? Weber's technique of excusing
his 'pure types' because of the 'complexity' of a social reality
they can only represent in a typified way rather than fully
describe permits the sociologist what is at best a temporary
respite. We can no longer ignore the significance for the
scope and limits of a specifically sociological understanding
characterized by a disembodied observation function of the
auspices and objectives of such a 'discipline' once this sort of
difficulty is brought to light. Indeed, it is precisely
through the category of 'traditional society' as the *real* opposite of the 'goal rational' society - the only type alleged to be
unrelated to tradition in Weber's scheme - that we are provided with the basis for our largely self-congratulatory distinction between 'culture' (them) and 'civilization' (us). (88)

The final residual moment of social reality as the result of
the operation of this disembodied observation function is more
specifically the property of anthropology - the category of
'primitive society' and the idea of the 'primitive' generally.
Goddard points out how utilization of this category as the
'other-side' of Western man and Western society provides a
parallel to traditional action and traditional society, yet goes
even further because of the consequences which arise out of
empiricizing these distinctions. (89)   Primitive man and primitive society, it is discovered, are code words for the way men
lived *before* there was an historical record. More than either
nature or tradition is the concept of primitivity the real
heart and soul of Western man as a disembodied observer who
claims to study external realities (other societies) and generate 'knowledge' about them as a consequence of being in
possession of the capacity for 'sense-experience'. To say he
is determined to learn about himself by reference to such a
category and such an understanding points to these distinctions and dichotomies as modal possibilities which, it turns
out, are 'available' in the form of 'extreme cases' within advanced industrial societies themselves. We pretend this is not
the case, yet reflection would compel us to realize how 'otherness' is in fact the unacknowledged-because-unknowable (given
the metaphor of knowledge as a grasp) way of conceptualizing

the totally familiar but (and because) incomprehensible.
Freud, more than anyone else, showed the relevance of this
particular fact to Western culture-as-civilization in 'Civilization
and its Discontents'. (90)

Primitive society is seen as the ground from which all conceivable conceptions of 'development' take their point of
departure. Being 'pre-historical', it is the bottomless pit
where all these characteristics which Freud pointed to can be
found. As such, it becomes the residual starting point on
the escalator for any theory of development as 'progress'.
In the case of sociology and anthropology, primitive society is
the beginning before beginning, the point of departure
against which all 'progress' as social and cultural *evolution* is
ultimately to be compared. An interesting aspect of this
evolutionary notion is provided by the later work of Talcott
Parsons on the 'evolution of societies'. (91) Parsons, following in the footsteps of numberless earlier students of 'primitive society', attempts to merge Max Weber's distinction, in
'Methodology of the Social Sciences', between progress understood as 'merely progressive differentiation' and as 'progress
of *technical* rationality in the utilization of means'. (92)
Parsons achieves this by taking advantage of the metaphor
that governs the notion of societal evolution itself: that of
the organism and of organismic evolution. Thus it is man's
status as a problem-solving animal which puts him at the top
of organismic evolution as a social creature capable of generating more 'complex' structures than any other animal. The
parallel that is taken advantage of given such a metaphor is
one which *uses* this point, then builds upon it in order to
state that modern Western societies are the most highly
developed. (93)

Thus man is to other forms of animate life as Western man is
to all other human types, past and present. Reconciliation
of progress as progressive differentiation with progress as
technical rationality in the utilization of means is achieved by
allowing the notion of organismic complexity to function as
evidence of higher development and to front for a distinction
between societies as cultures. Thus it is argued that ours is
a more 'advanced' society precisely because it is more complex
than 'primitive' (viz. tribal, undeveloped) societies in the
sense of being less integrated and more differentiated and
specialized. Even Durkheim honoured such a parallel, turning a sow's ear into a silk purse by supporting an effort at
'normalization'. Bad differentiation expressive of a complexity
that is characterized by differences which repel is turned into
good differentiation in the form of a complexity characterized
by differences which attract and complement one another.
Durkheim's formulation succeeds thereby in addressing the
issue of sensuous need, but only at the cost of deifying society

by reifying its demands and requirements. (94)   It is the
supreme ideological legitimation (rationalization) for sociology
as the science of *society*, fetishized as the only 'available' or
desirable form of collective life.   Finally, complexity as good
differentiation supports, and is thereby reconciled with, technical rationality when it is shown that the result of man's
evolution as a problem-solving animal is a form of rationality
- technique or goal-rationality - 'higher' and more 'advanced'
than all prior forms.   The social sciences thus rationalize
their technicization of practice by pointing to what a disembodied observation function has discovered in defence of its
autonomy.

Goddard makes the point I am driving at here far better
than I can.   I take the liberty of citing his analysis at
length.

But there are two immediate problems that must be faced
here.   The first is that there are almost no primitive societies [presently in existence] that do not have incredibly
complex social structures.   Insofar as this complexity resides in the kinship system alone - and this would mean that
kinship exhausts social structure - it might not be thought
too damaging.   The criterion of simplicity could be saved
by arguing that the kinship system had simply been elaborated over time without anything else changing.   But
such is not generally possible.   Where kinship is elabor-
ately organized, so are other institutions.   Most of the
large African societies, for example, maintain very complica-
ted religious, political and legal institutions which, while
apparently articulated with the kinship system, are to some
degree independent of it and often cut across it....

The second problem is partly contained in the first.   It
is that we are dealing with societies of a highly complex
nature that have endured for an unknown period of time....
Lacking a developed historical consciousness, primitive
peoples have no recorded history of their own.   History is
encapsulated in myth....   Clearly a society that has apparently existed for centuries has some form of history.   And
this is to say that it has *changed*, for it would be too much
to expect that it had not....   The main point at issue is that
it is very often assumed that any society which is genuinely
primitive does not change. (95)

I take Goddard's point, but in doing so, submit that primitive
society can only be a construct applicable to ourselves because
it appertains to the core, that which remains stable ('culture')
when 'everything else' has changed.   The idea which we
entertain in Western societies argues that ours is an innovative society where change is the rule rather than the excep-

tion. What is left is 'rationalized' (*vide* Durkheim) as 'respect for the individual' coupled with pre-industrial 'residues'.
Now we can see how primitivity addresses the taken-for-
granted foundation or essence out of which everything else
comes and into which all novelty (rationality; progress)
eventually is sedimented. (96)

We can also comprehend how both primitivity, and complexity as its 'other side', function as an observer's category or
conceptualization and/or as a one-dimensional depiction of unreal perfection at one end (primitivity as a totally integrated
culture) and all-too-real imperfection as development at the
other. Primitivity or simplicity is idealized as the unattain-
able which we can reference (but not know) because at *our*
source is precisely this essence which, however, has been
covered over by progressive differentiation and its more
human-centred upshot - technical rationality. That such
technical rationality feeds back into this forgetfulness
through its support for a disembodied observation function
and a resulting technicization of practice only underscores
the clear 'centre effects' of such a commitment to knowledge
as a grasp. Reflection suggests that in the final analysis
'primitivity', like 'nature' and 'tradition', is the simplicity
that is available in any collective for a member and participant. The fact that we can only comprehend such simplicity
as belonging to some hypostasized historical and cultural
'other' is poignant testimony indeed to the consequences of
society's rationalizing and de-enchanting agenda. We show
that we 'know' where we stand on this matter when we
address ourselves objectively in the form of the 'other' in
this way. We exhibit our 'longing' for this origin as goal
when we use even the most supreme indicators of rationalization and de-enchantment to make reference to this possibility,
even if this is done en route to convincing ourselves of our
superiority because of our greater differentiation and 'complexity'. (97)

IS RATIONALITY INNOVATIVE?

The initial answer to this must be that of course rationality is
innovative, if only because the innovative society has been
effectively *defined* as an advanced industrial society characterized by 'rational institutions' at its core and positive
individualism 'available' almost everywhere. I have, however,
quite obviously been at pains to take issue with such self-
satisfied speculation in the foregoing. Without rehashing the
different ways that rationality can be understood and formulated, it must be clear that our preoccupation with the presence
or absence of rationality in 'other cultures' is in truth a version of our own determination to address the limits of know-

ledge from inside these limits.   Horton makes this point, unambiguously, arguing that the desire to know is a recognition
of the need to render the complex simple and the diversified
a unity.   We address the limits of knowledge from inside
these limits when we objectify the other in order to see how
far we can go in our efforts, with Horton, Winch, Barnett
and Bourdieu, to 'understand a primitive society'. (98)

Beyond being true by definition, the question whether
rationality is innovative must therefore be answered - possibly.
Rationality is innovative when it avoids fetishizing the practical side of life by treating it too much in the abstract, as
Winch often appears to do, and when it shows its limits by
addressing what it could know as a self-steering recognition
of this limit vis à vis practice, life. (99)   This latter requirement is the way we speak to the limits of knowledge as a
grasp, something to be appropriated by and through the mastery and domination of externality.   In turning away from
the self-sufficiency of either the appropriative mode or one
premised on the special status of human being as that which
(unlike 'nature') must uniquely be 'interpreted' and 'understood', I have tried to display how theorizing defends the
legitimacy of the moment of sensuous need by displaying this
need in its authenticity.   It does this not by reifying the
moment of sense-experience which evidences the unfettered
sway of the disembodied observer, but by rendering it and
other distinctions topical so that what is empirically known will
reflect practice and life, not subvert it. (100)

CHAPTER 5

Culture: institutions and ideologies

If 'rationality', 'history' and 'progress' constitute the central code words whose meaning and relation to one another best summarize modern Western civilization as a 'culture', then the part played by operative assumptions regarding invention and innovation in the advanced societies today should help us to clarify this meaning and these relationships. This would mean that we could no longer rest satisfied with an analysis which confined itself to showing the difference between reason and rationality, where the former stood for some or another theoretical posture or 'ideal', and the latter for the present societal reality as it 'really' is. An effort to 'escape' the confines of a culture-as-civilization like ours committed to rationalism as both an ideal and a description, though clearly no less a part of this culture than more conformist practices, could only hope to show the limits of such understandings from 'inside'. This means that an emphasis on the non(or ir)rational, being simply the 'other side' of rationalism itself, is unsatisfactory. Indeed, I tried to show how it is precisely the concern for that which is beyond explanation in ourselves which leads us to ascribe to cultural and historical others the epithets of naturalism, traditionalism, and primitivism. Thus to ask whether innovation is rational or non-rational would require me to return to the problem cited at the outset - its incomprehensibility - in order to underscore what it really means to claim that it is an empirical property of a given: culture as civilization; society; organization; group; or individual.

This point can be made with greater force if I invert the above question, and ask whether (and if so, when) rationality is innovative, continuing the argument posed in Chapter 4. This was clearly a central question, perhaps even a fundamental one, for Max Weber, with his tension between the individual rational subject in possession of both principles and goals (as well as habits and feelings), and the increasingly organized collective ('society') under the sway of the so-called rationalization process. Weber would argue, as we shall see further on, that it is precisely the suppression of individual creativity emanating from the 'subject' which is endemic to the emerging order. One upshot of this all-too-successful effort to organize people in Western urban and industrial societies on the basis of what he called the 'rational mode of life' would be

that the 'innovative' would more and more be seen to lie in
activities, processes, and ideas which not only extended and
preserved the existing order but reflected the successful
'socialization' of those so characterized.   At this point, one
is reminded of the 'iron cage' prophecy which concludes 'The
Protestant Ethic and the Spirit of Capitalism', for here it is
predicted that eventually the truly individual and subjective
elements which can be stood against the emergent whole will
disappear, leaving a 'dead mechanism', 'mechanized petrification'.   It is precisely the way that Weber is compelled to
polarize the individual and society, giving to society what
passes for reason, while the individual is left with feelings,
which seems to support the view of many that he gave aid
and comfort, as it were, to caesarism and power-politics
(charisma) in post-First World War Germany.   In later sections I shall be concerned less with this issue, one already
dealt with extensively, and more with two related points: (1)
Weber's failure (or refusal) to see ubiquitous rationalization
as a basis for the emergence of a tradition, thus a 'culture';
(2) the way that Weber's isolated individual loses his status
as an autonomous goal-rational (not principled) subject, and
how this helps us see the 'problem' of invention and innovation in a new light. (1)

A CASE IN POINT

Let me press my point about the need to go 'beyond' reason
from inside our rationalistic tradition a bit further by looking
briefly at a study which will be discussed in greater detail in
the rest of this chapter - Wittgenstein's Remarks on Frazer's
'Golden Bough'. (2)   Here Wittgenstein speaks to the limits
of explanation by showing what is actually happening when
Frazer 'ex-plains' religious and magical practices on the operative assumption that those engaged in such practices are in
error.

> I think one reason why the attempt to find an ex-planation
> [for religious and magical practices] is wrong is that we
> have only to put together in the right way what we already
> know without adding anything, and the satisfaction we are
> trying to get from the ex-planation comes of itself. (3)

Wittgenstein thus views explanation as a form of self (and
collective self) reference where what is given and secure,
rather than what is strange and different, is central.   Philosophy shows the limits of explanation by unearthing the practices that underly the idea of a problem and its solution which
is given in the performance itself (e.g. ex-plaining).   We are
clearly reminded of what descriptions of the world 'really' tell
us ('Tractatus' 6.342), when Wittgenstein points out: 'And

here the explanation is not what satisfies us anyway.... And
that is the answer to the question why is this [human sacri-
fice] happening?: Because it is terrible.' (4)   Note that this
is neither an explanation nor even a 'reason'.   One is forced
to relate the problem of innovation as it is conceived in the
advanced societies today to the role of conceptual and theoretical innovation.   Is there, for example, a useful parallel
to be drawn between the impact of social and organizational
'structure' on invention and discovery as it relates to innovation (and 'diffusion') on the one hand, and the constraints
posed to conceptual and theoretical innovation by 'explanation'
on the other?

This largely rhetorical question continues the argument put
forward in the last chapter against Donald Schon's view that
invention and innovation are best understood as the result of
a 'displacement of concepts'.   To be sure, Barnett's (and
Tarde's) view of innovation as the result of a 'recombination'
or 'restructuring' rather than simply 'the addition and subtraction of parts', helped me address (not answer) the questions posed in criticism of Schon, namely, *what* concepts to
displace and *where* to displace them to.   But even here the
role of reason is not taken account of as it expresses itself
in the difference between the activity or process and its recognition.   Recognition, I argued, is no mere 'perception',
any more than invention and innovation can be grasped
through successful explanations.   Indeed, it is precisely the
intellectual component and the role of ideas embodied in the
act of recognition which points to the need for critique from
the inside by showing just what thought and language can
accomplish when this limitation is acknowledged. (5)   As an
example of this, notice the way Wittgenstein speaks of
Frazer's understanding of the 'natives' in 'The Golden Bough'.
Here he points not to Frazer's failure to ex-plain but rather
to what explanation means as a cultural (tribal) activity.   He
achieves his objective by showing us the problems implicit in
Frazer's explanation as an icon of what we ourselves might
hope to accomplish when speaking and writing, thinking and
talking.   Not only are the natives Frazer examines not 'in
error':   Frazer himself is not in error either.   His is not a
mistake for which another explanation is required, since the
idea of 'mistake' itself is appropriate only to practices which
are means to ends outside and distinct from them.

This is definitely not the case, Wittgenstein argues, with
religious and magical practices, where changes in behaviour
are a function of either 'conversion', gradual *collective* revi-
sion, or a reaction to cataclysms and unanticipated events,
rather than a process wherein each individual believer is
shown the error of his ways by an external observer, acknowledges his error, and changes his behaviour by rational deci-

sion. That religious and magical practices are not 'really'
carried out as an instrument or means to distinct ends (e.g.
rain, sunrise, fertility) is the most difficult thing for Western
peoples, with their commitment to disciplined observation, to
accept. Thus Wittgenstein cites the examples of praying for
rain when the rainy season comes, and celebrating the rites
of sunrise when the sun is about to rise. These practices
are not, then, in error: they simply reflect an interest in
an entirely distinct realm of human needs. Thus 'stupidity'
is not a valid way of addressing and evaluating these practices, whose persistence is attributed by Frazer to the fact
that it will rain sooner or later anyway and effectively confirm
the practice as 'successful'. Wittgenstein makes his case
against Frazer's judgment with the following remark: 'But
then it is queer that people do not notice sooner that it does
rain sooner or later anyway.' (6) The answer is that of
course they know this. The problem is our (e.g. the observer's) problem for two reasons. First, we are so conditioned
by our 'rationalistic bias' favouring individualism and an instrumental (means/end) norm of reason as rationality that we
cannot acknowledge how it would really be possible for people
to engage in activity 'for its own sake', especially if it involves pain, submission, or deprivation. Second, we are so unreflexive about ourselves (e.g. unacknowledged self and collective self-reference) that we fail to see that: 'A whole
mythology is deposited in our language.' (7)

Thus what is really important is the reasons why we *can*
know (e.g. Wittgenstein) what is actually happening, though
no account could ever serve to absorb the practices themselves. Wittgenstein shows numerous instances where the
connectives linking and tying together our sentences, as well
as the terms of derision we use to characterize 'primitive'
practices and beliefs (e.g. ghosts) simply draw attention to
the presence of ceremonies, observances, customs and conventions in Western societies which persist even though they
totally lack any instrumental justification whatsoever. It is
Wittgenstein's exemplary capacity to show how reason best
establishes its limits from inside the Western tradition which
provides some hope for the possibility that the common human
pattern will be acknowledged and recognized in a way which is
not subordinated to prevailing conceptions (and practices) of
'comparative advantage' as they are expressed in the extension
of the theme of domination of nature from non-human nature to
men. (8) At the same time, I cannot ignore the fact that it
is precisely what both Weber and Durkheim considered this
'tremendous development' which generates or makes possible
self- (and collective self-) reflection in the advanced societies.
This provides us with a basis for taking account of precisely
what it means when we, in contrast to Frazer's 'primitives',
'act from opinions', and rationalize these actions by reference

to the 'evidence', especially when the actions go against an established or customary pattern of behaviour. This then is the point of Wittgenstein's refusal to allow magical and religious practices in all cultures, including our own, to be construed as an error. He is saying *not* that they would only be an error for us to do them in 'our culture', but rather that: (1) we do engage in similar practices; (2) accept them; and (3) that this makes sense because no matter where they are found they are never mistaken.

In what follows I show (and display) why I think it makes sense to try to see 'industrial society' as a culture, not only by reference to sociological definitions (e.g. 'shared values', 'collective conscience') but in terms of traditions and conventions which so thoroughly permeate our language that it makes sense to call them a 'mythology' like Wittgenstein did. An emphasis on invention and innovation is central to this effort because it is here that certain themes relating to assumptions regarding rationality, history, and progress most clearly present themselves. That this occurs in both professional literature and in popular shibboleths suggests the all-pervasive character of its impact amongst the urban middle class in the advanced societies. It is the way that organizational and societal conceptions and understandings interact and interpenetrate under meritocratic auspices which justifies the extensive reference to Max Weber in what follows. The references to Wittgenstein are another matter, however. While Weber is a central figure in helping us analyse what we are doing by reference to the relation between rationality and domination, Wittgenstein shows us what it means to commit ourselves to such knowledge and knowing, and to transcend it by showing its limits from inside its authoritative auspices understood as a tradition and a culture.

INVENTION AND INNOVATION

I have argued off and on thus far for a view of innovation which sees it as a more 'available' version of invention where this latter is an outcome produced or generated by extraordinary individuals. I also noted the historical dimension of this cultural code word: it appears to *succeed* an emphasis on invention, even if invention remains necessary for subsequent innovation to occur. Paralleling this is the fact that an emphasis on invention, in addition to its manifest or latent technical bias, also expresses a commitment to the sort of 'negative' individualism which Durkheim found so problematic. (9) This in contrast to the clear focus on 'positive' individualism evident in the attempt to describe, explain and produce innovation in advanced industrial societies. This distinction generates still another effect, however. As a consequence of drawing our attention to the difference between negative and positive individualism, the distinction between invention and innovation also points to a significant shift in the nature of organizational decision-making away from hierarchy toward collegiality and away from the solitary individual at the top toward the team or group. While it is easy to overstate this argument - Galbraith is a good example - the shift away from a closed system model of top-down asymmetrical decision-making toward an open system approach based on collegial 'problem-solving' is, on the whole, a fact of life in the advanced societies which has been necessitated by the emergence of corporate capitalism with its specific contradictions. (10) It is not, then, a response to external factors but remains on the whole a pattern of behaviour consonant with the growth of the societal organism itself.

But this is not to argue that such collegiality contradicts the reality of a meritocratic social structure, where meritocracy *means* (with Weber) 'rational domination' rather than unassailed objectivity. The collegiality I have in mind here applies to just as narrow a segment of the society in its role as employees as does the norm of positive individualism and the more 'available' conception of innovation as group process and behaviour. Indeed, there is a sense in which the very restrictions which appertain to the possibility of being 'innovative' in the advanced societies take the form of group process in a formally organized and structured milieu. Collegiality, even when this is acknowledged, remains an overlay on structures where the hierarchical character of bureaucracy in its many and varied guises continues of necessity to hold sway. Bureaucracy, as the prototypical institution embodying legal-rational authority, becomes a model of the meritocratic structure that it so clearly presages. (11) As a closed system, it initially reflected the quite economically (and politically) 'correct' need to govern and control work relations from *within* the organization, whether public or private sector. This need corresponded to the era of early capitalism, with its 'anarchic' market relations, 'entrepreneurial' politics and still viable traditions, customs and pre-bourgeois institutions. An open-system approach, in contrast, reflects the extent to which norms of rationality formerly confined to work settings are increasingly 'system-wide'. While it may seem more amorphous for this very reason, this 'generalization' effect becomes all the more pervasive as an unchallenged *societal* principle, one where the supreme illusion remains the conviction by so many spread throughout the social fabric that meritocracy is not a form of domination at all. The question of 'availability' begins to reveal its compulsory aspect once even longitudinal choice mechanisms have been effectively institutionalized through socialization processes in the advanced societies. (12)

The question for writers on the subject of innovation has
been the extent to which, in following from invention, innovation displaces, perhaps even negates, it over time. Within
the limits provided by the contexts in which these processes
are seen to occur, the imbalance between a negatively individualistic phenomenon, particularly at the level of recognition,
like invention, and the collective and processual character of
innovation, understood as the diffusion of invention in formally
organized, and functionally related, settings, must be
clear. (13)   This imbalance suggests the likelihood that, over
time, the feedback effect of innovation on invention, given
the collective and blatantly organizational auspices of the
former, could effectively reverse the causilinear dependence
of innovation on specific inventions and discoveries which
someone wants to diffuse.   It is precisely the reciprocal
interdependencies between large-scale bureaucratic organizations, and a meritocratic social structure committed to generating 'rational social organization' using bureaucracy as its unacknowledged normative ideal, which helps make a case for
this reversal.   Secondary socialization renders 'innovation' as
behaviour and process increasingly 'available', albeit to
middle- to high-level salaried employees in formal organizations of one type or another.   Meanwhile, inventions continue
to take place, but are in their turn increasingly subject to the
prior commitments embodied in size, complexity and structure
and reflected in an organizationally-cum-societally available
norm of innovation. (14)   When Wittgenstein says that 'progress' is the form of our culture rather than one of its empirical properties, he means to point to it and related terms
(rationality; innovation) as first and foremost forms of life
rather than facts of life. (15)   In a later section I shall try
to show why I think that 'form of life' is the best way to
understand what I mean by 'culture'.

A most important way of arguing the question of invention
vis à vis innovation in advanced industrial societies would
begin with Schon's view of the relation between invention and
innovation in 'Technology and Change' and 'Beyond the Stable
State', and compare this attitude to that of S.C. Gilfillan,
writing 35 years earlier prior to the Second World War. (16)
While Schon's view takes as given the feedback effect I mentioned, Gilfillan is concerned in the mid-1930s with invention
in a period prior to the large-scale corporate (and governmen-
tal-military) interest which would show itself in extensive
financial support and funding in the period during and after
the Second World War.   Schon's studies essentially presuppose
invention as a state of affairs which is produced with sufficient regularity by organizational structures in advanced industrial societies.   Thus his problem is less with invention
than with innovation, which he defines as the 'diffusion' of
invention.   Note that for Schon there is no real sense in

which innovation constitutes the socio-cultural 'routinization'
of invention, since for him invention is now an organizational
production of the individual employee which is awaiting diffusion. Indeed, he is no more willing to allow the view that
invention is 'rational' in 'Technology and Change' than he is
to accept the rationality of innovation. (17) I have already
pointed out the serious difficulties which this argument poses
for him, here and elsewhere. What I want to do in what
follows is first compare his position to that of Gilfillan, then
try to argue for a view which relates invention to innovation
in a way expressive of Weber's somewhat ambiguous arguments
regarding the tug and pull between invention and innovation
in a collective experiencing increasing rationalization and
routinization. Finally, I want to tie this to managerial
ideology and an updated technical bias en route to forging an
acknowledgment of advanced industrial societies as 'cultures',
where by culture I understand what Wittgenstein meant by
'form of life'.

Gilfillan, writing in 1935 in the midst of an impressive career
as a scholar, teacher, museum curator, and consultant on
problems of technical invention, foresaw the need for a more
concerted effort to organize conditions appropriate to the
needs of inventors. In 'The Sociology of Invention', he
addresses his remarks in the main to the need for a social
science of invention and to those firms in the economy which
have both the resources and the interest. At the same time,
government is not altogether ignored. For example, Gilfillan
time and again makes reference to the *national* (American)
need for 'new fundamental invention of the sort that cannot
support itself economically'. He goes on to conclude his
book by saying:

> We have pointed out that the importance of invention has
> been much overrated by the class having most to do with it
> [engineers], and that no one has ever proved what its real
> value is, the share it has in originating social change.
> But still it is clear that invention is very valuable (espec-
> ially the working up though not the proposal of fundamental
> inventions), and that we should arrange our patent, bureau-
> cratic, philanthropic, commercial and educational systems so
> as to obtain a much faster flood of it, especially in the most
> needed directions. (18)

Gilfillan's final sentence advises 'social planning, not only to
guide the inventions, but also to meet their often hurt-bearing
impact'. (19) From most post-Second World War accounts of
invention and innovation, it would appear that the problem
anticipated by Gilfillan has been almost completely displaced by
innovation understood as the diffusion of invention. What
largely brought this state of affairs to pass, of course, was

the Second World War and its immediate aftermath.   The
upshot of these events brought both industry and government
to a realization that invention itself could and must be taken
in hand in the interests both of productivity and defence.
Indeed, industry and government first really learned to co-
ordinate their efforts during the Second World War, so this
pattern was essentially in place when the challenge of the
'cold war' presented itself after 1945.

The gradual shift to innovation requires some elaboration.
In a sense, the idea of diffusing inventions already in existence drew attention to uses, applications of already existing
things and processes.   This meant first that there was a
technical bias implicit in use of the term invention, and second
that innovation clearly had a broader meaning because it related to applications, deployments, etc. (20)   Indeed innovation is a less established term which appertains to novel uses
of something already in existence.   Thus the point made in
earlier chapters about the technical bias in innovation meant
to point to the role of tangible and concrete artifacts, and
techniques and processes constructed out of them, to show
how dependent the idea of innovation was on specific inventions up to the early 1960s.   My discussion of the development of a more autonomous notion of innovation beginning
between twenty and twenty-five years ago sought to take
account of two crucial events in the development of American,
and subsequently European and Japanese, industry: (1) its
increasing concentration and oligopolistic structure, particularly in manufacturing; (2) the vastly heightened dependence
upon applied science in the development of industrial, business, and military R & D.   Thus, looking at both events
for example, it is almost moot whether innovation is best
secured in an industrial structure which is competitive rather
than oligopolistic, because the issue really relates to 'surplus'
and the role of applied science in governing the pace and
type of invention as well as innovation. (21)

At the same time I have argued elsewhere that the societal
effects of a preference for large organizations, with their control of R & D and preference for applied science, may well
sacrifice long-term interests to short-term profitability or
middle-range 'market share'.   Here I focussed first on entre-
preneurship vis à vis a managerial caretaking function in
large organizations with vested interests in stifling inventions
and innovations which were seen to threaten the firm's comparative advantage.   The objective, of course, was to govern
the technical 'state of the art' in a given area.   Thus I was
concerned with the way that organizations, in co-operation
with other organizations and with the state, were in a position
to control entrepreneurial entry into given areas by encourag-
ing individuals and groups to sell off their ideas rather than

try to compete.   Regulation, anti-combines, taxation, special
subventions from government and a conservative banking and
financial system all favour established economic organizations
over small newcomers.   Paralleling this situation, and closely
bound up with it, was the largely managerial preference for
applied science and a narrowly technological bias over basic
research. (22)   While this was readily understandable for
firms whose first concern was 'development' out of R & D,
where scientific hypotheses were seen as potentially useful
vehicles taken from an existing storehouse, it became a problem when governments developed similar short-term, anti-
theoretical (e.g. anti-basic research) concerns, whether
because of impatience or unrealistic expectations, or in response to austerity.   I argued that a governmental commitment
of any duration to limiting support for basic research in science was problematic in the long run not only for science but
also for technology.   The idea that improvements in technique
could be sustained over the long pull by a science whose
basic research was not given priority in the funding and support of governments seemed to me to constitute a fundamental
misunderstanding of science with potentially calamitous consequences. (23)

In a sense, one would be justified in viewing invention as
increasingly the result of the application of science given an
interest in specific profit (or defence and space) related outcomes, with innovation either used interchangeably with invention, particularly in discussions of the large corporations, or
understood as the attempt (often the successful attempt) to
'diffuse' an already existing invention in the form of a technique, process or practice.   In 'Technology and Change',
Schon had distinguished both invention and innovation from
diffusion, as the following excerpt shows:

> I would like to use 'invention' to mean the process of bring-
> ing new technology into being, or again, the new technology
> created in the process.   'Technology' will mean any tool or
> technique, any product or process, any physical equipment
> or method of doing or making, by which human capability is
> extended.   'Innovation' will mean the process of bringing
> invention into use, and 'diffusion' the spread of its use
> beyond the first instance. (24)

Note first how readily Schon, in contrast to Gilfillan, could
assume the pre-eminent role of economic (and governmental)
organization in the 'production' of invention, to the point of
terming invention a '*process* of bringing new technology into
being or ... the new technology created *in the process*'.
Second, note the peculiar distinction between first 'use' (innovation) and subsequent ones ('diffusion').   Surely it is not
insignificant that in his next book, 'Beyond the Stable State',

published four years later in 1971, Schon virtually collapses
this distinction between innovation and diffusion altogether in
his concern to highlight the impact upon entire societies of a
pace of change generated by exponentially increasing rates of
diffusion. The threat to established institutions is alleged to
be grave, and denizens of the advanced societies are advised
to undertake immediate and large-scale 'public learning' in
order to avoid the perpetual disruption that goes with insur-
gency and invasion as the sole means of breaking 'dynamically
conservative systems'. (25)

What has in fact happened here is that invention has been
displaced by innovation, with the latter employed as a synonym for the former. The distinction between them is seen to
have little importance, now that the fusion and interdependence between what were formerly distinct activities speaks to
the ubiquity of 'process' itself. Diffusion, in turn, now
refers to all instances. What is important here is that it is
precisely the 'success' of what Schon had encouraged in 'Technology and Change', plainly on the horizon even before it was
published, which led to the situation described in 'Beyond the
Stable State'. Here we get a further development of Schon's
argument in the earlier work, where he states in his introduction the view that 'technological innovation belongs to us less
than we belong to it.' After pointing out the numerous institutions, professions, organizations and behaviour patterns
threatened by these relatively autonomous developments, he
falls back on a model of negative individualism, combined with
commitment to citizenship and public affairs, as a basis for
making public learning and subsequent accommodation possible.
To be sure, Schon is not interested in the sorts of accommodation and adjustment I cited as increasingly needed in Chapter
2. On the contrary. Further, his analysis fails to realize
that it is precisely post-war developments since 1945 *in the
West* which have underwritten the virtual collapse of a viable
citizen body in the advanced societies. In effect, it is really
the 'aggregate effects' of a tightly organized and highly 'innovative' economic, governmental, scientific-technological and
military structure of national-state (even international) dimensions which has produced the collapse of the stable state. (26)

I would argue, and shall further on, that here Mannheim is
a far better guide when he contrasts functional and substantial rationalities, arguing that increasing industrialization and
organization (functional rationality) *imperils* intelligent judgment and decision-making under changing conditions (substantial rationality). (27) Furthermore, I would argue that the
notion of the 'stable state' is too much of a straw man for
Schon, given his need to presume on the one hand 'total
system effects' but on the other an individual and collective
capacity to respond to these effects as though they had not

really happened at all.   I would suggest that Schon, like
Galbraith, makes far too much of this capacity, after showing
the overwhelming impact of an emerging political-cum-social
economy ('society') on practically everyone who could be expected to be helpful in the process of accommodation and
adjustment.   The alleged collapse of the 'stable state' not
only makes too much of 'stability' in the period prior to the
third industrial revolution (automated electronic technologies),
but treats the resulting revolution in largely technological
rather than socio-cultural and political terms. (28)   By this
I mean that Schon downplays or ignores the fact that such
changes may jeopardize an organization, particularly an economic organization, but not a society.   This does not mean that
'society', in the person of that 'culture-as-civilization' which I
have referred to as the advanced societies in the West, is not
threatened, just that the threat lies in the political and cultural area and is fundamentally international in character.   At
the same time, this threat has less to do with the Soviet Union
and its allies than with the difference between all industrialized nations and the so-called 'Third World' of developing and
newly independent countries. (29)

Without making too much of the terminological vagueness and
even acrobatics which punctuate Schon's account of invention,
innovation, technology and diffusion, it can be said that while
the 'Great Man' theory of invention, with its focus on technology, favoured by Schumpeter, has indeed been supplanted on
the whole by a focus on the cumulative impact of small (tangible and intangible) developments, like that found in Gilfillan
and Ogburn, this is not a mere correction of an earlier error,
as Schon implies. (30)   When I cited this distinction in Chapter 2, it was directed to pointing out how the shift in conception reflected the actual change in the way in which discovery
and invention were taking place as a consequence of the
growth of the industrial sector, the emergence of oligopolistic
and related forms of concentration, the subsequent organization of R & D activities (applied science) in firms (and governments), and increasing interdependence with the state,
particularly after 1945.   While I would be the first to acknowledge a 'lag' between developments in industry and business,
and the *perception* of these developments by social and administrative scientists, it must be quite clear that the 'Great Man'
theory generated by Schumpeter and others actually corresponded to the way that technological advance was occurring,
certainly up to the First World War, even in science.   My
argument for a greater 'availability' in invention, and particularly innovation, is not in any way taken account of by Schon's
reference to the Gilfillan-Ogburn view, since here too the emphasis remains on the technical or technological, albeit in an
emerging organization setting, or the distinct possibility of
one.   My concern was to show the essential *unity* of Western

development over the past 75 to 100 years, and to compare
this development with an emphasis on more ordinary activities
and processes (e.g. Tarde, Barnett, Bourdieu). Schon's
view, in contrast, not only remains tied to the conditions of
advanced industrial development, but is really seen to be a
property of salaried members of the urban middle class working in large organizations. The irony is that the problems
to which Mannheim drew attention are likely to be ones which
those *lacking* the opportunity and apparent capacity to 'inno-
vate' will be better able to respond to than those erstwhile
managerial and bureaucratic meritocrats who are assumed to be
leading the pack. (31)

RATIONALIZATION: TYPES AND LEVELS

In what follows I use the preceding discussion of invention,
innovation, and diffusion as a vehicle for addressing some
larger-order themes having to do with the emergence, modification and dismantling of institutions and ideologies in the
advanced societies. Schon's treatment in particular was
looked at as a central form of managerial ideology in these
societies since 1960. Not surprisingly, it is only after 1960
that 'innovation' begins to supersede invention. That this
constitutes both a reflection of actual developments and managerial ideology only seems difficult to accept where ideology is
presumed to be untrue, rather than simply an interpretation of
or gloss on events which construes them in a way supportive
of (or detrimental to) a given establishment or 'system'. (32)
I noticed earlier how it would be sensible to argue that in the
spatio-temporal relation between invention, innovation, and diffusion, the first two become absorbed organizationally (and
societally), while diffusion expands to mean all utilizations,
deployments, applications. Now let me relate this point to
one made in Chapter 2, where I noted that the aggregate
effects of organized invention and innovation over time create
an 'innovative society' in which both the problem to be solved
and its solution appear as the increasingly 'available' upshot
of such organized activity. Ellul and other determinists (not
excluding even Schon in some respects) are really drawing
attention to the way that the problem shifts from the opportunity presented by possibilities, to the recognition of side-
effects produced by solutions to problems relatively independently conceived, to increasing recognition of side (and centre)
effects produced by inventiveness and innovativeness themselves. (33)

Surely this was the purpose of 'Beyond the Stable State',
for here Schon recognizes precisely this point, one he himself
had strongly promoted in 'Technology and Change'. Ellul's
genius, evident in the original (French) edition of 'The

Technological Society', published in 1954, goes one step further
to point to the problems caused by the so-called 'technical
phenomenon', one whose societal consequences are best understood in terms of centre- rather than side-effects. This
means that the 'problems' which arise and allegedly demand
resolution are generated almost exclusively from *within* advanced industrial societies as a consequence of earlier inventions
and innovations and their economic and social consequences.(34) We can no longer presume that the advanced societies are made up of individuals, groups and organizations
whose prior problem/solution fixes, even given routinization
and sedimentation, simply disappear from sight. In fact what
really happens, as I argued earlier, is that *the idea* of a
problem/solution fix becomes sedimented in the form of pat-
terned responses to problems of adjustment, etc. through the
aegis of organized socialization processes in the advanced societies. It is as a consequence of this increasingly extended
and reinforced *structure* of secondary socialization in the
advanced societies that individuals internalize the idea that
problems are at one and the same time ubiquitous ('available'),
and readily soluble as a consequence. Indeed, I would claim
yet again that the 'solution' to problems is increasingly given
in their very formulation as problems, most significantly (for
my purposes) in the notion of crisis for which innovation (or
more and better innovation) is required. (35) Innovation, as
organized 'social' rationality, becomes the basic mode (form) of
affirmative orientation in a social structure where progress has
become a form of life, the basis of a culture, the only conceivable way of rendering the idea of 'tradition' sensible in this
context.

In turning to the concept of rationalization, both in its own
right and in terms of its necessary tie to invention and innovation, I shall be concerned not only with the organizational
consequences of this process and goal but with its societal
impact. Indeed, one point I want to make clearly in what
follows is that the prevailing entrepreneurial cum managerial
ideology regarding the relationship between organizations on
the one hand and society and state on the other is a seriously
deficient version of actual developments. Having discarded
the entrepreneurial mantle, save for occasional rhetorical
flourishes on worthy occasions, managerial ideology relies
heavily on the assumption of its prior empirical credibility in
order to justify its activities and undertaking in what is
alleged to be a 'post-industrial' society. (36) Even the term
'diffusion' is not adequately comprehended in terms of the
'application', 'utilization', and 'deployment' of invention and
innovation because this understanding fails to realize that the
progressive 'rationalization' of capitalism means that there
already exists a collective order (society) in which the likelihood of some sort of 'success' is almost total. (37) Rationali-

zation can mean nothing else but the process by which various 'rational' behaviours and ideas are (allegedly) institutionalized. The irony of Max Weber's use of this term was the way he drew attention to the problem of institutionalizing 'rationality' as one in which the individual's capacities would be fundamentally compromised in this effort to collectivize and structure the whole. The dialectical relationship between rationalization at the individual, organizational, and societal levels draws our attention not only to the tension between rationalization and rationality (the 'rationality question'), but to the concept of 'levels' as it relates to institutionalization and the emergence of advanced industrial societies as a 'culture'. (38)

While I would accept much of Weber's paradoxical rendering of rationalization, especially as it bears on the unavoidable tension with reason which is created by its extended ambit in the advanced societies, I would turn away from the pessimism which he largely justified precisely by reference to this inexorable process, with its unavoidable 'de-enchantment of the world'. Indeed, for me it makes much more sense to see in rationalization as a state of affairs observable in 'the world' the institutionalization of particular beliefs, attitudes, norms and values rather than a unilinear eschatology downwards in the direction of a 'dead mechanism'. The relationship between the three levels - individual, organizational, and societal - must be dialectical if we are to give adequate recognition to the interpenetration and interdependence between them. At the societal level, I mean by rationalization the increasing organization of collective life which results from society's ability to actually 'produce' individuals through standardized socialization agencies in the 'secondary' sector. Here the increased predictability of required and expected behaviours reflects the standardization of possible interaction situations in which the subject, increasingly conscious of 'himself', knows what is appropriate, expected, and required already. Work life and career development is where this consciousness most totally mobilizes itself, but its influence is increasingly system-wide, thus applicable to life as a whole in these societies. Once the individual becomes a socially produced product, work life and career become the other side of the institutions which produced him. What looks like a causal relationship takes on system properties (function; relation; interdependence) once the interest of large organizations in the production of such persons is understood to be central rather than peripheral to their actual production. (39)

At the same time, the process of rationalization, whether by the individual (self-rationalization), at the level of the organization of work and labour, or societally creates tensions and strains which underscore the failure of the effort at 'rationality transference' from the individual to the societal whole. (40)

Institutionalization, however, is not compromised as a process by this failed effort, if only because even the full-scale commitment to innovation and change reflects solidification.   The technical parallel to entrepreneurial or market capitalism as an approximatable ideal is invention conceived in negatively individualistic terms, while the technical parallel to organized corporate and managerial capitalism is innovation.   It is the 'social effects' of this system of socio-economic life, complemented by the impact of successful secondary socialization in producing non-resistant 'positive' individuals, which accounts for the systemic, that is, relationally interdependent, consequences of 'diffusion' on what is no longer unorganized externality at all. (41)   Like the obsolescence of a bourgeois ideology which attacked the values and norms of an already defeated class or status group, the latest chapter of managerial ideology must argue for 'diffusion' as both the problem and solution of invention and innovation in the dominant corporate organizations of advanced industrial societies.   Galbraith's 'technostructure', itself an embodiment of the fraudulence of 'dispersion of power' as ideal and reality, protects the manufactured (or manufacturable) 'success' underwritten by this latest phase of managerial ideology.   The very vastness of the corporate organization and its control of resources, coupled with its reciprocal interdependence with the state and political authority, guarantees that the problem of 'diffusion' will provide its own 'solution' ('success') just as readily as 'invention' and innovation did earlier. (42)

Normally, when we speak of the rationalization of an industry, industrial area, or any work system in whatever it consists, we have in mind a fairly 'objective' notion of technical rationality seen as a means in the service of already clear and unambiguous organizational objectives.   That this allegedly 'objective' goal is itself a desideratum should not blind us to the more fundamental, and continuing, goals which such objectives, and efforts in pursuit of them, serve.   In the first place it must be clear that economic, political (or military) goals or objectives really are primary, and that they must be stable and clearly formulatable if technical rationality ('technique') is to be put in their service.   In other words, rationalization can and does operate at several interdependent levels in work organizations of all types, given the fact that they are under two conflicting imperatives.   It is difficult even to keep specific economic objectives clearly defined and rank-ordered in terms of desirability when components of an organization's 'environment' are themselves shifting or in conflict. This is especially the case when, for one reason or another, a given organization feels it necessary to constantly monitor the relevant environments and import new knowledge and new skills into its structure in order to maintain or expand what it believes to be its 'comparative advantage'.   For in this case

it will find itself caught in the middle of a societal situation
which truly evidences the extent of society's emergence as a
social structure characterized by a 'normal' division of labour
as Durkheim understood it.   This points to what is clearly a
new order of sorts, but not one which can in any sense be
called post-capitalist.   In point of fact this order is evidence
of the thoroughgoing solidification of capitalism as a Western
system with global pretensions. (43)

Victor Thompson described the conflicting imperatives which
characterize the organization's position as an intermediary
between society and its other socialization processes over
twenty years ago in 'Modern Organization'. (44)   Here he
drew attention to the fact that organizations on the one hand
seek to 'rationalize' all possible internal tasks in the interests
of profitability through what he called task specialization,
while at the same time having to absorb elements in possession of new knowledge and skills into the organization as
person, rather than task, specialists.   Equating task and
person specialization with Durkheim's abnormal and normal
division of labour respectively, Thompson went on to argue
that in the tension and strain created by these conflicting
imperatives, the process of person specialization was emerging
victorious, at least in the United States at the time he wrote
(1961).   The very dynamism of organizations, which view
themselves as 'open systems' anxious to convert threatening
environmental elements into pawns in what is now seen as a
'domain' of organized action, is confronted by a defensive
need to protect the 'technical core' from invasion by unending
efforts at task rationalization favouring technology over
labour.   In order to carry this discussion a bit further in
recognition of subsequent social and organizational developments, however, we must begin by recognizing that this tension is necessary given the values and objectives of large-
scale economic organization in advanced industrial societies.
Even though task rationalization happens in the face of the
continuous importation of new knowledge and skills into the
organization, it happens over time, and at progressively
higher levels, only after the relevant values and objectives
have been accepted.   It is technical rationality given certain
broad economic (political or military) objectives which is the
court of last resort to which we must turn in order to understand how and why this is happening.

Indeed, it would appear necessary, in line with my earlier
point about the way levels interpenetrate and redefine or
influence one another dialectically, to see such organizations
as mediators functioning to convert discretionary skills at the
forefront of knowledge, technique, etc. into technologically
rationalizable tasks no longer directly dependent on even the
complement (or supplement) of 'labour power'.   To be sure,

there are numerous factors which stand in the way of such a
process becoming inexorable in Weber's sense, (45) though one
wonders whether the residual 'charisma' produced external to
the organization and available to stand against it is not at one
and the same time a clear social effect.   This becomes all the
more problematic when one reconceptualizes the rise of R & D
activities in large economic (and political/administrative)
organizations in order to see them as a central effort by these
organizations to capture and thereafter govern, and even *produce* as much as possible, the relevant technical (and other)
state of the art on which their position and advantage depend.
Technology as knowledge may approach objective status,
though even here we are basically 'inside' the cultural form of
life rather than independent of it, as both Weber and Wittgenstein pointed out. (46)   By comparison, the 'conversion' of
such knowledge into processes and structures of production,
administration, service, etc. is almost totally dependent on a
series of specific maximizing decisions in time and space which
are anything but automatic and objective.   Thus the real distinction is between the technically rational character of technology as knowledge and the economically or politically rational
character of efforts to convert such knowledge into end products, or into processes and structures which can be sedimented as organized work patterns, with the distinct possibility
of a subsequent impact on priorities and the rank-ordering
scheme. (47)

A somewhat different charismatic residual presents itself
when we look at the way the manager interprets these conflicting, or at least differing, imperatives when they affect his own
area, groups, or tasks.   The degree to which Wittgenstein
made sense when he referred to progress as the form, rather
than an empirical property, of our Western 'culture' is evident
from a prescient remark by Michel Crozier in 'The Bureaucratic
Phenomenon':

Progress in the organizational field meets a strong passive
resistance.   Bureaucratic systems persist and always find
new forms.   This is the result of two opposite and yet con-
vergent pressures.   On the one side, each individual,
each group and category within an organization, will always
struggle to prevent the rationalization and maintain the un-
predictability of their own task and function.   Their power,
the influence they can wield, depend on their amount of discretion, and, finally, on the uncertainty they have to face.
One can thus understand that they will fight rationalization
in their own field while trying to further it in other fields.
On the other side, the constant progress of rationalization
offers the possibility and temptation, to those responsible
for it, to push planning and standardization further than is
rationally feasible. (48)

Without commenting on the vagueness of Crozier's concluding
reference to 'feasibility' and 'rationality' as benchmarks in
deciding how far to push rationalization in given contexts, we
can see in this statement what Victor Thompson had in mind,
in both 'Modern Organization' and 'Bureaucracy and Innovation', when he criticized managerial reliance on the formal
authority built into a bureaucratic hierarchy which was in
ever greater conflict with 'ability'. Thompson was very
pleased that bureaucratic organizations of all types were
losing effective control of their job descriptions as a consequence of their increasing dependence on person specialists
(professional and technical personnel) trained *outside* the
organization in institutions of higher education and related
agencies. (49)

Thompson did not appreciate, however, that the tension
between authority and ability was something Weber had fully
anticipated in his attack on the meritocratic auspices of late
capitalism as synonymous with 'rational domination'. These
auspices seek the rationalization of both authority and task,
and rely on a fetishized notion of value-free, objective authority to legitimize the aspirations of what are in fact special-
interest groups operating under the same ideology of specialized competence and technical virtuosity that the bureaucrats
and managers now under attack by them had earlier employed.
Crozier's reference to the persistence of power interests and
the significance in modern organization of mystery and secrecy
in no way challenges the argument that one can actually
observe a set of collective and historical activities over time
and space which could usefully be collected under the term
'rationalization'. How could rationalization be comprehensible
as a continuous (unending?) process in the absence of new
raw material awaiting transformation? The question really
becomes (or remains) the extent to which norms of rationality
relevant to new knowledge and to change have been co-opted
by collective structures which permit of no more than a dialectic between society as a false totality producing positive individuals through its socialization agencies, and work organizations taking this partially formed product early in adult life
and completing the transformation (rationalization) in society's
name. It is this dimension of 'problem' which I have in mind
when I look at the literature on invention, innovation and diffusion with less, (or rather *more*) than thoroughgoing 'objectivity'. (50)

Just as the individual's substantial rationality is threatened
by the interpenetration and interdependence between early and
late socialization agencies, as Mannheim noted in 1935, so it
becomes necessary to address this problem by acknowledging
the different-level 'episodes' in which rationalization, understood as I have formulated it above, actually occurs. (51)   At

the same time, it would be ridiculous to abjure a dialectical understanding of these levels in favour of viewing them incrementally as steady aggregation processes beginning with the individual, moving through small groups to formalized activities in organizations, and on into society as 'culture'.   Such an approach conceals reality in the effort to speak plainly, especially when this latter standard demands that real social contradictions be 'smoothed' over with language rather than confronted through it. (52)   Rather than promote the fiction of such a steady growth process, one incomprehensible when the structure of society as an historically (and culturally) specific form of collective life is appreciated and understood, I have decided to focus on the problem of invention, innovation and diffusion by reference to the conflict and complementarity found in Weber's discussion of types of 'progress'. Here I accept Wittgenstein's view of 'progress' as the basis for comprehending a form of life, something to be elaborated further on.   At the same time, I do believe that Weber's discussion complements, even completes or 'fills in', Wittgenstein's remarks in a way which makes the best sense of what I have said in this section about rationalization.   What we shall discover, in fact, is that for Weber 'rationalization' is nothing less than a pessimistic interpretation of the doctrine of progress, one which appeared increasingly compelling to him given the fact that the rosy blush of the Enlightenment had irretrievably faded. (53)

When we consider the relation between rationalization at the individual, small group, intergroup, organizational, interorganizational and social levels, the first thing we must acknowledge is the impact of organizational, interorganizational and social pressures favouring rationalization on the lower levels of aggregation.   Even the novelty of unexpected knowledge, attitudes and practices must make itself 'available' in one way or another to economic and political interests, as Barnett pointed out.   This is no less a requirement for advanced industrial societies than it is for non-Western and historical collectives.   Barnett's reference to rejection underscores how contingent the modern technological order is because of its dependence on various sorts of allocation mechanisms and decisions reflecting real interests of an economic or political kind. Apart from the constraints on new knowledge, attitudes and practices posed by the problem of 'acceptance' where economic motives are pre-eminent, there is the threat to new knowledge posed by large organizations anxious to co-opt it onto already existing structures or suppress or rationalize it out of existence altogether.   Advanced industrial societies are problematic for the autonomy of the goal-rational individual precisely to the extent that they confront him with a structure of values and norms which have overcome 'pluralism' in the societal sphere in their movement toward totality.   The ubiquity

of 'socialization' as a social fact in both early and adult life
underscores the fact of totality in the person of 'society' and
suggests that only economic or military failure or collapse can
lead to real structural change. (54)   Mannheim's reference
to the adjustment and accommodation orientations of *all three*
basic individual responses to social (functional) rationalization
– 'self-rationalization' (e.g. discipline), 'self-observation' (e.g.
role conformity and rehearsal), and even 'self-reflection' – is
still fundamentally accurate, even though written in the early
1930s. (55)

Looking at Weber's discussion of the concept of progress,
and keeping in mind Wittgenstein's distinction between form
and property (form and fact), I can hopefully round out this
discussion of rationalization.   Speaking of the hortatory way
in which Americans in particular use the term 'progress', I
had noted that for Weber:

There is a recurrence here of the widespread confusion of
the three following meanings of the term 'progress': (1)
merely 'progressive differentiation', (2) progress of *technical rationality* in the utilization of means and, finally, (3)
increase in value.   A *subjectively* 'rational' action is not
identical with a rationally 'correct' action i.e., one which
uses the objectively correct means in accord with scientific
knowledge.   Rather, it means only that the *subjective*
intention of the individual is planfully directed to the means
which are *regarded* as correct for a given end.   Thus a
progressive subjective rationalization of conduct is not
necessarily the same as progress in the direction of rationally or technically 'correct' behaviour. (56)

I can deal directly with most of this excerpt, since it simply
restates Weber's determination to hold fast to the ethical norm
of autonomous (negative) individualism by contrasting a conception of rationality in terms of actor intent with one based
on conformity and adjustment to 'objective' technical requirements.   When Weber says that: 'An increase in subjectively
rational conduct can lead to objectively more efficient conduct
but it is not inevitable,' he makes this point clearly and unambiguously.   Anticipating Mannheim in 'Man and Society in
an Age of Reconstruction', he yet formulates his ethical norm
of the autonomous individual as a methodological postulate for
sociological investigation, and simultaneously deceives himself
(Loewith), while turning his back on the socially produced
character of the (then) emergent new men – Durkheim's positive individuals defined in terms of their occupations and
careers. (57)

I am more interested here in the first two understandings of
progress than in the third, since clearly this latter ('increase

in value') corresponds to the negative individual in possession
of an 'autonomous' value-rationality which disposes him against
the prevailing order, characterized as it is by 'rationalization'.
From the standpoint of Wittgenstein's claim that progress is
the form of our culture rather than one of its empirical properties, it must be clear that *all three* of Weber's possible
understandings play their part.   To be sure, at the outset
I need to acknowledge the complementary role of technical
rationality and progressive differentiation, the first corresponding nowadays to an organizationally induced initiative,
and the second to a societally induced one providing a basis
for increases in technical knowledge while increasingly dependent on these very developments.   When modernization and
development theorists focus on differentiation, specialization
and emergent complexity in their efforts to evaluate the 'progress' of Third World countries along our (alleged) path of
development, eschatologically conceived, they are revealing
the extent of their commitment to Durkheim's project – an
occupational and organizational society of positive individuals
inhabiting (and sustaining) a 'normal' division of labour.
The 'merely' in Weber's first meaning conceals the central
societal role played by progressive differentiation and the
emergence of more complex types in both organic and human
collective life.   The evolutionary metaphor here, as in the
case of levels, is of the greatest significance in appreciating
the tension and complementarity between work settings and
society as a whole, with its more specific agencies of secondary socialization. (58)

When Weber contrasts 'merely progressive differentiation' to
'progress of technical rationality in the utilization of means',
he intends to draw attention to the causilinear auspices of the
latter, the only kind of development which appears to him both
man-induced and 'objective', that is, free of capriciousness in
his judgment.   Only here, Weber argues, are terms like
'correct' and 'incorrect' appropriate.   While it might appear
that Weber is at one with Wittgenstein on the limited sphere of
applicability of this particular type of reason and progress, it
must be stated that he was far more ambiguous about this
than Wittgenstein.   Indeed Wittgenstein would see progressive
differentiation more the 'natural' ally of progress as 'increase
in value', whereas for Weber, the ambiguity lies in the way
that value could and often did coincide with technical correctness and progress. (59)   If one keeps in mind the point made
earlier regarding Weber's encircled yet (allegedly) autonomous
subject as simultaneously a goal-rational and a principled (e.g.
value-rational) actor, it must be clear from the definition that
follows how easily technique could square with the actor's
values.   The dependence on a prior empiricization of the
dichotomy between ends and means is also significant.

Given a specified end, then it is possible to use the terms 'technical correctness' and 'technical progress' in the application of means, without any insuperable dangers of ambiguity. ('Technique' is used here in its broadest sense, as rational action in general: in all spheres, including the political, social, educational, and propagandist manipulation and domination of human beings.) Only when a specified condition is taken as a standard can we speak of progress in a given sphere of technique, for example, commercial technique or legal technique. (60)

Weber acknowledges in the next sentence that:

We should make explicit that the term 'progress' even in this sense is usually only approximately precise because the various technically rational principles conflict with one another and a compromise can never be achieved from an objective standpoint but only from that of the concrete interests involved at the time.

Though this point is also made at the outset in his discussion of 'types of authority and bases of legitimacy' in 'Theory of Social and Economic Organization', (61) the essence of technical progress is the assumption that real interests are given, stable and unproblematic in their rank-ordering. This is precisely what makes heightened efficiency through 'rationalization' possible as the objectively correct type of behaviour for those desirous of acting in a technically rational way. To be sure, Weber tends to carry the model of the individual actor too far when exemplifying technical rationality, in line with his view that organized collectives could only compromise *both* economic and technical rationality through their commitment to structure, formalism and non-productive vested interests. Weber perhaps best summarized his attitude on this matter when he stated that

the formation of cartel agreements, no matter how rational their basis in relation to the market situation may be, immediately diminishes the stimulus to accurate calculation on the basis of capital accounting, because calculation does not take place at all, or with a high degree of accuracy, in the absence of an objective need for it. (62)

The issue of values which Weber's negatively individualistic anti-social sociology thus highlights is to be discovered not so much in the clash of principles and rationalization as in the conflict between the goal-rationality of certain actors and the organized and collective 'functional' rationality of the whole, or some significant subset of it. Looked at from the standpoint of Weber's almost pantheistic support for pluralism and an 'antagonism of values', the problem can perhaps be more

accurately construed in light of twentieth-century developments.   It is precisely the way that a pluralism of sorts has
been displaced by an increasing homogeneity of values, converted into stable ends and stable mechanical rank-orderings
of ends by those organizations at the forefront of the so-
called rationalization process, which suggests the need to
transcend Weber's distinction between goals and principles
when trying to isolate the most significant and persistent
features of 'society' as an historically and culturally specific
form of collective life rather than a synonym for collective life
itself.   It is therefore not only possible but necessary to
realize that value-homogeneity, far from being impossible
under conditions of ever greater structural and relational
('emergent') complexity and differentiation, is absolutely
necessary if such an 'abstract' society of roles and statuses
is to hang together at all. (63)   Only Weber's determination
to keep principles and values rigidly separated from the goals
and ends of an economizing capitalistic (negatively individual)
mode of activity gone wrong as a consequence of its very
'success' could cause him to refuse to see this homogeneity as
an unavoidable by-product of rationalization itself.

I said earlier that Wittgenstein's point about progress comprehended all three of Weber's meanings, and now we can
perhaps better see how this makes sense.   As a form of life
rather than a fact of life (empirical property), 'progress'
shows the essence of a culture in the way that these three
understandings interpenetrate and thereby gain significance
by reference to one another.   This may be easier to see in
the case of 'progressive differentiation' and 'progress of technical rationality in the utilization of means' than in the case of
'increase in value', yet we could only treat the latter meaning
as one independent of the culture if we admitted to the same
sort of full-scale alienation from industrial society which Weber
himself clearly felt.   This, as I suggested, is based upon the
split between values on the one hand and ends or goals on the
other which is built into his behaviour and authority typologies, and conditions his conception of rationality in terms of
actor intent, where such intent reflected the individual's dis-
satisfaction with the prevailing 'rational' order. (64)   The
irony of Weberian rationalization is to be discovered in what
its reality means for Weber the sociologist: he cannot stand
against the process he claims to see as a sociologist whose
business requires him to be free of values and in pursuit of
the objectives of an 'empirical discipline' created by this very
process.   In the final analysis, then, Weber's very characterization of his own opposition (and that of others) to the
emerging order as 'values' or 'principles' would require him to
acknowledge an argument like mine as fundamentally 'correct'
on all counts: the resisting subject as *a participant* in the
culture as a 'form of life'. (65)

INSTITUTIONALIZATION AND CHANGE

My emphasis on rationalization in the last section was not intended to ignore the role of 'new knowledge'. Rather, I wanted to draw attention to the way that the novelty or newness of knowledge generated within advanced industrial societies is *increasingly* conditioned by the reality of structure, organization and reciprocal (and unending) socialization. What is really 'outside' the predefinitional capacities of these societies only serves to underscore the problem of acceptance or rejection cited for all collectives by Barnett by adding yet another dimension to it. (66)   Invention, innovation, diffusion: the less likely they are, the more available they become, and the more it is really believed possible to produce and anticipate them, and thus to no longer be surprised in any meaningful way by their 'untimely' appearance.   The 'new knowledge' to which Victor Thompson refers, particularly in 'Modern Organization', for instance, readily reveals itself as professional and technical competences often produced by socializing, and training and certifying, agencies *outside* the large corporation or public bureaucracy.   To the extent that the 'normal' division of labour approaches systemic capacity, the reciprocity to which I drew attention earlier allows the organization to trade off its prior closure only if the society as a whole gives up its unorganized and pluralistic character and embraces closure.   This is the real meaning of meritocracy, and it is why Weber refused to see such a structure as open and pluralistic, focussing instead on its most ironic, yet central feature: 'rational domination' under the guise of 'objective' processes of technical, functional, and organizational rationalization.   That he could do this only obliquely and by reference to his own values spoke to sociology's origins, goals and limits more than anything else. (67)

There are very few places in Weber where it possible to see any reference to change possibilities for Western industrial societies, ways in which we could take account of the factor of institutionalization and sedimentation as a combination of rational design and (mostly) spontaneous development.   Weber discussed change all right, but only for all other cultures and the West in the early modern period, never in the present and future.   His pessimism probably goes a long way toward explaining this rather distinctive feature of his work. (68)   We find out (in spite of Weber) how his beloved entrepreneurial and market capitalism, characterized by the dominance of bourgeois class principles and values conditioning straightforward economizing and goal-rational behaviour, actually produces its opposite by adherence to its ground rules, but little else regarding change possibilities that might deny the rationalization (and de-enchantment) process its ultimate and largely pyrrhic victory.   Yet it is because Weber's remains on the

whole the master analysis of these developments, anticipated
during and often prior to, their full-scale emergence, that, it
is necessary to see how far we can go in our effort to use
his work as a basis for clarifying the notion of a culture, a
form of life, in Wittgenstein's sense.   There is a compelling
point about Weber's analysis, with its tension between organization and disorganization, rationality and rationalization,
structure and process, charisma and technical and intellectual
competence, that demands this effort, given my view of invention, innovation and diffusion as local episodes produced and
sustained by 'progress' with its accompanying archetypal concepts – rationality and history. (69)

One problem I must acknowledge at the outset is my very
rationalistic and individualistic tendency to see change as activities and events opposed to institutionalization processes
rather than embodied in them.   Here it would be the view of
most that events occurring largely 'independent' of our control (as 'external' observers) really do not qualify as change,
but actually make it more difficult for change to take place.
Such an argument would simply serve to reveal how committed
we are to the idea that 'real' change can only be the sort of
thing which is consciously and purposively man-induced or at
least the result of the unanticipated consequences of (our)
human activity.   Weber was fully caught up in just such a
commitment, choosing to make his stand for the individual on
the issue of actor intent versus objective consequences.
Thus Weber argued that rationality was 'really' only a property
of individual actors who intended to realize certain objectives
and organized and released their behaviours accordingly.
Whether their efforts were successful, while important, did not
enter into the assessment of rationality at all, for failure
could be accounted for by incomplete information or unanticipated factors intervening. (70)   A 'dynamic' society is one
full of people who only acknowledge change as a property of
the agent, now expanded to include groups and organizations,
in line with the rise of positive individualism and a 'normal'
division of labour.   Institutionalization is something that other
(less 'advanced') societies (e.g. 'cultures') *reflect*, and it is
believed that only through the modernization experience will
these peoples become capable of appreciating the value of
change.   It is our disciplined observation of 'other cultures'
that gives us the impression that change and institutionalization are radically different, even conflicting, processes, with
the first the result of conscious 'rational' decision and action,
and the second a consequence of uncontrollable and fundamentally non-rational factors barely related to human activity at
all.   It is a triumph of sociological, managerial/bureaucratic,
and meritocratic ideology that we believe this, almost without
cavil, and it already is having serious consequences for us in
the international economic and political arena. (71)

When I analyse Weber's scholarly work, I find a clearly ambiguous attitude toward acknowledging the role of institutionalization in his own historical collective - the industrial society
of Western Europe at the turn of the century. Rationalization
sits somewhere between the conscious and purposive rational
action of the autonomous subject and institutionalization.
Even in his most pessimistic of pessimistic moments, Weber
must maintain the distinction between 'them' and 'us'. The
determinism that lies not far beneath the surface in Weber's
conception of rationalization still has the flavour of something
specifically 'rational' about it. (72)   It is not, after all,
'mere' institutionalization.   This attitude is something one
finds permeating practically the whole of Western development
and modernization theory, not the least in that most Weberian
of contemporary thinkers, Shmuel Eisenstadt. (73)   Weber's
example is clearly in the forefront for these theorists when
they try to deal with the factor of tradition, custom and convention.   What do we learn about sociology, and the social
(and related) 'sciences' as a whole, from the fact that they
are plainly incapable of 'handling' this category?   I already
pointed to Weber's disastrous attempt to make sociological
sense of tradition, whether in the typology of behaviour/action,
or in the discussion of types of legitimate authority. (74)   I
also argued that this category really points to that which we
'know' about ourselves below the 'rational' surface but cannot
articulate.   That it only underscores the importance of the
'common human pattern' is well brought home by Wittgenstein's earlier remark: 'A whole mythology is deposited in our
language.' (75)

What about the idea of a 'rational' institution'?   Weber's
ambiguous legacy is in significant part the result of his determination to maintain the difference between rationalization and
institutionalization, while at the same time attacking the idea
that these processes, however empirically observable they may
be, are really 'rational' after all.   Here the picture of an un-
winding mainspring terminating in a dead mechanism speaks to
the way that individual actors with purposes expressing principles and goals (change), create structures of power and influence whose permanence can only be challenged by the likelihood of mechanized petrification, never by revolution.
Indeed, revolution would have to appear no less alien to occi-
dental reason than the socialism which was supposed to issue
from it.   Looked at in terms of the tension between institutionalization and change, revolution would have to sit in the
middle as the 'other side' of rationalization.   Even here, however, Weber is determined to deny his enemies their ideal
(socialism) because he cannot have his (capitalism). (76)   'Increase in value' is best understood as Weber's resistance to
the very sociology (and society) to which he felt himself
bound 'with the certainty of a fate'.   This means that it is

no less a property of modern Western civilization as a culture
or form of life than the other two meanings of 'progress' he
isolated - 'progressive differentiation' and 'increase in technical rationality in the utilization of means'.

If we want to extract from Weber's writings the very most
that he could have agreed to regarding institutionalization and
change in industrial societies, we shall have to look at the
'bases of legitimacy', and compare what for him are the two
factors which account for the emergence and persistence of
organized structures based on functional and technical standards and requirements. Here I must acknowledge Weber's
understanding of his notorious 'ideal types' as controlling for
my comprehension of his meaning. No 'real world' collective
situation is ever found resembling one 'pure type' to the exclusion of others. They are always admixed, and the real
question concerns which one is pre-eminent, and the ratios in
which given admixtures of all the types occur in empirically
observable real world situations. (77) The two factors to
which I refer are first the role of legal-rational authority and
constitutionalism in the emergence of an organized and structured society, and second the role of that elusive phenomenon
- the routinization of charisma. (78) While the lion's share
of attention has always been directed to the first, much of
the rationale for this emphasis has lain with the determination
to explain ourselves by reference to *distinctive*, yet self-
generated, collective phenomena which allegedly provide the
basis for our transcending 'mere' institutionalization, as we
conceive of it, in favour of change. Routinization of charisma
must on reflection be considered a far deeper and more
'general' human phenomenon than the historically (and culturally) specific emergence of legal-rationalism and constitutionalism. Treatment of this phenomenon parallels strikingly the
way that Western thinkers deal with tradition, custom and convention, and is worthy of sustained treatment by reference to
the common human pattern for this reason.

Weber's discussion of legitimacy has never really been superseded, as even the recent work of Habermas shows. (79)
Weber wants to preserve the negatively individualistic component of 'voluntarism', which is reflected in the methodological
constructivism that requires sociologists to take account of
actor intentionality in assessing the presence and nature of
'rationality' as exhibited by the autonomous subject. A further indication of the persistence of this theme in Weber is the
way his understanding of 'imperative co-ordination' (*Herrschaft*)
stresses 'the *probability* that a command with a specific content
will be obeyed by a given group of persons.' (80) Even when
his subjects are in the midst of the process of rationalization,
Weber insists that the sociologist not forget that all social
relationships, including large-scale formally organized groups

(*Verband*), are to be understood as aggregations 'built up' out
of individual subjects who are the real 'concrete' structures in
any sort of collective. (81)   I am less concerned with the
way this attitude is reflected in Weber's polarization of virtually all collectives vis a vis the individual as autonomous
subject than with the contradiction between his notion of a
collectively and historically self-generated 'fate' - rationalization - and his insistence that sociology honour a methodological postulate thoroughly out of kilter with social reality. (82)
Such a requirement could have no other upshot than to force
sociology gradually into a position in which it would have no
choice but to endorse Durkheimian 'positive' individualism.
This would be the only alternative to a life-defeating pessimism which would make of the social theorist himself a 'dead
mechanism'.

Weber's conception of legitimacy is broad enough to comprehend the idea that legal-rational authority is only one basis for
exercising imperative control based on the voluntary acquiescence of the individual subject. (83)   The concept of voluntarism to which Weber off-handedly subscribes in this particular typology is of the greatest importance, because it clearly
disputes the emphasis on actor intent so fundamental to his
discussion of 'rationality' as a behavioural category in sociology.   Indeed, the idea that individuals might view either
charismatic or 'traditional' forms of imperative co-ordination as
'legitimate' could only be reconciled with the reality of rationalization as the central 'uniqueness in which we move' as
Western peoples if a schema of progress in terms of both progressive differentiation and technical rationality in the utilization of means were presumed in the final analysis to square
with 'increase in value'. (84)   This is the hidden irony of
Weber's three meanings of progress of which he must have
been supremely aware: increase in value *must* accord with the
reciprocal interdependence of the first two understandings
rather than stand in opposition to them.   Nietzsche had
already made plain what it really meant to speak of 'value' at
all.   Only those who had altogether transvalued value could
bring it into the world as a nameable, describable entity or
phenomenon.   Weber's (alleged) achievement of complete
'objectivity' on this score can have no other upshot than to
render the idea of opposition to the prevailing order (e.g.
rationalization) absurd as an interpretation of what he means
by 'increase in value'.   It is Weber's commitment to the authority of Western cultural self-determination which ultimately
undoes him, even if the price paid for such collective (and
historical) self-responsibility is an unwound mainspring as a
culmination and a fate.

Still, there is much to be learned from Weber's discussion of
'bases of legitimacy' and their relation to types of 'imperative

control'.   It reveals why he must be seen as an icon of
Western attitudes and contradictions, rather than an eccentric
and idiosyncratic minority of one.   If I stay with the idea of
admixture given the pre-eminence of one base over the other
two, I still must account for the claim that the routinization
of charisma tells us more about the common human pattern
than the historically and culturally unique phenomenon of
legal rationalism and constitutionalism.   My reason for underscoring this point is related to the persistence of episodic
forms of charismatic routinization at all levels on and off over
and over again in the organized structures of advanced industrial societies. (85)   It also appears to be related to the process of articulation between given contexts, settings and levels.
When I argued that the shift in emphasis from invention to
innovation spoke to the rationalization of invention in these
structures, I meant to point to rationalization as the result of
the socialization and subsequent organization of the subject's
voluntarism in a way plainly reminiscent of Durkheim.
Rationalization gives the gloss of both rationality and difference to what is in fact a process of institutionalization differing in no significant respects from the perennial ways that
newness and difference are routinized and sedimented through
the operation of cultural symbols, expressions and controls.
Standing beneath the rational mythology that lies deeply
deposited in our language are basic human needs and feelings
which one finds it difficult to believe will ever be displaced or
fundamentally changed.

In effect, we need to see 'change', understood as the mortal
enemy of institutionalization because it *defends* the autonomy of
the subject (thus the superiority of civilization over culture),
as a superficial ideological rendering intended to convince us
that processes of institutionalization associated with routinization and sedimentation are properties of 'lower-level' cultures
which Western peoples have (along with tradition) transcended.
Development, under such an *ideology of development*, is viewed
as the way everyone can progress from pre-civilized states or
conditions to modernity in an 'objectively' real way, rather
than the procedure by which forgetfulness is ensconced in
consciousness as the pre-eminent basis for knowledge and
knowing.   Suppression of the common human pattern, while
problematic, is not cited here in order to defend the idea of
some unchanging entity called 'human nature'.   It rather
draws attention to the way that that which is actually responsible for absorbing change and difference over time and space
is passed over in favour of the changes or differences themselves. (86)   We change, while 'they' either institutionalize
or reflect already established institutional patterns.   Development is seen as a way they become more like us, albeit in the
most superficial aspects, rather than the way that a particular process of institutionalization favours the 'global reach' of

one ideology-in-practice over those less differentiated and
less technically sophisticated, thus (alas) from our standpoint
less valuable. (87)   We only have to try to think of what
value and tradition must mean to us when they have been
'successfully' formulated as empirically observable categories
'available' in the world to see how our starting points for
knowledge and knowing must be adjudged false beginnings,
beginnings which begin by acknowledging chosen boundaries
as limits rather than achieving limit by ending in it.   What I
have said of value and tradition could be extended to show
how senseless the idea of a 'rational institution' must be, yet
it constitutes the cornerstone of sociology as the science (or
logic) of society.

Weber's attitude to institutionalization equates it with routinization, sedimentation, and the emergence of what he refers
to as 'traditional' modes of authority and behaviour. (88)
Whether he studies institutionalization as an already present
state of affairs (elsewhere), or something which might come
into being in the face of collective historical and cultural
developments *anywhere*, he treats it on the whole as something
which leads to or is equated with (individual) human passivity.
In clear contrast, I noticed, was *change*:   it means the conscious and concerted efforts of 'rational' purposive actors
based on the intent to realize a given objective or state of
affairs.   A type case of such change for Weber would be a
situation in which unabashedly goal-rational behaviour reflected clear religious (Protestant) and secular moral principles
like 'duty, honour, the pursuit of beauty, a religious call,
personal loyalty, or the importance of some "cause" no matter
in what it consists'. (89)   Though Weber makes it clear that
principled ('for its own sake') and goal-rational action are different, his type case of entrepreneurial market capitalism does
combine the two, thereby confirming his already-noted observation that 'it would be very unusual to find concrete cases
of action, especially of social action, which were oriented only
in one or another of these ways.' (90)   My dispute with
Weber here would point to the unacknowledged ideological content of a schema of behaviour/action which insists that there
are forms of action which are *not* social in their nature.
Without making society an absolute totality having nothing
lying outside it as possibility, the difficulty inherent in such
an attempt to preserve the negative individual from the role of
collective influence must nevertheless be clear.

When it is Weber's values and ideals that are being realized
through the actions of his (negative) individuals, Weber
speaks of, or alludes to, change and basically denies the role
of collective factors related to training and socialization altogether.   Only institutionalization contravenes the ideal of
activity for Weber, and here we talk of states of affairs either

elsewhere, or the worst sort of passivity that could possibly befall us given our alleged drift toward total rationalization and world de-enchantment. Still, as noted, Weber is loath (like us) to give up the 'special' character of our own collectively and historically self-induced 'tremendous development', so chooses to steer a middle path between the extremes of active individual change and passive collective institutionalization by pointing to ubiquitous and faceless rationalization. Rationality is quite literally petrified into the 'structure' of both the process and the word which denotes it. This is what happens to rationality when it loses its individual dynamism as an activity changing and transforming the world, and becomes a collective and corporate structure of power and vested interest trying to retain the outward appearance of change while as empty of real content as only a 'dead mechanism' can be. What is tradition and routine in advanced industrial societies *for Weber* if not the unanticipated, or undesired, consequences of the process of incipient rationalization as an expression of a type of institutionalization which overtakes the individual rather than sedimenting and making sense of his behaviour and action in a collective historical setting? (91)

At this point I want to look at the way Weber deals with what is alleged to be our 'institutional' essence even as we undergo rationalization and de-enchantment - legal-rational authority and its quintessential collective embodiment - bureaucracy. In the first case - legal-rational authority - I begin with the notion of imperative control built-in to its exercise, where what is virtually given in its pre-eminence is the presence and central role of an administrative staff. (92) Bureaucracy constitutes its collective formal embodiment and, though the only alternative to dilettantism in the field of administration, can hardly be looked at in any other way but as an organized, hierarchical and institutional structure. Weber qualifies this to some extent by reference to the categories relating to 'ability' that are evident in a delineation of the key characteristics of the (generalizing) ideal type. Thus there is concern about specialization, technical competence, professional qualifications, and selection and advancement on the basis of 'merit'. Yet Weber never appears to deal with these allegedly 'objective' factors as collectively produced, sustained and situated, in fact as the essence of society as an historically and culturally specific form of collective life, even though he does snipe at them from the sociological sidelines occasionally. (93) Legal-rational authority is similarly 'rational' to the extent that it realizes the sort of stability which is apparently generated as a collective reality by the need for active individuals exercising purposive behaviours (change) to have an infrastructure and system of rules supportive of their maximizing activities. It is when goal-rationality becomes absorbed into organized structure that its earlier alliance with principle is sundered, leaving principle intact mainly as values standing in opposition to the emerging collective reality.

The fates of goal-rationality and of principled action are thus complementary - different fates but ones caused by the institutionalization of both which effectively negates each one in different ways. Think, for example, of the fate of principled action in particular: it alone fails to make the transition to a type of imperative control or authority from the behaviour/action schema. That traditional behaviour and affective behaviour become traditional authority and charismatic authority respectively may seem persuasive, but something of consequence is missing here. First, we need to reformulate the relation between the two typologies so that the latter is seen to be conceptually and historically prior, in contrast to the way they appear in 'Theory of Social and Economic Organization'. (94) Next, it is necessary to see both goal- and value-rational (i.e. principled) actions rendered problematic as a result of 'rational'(ized) institutionalization. The *sine ira et studio* character of bureaucracy *and sociology* reflects the impersonal, therefore allegedly 'objective', character of legal-rational authority in industrial societies. Weber's 'individuals', it turns out, can only be preserved as active, world-building beings by a methodological postulate of sociology because of the substantive consequences of the emerging infrastructure, which renders only charismatic authority truly individualistic, and seriously 'unstable' and undistributed as a consequence. The idea that Weber could put such stock in stability, particularly when it serves to demonstrate the similarity between legal-rational and traditional authority, in contradistinction to charisma, provides us with a most important opening in any discussion of the relation between rationalization and routinization. (95)

If we compare rationalization, and its social psychological upshot - de-enchantment - to the routinization of charisma and its social psychological upshot - traditionalization - we see how significantly they relate to the first two meanings of progress already mentioned. 'Progress' as the *form* of Western civilization-as-culture, to be sure, combines all three understandings, but here it is the distinction between progressive differentiation and the progress of technical rationality in the utilization of means which mainly concerns me. Forced to choose which of the two he would prefer as an autonomous subject extolling 'increase in value' in the face of the failure of principled action to sediment itself as a form of 'legitimate' authority, Weber has no choice but to stand with technical rationality, however formalized and functionalized it had become, over 'mere' progressive differentiation on its own. Of the two, technique

clearly favours change and the capacities, interests and intentions of negatively individual actors more than 'progressive
differentiation', even if the progress of technique leads invariably to rationalization.   Indeed, progressive differentiation
has a far more deterministic aura about it than either technical rationality or increase in value.   This no doubt is in
part due to the unambiguous evolutionary overtones given in
the idea of 'differentiation', a concept from biology which has
been adopted, largely metaphorically (Schon), by sociology
and anthropology.   Thus differentiation, as an indicator of
'development' and 'modernization', trades on speciation in evolutionary theory when it argues that collectives at a higher
'level' are more 'advanced', 'developed', 'mature', and 'civilized'.   Culture becomes a negatively charged word in this
equation when compared to its alleged opposite – civilization,
and the sort of 'normalization' counselled by Durkheim is
pointed to as authority when it encourages us to heal or
repair pathological differentiation by making Weberian negative
individualism 'functional' rather than dysfunctional for work
and labour activities in large organizations, and in society as
a whole. (96)

Reflection on this metaphoric parallel between biological and
social differentiation, where the latter trades on an evolutionary conception of the emergence of ever higher levels in
human collective life, reveals precisely the sort of fallacy
which Weber's defence of principle, value, intent and the
negative individual was intended to confront and challenge.
Weber's point is that differentiation as a background standard
for defining progress falls into the very trap that is implicit
in the transfer of goal-rationality from individuals to organized
structures of power and interest.   It is in the act of producing properly socialized 'positive' individuals that rationalization
reveals its true colours.   Such a collective is alleged by
those who promote progress as progressive differentiation to
be 'higher' than the stage of negative individualism which precedes it, yet for Weber such an evaluation is absurd.   Weber
considers it not only possible but (in this case) *likely* that
Western civilization will 'fall back' into organized status structures whose effect will be to inhibit mobility and change or
annihilate it altogether. (97)   Still, we did it ourselves: it
is not mere 'routinization', mere 'tradition'.   Weber will only
allow the first to survive in the form of microcosmic episodes
within organized structures, since there is nothing for him
outside advanced industrial society that can affect its dynamic
drift toward 'mechanized petrification' in any way.   Even
technical change, once captured by these organized structures
in order to minimize uncertainty and risk (R & D), ceases as
a consequence to really constitute change at all, becoming
instead part of the process of rationalization between his ideal
(free market capitalism) and that outcome that awaits all 'other
cultures' – institutionalization.

I would like to conclude this section by addressing the relationship between the common human pattern that receives
what is routinized, traditionalized, sedimented, even 'rationalized', and Weber's tension between institutionalization and
change as an icon of Western thinking on the subject.
Weber's conception of change always generates its effects on
collective life and social relations in a somewhat ambiguous
way.   The actor as negative individual is at one and the
same time a 'member' of the collective in question, while he
seems to operate as an external force from 'outside' it.   His
reason may be rationalized, but it is never institutionalized,
since this only appertains to charisma, which is (eventually)
routinized and traditionalized.   Collective self-destruction
ordained from within is the pattern Weber isolates for modern
Western civilization.   Charismatic routinization is at best
episodic given its non-rational character as that basis of
legitimacy which combines the value-rationality of leaders with
the affectivity of followers en route to the inevitable transmogrification into tradition. (98)   The question here must be
whether those who confer legitimacy behave any the less
rationally when they support charisma, whether at the highest collective level, or episodically in subsystemic structures,
than those whose preference is for an ethics of responsibility
over one of ultimate ends.   Indeed, we are again reminded
of the failure of principled or value-rational action to sediment
itself as a form of legitimate authority, given Weber's subtle
shift of meaning in his notion of 'ultimate ends' away from
principle and toward charisma and affectivity. (99)

Principled action, even more than goal-rationality, it turns
out, is 'unsocializable' in the extreme, for even goal-rationality
can be organized and 'transferred' to organized structures,
which themselves become 'persons' of a sort, even 'actors'
(e.g. corporations).   The question which persists and remains unanswered in this the most intriguing and culturally
significant effort to deny the cultural reality of Western civilization in the person of advanced industrial society is whether
institutionalization and change are really comprehensible as
historical and empirical (not just conceptual) opposites.
Weber shows us what happens when the most 'competent' conceivable sociological analysis of the genesis and development
of modern Western civilization is forced to evaluate its subject
matter by reference to properties which are both uniquely
world-historical and indicative of the common human pattern
lying beneath the rhetoric of rationality, function, organization, and individualism.   I would submit that the preference
for idiosyncrasy over commonality, change over institutionalization, routinization and tradition, makes an assumption about
their empirical and historical coevality which will not hold up
under close scrutiny.   Looked at in the most dispassionate
possible way, we realize that sociology's problem is really that

it is not objective enough.   Objectivity favours not idiosyncrasy but commonality, as would befit a real science which put
man before a denatured nature which turns out to include
'everything (and everyone) else'. (100)   And with this we
see the way that 'change' operates superstructurally as a way
of 'rationalizing' an historically unique process of institutionalization which may not, it is to be hoped, culminate in a
dead mechanism after all.

CULTURE AS 'FORM OF LIFE'

I am now ready to conclude by returning to Wittgenstein, in
particular his discussion of 'form of life' (*Lebensform*) in the
later philosophy and its relation to the idea of a 'natural history'. (101)   The concept of culture which I have focussed
upon off and on throughout this chapter is probably best captured in the meaning which seems to attach most securely to
the idea of a 'form of life'.   Before unravelling this notion,
however, I need to be clear on the way Wittgenstein relates
'historical' types of explanations of human affairs to both
'forms of life' and the idea of 'natural history'.   To the
extent that one sought to treat human collective life as
nothing more than mere biological evolution out of 'lower'
animate forms, he would be indulging in a 'developmental'
type of explanation for Wittgenstein.   Indeed, Wittgenstein
would admit that this would be the most likely candidate if he
were trying to ex-plain rather than address the 'ground'
within which explanations occur and take on their general
and peculiar properties.   In effect, Wittgenstein, consistent
with his criticisms of Frazer, and his total rejection of
Frazer's attempt to 'ex-plain' religious and magical practices,
turns away from such hypothetical ('every explanation is an
hypothesis') notions (*Entwicklungshypothese*) altogether in
favour of an approach which focusses on grasping the formal
connections among things.   Thus the sociological claim to
differ from 'mere progressive differentiation' by dint of a history which includes both 'progress in technical rationality in
the utilization of means' and 'increase in value' is repudiated
by Wittgenstein. (102)

   The difference here hides the key similarity: all are explanatory efforts, therefore hypotheses.   All that can be said
of 'progress' as a peculiarly human historical category is that
it is expressive (not descriptive) of the form of our life,
that is, a way into grasping the formal connectedness, the
ground within which particular cultural explanations are
framed.   As for 'increase in value', Wittgenstein had from the
very outset refused to permit the formulation of value in the
person of religious, magical, etc. practices to inhabit any and
all nameable/describable worlds. (103)   The furthest he would

go with Weber in this regard was to agree that no 'form of life' (which includes but is not exhausted by 'language-games') could ever be reduced to overt behaviour which would serve to define human language under the norms of a propositional logic. Indeed, this realization was a central reason for abandoning aspects of the scheme set down in the 'Tractatus', and is related to Sraffa's reference to how exactly one would fit either purely expressive behaviour or concealed intention into such a scheme. 'In ironic behaviour the gestures and expressions would not correlate at all with the concealed intention. In other words, a form of life cannot always be reduced to a form of overt behaviour.' (104) The fact that Wittgenstein here claims to be interested in explaining nothing at all may appear confusing, but one can argue that it is precisely the attempt to view such efforts as explanatory which has led to the sort of confusion that defines 'form of life' in terms of either biological adaptation and evolution, causilinear history, or behaviour packages, or sees forms of life (with Malcolm) as virtually synonymous with language-games. (105)

Wittgenstein, consistent with his critique of Frazer's 'Golden Bough' discussed at the beginning of this chapter, understands by 'form of life' that which in general grounds the customs and practices of any 'culture', and the specific sorts of customs and practices which express (not describe) these deeper grounds in particular cultures. It is his combined interest in formal connectedness and concern for what lies below the surface of idiosyncratic cultural practices (e.g. genuflection rather than ritual sacrifice) that leads him to turn away from historical patterns of explanation because they are, after all, patterns of explanation, and like other specific and culturally idiosyncratic practices, only display the deeper commonality that grounds them. They express the presence of a form of life that grounds and organizes particular facts of life, for example, the propensity in a given culture (e.g. Weber's 'modern Western civilization') to explain itself and others by reference to rationality, history and progress (and its sub-categories - invention and innovation). In line with this emphasis on formal connectedness and deeper ground went an equally total repudiation of 'merely progressive differentiation'. Here what is specifically human can only be explained by reference to evolution and adaptation, never grounded. For example, Wittgenstein would argue that because humans have a 'natural history' of their species, no attempt to search out these connections can ignore man's status as an animal. Yet this is only a necessary condition, not one sufficient for the task. Indeed it is clearly meaningless, if not totally absurd, to simply redefine these very capabilities as merely 'animal' gestures and behaviours.

All Wittgenstein is doing here is refusing to accept the split between nature and culture that was so fundamental to efforts like Frazer's, who viewed his 'primitives' as living beings outside the pale of real human being. As social thinkers heavily informed by philosophies replete with human *hubris*, both Marx and Weber are remarkable for *not* having accepted the empirical and historical character of the alleged distinction between nature and culture. An example in defence of the need to recognize man's animality would be colour-blindness, which makes it impossible for individuals to learn 'the language game of normal colours'. (106) Indeed neither our perceptive capacities nor our reliance upon memory are rule-governed, in the sense of being dependent upon customs or institutions for their expression. To be sure, culturally specific forms of life defining the significance to be attached to particular perceptions, experiences, concepts and memories may lead us to give a quite legitimate emphasis to difference and idiosyncrasy in our discussion of human collective life in time and space. It was precisely Wittgenstein's membership in that general historical culture which Weber termed 'modern Western civilization' that led him to address the common human pattern lying beneath the surface of difference. In effect, Wittgenstein would say that difference is grounded in commonality, and would include in his understanding of this the distinction between explanation (difference; surface, facts of life) and ground (commonality; depth; form of life). It is my support for this understanding which led me to be sceptical of any focus on uniqueness which favoured an emphasis on change, as the manifestation of rationality, history and progress, over institutionalization. Institutionalization expresses both the ground, and the return to the ground in time and space, as a counter-understanding to Weberian hubris in the person of rationalization and de-enchantment.

The best way of reconciling this concern for form, depth, and ground with the refusal to rest content with *any* explanation, whether evolutionary or human/historical (thus effectively 'customized'), would be to look briefly at instances which would compel us to treat men as animals (necessary condition) but something more (sufficient condition). Here I would be acknowledging Wittgenstein's understanding of the limits of saying relative to showing, 'the world' as nameable *and describable* relative to what grounds all such descriptions and explanations, namely perception, language and memory. (107) Here what I want to say is that perception, language and memory are the uniquely human bases for producing forms of life, and thus that forms of life are not something shared by other kinds of animals at all. These capacities are to be distinguished from the somewhat different need to express something for Wittgenstein, as I noticed earlier. (108) This need to express is no less uniquely human than perception, language and memory, however. It

is rather the way that this need is related to the latter three
capacities which helps us appreciate the phenomenon of
naming, describing and explaining as activities which are
grounded in specific forms of life, thus expressive of particular cultures (not just 'ours', except in the broadest, largely
self-defining, sense). Thus, for example, when Wittgenstein
says that: 'The characteristic feature of primitive man is that
he does not act from opinions,' he means to underscore his
earlier point that: 'Every explanation is a hypothesis,' where
a hypothesis is synonymous with an opinion. We *do* act from
opinions, and this fact turns out to be the central one in distinguishing science from magic. 'Simple though it may sound,
we can express the difference between science and magic if
we say that in science there is progress but not in magic.
There is nothing in magic to show the direction of any development.' (109)

Wittgenstein's point, then, is that there is a clear formal
difference between an animal world and a human world. This
does not, however, dispute our origins and animal characteristics and needs, but instead underscores the kind of animal
we are (Marx). Here the example of feral children remains
instructive, but not for the reasons cited by ethnocentric
sociologists and psychologists. Thus we cannot dispose of
the difference between human beings and the rest of animate
nature by simply referring to a biological evolution process
which produces human beings who see themselves in terms of
rationality, history and progress. This has the not-wholly-
unintended effect of differentiating Western man from 'primitive' man, and of lumping the latter with the rest of animate
nature rather than with human beings. Defined sufficiently
narrowly, such 'primitives' turn out to have little or no
'human' world at all. Apart from the way this explanation
skips over the matter of our real kinship is something less
obvious. Wittgenstein had noted that: 'There is an entire
mythology deposited in our language,' and two points are
important here. (110) The first is that language is an
activity which all humans share regardless of time or space
or culture, and thus that the fact of mythology in this the
key expressive basis (not synonymous with 'language games')
for forms of life is a common characteristic as well. Second,
as the essence of our form of life as a culture, rationality,
history and progress (and their offspring) are the essential
orienting concepts of our particular mythology.

A final point would return to the distinction between necessary and sufficient conditions, and would cite narrow evolutionary and human/historical explanations as insufficient
because of the way they repudiate the common human pattern,
with its emphasis on form, depth and connectedness. As a
student of 'forms of life' recently put it:

Although we can train a smart dog to do many clever tricks,
we can never train him to be sincere, to pretend, or to
hope. Why, according to Wittgenstein, are these 'adapta-
tions' not possible? It is clear that the reason is not anything organic or anything to do with the capacity for
learning. A dog cannot simulate pain because the 'sur-
roundings' (*Umgebung*) which are necessary for this behaviour to be real simulation are missing. Millions of dogs
and humans have lived intimately together for thousands of
years in the same physical environment, but dogs have not
adapted to human life forms. Like lions who could talk,
talking dogs would still be excluded from human
lebensformen. (111)

The human environment (*Umwelt*) is therefore qualitatively distinct, which is to say that there are specific forms of life in
which are embedded specific language games which human
beings can share together but which humans cannot share
with animals. There is a formal difference between a human
world and an animal world which is not captured by alluding
to a mere empirical difference ordained by evolution and subsequent history. As an example of this point, think once
more of Wittgenstein's criticism of Frazer: 'What is really
important is that Frazer has the word "ghost" *available in*
his language-game as part of his form of life', not the empirical and historical difference between believing in magic and
believing in science.

I wish to say: nothing shows our kinship to those savages
better than the fact that Frazer has at hand a word as
familiar to us as 'ghost' or 'shade' to describe their views...

What is queer in this is not limited to the expressions
'ghost' and 'shade', and too little is made of the fact that
we include the words 'soul' and 'spirit' in our own civilized
vocabulary. Compared with this, the fact that we do not
believe our soul eats and drinks is a minor detail. (112)

The tension between formal connectedness and empirical
explanation is well-captured in the surface character not only
of an evolutionary hypothesis, but of one premised on human
life as history. Indeed, when the two are put together, one
sees that the essence of both efforts is to explain by reference to development. In this regard Weber simply inverts
the Enlightenment eschatology, while retaining the hubris
associated with our superiority at the top of the evolutionary
process of adaptation and selection (where else?). The effect
of this has not been to overcome an empiricized man/nature
distinction, but rather to shore up both the commitment to
human difference and consequent superiority and to distend
and distinguish ourselves from earlier and contemporary

'primitive cultures'. Even institutionalization is looked at as a property of primitives who have cultures rather than civilizations, thus of a situation in which men effectively lack 'rational' control over the direction of their lives. In the absence of such control, they are, in effect, consigned to a world of brute determination which is simultaneously a world of brute indetermination. (113) The tension between change and institutionalization is nothing less than the tension between surface and ground, explanation and the forms of life that ground such explanations in the sense of making them possible as things which have meaning for us in terms of perception, language and memory. Perhaps most ironically, it is only by turning away from development hypotheses that we are able to return to the ground by stressing the formal connections which lie at the heart of the common human pattern. Our 'culture' may be an historically specific form of life, but we could only claim to know this if we had returned to the ground from which all forms of life emerge, generating different possible 'worlds', different 'facts of life'.

CHAPTER 6

Summary and conclusions

In what follows, I first summarize the main points of my
argument in order to provide the reader with as much of a
step-by-step picture as is possible under the circumstances.
Then I conclude with some specific remarks directed to the
relationship between innovation and 'rationality', 'progress',
but particularly history as development.   In a sense, the
core of the modern (Western) teaching is the idea of history
as a human-centred version of the development hypothesis
(*Entwicklungshypothese*) which we encountered in our discussion of Wittgenstein in the last chapter.   It is the sanction
this particular idea provides for the modernization project
presently being attempted by multinational capitalism and by
socialism, along with the developing countries themselves,
which compels me to state my own specific hypothesis on the
matter: that the limits of any possible pattern of action are
not to be discovered in the limits posed by language as a
basis for speaking what we think, and that therefore our
challenge lies in seeing whether the 'what we have no choice
but to be' can possibly include an acknowledgment of limit or
falls short of it.   Do the thoughts that our speech puts forward as possibilities in the world show the idea of limit given
in real possibility, or are we consigned by our form(s) of life
to attempt to produce life as the world through unreflexive,
but disciplined, observation?

SUMMARY

A sketch of the main points of the book thus far would include
the following arguments, ideas, and observations.

I

Given Wittgenstein's point that 'Every explanation is a hypothesis', I began with his observation that 'progress' was best
understood as a 'form of life' in advanced industrial societies
rather than one of its empirical properties (e.g. a 'fact of
life').   At the same time, I took issue with his insistence that
philosophy as such should be concerned (ideally) with 'absolute clarity' for its own sake.   I was far less ready at the
outset to deny factual status to any and all development

186

hypotheses than Wittgenstein seemed to be insisting on when
he refused to support any broadly 'political' or 'humanitarian'
concerns on the part of thought. Now I can see that my commitment did in fact constitute an expression of rationality,
history and progress as the key code words of our particular
form of life, so my problem at this point was how to face
this fact, and the role of thought in any such effort. I
made, as it turns out, more of the notion that there are two
Wittgensteins than I should have. M.O'C. Drury is our best
guide here when he says:

> I think perhaps the remark that Wittgenstein made, that
> after his conversations with Sraffa he felt like a tree with
> all its branches lopped off, has been misinterpreted. Witt-
> genstein chose his metaphors with great care, and here he
> says nothing about the roots or the main trunk of the tree.
> These - his fundamental ideas - remain I believe un-
> changed. (1)

None the less, the introductory section tells the reader that
Wittgenstein's prohibition against 'ethical talk' of the sort
given in the commitment to *any* development hypothesis is too
much of a constraint on our speech as an expression of what
we think, and that I shall therefore proceed without being so
bound. The assumption here was that if I was wrong it
would show through.

I went on to say that I intended to treat a focus on 'innovation' as an opportunity precipitated by a crisis, where by
crisis I understood a problem *and its solution*. My guide
here was Wittgenstein's statement in 'Tractatus Logico-Philosophicus', where he says: 'For doubt can exist only where a
question exists, a question only where an answer exists, and
an answer only where something can be said.' (2) In addition, however, I was anxious to argue that something can
exist and yet be incomprehensible, thus that my speech on
the subject of 'innovation' would take the form of addressing
the phenomenon it attempts to capture. After showing the
very limited assistance which the fact-value dichotomy as an
empirical distinction could provide us with - in any and all of
its manifestations - I suggested that the heart of this tendency
to empiricize analytical distinctions was to be discovered in a
view of reality which equated it with nameable/*describable*
worlds only. Thus, for my purposes, both the distinctions
between referential and condensational symbols and between
nominal and real definitions were more of a problem because
they began by presuming the very conceptions of reality, concreteness and abstractness, and the 'empirical' which I considered so problematic. That this was the case, of course,
helped make my point by showing me where I could not turn.
My temporary way out attempted to show why concepts must be

comprehended as universals rather than merely words in need
of adequate definition, and how this offered support for the
idea that concepts must *not* be presumed capable of absorbing
their objects rather than disputing it.   The truncated role
for thought and theory ordained by instrumentalist and functionalist approaches to conceptualization was briefly illustrated
by Max Weber's notion of 'ideal types' as 'heuristic' devices
which did not, he claimed, exhibit any particular 'rationalistic
bias' on the order of a form of life.   Reference to the current notion of 'intelligence' as a stable entity subject to measurement underscored my point about the incomprehensible and
its role in our form of life, and I concluded by pointing out
the sense of yet another apparently contradictory claim: that
ideas might reasonably be understood to be socially determined
in a certain sense, while yet being prior to the act of innovation, or at least its recognition.   Given in the idea of a nameable, describable world of human activities is the limits of this
world vis à vis life, which I wanted to try to show by addressing the phenomenon of innovation as a proximate expression
of the key concepts which mark our form of life - rationality,
history, and progress.

II

I began Chapter 2 by distinguishing between two views of innovation, generally speaking, which I would eventually recast
as the distinction between invention and innovation.   The
first was chronologically prior, and argued that innovation
was best understood as an undistributed possession of 'special'
persons, thus exclusive.   In accordance with this, I pointed
to the unmistakable emphasis on tangible outcomes which such
a position favours, then contrasted it to a second view which
stressed behaviour and process rather than tangible outcomes,
and availability rather than exclusivity.   I then noted a
gradual shift away from exclusivity evident in the greater
stress put on behaviour and process vis à vis tangible outcomes.   This would later develop into a clear preference for
a group rather than an individual-centred focus, something
which brought a highly significant parallel to my attention.
In this regard I contrasted bourgeois 'negative' individualism
to the sort of 'positive' individualism which Durkheim was convinced must succeed the earlier type.   Here emphasis was on
the theory of society, seen as an historically and culturally
specific form of collective life, which needed to be reformed in
an ameliorative way by the joint efforts of sociologists and
occupational groups committed to 'normalizing' the allegedly
pathological division of labour that had resulted from Western
(capitalist) industrialization.   The key to this normalization
effort was the requirement that individualism be made 'functional' rather than dysfunctional for the emerging form of

collective life, thus that the individual be co-ordinated into group and occupational activity as a 'person' who sees his individuation in the maximal performance of organizational and occupational functions and roles. In addition to this 'sociali-zation' of the individual, I noted the fact that this could be seen as a single dynamic development whose effects in the field of invention and innovation would serve to redefine the individual as a disciplined observer whose behaviour always had a 'social' referent, but one 'inside' as well as external to him. Tarde's notion of imitation/counter-imitation was next addressed, in order to show both how invention and innova-tion were seen to differ from it, and how such a view could still be sympathetic to the sorts of commonsense understand-ings prominent in the work of Barnett and Bourdieu, among others. Whereas Durkheim had associated similarities and likenesses with 'primitive', or at least pre-modern, collectives (e.g. mechanical solidarity; common conscience), Tarde points to these features as the only true basis for the social scien-ces, in clear contrast to Durkheim's exclusivism. The idea that Western 'culture-as-civilization' might generate behavioural categories like disciplined observation in order to underscore its idiosyncratic, 'special' character, even in the face of what appeared to be an emphasis on availability in the form of behaviour and process rather than tangible outcomes, struck me as highly significant. It meant that the alleged 'turn' away from exclusivity and tangible outcomes toward availability and behaviour and process was really no turn at all. The reason why innovation seemed increasingly like organized in-vention could be seen in the way in which individualism itself had been transformed. No longer needed to battle retrograde pre-bourgeois (and pre-capitalistic) remnants, the fate of the inventor whose conception of technology was essentially pre-scientific all too readily parallels the clear 'obsolescence' of negative individualism. Finally, it must be noted that neither of the twin claims of greater availability and an emphasis on behaviour and process rather than tangible outcomes were quite what they seemed. First, availability is rigidly con-fined to those urban middle-class employees of large organiza-tions whose managerial ideology has become so central to advanced industrial societies. Second, what appears to be a de-emphasis on tangible outcomes only highlights the extent to which technique and technology has been sedimented into all the organized structures which collectively comprise advanced industrial societies. (3) I concluded this chapter by addres-sing our 'technical bias', what this really means relative to economic and political interests, as well as science, and the difference between an internal dynamic in the later middle ages making Western development possible, and the present external influences on Third-World countries which are becom-ing increasingly internalized in the form of their own 'good (internal) reasons' for developing and modernizing rather than adapting to change. A scenario was set down in which the likelihood of common cause in the face of differential rates and processes of industrialization by Third-World countries was addressed, and less than optimistic conclusions were reached regarding such a possibility.

III

My concern here was with the relationship between practice, particularly collective (social) practices, and thought and theory addressed to such practices. The central role of disciplined observation was cited as a vital ingredient in the thoroughgoing reformulation of practice in the advanced societies. Complementing this was the refusal to support theoretical efforts favouring reflexivity and dialectic. The indisputable effect of the emergence of disciplined observation vis à vis both practice and theory was what I labelled the 'technicization' of practice. Once practice is fetishized as a category coincident with tradition, custom and convention as these terms are understood in the social sciences, it is inevitable that such activity will be seen to be denuded of reason and rationality. These latter terms will in turn be seen to apply to specific modes of institutional training and certification alone, as if such an understanding could possibly be meaningful in the absence of the actual reference which makes such derivative notions comprehensible to us. A technicized practice is therefore best understood as that 'one-dimensional' form of life which is reflected in the ideal collective as it is produced by the disciplined observer - 'society'. Here what is important is less any discrepancies between ideal and reality as it is configured 'empirically' by the social scientist, and more the way that modes of 'secondary socialization' seem to be narrowing the distance between them, thus the difference between ideal and reality itself. In attempting to address this problem, I argued that thought is only marginally better served by the utopian ideal of critical thinking than by the presentist notion which addresses the societal agenda itself for the disciplined observer, whether specifically a social scientist or one socialized in a vision of proper social relations which honours these disciplines as 'distant models'. It is the tendency to equate the practical and the technical under 'norms of rationality' as they are formulated in advanced industrial societies which leads social scientists to confuse what they believe to be a bona fide description of what passes for practice in the form of custom, convention, and tradition (one which they claim to have produced *sine ira et studio*) with what is nothing less than legislation anticipating developments endemic to the auspices of their disciplines. Thus, it is the way that the social sciences function as both a light infantry and an advance guard producing normative 'ideal type' concep-

tions of proper collective (social) behaviour in the guise of
'descriptions' requiring only 'frameworks' and 'heuristic
devices' which points to the mission of disciplined observation
in its twin but interdependent tasks vis à vis practice (reformulation) and theoretical reflexivity (annihilation). (4) Technicization, in line with the technical bias reflected in the idea
of instrumentalism as the prototype for reason and rationality
in society, functions as the effective 'other side' of disciplined
observation in this regard. I cited Bourdieu in particular as
someone who underscores the seriousness of this particular
development once it is transferred into the analysis of 'other-
cultures' on the assumption that the disciplined observer is
able to secure his 'own-culture'. It is here that I was able
to address the dilemma of what I called an 'unhinged observation function' perhaps most directly. A notable feature of
this unhinged function and the technicized conception of practice and the practical which is its necessary other side was
the tendency to 'empiricize' dichotomies and dualisms so that
they lose their original status as topics and moments of the
whole and become code words for describing the world as an
observable yet abstract totality made up of 'concrete' parts-
as-facts-as-events in the form of empirical particulars. It is
precisely this tendency toward empiricization on the part of
the disciplined observer's unhinged observation function which
led me to argue that the social sciences' problem is that they
are not objective enough. Reality as a concrete totality
always requires that what addresses it by reference to the
code word 'practice' see in such reference a moment of the
whole which simultaneously constitutes this whole as an external abstraction relative to the static particulars of empiricism
which aggregate to comprise 'the world'. (5) I concluded by
noting how unreflexive reference to this empirical convention
made it almost impossible for us to see the need for reflexivity
to excavate and make sense of innovation relative to custom,
convention and tradition. The idea of an 'innovative society'
avoids becoming a contradiction in terms only where the original notion of what innovation might be is thoroughly jettisoned,
in favour of one which equates it increasingly with what in
'other' cultures would in fact be called tradition. This is
only underscored by the recent need for advanced industrial
societies to adapt to external developments in the face of their
inability to dictate and determine them.

IV

Having made reference off and on throughout the text to
reason and rationality, in particular my hostility to the instrumentalist conception which functions as a norm in advanced
industrial societies, I wanted to discuss it further in light of
the tension between practice, theory and disciplined observa-

tion.   To present my concerns in the form of a 'rationality
question' was seen as a way of addressing the concept-become-
norm of reason as rationality.   Here I could generate not only
an ideal but also a method of evaluating member's practices in
advanced industrial societies.   The fact that innovation had
been focussed upon by social theorists anxious to establish
either its rational or non-rational properties seemed to constitute an opening wedge in any attempt to discover the real
relation being asserted between innovation and rationality.
The question: 'Is innovation rational?' began with certain
presumptions about the nature of the world given in the empirical convention, disciplined observation (unhinged observation function) and an essentially one-dimensional (technicized)
conception of practice which would be absent from the brief
query which concluded the chapter, namely: 'Is rationality
innovative?'   In the first case, I needed to clear the ground
by disentangling reason from rationality, showing how the
latter constitutes an attempt to reformulate practice in certain
settings so that reason is seen to be an empirical property of
the action of individuals and the behaviour of collectives of
various types.   Weber's typology, while helpful in certain
respects, became problematic to the extent that his so-called
'methodological device' was revealed to have all-too-obvious
substantive consequences in the form of a preference for negative over positive (occupational) individualism.   A.J. Greimas's scheme was cited as an interesting way of unearthing
what Jameson called the 'narrative structure' present in
Weber's studies by reference to the idea of a 'semantic rectangle'.   Here what is important is the difference between the
contrary of a particular term and its simple negative, for example between value-rational or principled action and affectivity respectively in their relation to Weber's sociologically 'concrete' concept of goal-rational action.   In contrast to the
boundaries which Weber the sociologist allows to stand as limits
in his conceptual scheme, there is the theorist always on the
verge of breaking through but rarely able to overcome the
sense of duty which keeps him at his post 'in spite of all'.
In the face of the reality of rationalization and de-enchantment,
all Weber can do is recommend either 'facing the music' or
falling back into tradition, religion, dilettantism, etc.   It is
the way that innovation appears so absurd for Weber in the
light of his pessimism that compels him to see an option to
rationalization and routinization only in charisma and the political field.   The fact that this is never developed in preference to an ethics of responsibility cannot detract from the fact
that it was, after all, 'available' as a valid interpretation of
his work.

In the two sections in which I sought to open out the question: Is innovation rational? I was as concerned with what the
asking of such a question must presume as in any possible,

sanctionable answer I might generate to it.   Thus, the issue
for me really was one of how I could possibly feel more secure
with the notion of reason/rationality than with innovation.   I
would have to presume reason and rationality to be 'in hand'
in order to answer the question at all.   Otherwise, I would
be forced back on the question itself - what form of life its
asking manifested.   In the two sections devoted to this question it became necessary first to point out our 'stake' in the
idea of uniqueness and 'difference' as a basis for the security
necessary in order to even ask the question.   Here rationality was seen to be an empirical property built into the internal dynamic of Western development understood as 'progress'.
In contrast to both the ancient teaching, and the emphasis in
some modern thinkers on commonality (Vico), reason was seen
to be increasingly manifested within Western development.
This supported the notion that one could assert the superiority
of the West over 'cultures' either earlier in time or contempor-
aneous with it.   In a way what such an historical argument
did was generalize the sort of claims which cannot help but
emerge from the conviction that reason is best comprehended
by reference to an instrumental and goal-rational 'concrete'
type (Weber).   The ideal model of progress - technical rationality in the utilization of means - serves to reconcile goal
rationality as the paragon type of individual action with the
idea of a unilinear historical process (Enlightenment), or even
a dialectical one (Hegel; Marx).   It is only within these confines that one can make sense of an argument asserting the
alleged non-rationality of innovation (like Schon's), for it
depends on the presence of the very organized structures which
have spearheaded the norm of occupational individualism (Durkheim).   Here the tension so central to Mannheim's analysis is
ignored by assuming that the question: Is innovation rational?
contains its own (obvious) answer, one virtually given in the
asking.   It is the latent idea that reason/rationality lies in
the organized structures themselves which makes reference to
the idea of innovation's alleged non-rationality even possible.
And it is the way such a position ignores the distinction
between the event and its recognition, perhaps by someone
else, which underscores the problematic nature of the question
as an empirical query with an 'available' (but external) answer.
I thereafter addressed three key code words which have been
allowed to function in a residual way (otherness) for Western
thought - nature, tradition, and the primitive - in order to
show how they really indicate our own concern about the
'ground' which lies beneath the idiosyncratic ideas which we
emphasize when discussing our culture-as-civilization.   It is
Goddard who shows us this deep problem in his critical reflections on the idea of the primitive, where the idea is seen to be
a false residue ('other') for the social sciences after all.   As
for 'nature', the dehumanized view of natural science is similarly seen through by Marx when he shows, like Wittgenstein

after him, how problematic the very necessary observation function is once it becomes unhinged from theory, disavows reflection, and seeks to reconstitute practice in its own image (society).

V

I concluded Chapter 4 by posing the question whether 'rationality' itself was intellectually innovative, after showing the way an unhinged observation function fetishizes nature, tradition, and the primitive by viewing them exclusively as empirical properties ('facts of life') of 'other cultures' (or culture per se).   I then tried to focus more specifically on some key institutional and ideological features of advanced industrial societies as cultures in their own right, as well as a civilization which (among other things) observes 'cultures'.   Here I was particularly concerned with institutions and ideologies which disciplined observation, 'free' of both practice and theory, simultaneously fetishizes and makes both the model of its tasks ('rational organization' as the normative ideal for collective life in the person of society) and its pre-eminent object of study.   The two main figures here were (once again) Weber and Wittgenstein.   I first utilized Wittgenstein's critique of Frazer's 'Golden Bough' in order to underscore the extent to which social-scientific modes of knowledge had repudiated theoretical reflection, and how such repudiation revealed their mission (society) and some of its most serious consequences (reconstitution of practice).   I then turned to the example of invention, innovation and diffusion as successive 'problems' which could only be articulated once their 'solution' was seen to be readily at hand.   Here it was the idea that the problem of innovation presupposed solution of the problem of invention, and that of diffusion solution of the problem of innovation, which suggested one way that rationality was seen to be increasingly sedimented (Weber would say petrified) into our civilization as a 'tradition'.   Following my earlier discussion of Schon, I noted his presumption of organized functional rationality (Mannheim) which is at hand to pose new problems resulting from its 'solution' of the problem of invention (Gilfillan).   Here the problem was seen to be no less 'social' than technical, in the sense that what was really at stake was the tension between negative (Weber) and positive (Durkheim) individualism as I had seen it take shape in the contrast between an exclusivist (outcomes) and a 'more available' (behaviour/process) notion of innovation earlier.   I concluded this section by arguing that Mannheim may have been seriously mistaken when he suggested that those in directive and managerial roles are most likely to benefit substantially from increases in functional rationalization.   It is the very impact of the contemporary ideology of innovation/

diffusion in advanced industrial societies, particularly as it
takes shape in organized work settings, which leads me to be
sceptical of Mannheim's observations regarding the superior
substantial rationality of this elite class fragment.

At this point I returned to Max Weber, in particular his
central orienting concept of rationalization, in order to suggest another critique besides the one subsequently mobilized
by Marxian and critical thinkers like Marcuse and Habermas.
This was not, however, a turning away from the preceding
concern, but rather an attempt to set it in a perspective in
which it might be rendered sensible by reference to the tension between rationalization (the way we destroy ourselves by
playing out our hand) and institutionalization (what happens
in 'other cultures' – or rather cultures).   In the case of
rationalization I was particularly interested in the view that
what was admitted by Weber to be a petrified form of rationality could still claim to be an expression of (Western or occi-
dental) reason.   We are permitted a bad end only so long as
it is seen to be our own doing (or undoing), something
rooted in our origins ('rational mode of life') rather than the
result of the same sort of external influence that is so central
to explaining Western domination over the Third World, even
(or especially) when one or a group of countries in the latter
category appear to be 'in the driver's seat' ('oil crisis'; *vide*
Chapter 2).   This 'other side' of technical progress, a simple
inversion of the Enlightenment vision (whose blush has irretrievably faded), leads through the *fulfilment* of its inner
character based in origins (Calvinist religiosity; predestination and doom) to the 'iron cage' as an unwound mainspring,
a 'dead mechanism' whose petrified character reflects the fact
that it does not gain in strength from appropriating all manner
of externality standing against it, but is rather exhausted and
spent as a result of this activity.   Weber is an archetypal
icon of non-critical criticism – the theorist who can only attack
his culture by simultaneously requiring its destruction, while
insisting in the name of its idiosyncratic superiority that this
destruction be/is collectively (and historically) self-ordained.
A less-loaded approach to rationalization based on a more
proximate and empirical conception sought to tie Weber's 'systemic' notion to the issue of the relation between invention and
innovation presented earlier.   Here I was concerned with the
way that large organizations (Weber's 'bureaucracy') functioned
as intermediaries both socializing and receiving those already
socialized, and with the parallel tension between seeking to
rationalize core technologies and the need for new knowledge
from those trained by institutions outside the organization.
The next section addressed the tension between institutionalization and change, in order to show how even an optimistic
turn on the matter of development tended to see change as a
dynamic process unique to the advanced societies and opposed

diametrically to institutionalization, rather than constituting a
form of institutionalization central to the production of particular traditions expressive of a culture.   Weber, somewhat in
contrast, treats rationalization as a middle way between institutionalization (them) and freedom.   It denies us both the
Western ideal of individual action, whether of the principled or
goal-rational variety (without however admitting that this is
its source, e.g. 'rational mode of life'), and the opportunity
to interpret developments by reference either to routinization,
or adaptation forced on us 'from the outside'.   The concluding section sought to tie the chapter together by seeing the
idea of culture as one which might be made more meaningful
by reference to Wittgenstein's notion of 'form of life'.   A
particular interpretation of this most controversial term was
defended and the real relationship between forms of life and
facts of life suggested.

CONCLUDING REMARKS

I

It now remains for me to tie together some final thoughts
either stated explicitly in the text or strongly suggested by
it.   First, there is the way I have made reference to invention and innovation throughout this study.   My early claim to
be at least as interested in 'tradition' as in 'innovation' can
now be better appreciated.   Indeed, what should come out of
such an effort is the realization that comprehension of what
innovation 'really' means is bound up with tradition, in contradistinction to either practice or to disciplined observation
in its disembodied form.   Regardless of how essential the
observation function remains as a quite essential supplement,
even prerequisite, to human social thinking, it is clearly its
increasing autonomy which is responsible for our inability to
see through key code words (rationality, history, progress)
and their more proximate material and processual manifestations
(invention, innovation, diffusion).   I have little choice but to
return to the point I made at the very beginning: that something can exist which we capture to some extent in a name
while at the same time being *incomprehensible, however much
described and defined*.   For me, innovation fitted this bill,
no less than perception, language and memory did for Wittgenstein. (6)   At the same time, this realization emerged as a
deeper understanding increasingly threatened by the determination to suppress such understanding by simply asserting that
innovation, like invention before it and diffusion afterwards,
was a 'problem' with its own solution essentially built-in
('crisis').

Here the way out was to invoke correspondence rules and an

empirical convention, albeit in an inverted form. The result was what Ogden and Richards had noticed as the tendency to assume that any term we use must correspond to a nameable and describable state of affairs occurring in 'the world'. (7) Any opportunity to address what answers are presupposed in the questions we ask is suppressed by such a decision. The result is at once to obscure what is happening to those who accept innovation as an 'obvious' fact of life, and to provide theoretical reflection with what it must have if it is to show how innovation is the key contemporary code-word comprehending a culturally specific form of life as it is expressed in and through rationality, history, and progress. At the same time, the decision to treat the observation function as both disembodied and disciplined (neutral and objective), thus independent of both practice and theory, was allowing the demands of the correspondence requirement under an empirical convention to produce as a central aspect of this form of life the growing public belief that innovation *really is* comprehensible in functional terms by reference to 'displacement of concepts' and the portability of analogues and metaphors. (8)

And now we can perhaps see more clearly how we might usefully (and validly) relate and effectively tie together the early and the later Wittgenstein. This would likely be disagreeable to Wittgenstein, I readily admit. Indeed, the exercise itself, apart from the way it is carried out, would be anathema to him. For me, however, there still remains the problem which emerges from my inability, stated at the outset, to support perfect clarity 'for its own sake'. This in spite of the fact that I have quite clearly repudiated (or am in the process of repudiating) some of the key baseline assumptions that underlie and fuel instrumentalism, incrementalism, and interventionism, elements central to an unhinged observation function and a technicized practice. (9) This is connected with a point raised elsewhere in greater detail than I can do here: the issue of whether one tries to speak what cannot, in the strict sense of 'Tractatus', be 'said', or allows this boundary to function as limit. I would argue that this latter outcome was denied even in the 'Tractatus', as Wittgenstein observed near the end when he stated of his propositions that 'anyone who understands me eventually recognizes them as nonsensical....' (10) When I address this difficulty further on we shall see how significant is its relation to the very 'political' issue of the link between ethical talk and ethical action.

First, however, let me use my earlier attempt to tie together the 'two Wittgensteins' in order to display the sense that such an effort provides for my analysis and argument regarding 'innovation', and the more 'abstract' notions that its proximate expression stands for - rationality, history and progress.

Wittgenstein had written to Ficker regarding possible publication of the 'Tractatus' stating that, 'my work consists of two
parts: the one presented here plus all that I have not written.   And it is precisely this second part that is the important one.' (11)   If this was in fact a conscious strategy,
then of course the point made above is underscored in its significance.   If we treat it as something which appears to its
author on the completion of his work, rather than something
which informed the actual writing, which is equally (if not
more) likely, then we gain an insight into the significance of
'Tractatus' for the mind/body problem as it had been initially
formulated by Schopenhauer.   In either case, I can suggest
a possible tie of the greatest significance betweeen the 'logical
atomist' conception of 'the world' in 'Tractatus' and the concept of *lebensform* which is found in later work after 1933,
and particularly in the 'Philosophical Investigations'.

Wittgenstein's conception of 'the world', while more complex
than the logical atomist claim makes it, probably has more
room in it for this view than for any other.   Thus 'the
world' is a natural realm rather than a 'social' one, where
objects in relations as 'states of affairs' only become 'facts of
life' under certain specific conventions like empiricism (concrete facts and abstract whole), causality (with other types of
explanation a 'deviation' from causality), correspondence rules
(of which the so-called 'picture theory' in 'Tractatus' was a
defence) and a distinct (but not autonomous) observation function. (12)   What provides us with the missing link between
this notion, conditioned though it was, and the later concern
for 'forms of life' is the idea of a disembodied observation
function, one unhinged from reflexivity and directed to the
technicization of practice as a one-dimensional activity of the
disciplined observer whose prototype is to be discovered in
the social sciences and related disciplines.   It is here that
we are at last provided with a way of making sense of *lebensformen* in terms of the early Wittgenstein, particularly as he is
found in 'Tractatus'.

It would seem fairly clear, at least, that an emphasis on
'forms of life' expresses its author's realization (and concern)
that one particular culture-as-civilization has as one of its
central features the commitment to producing through disciplined observation 'facts of life'.   To be sure, Wittgenstein
never thinks in terms of this observation function becoming a
'model' for collective practices, something which will one-
dimensionalize practice as a consequence of its effective 'unhinging'.   But he does notice the assault on perception,
language and memory as it takes shape in the activity of disciplined observation by social and behavioural scientists, who
persuade themselves of the empirical significance of the inside/
outside distinction, then argue that theirs is the one and only

'progressive' approach because it works from the outside in as privileged testimony must. The two intellectual enterprises which Wittgenstein always totally repudiated - dialectical reflexivity and the so-called 'development hypothesis' (*Entwick-lungshypothese*) - are precisely what inform my view of the situation and my concern in these pages about a disembodied observation function and a technicized practice. (13)

Without doubt, aspects of this concern were clearly apparent both in Wittgenstein's Remarks on Frazer's 'Golden Bough' and in his transitional Lecture on Ethics. (14)   Nevertheless, such claims were essentially unsayable, and remained so for the author of the 'Investigations' no less than for the architect of the 'Tractatus'.   Remember how I made reference to what lies beneath the surface in our (Western cultural) efforts to reduce the world to explanations about it, according to Wittgenstein?   What is important here was the way that our special character as a culturally (formal connexion) rather than an historically (development hypothesis) specific form of life *values* explanations in the form of facts of life where only the ongoing reality of life serves to put in proper perspective all the explanations we generate in the absence of an acknowledgment of their hypothetical character.   Here our guide is to be discovered in 'Tractatus', where Wittgenstein shows us that what explanations (in contrast to thought) really tell us about life is that life includes such efforts. (15)

It is his analysis of Frazer which must have been instrumental, carried out as it was in 1931, and later in 1936, in bringing Wittgenstein to the realization that his claims only make sense in and for one particular culturally specific *lebensform* - what Weber called 'modern Western civilization'.   Thus, as he argues, we are unique in the way we act from opinions given the doctrine of progress (increasing rationality through history) and the 'fact' that science alone, in contradistinction to magic, progresses. (16)   Similarly, explanations become part of the fabric of collective life, as Popper later pointed out, to the extent that they are themselves treated as finished 'states of affairs' rather than hypotheses.   In order to go any further than this, it is necessary to try to say what allegedly cannot be said, and therefore to turn to a dialectical reflexivity informed by some sort of development hypothesis which, however, is not committed to the doctrine of progress through historical time, but only to the possibility of such progress (and regress, *vide* Weber and Collingwood). (17)   It is the above constraints which always made it impossible for Wittgenstein to say what allegedly could not be said, but I have felt it necessary to challenge his idea of sense and nonsense, tied as it is to 'the world' as a particular *lebensform* philosophically produced solely by and through 'formal connectedness'.

Yet it is to a significant degree Wittgenstein's own work, particularly the concluding section of 'Tractatus' (6.4-7) and his Remarks on Frazer's 'Golden Bough', which provide me with so much support for treating aspects of the notion of sense and nonsense as part of the above conventions rather than a basis for reflecting on them. Think of what his analysis of magical and religious practices means for the idea of what we (and others) term a 'common human pattern', something only underscored by what would seem to be the best understanding of the concept of *lebensform*. Think of those terms which 'we all know' (ghost; prayer; curse), and the gestures we employ not only in a religious (genuflection) but a secular (handshake) setting as surface phenomena reflecting this deeper commonality. This even as we use the former in particular (Frazer) as a way of producing the idea of the 'primitive' as not only an 'other', but an inferior other, when what it really reveals is our concern, wholly legitimate but often culturally embarrassing, with our origins and the mystery of being and existence as it is 'discovered' in the operation of our three most 'mundane' faculties - perception, language and memory. The point which my emphasis herein on innovation and related terms as a 'type case' makes unambiguously is the collective consequences of being 'what we alone can be' as a culturally specific form of life. We are that culture-as-civilization which acts on opinions which are treated as finished explanations, even those opinions concerned with perception, language and memory as they are allegedly seen from a privileged position 'outside' them. (18)

Surely, we can now see what Adorno and Benjamin meant when they argued that the social sciences were not objective enough, and that any repair would entail a dialectical reflexivity committed to recognition of the development hypothesis in general. Take my critique of Weber's thoroughly unreflexive conception of custom, convention, and tradition, formal categories having the status of 'non-starters' in sociology and related disciplines. Wittgenstein makes the point that what is 'deep' in such observances and gestures cannot be reached through explanations aimed at uncovering origins. Their real meaning lies in what those who observe and honour them feel. To be sure, many such practices become 'ritualized', carried on at the borderline of conscious action, as Weber noted, but I would argue that this may well be a culturally specific dilemma of our culture-as-civilization, committed as it is to the mastery of human and non-human externality, more than anything else. Indeed, there is a clear concern for resisting such 'routinization' in many 'primitive' cultures. The search for origins, apart from what it shows us about the real needs we feel and have in common with 'other cultures', tells us more about our 'own culture' as one determined, indeed driven, to explain (the world, states of affairs, 'facts of life') than it

does about the customs themselves. A radical example in-
voked by Wittgenstein reaches my general and specific concerns in this study better than any other: the idea of
inventing a festival! (19)

The problem with explanations, apart from their clear one-
dimensionality, is the way they lose their status as hypotheses (*contra* Popper) and become a permanent part of a particular form of life. (20) As such their sheer proliferation
under specific social conditions, and the apparent 'success'
that underwrites such proliferation, generates a belief in the
value of disembodiment - an unhinged observation function
whose show of apparent discipline (objectivity; neutrality)
serves to legitimize its effect if not intent. This effect is,
of course, the 'practical/technical' *social* criticism of reflexivity as irrelevant (Bacon) or dangerous (Popper), a clear and
correctly perceived barrier to the reconstitution of practice in
the image of the disciplined observer (society). As I have
argued in considerable detail elsewhere, the social sciences,
even in the presence of the formal requirement of 'tolerance',
fundamentally resist dialectical thinking because it draws
attention to the lack of real openness to be discovered in
Popper's paragon 'open society'. (21) It also reveals the
dire superficiality of our sensory capacity as it is reflected in
the near-total domination of the visual mode as a basis for
analogy and metaphor in thought. Our problem is that we
increasingly believe that we really can invent festivals, and
that every day more and more of the rest of the earth agrees!
Ours is the burden of history, where the 'progress' that its
claim of increasing rationality allegedly guarantees has as one
of its most problematic upshots precisely the 'success' of such
thinking in terms of its acceptance by 'other cultures'. Here
we can see a most significant, but not generally appreciated,
confirmation of an argument like Barnett's in 'Innovation'. (22)

II

Let me now return to the notion of saying and showing, and
the corollary issue of the relationship between ethical talk and
ethical action, and conclude thereafter. I noted in the last
chapter how significant was our basic inability to appreciate
the point Wittgenstein had made at the very beginning of
Remarks on Frazer's 'Golden Bough': that religious and magical practices are not carried out as an instrumental means to
ends outside them. While we might be able to grasp this
when applied to 'own culture' religious practices because
society (and therefore sociology) is predicated on the contrast
(Parsons) between an instrumental (read 'rational') sphere and
an expressive one, we appear certain that 'primitive' magical
rites and practices connected with rain really are attempts to

generate rain as an effect of such activity, either directly or
as a consequence of divine intervention.   Wittgenstein forced
us to consider the more likely possibility that here we have
propitiation for the rain that God(s) will bring, given the fact
that this is the rainy season. (23)   The point here is that
any request which implores God to make it rain would be
based upon a disruption of the routinely given (e.g. the
rainy season that does not come), and might even constitute a
violation of authentic religious practices for those people.
Think of this as a way of talking about a religious version of
'inventing' a festival, where such activity, even if it happened, would be a bridge between practices based on experiences
which no longer occur and the practices which will emerge if
the situation does not return to normal but 'permanently'
changes.

Here I am thinking of the way those instrumental, incremental and interventionist biases so fundamental to our particular
form of life make it extremely difficult to 'see through' the
technicized practice being produced by a disembodied observation function in the advanced societies.   This means that the
real objectivity which only openness to thought can provide us
with on these matters is either lacking altogether or greatly
hemmed in.   In its place we have the normative ideal of
society continually being reproduced in and through the research and teaching of the social sciences and related disciplines.   By 'research' here I understand methodical empiricism and structurally decomposed theories, allegedly in the
form of hypotheses, which are really fixed explanations precisely because their answer is virtually given in the way they
are presented as 'problems' or 'questions'. (24)   Wittgenstein's resistance to such thinking, noted by Engelmann, (25)
is expressed in the distinction between saying and showing so
central to the 'Tractatus' in particular, but also found in many
of his later writings as well.   I have argued elsewhere that
this acknowledgment on his part was to some extent premised
on his sceptical attitude toward versions of the 'knowledge is
power' dictum as it takes shape in the commitment to explanation as both a form of mastery and a prelude to its 'material'
expression through instrumentalism, incrementalism, and interventionism.   Thus, instead of seeing in ethical talk an instrumental prelude to ethical action, Wittgenstein saw the
former as an effective substitute for the latter in the form of
a 'sublimation' (Freud). (26)

The idea of a 'great sublimation' may appear strange to us,
yet the sense we do in fact derive from seeing it standing in
clear opposition to the more 'open' causilinear notion of the
relation between speech and action suggests the distinct possibility that substitution, or rather sublimation, may be sensible to us as an interpretative explanation of our behaviours

(and that of others) precisely because it 'corresponds' to experiences that we have learned to interpret in just this way.
Ignoring for the moment the details of Wittgenstein's 'respect'
for Freud's cleverness, as it appears in the 'Lectures and
Conversations' and elsewhere, it is quite clear that this respect was addressed to Freud's capacity simultaneously to make
sense in a highly interesting way (cleverness), and to reflect
his own membership in a particular form of life by his capacity
for producing a credible and 'powerful' mythology, such as
one could discover at the intellectual centre of any and all
lebensformen. (27) Freud meets the first condition by his
appeal to origins, and also by the way he formulates and
uses the parallel between ontogenesis and phylogenesis. (28)
The upshot of this is that sublimation too becomes eminently
acceptable as an interpretation of 'cultural' events, something
of more than ephemeral importance. Seen in this light, the
idea that ethical action might well be frustrated, even negated
altogether, by ethical talk, rather than spurred on by it,
appears eminently reasonable given the fact that such notions
are in fact 'reflections' of the form of life that makes them
possible, and which they apparently 'display' whether willingly
or in spite of themselves. It is our fear of the accuracy of
such an interpretation, as it stands in opposition to its more
open and unilinear opponent, that compels us to note the
sense of such a claim, based as it is on our own experience.
Ethical talk in general inhibits ethical action by individuals, at
least in 'our culture', because it allows them the luxury of a
substitution which functions as an effective sublimation. This
particular interpretation would, of necessity, have to be resorted to in the final analysis (if not sooner) in order to
render sensible Wittgenstein's notion of a highly restricted
'speech that says', in contradistinction to mere 'gassing'. (29)

When I alluded earlier to the way that my commitment to dialectical reflection required me to endorse some notion of development, albeit as a possibility rather than something certain
(thus essentially given), I meant to underscore the way that
an emphasis on formal connectedness like Wittgenstein's seems
to involve of necessity the idea of something which may, in
future if not now, be understood as an origin of some subsequent phenomenon. Here I am addressing the dependence,
manifest or latent, of dialectical thought or theoretical reflection on some sort of development hypothesis. Thus, the idea
of acquiring a recognition of and sensitivity to the meaning of
our commitment as a form of life to the disembodied observation and registry of congeries of 'facts of life' depends greatly
upon what we conclude regarding the relationship between
social and cultural *change* and the persistence of our particular form of life. If it is precisely our capacity to produce
and reproduce such states of affairs, and offer them as explanations of phenomena and events which we experience, which

204   *Summary and conclusions*

marks out our particular form of life, then the question of the point at which, to quote Wittgenstein, 'my spade is turned' becomes of central importance. (30)   Seen in this light, perhaps the most realistic recommendation would not seriously argue for displacing such a deep-seated cultural enterprise *in toto*, but would rather address itself to getting the very necessary and very human observation function back in harness relative to practice by acknowledging the important role reflection has to play as a primordial human capacity in what remains after all, human affairs.   But such a recommendation, however much it is premised on the very sensible idea that every human being is a 'theorist', regardless of culture, nevertheless constitutes a less explicit acknowledgment of some notion of development and change, however non-linear and however much in opposition to the presumption of automatic 'progress' it is alleged to be.

It is the way that the emphasis on formal connectedness would be employed in advanced industrial societies which draws our attention to the relationship, unavoidable so it would seem, between this idea or notion and social change itself, and helps us understand why men attach a positive value to 'development' over time.   By this I mean that our commitment to the production of facts of life remains central even in our effort to show its limitations as a form of life by invoking such 'deep structures'.   It is the value that human beings put on their activities, including the accumulation (and investment) of knowledge (such as it is), which leads them to build up their hopes and expectations about tomorrow.   Some people, indeed most people, in these societies may by now have effectively internalized the presumption cited by Wittgenstein which acted as my point of departure for this study, namely, that progress is *built-into* the notion of change in 'our culture'.   At the same time, this apparent fact of life is all too rarely understood to be expressive of our form of life as well as one of its empirical properties.   Think of the idea of effort, trial and error and commitment to work and labour activities of all types in these societies.   Does it not seem eminently sensible for these individuals to approach such activity with the idea that things will be improved and made better as a result of it?   The idea that such activities would be viewed as simply 'carrying on' is most unlikely because it would simply generalize the claim of alienation which is today to be found across all too vast a range of organizations, occupations, and tasks. (31)   The problem which I addressed myself to on and off throughout this study is the way the collectivization and organization (rationalization) of more and more activity in these societies seems to require the operation of an unhinged observation function which tries to compensate for the failure of existing agencies of 'secondary socialization' to achieve a bridge between the individual, family and peer

group and more complex and formalized social and institutional
levels. (32)

Reference to the common human pattern throughout this
study was made immensely clearer by Wittgenstein's Remarks
on Frazer's 'Golden Bough', for here we were able to see some
of the more glaring consequences of our particular obsession
with difference, uniqueness, idiosyncrasy. Yet here the tie,
only underscored by our commitment to utilize what we
thought we knew, between the concern for formal connectedness and an implicitly (or explicitly) accepted development
hypothesis, became more and more obvious. Even my concern that reflexivity be acknowledged could only go so far in
repudiating the cultural dynamic that to some extent had made
me possible. For here I was claiming that the social sciences
and related disciplines were more a part of the problem than
an element in its 'solution' (except in terms of 'crises') precisely because their own commitment to an unhinged observation function had generated what at best might be called a
false objectivity. In the absence of reflexivity, the social
sciences' particular combination of theory and method was not
objective enough! My suggestion would thus take the form of
an attempt to use reflexivity to overcome facile notions of
development as progress while allowing us to retain the sort
of optimism on which effort and commitment so much depend.
Far from being repudiated, the observation function could
then be returned to its proper role, thereby increasing the
likelihood that practice could be revived by being de-technici-
zed.

The question coming out of all this would still, however,
have to be the following: Is this itself a basis for the trans-
cendence of the culture-as-civilization which I have addressed
by reference to the notion of 'form of life', or is it rather a
way of preserving our idiosyncrasy over time in light of the
reality of 'developments' in the Third World leading simultaneously to the distrust of the West and to the ever greater
embrace of its values and central institutions? Seen in this
light, even Wittgenstein's incomparable drive for 'perfect
clarity' could only euphemistically be distended from that version of progress which is itself committed to mastery, broadly
conceived and understood. Further, the idea of newness or
novelty as well is strongly challenged by being 'put in its
place' as a consequence of my support for the idea of civilization as culture and culture as form of life. It is not simply
the way that invention and innovation are tied to rationality,
history and progress as their contemporary proximate material
and processual manifestations, but also the significance of my
claim that something can exist yet be incomprehensible beyond
the naming and describing. Is there an answer lying hidden
below the surface of the question: What could such a notion
mean?, and if there is then what does *this* mean?

CHAPTER 7

Reprise

In this brief study, I have addressed 'innovation' as a phenomenon the incomprehensibility of which, beyond the naming and describing, points to its essentially ideological function in a language game which is fundamental to our particular form of life - Western rationalism.

I have tried to show how its address points up family resemblances between it and the key code words of our 'culture-as-civilization' - rationality, history, and progress. It is a younger sibling, along with invention and discovery, in a family which stands at or near the top of what is nothing less than a hierarchy of language games whose ordering and change is absolutely central to understanding the cultural character of 'civilization' as that (alleged) anti-culture which observes and depicts everything it believes to be 'other' to it. Innovation qualifies as a younger sibling in this regard in terms both of its age and its processual and organizational specificity relative to its 'parents'.

It has been argued that changes in the way terms like invention and innovation have been used away from relative exclusivity towards greater 'availability' parallel efforts in the social, behavioural, and administrative/managerial sciences to render individualism itself more available by making it coincident with society's interest in functional role performance rather than inimical to it. The upshot of this is that an organized, corporate and managerial capitalism heavily dependent on science-based technology and substantial and continuing state intervention is provided with further efforts at legitimation at precisely the point in time when technical progress and social welfare often seem less than fully capable of delivering the material basis for such legitimation on their own.

I also focussed on the services delivered by the social sciences to this end by pointing to their commitment to the ideal of a disembodied observation function - disciplined observation - and the way this commitment leads to and reinforces what is essentially a one-dimensional and technicized conception of practice. Their effort to reconstitute practice in their own image by reference to a largely unacknowledged technical bias is all too often complemented by a parallel attempt to extirpate theoretical reflexivity by arguing either for its sterility (Bacon) or danger (Popper). I then simultaneously argued for and endeavoured to display the need for reflection as I understand it as an antidote to the objectives and promises of these disciplines but in the interests of practice.

Attention thereafter to the archetypal 'problem of rationality' suggested the significance of presuming the describability of whatever is named on the assumption that whatever can be named must 'exist'. Family connections between innovation and rationality were explored in order to draw attention to the consensual and group-bonding role of questions like: 'Is innovation rational?' Here the presumption that rationality was well in hand as a basis for posing the question was shown to be the basis of a far more substantial problematic. I then treated nature, tradition and the primitive as the 'other side' of empiricized, thus one-dimensionalized, dichotomies whose retopicalization suggests how thoroughly ignorant of the 'familiar' in ourselves we are and how confusing life is made by projecting these categories on to cultural 'others' rather than acknowledging that it is their origin in ourselves which is supremely important.

The idea of our civilization as a culture doggedly determined to deny such a characterization was then shown to be central rather than peripheral to our form of life. I addressed this topic by pointing to the tension in Max Weber first between reason and rationalization and thereafter between institutionalization and change. Weber is clearly an intellectual fulcrum in this regard, as is evident from the way he sponsors a non-critical criticism of the social sciences as a creature of society while simultaneously attacking reflexivity (with Durkheim) as 'dilettantism' or (on his own) as cowardice.

Weber also revealed his colours by invoking a pessimism which refuses to accept 'change' in its various empirical and normative guises (rationality, history, progress, invention, innovation, etc.) as a form of institutionalization once it is seen to be produceable and manageable because that would be tantamount to admitting that modern Western civilization (or discrete periods therein) is a culture after all. He completes this posture as a centrepiece in his thinking by insisting that we are fated to produce our own bad end through the working out of an inner dynamic rather than as a result of external influences. The historical basis of this dynamic is the so-called 'rational mode of life' inaugurated by Protestantism and reflected subsequently in capitalism and science, and it is this 'inner logic', socialized and institutionalized, which must be seen to run its course through to the total rationalization and de-enchantment of the 'iron cage'.

Finally, Wittgenstein's critical notes on Frazer's 'The Golden

Bough' was cited as a case in point showing our bias toward instrumental (ends/means) rationality and the consequences of this bias for our understanding of the religious and magical practices and traditions of 'primitive' peoples. I concluded by addressing the issue of whether even reflexivity, in contrast to disembodied observation, provides a basis for transcending certain cultural and institutional trends or only completing them. Innovation, I conclude, is the solution to a problem which is false because it fails to address its auspices, in particular the bourgeois conception of crisis so well articulated by Mannheim. This brings us full circle and returns us to our original dilemma – the need to formulate more meaningful questions and problems less hostaged to the very project whose 'values' are under consideration.

At the same time that I acknowledge, with Wittgenstein, that progress is indeed our cultural form of life rather than simply an empirical fact of life, I thus have no choice but to dispute his view of any and all development hypotheses as ultimately nonsensical precisely because of the way sense is defined in and by a cultural form of life committed to rationality, history and progress, and thus to invention and innovation as well. It is therefore the realization that we possess disciplines, occupations and institutions committed to appropriating 'facts of life' which is central to understanding our uniqueness as a culturally specific form of life – advanced industrial society.

NOTES

CHAPTER 1 RECONNAISSANCE

1   Cited in M.O'C. Drury, 'The Danger of Words' (London: Routledge & Kegan Paul, 1973), pp. ix-x.
2   'Tractatus Logico-Philosophicus', 5.632.
3   Ibid., 1.000.
4   This is the impression one gets from Max Weber.   See particularly, Weber, Science as a Vocation, in 'From Max Weber', edited by Hans Gerth and C. Wright Mills (NY: Oxford University Press, 1946), pp. 137-40.   In the 'Tractatus', however, Wittgenstein counters such a claim by stating that what is mystical is that the world exists at all! (6.44).
5   Friedrich Nietzsche, 'Zarathustra', Part II; 'Beyond Good and Evil', Section 211.
6   'Tractatus Logico-Philosophicus', 6.54.   Also see Wittgenstein, Lecture on Ethics, 'Philosophical Review', vol. 74 (January 1965), pp. 3-12, 12-26.
7   Ibid., 5.633; 5.641.   Also see generally Arthur Schopenhauer, 'The World as Will and Representation', 2 vols (NY: Macmillan, 1968), originally written in 1843.
8   'Tractatus Logico-Philosophicus', 3.02; 4.   Also note 'the impossibility of illogical thought' at 5.4731.
9   See Alfred Kroeber, 'Configurations of Culture Growth' (Berkeley: University of California Press, 1944), but particularly H. Barnett, 'Innovation: the Basis of Cultural Change' (NY: McGraw Hill, 1953), p. 9, where this definition of innovation is given.
10 This is discussed in my Knowledge and Totality (unpublished manuscript), especially chapter 5.
11 'Development' has to be defined narrowly in terms of technique and technology for this claim of superiority to hold.   Max Weber, 'Methodology of the Social Sciences' (Chicago: Free Press, 1949), pp. 27-36 at p. 34.   This notion of 'availability' is central to Weber's conception of de-enchantment, not because we already know all that interests us, but rather because we can 'find out' without having to reflect or remember. See Weber, 'From Max Weber', pp. 138-40, particularly the reference to the difference between riding on a streetcar and knowing how it 'works'.   More generally, see J.B. Bury, 'The Idea of Progress' (NY: Macmillan, 1932); Carl L. Becker, 'The Heavenly City of the Eighteenth Century Philosophers' (New Haven: Yale University Press, 1932); John Baillie, 'The Belief in Progress' (London: Oxford University Press, 1951); Ronald V. Sampson, 'Progress in the Age of Reason' (London: Heinemann, 1956); Raymond Aron, 'Progress and Disillusion' (NY: Praeger, 1968); Leslie Sklair, 'The Sociology of Progress' (London: Paladin, 1971); W. Warren Wagar, 'Good Tidings' (Bloomington: Indiana, 1972); Robert Nisbet, 'History of the Idea of Progress' (NY: Basic Books, 1980); and Krishan Kumar, 'Prophecy and Progress' (Harmondsworth: Penguin, 1978).
12 In this regard see Karl Mannheim, 'Ideology and Utopia' (NY: Harcourt, Brace, 1936), pp. 5-53, 105-8.
13 John Gardner, 'Self-Renewal: The Individual in the Innovative Society'

(NY: Harpers, 1963), pp. 27-42.   Compare the following remark by Wittgenstein: 'The sickness of a time is cured by an alteration in the mode of life of human beings, and it was possible for the sickness of philosophical problems to get cured only through a changed mode of thought and of life, not through a medicine invented by an individual.' Wittgenstein's effort to address causal reasoning as a Western cultural artifact is discussed in Chapter 5 and in H.T. Wilson, Knowledge and Totality, chapters 1 and 2.   Wittgenstein is saying that ultimately problems in collective life can never be 'solved' at all, but rather just go away and are replaced by others.

14   See generally Hannah Arendt, 'The Human Condition' (Chicago: University of Chicago Press, 1958); and H.T. Wilson, 'The American Ideology' (London: Routledge & Kegan Paul, 1977), chapters 1, 2 and 10. On the latent metaphors of scarcity and surplus, and the sustaining rhetoric, see Peter Wiles, The Necessity and Impossibility of Political Economy, 'History and Theory', vol. 11 (1972), pp. 3-14; and H.T. Wilson, Capitalism, Science and the Possibility of Political Economy (unpublished paper).

15   See Peter Zinkernagel, 'Conditions for Description' (London: Routledge & Kegan Paul, 1962).

16   Ludwig Wittgenstein, 'Tractatus Logico-Philosophicus', new translation by D.F. Pears and B.F. McGuinness, incorporating Bertrand Russell's 1921 introduction to the first English edition (London: Routledge & Kegan Paul, 1961), 2.02331; 3.144; 3.24; 3.317; 4.023; 4.0641; 4.26; 4.5; 6.341.

17   Ludwig Wittgenstein, 'Philosophical Investigations' (NY: Macmillan, 1953), no. 78.

18   Compare to Wittgenstein, 'Tractatus', 5.632.

19   This is essentially the argument I make against Popper's analysis in 'The Poverty of Historicism' (London: Routledge & Kegan Paul, 1957) in 'The American Ideology', chapters 1, 2 and 5.

20   Karl Popper, Epistemology Without a Knowing Subject, and On the Theory of the Objective Mind, in Popper, 'Objective Knowledge' (London: Oxford University Press, 1972);   and Popper, The Worlds 1, 2 and 3, in Popper and J.C. Eccles, 'The Self and its Brain' (1975).

21   Popper, 'Objective Knowledge', pp. 115-19;   156-61.

22   Ibid., pp. 118-19;   Popper and Eccles, op. cit., pp. 36-50.

23   Popper, 'Objective Knowledge', pp. 119-25;   Popper, 'Logic of Scientific Discovery' (London: Routledge & Kegan Paul, 1959);   and Popper, 'Conjectures and Refutations' (London: Routledge & Kegan Paul, 1963).

24   George Spencer Brown, in 'Laws of Form' (London: George Allen & Unwin, 1969), p. 126, says the following thing about 'ex-planation':
   To ex-plain, literally to lay out in a plane where particulars can be readily seen.   Thus to place or plan in flat land, sacrificing other dimensions for the sake of appearance.   Thus to expand or put out at the cost of ignoring the reality or richness of what is so put out. Thus to take a view away from its prime reality or royalty, or to give knowledge and lose the kingdom.

25   See generally Murray Edelman, 'The Symbolic Uses of Politics' (Urbana, Illinois: University of Illinois Press, 1964), particularly his discussion of Sapir, Fensterheim and Himmelstrand.

26   Robert Merton, Manifest and Latent Functions, in Merton, 'Social Theory and Social Structure' (NY: Macmillan, 1957), pp. 19-84.

27   The phenomena of objectivation and reification have been carefully (and persuasively) examined by Peter Berger and Stanley Pullberg, Reification and the Sociological Critique of Consciousness, 'History and Theory', vol. 4 (1965), pp. 196-211.

28   See G.H. Von Wright, 'Explanation and Understanding' (Ithaca, NY: Cornell University Press, 1972), chapter 2;   and Von Wright, 'Causality and Determinism' (NY: Columbia University Press, 1974), particularly those pages where he distinguishes action or agency from causality, and causal inference from causal explanation.

29 'Innovation' would seem to belong to a special category of word precisely because it contains all these variegated significations, meanings, possibilities, and values.
30 See my Reading Max Weber: the Limits of Sociology, 'Sociology', vol. 10, no. 2 (May 1976), pp. 297-315.
31 The work of Herbert Blumer within sociological theory is particularly valuable in this regard. See Blumer, 'Symbolic Interactionism' (Englewood Cliffs, NJ: Prentice Hall, 1969), especially pp. 140-82 on the 'concept' in the social sciences. Blumer's work is discussed in some of its aspects further on.
32 Robert Bierstedt, Nominal and Real Definitions in Sociological Theory, in 'Symposium in Sociological Theory', edited by Llewelyn Gross (NY: Macmillan, 1959), pp. 121-44. Also see generally, C.K. Ogden and I.A. Richards, 'The Meaning of Meaning' (London, 1924), on 'referrents'.
33 Bierstedt, op. cit., pp. 124-5.
34 As I suggest further on, even Blumer's critique of nominal definitions is conditional: as vehicles they are necessary, but they become a real problem when they are allowed to stand as a description.
35 Barnett, op. cit., p. 9.
36 See Felix Kaufmann, 'The Methodology of the Social Sciences' (NY: Oxford University Press, 1944) on 'protocols'. On causality see sources cited in note 28, this chapter. Also Mario Bunge, 'Causality and Modern Science', 3rd revised edition (NY: Dover Publications, 1979); J.L. Mackie, 'The Cement of the Universe: A Study of Causation' (Oxford: Clarendon Press, 1974); R. Harré and E.H. Madden, 'Causal Powers' (Oxford: Basil Blackwell, 1975); and H.T. Wilson, Knowledge and Totality.
37 Bierstedt, op. cit., pp. 126-7.
38 Ibid., pp. 127-8.
39 Wittgenstein, 'Tractatus', 5-5.132; 5.4731.
40 Bierstedt, op. cit., pp. 129-30.
41 To be sure, a description of innovation may be, and often is, attempted in the literature. But such an effort is hardly to be equated with successful capture. This is not to say that descriptions are not possible, but rather to point to precisely what a description is *when it is achieved*!
42 Wittgenstein, 'Tractatus', 6.342. A remark by Jacques Ellul is also pertinent to this point. 'It is exactly like a man who claims he can explain how a painter creates his work. The man takes a puzzle representing a canvas by that painter and starts to piece the puzzle together. He will wind up with the picture all right, but he will have shown only how a puzzle works and not how an artist paints.' This distinction is directly relevant to the contrast between the phenomenon on the one hand and its description or explanation on the other. See Ellul, 'The Technological System' (NY: Continuum, 1980), p. 27.
43 Blumer, op. cit. On concatenation, see particularly The Methodological Position of Symbolic Interaction, op. cit., pp. 1-60.
44 H.T. Wilson, Science, Critique and Criticism: The 'Open Society' Revisited, in 'On Critical Theory', edited by John O'Neill (NY: Seabury Press, 1976), pp. 205-30.
45 This point is put at centre stage by Stanley Rosen in 'Nihilism' (New Haven: Yale University Press, 1969). Also see Sanley Raffel, 'Matters of Fact' (London: Routledge & Kegan Paul, 1979). This charge of equating the ideal speech situation with silence has been brought against Jürgen Habermas. See particularly Habermas, Towards a Theory of Communicative Competence, in 'Recent Sociology', no. 2, edited by H.P. Dreitzel (NY: Macmillan, 1970), pp. 114-48; and 'Communication and the Evolution of Society' (Boston: Beacon Press, 1979).
46 On Bacon, see my 'The American Ideology', pp. 58-60, 70-4. Popper may dispute Bacon fundamentally on 'induction', but he clearly agrees with him on the uselessness of certain forms of contemplation, only

radicalizing this concern in his strictures on 'utopian' patterns of thought and thinking like holism and historicism.

47 Crediting Humboldt, Marcuse makes this same point in 'One Dimensional Man' (Boston: Beacon Press, 1964), pp. 209-14.

48 Wilson, 'The American Ideology', pp. 171-99.   Also see Alan F. Blum, Criticalness and Traditional Prejudice, 'Canadian Journal of Sociology', vol. 2, no. 1 (1977), pp. 97-124.

49 For a critique of legal-rational speech, Alan F. Blum, 'Theorizing' (London: Heinemann, 1974).   For an example of this mode of thinking at a very high level, sociologically speaking, Paul Diesing, 'Reason in Society' (Urbana, Illinois: University of Illinois Press, 1962).

50 See Arendt, The Public and Private Realm, in 'The Human Condition', particularly pp. 39-46.   On Weber's parallel analysis of bureaucracy and sociology, Wilson, 'The American Ideology', pp. 145-70;   and Blum, 'Theorizing', pp. 228-41.

51 Marcuse, 'One Dimensional Man', p. 135.

52 Karel Kosik, 'Dialectics of the Concrete' (Dordrecht: D. Reidel, 1976).

53 Wilson, 'The American Ideology', chapters 1, 2, 5 and 10 on the squeeze put on *both* theory and practice by disciplined observation and methodical empiricism (the social sciences).   See particularly pp. 240-8.   Also Wilson, The Meaning and Significance of 'Empirical Method' for the Critical Theory of Society, 'Canadian Journal of Political and Social Theory', vol. 3, no. 3 (Fall 1979), pp. 57-68.

54 Theodor Adorno, 'Negative Dialectics' (NY: Seabury Press, 1973), p. 5. Also see pp. 192-7.

55 See Wittgenstein, 'Tractatus', 5.632;   David Keyt, Wittgenstein's Notion of an Object, 'Philosophical Quarterly', vol. 13 (January 1963), pp. 13-25.

56 Max Weber, 'Theory of Social and Economic Organization' (Chicago: Free Press, 1947), pp. 91-2;   Weber, 'Methodology of the Social Sciences' (Chicago: Free Press, 1949), pp. 90-2.   Also my Reading Max Weber: the Limits of Sociology, op. cit.

57 Weber, 'Theory of Social and Economic Organization', p. 186.   See Blum, Criticalness and Traditional Prejudice, op. cit.

58 Karl Loewith, Weber's Interpretation of the Bourgeois - Capitalistic World in terms of the Guiding Principle of Rationalization, in 'Max Weber', edited by Dennis Wrong (Englewood Cliffs, NJ: Prentice Hall, 1970), pp. 101-22.

59 Weber, 'Theory of Social and Economic Organization', pp. 93-104, 106-9.

60 Weber, Science as a Vocation, in Weber, 'From Max Weber', edited by Hans Gerth and C. Wright Mills (NY: Oxford University Press), p. 139.

61 Blum, 'Theorizing', pp. 227-8.

62 Weber, Science as a Vocation, op. cit., p. 138.

63 Eddy Zemach, Wittgenstein's Philosophy of the Mystical, 'Review of Metaphysics', vol. 18 (1964-5), pp. 38-57;   B.F. McGuinness, The Mysticism of the Tractatus, 'Philosophical Review', vol. 75 (July 1966), pp. 305-28;   Stanley Rosen, op. cit.

64 Blumer, op. cit., p. 175.   Also see Stephen Jay Gould, 'The Mismeasure of Man' (NY: Norton, 1981).   Compare Blumer's reference to 'nature' in the foregoing to that of Harré and Harré and Madden, op. cit.   Also see the examples provided in M.O'C. Drury, op. cit., pp. 57-8.   Hannah Arendt makes a similar point about 'the modern astrophysical view', and 'its challenge to the adequacy of the senses to reveal reality', which, has 'left us a universe of whose qualities we know no more than the way they affect our measuring instruments.' According to Eddington these qualities bear essentially the same relation to the instruments which measure them 'as a telephone number ... to a subscriber'.   See Arthur Eddington, 'The Philosophy of Physical Science' (Cambridge: Cambridge University Press, 1939);   and Arendt, 'The Human Condition' (Chicago: University of Chicago Press, 1958), p. 261.   For a reconstruction of 'nature' as the familiar, see Chapter 4, section titled 'Nature, tradition, and the primitive'.

65 Harold Fallding, Only One Sociology, 'British Journal of Sociology', vol. 23, no. 1 (March 1972), pp. 93-101.
66 But see Albert W. Levi, Wittgenstein as Dialectician, 'Journal of Philosophy', vol. 61 (13 February 1964), pp. 127-39. Thus Bierstedt's view of real definitions as descriptions of an empirical world.
67 This is Marx's critique of Kant, and idealism generally. Mannheim puts his argument most comprehensively in 'Ideology and Utopia'. For a critique, Theodor Adorno, The Sociology of Knowledge and its Consciousness, in 'Prisms' (London: Neville Spearman, 1967), pp. 37-49. Also see Martin Jay, The Frankfurt Critique of Mannheim, 'Telos', no. 20 (Summer 1974), pp. 72-89.
68 See generally Gabriel Tarde, 'Laws of Imitation' (NY: Henry Holt, 1903); Mary Hesse, 'Models and Analogies in Science' (Indianapolis: University of Notre Dame Press, 1966); Donald Schon, 'The Displacement of Concepts' (London: Tavistock, 1963); Schon, 'Technology and Change' (NY: Delta, 1967); Arthur Koestler, 'The Act of Creation' (London: Hutchinson, 1969). Also see Florian Znaniecki, 'The Social Role of the Man of Knowledge' (NY: Columbia University Press, 1940).
69 Karl Marx and Friedrich Engels, 'The German Ideology', excerpts in 'Marx and Engels: Basic Writings on Politics and Philosophy', edited by Lewis Feuer (Garden City, NY: Doubleday Anchor, 1959), pp. 246-61.
70 See particularly Jane Jacobs, 'The Economy of Cities' (NY: Random House, 1969), pp. 49-121, as well as my 'The American Ideology', pp. 137-44. On innovation, Wilson, Innovation: the Practical Uses of Theory, in 'Social Change, Innovation and Politics in East Asia', edited by Y.S. Yim, H.T. Wilson, and R.W. Wilson (Hong Kong: Asian Research Service, 1980), pp. 9-29; and Wilson, Science, Technology and Innovation: the Role of Commonsense Capacities, 'Methodology and Science', vol. 15, no. 3 (1982), pp. 167-200.

CHAPTER 2 AVAILABILITY/BIAS

1 See generally Jacques Ellul, 'The Technological Society' (NY: Alfred Knopf, 1964); Ellul, 'The Technological System' (NY: Continuum, 1980); and my critique in The Sociology of Apocalypse, 'Human Context', vol. 7, no. 3 (Autumn 1975), pp. 474-94. On specific historical and institutional developments, S.C. Gilfillan, 'The Sociology of Invention' (Cambridge, Mass.: MIT Press, 1935), and Nathan Rosenberg, 'Perspectives on Technology' (Cambridge: Cambridge University Press, 1976).
2 Max Weber's pessimism is fuelled by the very ambiguity of his position on these matters. Critical of the process of rationalization and de-enchantment, albeit in a non-critical (e.g. non-dialectical) way, Weber is yet determined to 'stay at his post' and 'do his damned duty in spite of all'. People unable to exercise such discipline should return to the churches, which will embrace them with open arms. This attitude is expressed initially in 'The Protestant Ethic and the Spirit of Capitalism' (NY: Scribners, 1952), where Weber develops his thesis on 'innerworldly asceticism', as a response to the doctrine of predestination and human depravity in Calvinism and Pietism in particular. His subsequent analysis of the secular institutions which serve to define modern Western civilization - science, science-based technology, capitalism, the rule of law, bureaucracy and the social sciences - can be found in 'From Max Weber' (NY: Oxford University Press, 1946); 'Theory of Social and Economic Organization' (Chicago: Free Press, 1947); 'Law in Economy and Society' (Cambridge, Mass.: Harvard University Press, 1954); and 'Methodology of the Social Sciences' (Chicago: Free Press, 1949). For commentary, Karl Loewith, Weber's Interpretation of the Bourgeois - Capitalistic World in terms of the Guiding Principle of Rationalization, in 'Max Weber', edited by Dennis Wrong (Englewood Cliffs, NJ: Prentice Hall, 1970), pp. 101-22; Gabriel Kolko, A Critique of Max Weber's

Philosophy of History, 'Ethics', vol. 70, no. 1 (October 1959), pp. 21-36;   Frederic Jameson, The Vanishing Mediator: Narrative Structure in Max Weber, 'New German Critique', vol. 1 (1973), pp. 52-89;   H.T. Wilson, Max Weber's Pessimism, 'International Journal of Contemporary Sociology', vol. 8 (April 1971), pp. 183-8;   and Wilson, Reading Max Weber: the Limits of Sociology, 'Sociology', vol. 10, no. 2 (May 1976), pp. 297-315.   The tension between development and institutionalization in Weber is given detailed discussion in Chapter 5.

3   For example, John Gardner, 'Self-Renewal: the Individual in the Inno-vative Society' (NY: Harpers, 1963).

4   This tension is evident in Donald Schon's work.   See 'The Displace-ment of Concepts' (London: Tavistock, 1963), but compare his 'Tech-nology and Change' (NY: Delta Books, 1967), to 'Beyond the Stable State' (NY: W.W. Norton, 1973).   Also see Chapters 4 and 5.

5   See particularly David Noble, 'America by Design: Science, Technology and the Rise of Corporate Capitalism' (NY: Oxford University Press, 1977).

6   On the decline of the solitary individual and the rise of the group or team see William H. Whyte, 'The Organization Man' (Garden City, NY: Doubleday, 1956), chapters 1-5;   and J.K. Galbraith, 'The New Indus-trial State' (Boston: Houghton Mifflin, 1967), chapters 1-6.

7   On meritocracy, H.T. Wilson, 'The American Ideology', chapter 9; Wilson, Elites, Meritocracy and Technocracy: Some Implications for Representation and Political Leadership, in 'Political Leadership in Canada', edited by Hector Massey (forthcoming).

8   H. Barnett, 'Innovation: the Basis of Cultural Change' (NY: McGraw Hill, 1953).   An excellent example of just this sort of adaptation in the contemporary context is the response by organization theorists to the way economists have approached innovations as *formally* incompat-ible with existing theories of the firm.   Disputing both the convention-al wisdom and the 'innovation-in-the-face-of-adversity' hypothesis, Cyert and March endorse a focus on 'organizational slack'.   Here the authors simply assert that 'significant technological improvements' reveal the presence of slack rather than scarcity, but that innovations occur whether they are 'successful or unsuccessful'.   The distinction between innovations as responses to specific problems and 'slack inno-vation' cannot dispute the fact that *both* kinds of innovation are the result of 'organizational slack', according to the authors.   Further on in this and subsequent chapters I discuss both types as instances of a conservative and organizational mode of thinking which sees the social division of labour as the guarantor of novelty rather than an obstacle to it.   See Richard Cyert and James March, 'A Behavioural Theory of the Firm' (Englewood Cliffs, NJ: Prentice Hall, 1964), especially pp. 278-9.   Compare to Jane Jacobs, 'The Economy of Cities' (NY: Random House, 1969), particularly her discussion of the relation between inno-vative ideas and the development of 'new work' at pp. 49-121.   Also see Edwin Mansfield, Technical Change and the Rate of Imitation, 'Econ-ometrica', vol. 29 (1961), pp. 741-6.   For a useful conceptual scheme distinguishing innovations as 'reforms' from innovations as 'revolutions', see L.A. Boland, An Institutional Theory of Economic Technology and Change, 'Philosophy of the Social Sciences', vol. 1, no. 3 (1971), pp. 253-8.

9   H.T. Wilson, Innovation: the Practical Uses of Theory, in 'Social Change, Innovation, and Politics in East Asia', edited by Y.C. Yim, H.T. Wilson, and R.W. Wilson (Hong Kong: Asian Research Service, 1980), pp. 9-29.   This point is particularly pertinent to the remarks made in the preceding note.

10 On the mediation of capital between science and technology, H.T. Wilson, Science, Technology and Innovation: the Role of Commonsense Capacities, 'Methodology and Science', vol. 15, no. 3 (1982), pp. 167-200.   On managers as 'private bureaucrats', Charles Lindblom, 'Politics and Markets' (NY: Basic Books, 1977).   On technocracy as post-

bureaucratic administration, H.T. Wilson, Technocracy and Late Capitalist Society: Reflections on the Problem of Rationality and Social Organization, in 'The State, Class and the Recession', edited by Stewart Clegg et al. (London: Croom Helm, 1983), pp. 152-238. On the role of the social, behavioural and administrative sciences, H.T. Wilson, Rationality and Decision in Administrative Science, 'Canadian Journal of Political Science', vol. 6, no. 3 (June 1973), pp. 271-94; and Wilson, 'The American Ideology', chapters 2, 5 and 10.

11 That Marx was *not* supportive of a unilinear and deterministic explanation is clear from a close reading of Karl Marx and Friedrich Engels, 'The German Ideology' (London: Lawrence & Wishart, 1965). Such a view would be far more appropriate in the case of Max Weber. See particularly Kolko, A Critique of Max Weber's Philosophy of History, op. cit.

12 See Peter Wiles, The Necessity and Impossibility of Political Economy, 'History and Theory', vol. 11 (1972), pp. 3-14; and a critical response in H.T. Wilson, Capitalism, Science and the Possibility of Political Economy (unpublished paper). A good debate on the issue of negative vs positive freedom took place between David Spitz and Michael Walzer in 'Dissent' during the years 1965 and 1966.

13 See particularly Emile Durkheim, 'The Division of Labour in Society', translated by George Simpson (NY: Macmillan, 1952), originally published in 1893.

14 Ibid., pp. 200-12.

15 Ibid., p. 229.

16 I make this claim in Innovation: the Practical Uses of Theory, op. cit. But see especially Jane Jacobs, 'The Economy of Cities' (NY: Random House, 1969), pp. 49-144. This point is not an argument against the 'cross-cultural' view of innovation as ordinary and commonplace. See Imitation/counter-imitation and A cross-cultural approach further on in this chapter.

17 Durkheim, op. cit., pp. 407, 403. Very much to the point of this idea of a more 'available' norm of individualism and innovation is Ivan Illich's 'Gender' (NY: Pantheon, 1982). This excellent study reached me too late to be incorporated into the text. It provides eloquent evidence of the impact that capitalism, with its allied notions of surplus and scarcity, has had on women in particular through the *de-gendering* of collective life. In the place of gender, one finds sex and sexuality as the basis for late capitalism's drive to equality through the commodification of gender. Reduction to the status of 'individuals' as a consequence of such de-gendering serves civil society not only in its work and labour aspects, but from the standpoint of consumption and leisure as well. Women, Illich argues, will never be able to compete equally in a de-gendered collectivity, something which many feminists seem to realize, if their present efforts to combine gender and sexual identification in both their occupational and 'private' lives is to be accorded any significance. At pp. 65-6 Illich states:
Economic discrimination against women appears when development sets in. It does not then go away: nothing indicates that it ever will. ... I came to the conclusion that the struggle to create economic equality between genderless humans of two different sexes resembles the efforts made to square the circle with ruler and straight-edge.
Further on, I treat the disembodied observation function so central to our obsession as a form of life with 'facts of life' in a way which plainly shows that it presupposes the annihilation of gender, no less for those who observe than for those who must submit to such observation. It is because we have not really 'forgotten' gender at all, even in the face of the system's relentless drive to the sexualization or commodification of gender, that disciplined observation must eschew reflexivity in its effort to reconstitute practice in a form more appropriate to society as a culturally and historically specific *form* of collective life rather than a synonym for it. Above all it must not do anything to encourage

remembrance, thus the real reason for the prohibition against reflexivity. Reconstitution of practice, the real objective of the social sciences in their mission for society, has at its core a commitment to an 'available' norm of individualism (and innovation) which demands the substitution of sexuality for gender. These parallel themes are developed further in the remainder of the book. For the role of discipline in the growth of civil society, see Michel Foucault, 'Discipline and Punish' (NY: Random House, 1978); and John O'Neill, Defamilization and the Feminization of Law in Early and Late Capitalism, 'International Journal of Law and Psychiatry', vol. 5, no. 3/4 (1983).

18 Ibid., pp. 364-5.

19 Ibid. See especially the preface to the second edition, added nine years after original publication, in 1902, A Note on Occupational Groups.

20 Discussed in Wilson, 'The American Ideology', pp. 171-99; and in Wilson, Functional Rationality and 'Sense of Function': the Case of an Ideological Distortion, in 'International Yearbook of Organization Studies', edited by David Dunkerly and Graeme Salaman (London: Routledge & Kegan Paul, 1981), pp. 37-61.

21 Durkheim, op. cit., pp. 408-9.

22 Ibid., pp. 33-6, 408-9, on the need for sociologists to develop a 'moral code' for themselves as 'responsible intellectuals' committed to intervention in the interests of reform. On the insufficiency of this position given the central role of the social sciences and related disciplines in advanced industrial societies today, H.T. Wilson, Anti-Method as a Counter-Structure in Social Research Operations: Critique as Subversion of Established Professional Practices, in 'Beyond Method: A Study of Organizational Research Strategies', edited by Gareth Morgan (Los Angeles: Sage Publications, 1983), pp. 247-59.

23 Wiles, op. cit., remains confident, but Weber's view was perhaps prescient in associating a commitment to economics as the paragon social science with support for negative, rather than positive, individualism. This would simply constitute the 'other side' of Durkheim's quite legitimate association of sociology with positive individualism, in op. cit. See Max Weber, 'Methodology of the Social Sciences', sections concerned with economic analysis.

24 Durkheim, op. cit., pp. 54-6, builds his theory of the development of the social division of labour on three basic kinds of dyadic sociation: (1) likenesses that attract (mechanical solidarity based on the 'collective conscience'): (2) differences that repel (abnormal division of labour following on Western industrialization); and (3) differences that attract (organic solidarity based on functional interdependence expressive of 'positive individualism').

25 On the observation function see Wilson, 'The American Ideology', chapters 2, 5, 8 and 10; and Knowledge and Totality, chapter 4. For the distinction between agency or action and causation with special reference to laboratory experimentation in science, see G.H. Von Wright, 'Explanation and Understanding' (Ithaca, NY: Cornell University Press, 1972); and 'Causality and Determinism' (NY: Columbia University Press, 1974).

26 Here I am making a distinction between the 'conflict within consensus' approach of early industrial capitalism embodied in legal and juridical theory, and the later to emerge 'socialization and norm internalization' model of the contemporary period, corresponding to the primacy of economics and sociology respectively. This is discussed in H.T. Wilson, The Problem of Discretion in Three Languages, research document, Judiciary Project, University of Paris, Paris, France (March 1980).

27 Wilson, 'The American Ideology', especially chapters 5, 8 and 10. On the observer's limited notion of practice in anthropology, Pierre Bourdieu, 'Outline of a Theory of Practice' (Cambridge: Cambridge University Press, 1977), especially pp. 1-71.

28 I would submit that this is the real upshot of John Gardner's argument

in 'Self-Renewal: The Individual and the Innovative Society' (NY: Harper, 1963), cited in note 2, Chapter 2.

29 Elton Mayo, 'The Human Problems of an Industrial Civilization' (Cambridge, Mass.: Harvard Business School, 1933).

30 Wilson, Functional Rationality and 'Sense of Function' ..., op. cit.

31 Durkheim, op. cit., pp. 32-3. For a parallel statement by Weber indicating his hostility to such an orientation for sociology, and the social sciences generally, see 'Methodology of the Social Sciences', p. 13, where he says:

> On the contrary, I am most emphatically opposed to the view that a realistic 'science of ethics' i.e. the analysis of the influence which the ethical evaluations of a group of people have on their conditions of life and the influences which the latter, in their turn, exert on the former, can produce an 'ethics' which will be able to say anything about what *should* happen.

32 Wilson, The Problem of Discretion in Three Languages ..., op. cit.

33 Gabriel Tarde, 'Laws of Imitation' (NY: Henry Holt, 1903), originally published in 1890. Also see 'La Logique Sociale' (1895); and 'L'Opposition universelle' (1897).

34 In this regard, see 'Laws of Imitation' preface to the second edition, pp. xiii-xxiv.

35 'Laws of Imitation', pp. 1-58. Also see Pierre Bourdieu, 'Outline of a Theory of Practice' (Cambridge: Cambridge University Press, 1977), pp. 96-158, particularly his discussion of 'limited invention', ordinary and extraordinary, and the habitus.

36 Ibid., pp. xiii-xiv.

37 This is discussed in Wilson, Innovation: the Practical Uses of Theory, op. cit.

38 'Laws of Imitation', pp. xiv-xv.

39 Ibid., p. xv.

40 This argument was first articulated by Kingsley Davis. But see the article on functional analysis in I.L. Horowitz, 'Professing Sociology' (Chicago: Aldine Press, 1968). It is a somewhat less critical approach to that presented in Wilson, Functional Rationality and 'Sense of Function' ..., op. cit.

41 See Durkheim, op. cit., p. 403.

42 H.T. Wilson, Functional Rationality and 'Sense of Function': The Case of an Ideological Distortion, 'International Yearbook of Organization Studies, 1980', edited by David Dunkerly and Graeme Salaman (London: Routledge & Kegan Paul, 1981), pp. 37-61.

43 Here I am reminded of the following remark by Giambattista Vico, in 'The New Science', paragraphs 332-3, regarding 'the universal and eternal principles (such as every science must have) on which all notions are founded and still preserve themselves'. He says that there are only three universal customs - religion, solemn marriage, and burial. Since he accepts the axiom that 'uniform ideas, born among peoples unknown to each other, must have a common ground of truth', it is these common human customs on which the 'new science' must be built.

44 Wilson, Science, Technology and Innovation, op. cit.; H.T. Wilson, Technology and/or/as the Future (review essay), 'Philosophy of the Social Sciences' (forthcoming).

45 Central to the idea of a 'unit of analysis' in social theory is the role of members' practices as a built-in feature of this theory. Though Weber evidenced an historical concern for the lived attitudes and practices of the populations and cultures being studied, and encouraged an interpretative sociology and *verstehen* to this end, he undercut this position to a large extent by his rigid split between the substantive and the methodological. As a result, his 'unit of analysis' took the form of the well-known 'ideal type', whether of the individualizing (Protestantism) or the generalizing (bureaucracy) variety. Weber's commitment to comparative research, so central to his work, nevertheless depends on protocols which treat such ideal types as 'methodological devices' for

purely 'heuristic' purposes which allegedly express no necessary 'rationalistic bias'.   See Weber, 'Theory of Social and Economic Organization', translated and introduced by Talcott Parsons (Chicago: Free Press, 1947), pp. 87-123, where aspects of this inconsistency are in clear evidence.   This point is made with great force by: Karl Loewith, Weber's Interpretation of the Bourgeois-Capitalistic World in terms of the Guiding Principle of Rationalization, in 'Max Weber', edited by Dennis Wrong (Englewood Cliffs, NJ: Prentice Hall, 1970), pp. 101-22; H.T. Wilson, Reading Max Weber: the Limits of Sociology, op. cit.; and Wilson, 'The American Ideology', chapters 2, 6 and 7.   Also see Alfred Schutz, 'Phenomenology of the Social World' (Evanston, Illinois: Northwestern University Press, 1967), pp. 3-44.

Marx, refusing to honour the 'objective' validity of (subsequent) academic specialization on which Weber's distinction between substantive and methodological is largely based, does not treat lived experience in the form of members' practices as a procedural matter or methodological protocol.   Having criticized Kant in particular for treating the practical side of life too much 'in the abstract', and thereby speaking to the *de facto* supremacy of theory over practice, Marx's 'unit of analysis' was a dialectically informed interpenetration of the theoretical, observational and commonsensical which he called a 'social formation' (e.g. feudalism, capitalism, etc.).   'Social formation' comprehends a critical and totalistic, as well as a methodological and strategic, element.   'Industrial society' is clearly too narrow and narcissistically self-contained a 'unit of analysis' for it to function in a useful comparative way.   See Theodor Adorno, 'Negative Dialectics' (NY: Seabury Press, 1973), note (*) at p. 152.   A recent effort to merge aspects of these two conceptions of 'unit of analysis' is provided by Pierre Bourdieu, op. cit., in particular his notion of 'habitus'.   See especially the definition at p. 78.

46   See 'Rationality', edited by Bryan Wilson (Oxford: Basil Blackwell, 1970), where a debate on the matter of rationality as it relates to members' practices in non-Western tribal societies is thrashed out.   See particularly the contributions of Peter Winch (2), Robin Horton, and J.H.M. Beattie, which bear on this issue of 'understanding other cultures' as well as 'our own'.   An excellent, if largely unrecognized and unheralded, effort to do just this using both disciplined observation and sensitivity to members' practices and understandings is provided by H. Barnett, 'Innovation: the Basis of Cultural Change' (NY: McGraw Hill, 1953).

47   Wilson, Knowledge and Totality, chapters 1 and 2.   R.G. Collingwood made my point clearly and unambiguously in 'Principles of Art' (London: Oxford University Press, 1937), p. 67 when he said:
   Savages are no more exempt from human folly than civilized men, and are no doubt equally liable to the error of thinking that they, or the persons they regard as their superiors, can do what in fact cannot be done.   But this error is not the essence of magic; it is a perversion of magic.   And we should be careful how we attribute it to the people we call savages, who will one day rise up and testify against us.

48   For a critical appraisal of several concepts aimed at understanding the tribal (or class) 'other' see H.T. Wilson, Notes on the Achievement of Communicative Behaviour and Related Difficulties, 'Dialectical Anthropology' (1983).

49   Barnett, op. cit., p. 7.

50   Compare James March and Herbert Simon, 'Organizations' (NY: Wiley, 1958) to James Thompson, 'Organizations in Action' (NY: McGraw Hill, 1968).   For commentary, H.T. Wilson, Rationality and Decision in Administrative Science, op. cit.; and 'The American Ideology', chapters 6-8.

51   See 'The American Ideology', chapter 8.   I argue that an open systems approach to the study of organizations not only is in harmony with, but

expressive of, a view of 'society' as an increasingly closed 'macro-system'. This perhaps helps to explain the obsession with 'industrial society' as the exclusive unit of analysis. It is society as a 'rational-(social)organization' which is the hidden, if historically explicit, notion here. This does not dispute the rise of international markets and business cycles, but rather focusses on the nation-state-as-firm that this development requires.

52 The case of Canada as an exporter of its natural resources to the United States, which even today has many or most of them in abundance, is a case in point. This suggests that there are at least three kinds of 'scarcity' (like 'limit'): real scarcity, scarcity at the price, and scarcity resulting from the refusal to extract or exploit one's own resources in favour of those found in some developing country that later decides to nationalize foreign holdings.

53 Compare in this regard Paul Diesing, 'Reason in Society' (Urbana, Illinois: University of Illinois Press, 1962), where 'technical rationality' functions as the 'methodological' standard, to Weber's simultaneous endorsement in 'Theory of Social and Economic Organization', pp. 87-123, and criticism in 'Methodology of the Social Sciences', pp. 27-36. This is discussed in detail in Wilson, 'The American Ideology', particularly chapter 8.

54 Barnett, op. cit., p. 2. On Worlds one-three, see notes 20, 21, Chapter 1, 'Reconnaissance'.

55 This role, to be sure, is at variance with their stated ideology. Far from leading the entire developed world into a socialist stage beyond capitalism, their attraction for the Third World resides to a large extent in precisely their overall backwardness. At best, these societies possess industrial superstructures built on a feudal base, whereas Marx stated that an industrial ethos must permeate the base as substructure as well before the transition (or revolution) could even be contemplated seriously.

56 Diesing, op. cit., pp. 1-13; and Weber, 'Methodology of the Social Sciences', pp. 27-36. On the difference between 'knowing how' and 'being able', see H.T. Wilson, Science, Technology and Innovation ..., op. cit.

57 Marion Levy, 'Modernization: Latecomers and Survivors' (NY: Basic Books, 1972), p. ix.

58 On the idea of limit in regard to the technical bias vis à vis a cross-cultural approach, Bourdieu, op. cit., pp. 124, 129, 137, 164, 166; and Winch, Understanding a Primitive Society, in 'Rationality', edited by Bryan Wilson, pp. 107-11. For evidence of the shift noted within 'industrial society', see Schon, op. cit.; and a criticism in Wilson, Innovation: the Practical Uses of Theory, op. cit.

59 Barnett, op. cit., pp. 7-8.

60 Ibid. (passim).

61 See note 54 on Barnett and Popper.

62 Barnett, op. cit., p. 9. He discusses 'innovative processes' at pp. 181-289, following, but at the same time improving on, Tarde.

63 See particularly, J.B. Bury, 'The Idea of Progress' (NY: Macmillan, 1932).

64 On seeing the West as a 'culture' or cultures, Alfred Kroeber, 'Configurations of Culture Growth' (Berkeley: University of California Press, 1944). Compare to the work of Alfred Weber, in which European 'culture' is distinguished from (North) American 'civilisation'.

65 See note 55. This is not to ignore the other side of this 'balance of power' equation, that is, that the West's very pre-eminence protects many Third World countries from incursions by the Soviet Bloc countries. I only seek to draw attention to the less obvious role of the latter in tacitly or explicitly restraining the former.

66 Jacques Ellul, 'The Technological Society' (NY: Alfred Knopf, 1964), originally published in French in 1954; Ellul, Ideas of Technology, in 'The Technological Order', edited by Carl Stover (Detroit: Wayne State

University Press, 1963), pp. 10-37; and Ellul, 'The Technological
System' (NY: Continuum Books, 1980). For critical commentary, H.T.
Wilson, The Sociology of Apocalypse: Jacques Ellul's 'Reformation' of
Reformation Thought, 'Human Context', vol. 7, no. 3 (Autumn 1975),
pp. 474-94.

67 H.T. Wilson, Science, Technology and Innovation: the Role of Commonsense Capacities, 'Methodology and Science', vol. 15, no. 3 (1982), pp.
167-200.
68 H.T. Wilson, Science, Critique and Criticism: the 'Open Society' Revisited, in 'On Critical Theory', edited by John O'Neill (NY: Seabury
Press, 1976), pp. 205-30.
69 Wilson, Science, Technology and Innovation ..., op. cit.: and Wilson,
Response to Ray, 'Philosophy of the Social Sciences', vol. 11, no. 1
(March 1981), pp. 45-8, and vol. 13, no. 1 (March 1983).
70 Kroeber, op. cit. This is probably the real reason why in Weber's
work the rationalization process, extended globally, must produce 'world
de-enchantment' (*Entzauberung*). Also see I.L. Horowitz, The New
Fundamentalism, 'Transaction: Social Science and Modern Society', vol.
20, no. 1 (Nov./Dec. 1982), pp. 40-7.
71 Thus the paradox of André Gunder Frank's criticism of the advanced
countries in 'Capitalism and Underdevelopment in Latin America' (NY:
Monthly Review Press, 1967). For a conflicting point of view, see
Michael Novak, Why Latin America is Poor, 'Atlantic' (March 1982),
pp. 66-75.
72 Compare to Levy's cogent discussion at op. cit. For a useful summary
assessment of the serious, though largely predictable, difficulties facing
OPEC countries now and in the foreseeable future, see Daniel Pipes,
The Curse of Oil Wealth, 'Atlantic' (July 1982), pp. 19-20, 22-5.
73 Fernand Braudel, 'Capitalism and Material Life, 1400-1800' (London, 1973).
74 Wilson, Science, Technology and Innovation, op. cit.
75 See John Hicks, 'A Theory of Economic History' (Oxford: Clarendon
Press, 1969). For a contemporary classification scheme, Charles
Perrow, A Framework for the Comparative Analysis of Organizations,
'American Sociological Review', vol. 32 (1967), pp. 194-208.
76 Braudel, op. cit. Compare to Ellul's rendition of 'traditional techniques' in the pre-modern period in 'The Technological Society', pp.
64-76. Also see H.T. Wilson, The Sociology of Apocalypse ...,
op. cit. for critical commentary.
77 Hicks. op. cit.; Immanuel Wallerstein, 'World Systems, 1600-1900' (NY,
1977).
78 Karl Marx, 'Capital', vol. III. Also see Karl Polanyi, 'The Great Transformation' (NY: Oxford University Press, 1964).
79 Jane Jacobs, 'The Economy of Cities' (NY: Random House, 1969), pp.
49-144.
80 Coch and French, Resistance to Change, 'Human Relations', vol. 1
(1948); Alvin Toffler, 'Future Shock' (NY: Ballantine Books, 1970);
J. Sheehy, 'Passages' (NY: Knopf, 1976). Surely one point relevant
here is that, far from 'improving' in our capacity to handle complexity,
tension, change, etc. we get worse, or at best stay the same. This
would present a strong case in support of Ellul's, Arendt's and Levy's
claim that society is an unnatural and artifical aggregation which we
cannot hope to 'humanize' from within.
81 John Goldthorpe, Theories of Industrial Society: On the Recrudescence
of Historicism and the Future of Futurology, paper read at the World
Congress of Sociology, Varna, Bulgaria, June 1970. Compare to John
Rex, 'Sociology and the Demystification of the Modern World' (London:
Routledge & Kegan Paul, 1973).
82 Anton Zijderveld, 'The Abstract Society' (Garden City, NY: Doubleday,
1970); and Robert Merton, The Role Set, 'British Journal of Sociology',
vol. 18 (1957), pp. 106-20.
83 See L.J. Henderson, 'Pareto's General Sociology' (Cambridge, Mass.:
Harvard University Press, 1935); 'The Fitness of the Environment'

(Boston: Beacon, 1958); Karl Mannheim, 'Man and Society in an Age of Reconstruction' (London: Routledge & Kegan Paul, 1940); and Thomas Schelling, On the Ecology of Micromotives, 'The Public Interest', no. 25, (Fall 1971), pp. 59-98.

84 Ellul, Ideas of Technology, op. cit., and Schelling, op. cit.

85 In 'The American Ideology', I accept this dynamic but refuse to support the idea that it is premised on a 'technical interest'. Note that this suggestion can only work if, as a consequence of giving more attention to adaptation or accommodation, a more critical and reflexive *public* posture toward capitalism and development results. On 'nature' and 'other cultures' as raw material, Herbert Marcuse, 'One Dimensional Man' (Boston: Beacon Press, 1964), particularly pp. 144-69.

86 In 'Tractatus Logico-Philosophicus', Wittgenstein makes the following point at 6.51: 'For doubt can exist only where a question exists, a question only where an answer exists, and an answer only where something can be said.'

CHAPTER 3 PRACTICE/THEORY

1 See my Science, Technology and Innovation: the Role of Commonsense Capacities, op. cit. Also David Noble, op. cit.; and J.R. Ravetz, 'Scientific Knowledge and its Social Problems' (NY: Oxford University Press, 1973).

2 Charles Perrow, A Framework for the Comparative Analysis of Organizations, 'American Sociological Review' vol. 32 (1967), pp. 194-208. The association of practical capacity with the ability to respond to 'crises' in everyday life is discussed by Karl Mannheim, in 'Man and Society in an Age of Reconstruction' (London: Routledge & Kegan Paul, 1940), pp. 55-60.

3 Jurgen Habermas, 'Toward a Rational Society' (London: Heinemann, 1971); Habermas, Toward a Theory of Communicative Competence, in 'Recent Sociology, No. 2', edited by Hans P. Dreitzel (NY: Macmillan, 1970), pp. 115-48; and Habermas, 'Communication and the Evolution of Society' (Boston: Beacon, 1979). My critique of Habermas can be found in Science, Critique and Criticism: the 'Open Society' Revisited, in 'On Critical Theory', edited by John O'Neill (NY: Seabury Press, 1976), pp. 205-30; The Poverty of Sociology: 'Society' as Concept and Object in Sociological Theory, 'Philosophy of the Social Sciences', vol. 8, no. 1 (March 1978), pp. 187-204; and Response to Ray, 'Philosophy of the Social Sciences', vol. 11, no. 1 (March 1981), pp. 45-8, and vol. 13, no. 1 (March 1983), pp. 63-5.

4 Hannah Arendt, 'The Human Condition' (Chicago: University of Chicago Press, 1958). That her attitude to theorizing presumes that the dichotomy between thought and activity is empirically real is something I respond to in 'The American Ideology' (London: Routledge & Kegan Paul, 1977), pp. 171-6.

5 See Arendt, 'Between Past and Future' (NY: Viking Press, 1968), particularly her discussion of Plato's repudiation of politics in favour of statecraft.

6 H.T. Wilson, 'The American Ideology', pp. 236-41, 245-53.

7 Herbert Marcuse, The Affirmative Character of Culture, in 'Negations' (Boston: Beacon, 1968), pp. 88-133 at p. 88.

8 See Alan Blum, 'Theorizing' (London: Heinemann, 1974), pp. 1-63.

9 For a critique which locates phenomenology as one of the most recent phases of German idealism, see Marcuse, The Concept of Essence, in 'Negations', pp. 43-87. The idea that disciplined observation is the prototypical *activity* in advanced industrial societies is explored in Wilson, 'The American Ideology' and in Knowledge and Totality.

10 Marcuse, 'One Dimensional Man' (Boston: Beacon, 1964). Theodor Adorno makes my point concisely in Scientific Experiences of a European Scholar in America, in 'The Intellectual Migration: Europe and America,

1930-1960', edited by D. Fleming and B. Bailyn (Cambridge, Mass.: Belknap Press, 1968), p. 353, when he says:

> My own position in the controversy between empirical and theoretical sociology, so often misinterpreted, particularly in Europe, I may sum up by saying that empirical investigations are not only legitimate but essential, even in the realm of cultural phenomena. But one must not confer autonomy upon them or regard them as a universal key. Above all, they must terminate in theoretical knowledge. Theory is no mere vehicle that becomes superfluous as soon as the data are in hand.

Also see Wilson, The Meaning and Significance of 'Empirical Method' for the Critical Theory of Society, 'Canadian Journal of Political and Social Theory', vol. 3, no. 3, (Fall 1979), pp. 57-68.

11 Karl Popper, 'The Poverty of Historicism' (London: Routledge & Kegan Paul, 1957). For a critique see my Science, Critique and Criticism ..., op. cit.; and 'The American Ideology', particularly pp. 101-21.

12 On 'society' as an historically and culturally specific form of collective life, Theodor Adorno, Society, in 'The Legacy of the German Refugee Intellectuals', edited by Robert Boyers (NY: Schocken Books, 1969), pp. 144-53.

13 This juxtaposition of actor and observer is discussed in my Knowledge and Totality, chapter 4.

14 Pierre Bourdieu, 'Outline of a Theory of Practice' (Cambridge: Cambridge University Press, 1977), pp. 1-9. Compare to George Boas, 'The Limits of Reason' (NY: Harper & Bros, 1961).

15 Ibid., pp. 5-6.

16 Such an analysis of 'openness' could be neatly paralleled by our critique, and that of others, of Popper's 'open society', since in both cases it is the disciplined observer as neutral and objective 'outsider' bringing real sense to proceedings which are patronized as conventional and traditional who is my chief antagonist, as well as Bourdieu's. Compare Bourdieu on this score to Barnett's discussion of the sociological (anthropological) observer in H. Barnett, 'Innovation: the Basis of Cultural Change' (NY: McGraw Hill, 1953), p. 7. On the advanced societies and Popper, see Wilson, Science, Critique and Criticism ..., op. cit.; Everett Knight, 'The Objective Society' (NY: George Braziller, 1959); and Herbert Marcuse, Karl Popper and the Problem of Historical Laws, in 'Studies in Critical Philosophy' (Boston: Beacon, 1973), pp. 193-208. Also see Danté Germino, Karl Popper's Open Society, 'Political Science Reviewer' (1979), pp. 21-61.

17 I encounter Popper's support for a 'unity of method' as it appears in 'The Poverty of Historicism' in 'The American Ideology', particularly pp. 101-21, and argue that it is the objective, *truth*, which must hold for both the natural and social or cultural sciences. This means that the method in the latter case must be different from that appropriate to the natural sciences.

18 Jacques Ellul, 'The Technological Society' (NY: Vintage, 1964), published originally in 1954; Ellul, Ideas of Technology, in 'The Technological Order', edited by Carl Stover (Detroit: Wayne State University Press, 1963), pp. 10-37.

19 Ludwig Wittgenstein, 'Tractatus Logico-Philosophicus', translated by D.S. Pears and B. McGuinness (London: Routledge & Kegan Paul, 1961), containing the original introduction by the first English translator, Bertrand Russell, published in 1922. Also, my discussion in Knowledge and Totality, chapter 1, section II, on causality, lawfulness and the problem of description.

20 Durkheim, in 'The Division of Labour in Society', sees such an outcome as synonymous with the emergence of a post-anomic 'organic solidarity', of course, but needs to treat his 'normal' division of labour as the realization of 'functional interdependence', conceived as an objective social fact. See H.T. Wilson, Functional Rationality and 'Sense of Function': the Case of an Ideological Distortion, op. cit.

21 Max Weber, 'Methodology of the Social Sciences' (Chicago: Free Press, 1949), p. 34.   More significant still is Wittgenstein's remark, recorded by one of his students, M.O'C. Drury, in 'The Danger of Words' (London: Routledge & Kegan Paul, 1973), pp. ix-x and cited in the preface:
> Our civilization is characterized by the word progress.   Progress is its form: it is not one of its properties that it progresses.   It is typical of it that it is building, constructing.   Its activity is one of constructing more and more complex structures.   And even clarity serves only this end, and is not sought on its own account.   For me on the other hand clarity, lucidity, is the goal sought.

22 Discussed in Frederic Jameson, The Vanishing Mediator: Narrative Structure in Max Weber, 'New German Critique', vol. 1 (1973), pp. 52-89, with special reference to the influence of Nietzsche on Weber. Also see H.T. Wilson, Value: On the Possibility of a Convergence between Economic and Non-economic Decision Making, in 'Management under Differing Value Systems', edited by G. Dluges and K. Weiermair (Berlin and NY: Walter De Gruyter, 1981), pp. 37-71.

23 H.T. Wilson, Reading Max Weber: the Limits of Sociology, 'Sociology', vol. 10, no. 2 (May 1976), pp. 297-315.

24 Wilson, 'The American Ideology', pp. 145-70.   On Weber's determinism, see Gabriel Kolko, A Critique of Max Weber's Philosophy of History, 'Ethics', vol. 70, no. 1 (October 1959), pp. 21-36.

25 Mannheim also accedes to such nostalgia in 'Man and Society in An Age of Reconstruction', pp. 53-9 when he equates 'pluralism' with a combination of many small sellers in the 'free market' *and* an unattached and 'free-floating' intelligentsia.

26 For a comparison between Ellul and Weber on the role of technique versus rationalization in generating and sustaining advanced industrial societies, see my The Sociology of Apocalypse, 'Human Context', vol. 7, no. 3 (Autumn 1975), pp. 274-94.

27 Thus for Weber, the 'substantively rational' man, in the final analysis, is a category restricted to those who stand against and oppose the rationalization process.   See my comparison of Weberian substantive rationality and Mannheimian substantial rationality in Reading Max Weber ..., op. cit., pp. 310-12.

28 Herbert Marcuse, 'One Dimensional Man', pp. 144-69.

29 G.H. Von Wright does this when he distinguishes action or agency from causation in Von Wright, 'Explanation and Understanding' (Ithaca: Cornell University Press, 1972), pp. 34-82; and in 'Causality and Determinism' (NY: Columbia University Press, 1974).   I show how essential the distinction is to any attempt to make sense of causal explanation in Knowledge and Totality, chapters 1 and 4.

30 Weber's view of the labourers who constructed the pyramids would now appear to constitute an instance of his own failure to adequately put himself in the position of his historical subjects.   See Peter Green, Tut, Tut, Tut, in 'New York Review of Books' (11 October 1979).

31 On the hierarchy of activities, Hannah Arendt, 'The Human Condition'. On reformism and intervention through 'piecemeal social engineering', Wilson, 'The American Ideology', pp. 101-21 and passim; and Knight, op. cit., particularly the concluding paragraph.

32 This is discussed in Chapter 1.   On 'crisis' as an intellectual category and problem, see Karl Mannheim, 'Ideology and Utopia' (London: International Library of Psychology, Philosophy and Scientific Method, 1936), pp. 5-53, 100-8, 144-52.

33 C. Wright Mills, Types of Practicality, in Mills, 'The Sociological Imagination' (NY: Grove Press, 1959).

34 Bourdieu, op. cit.   The essays by Winch (2), Horton and Beattie all occur in 'Rationality', edited by Bryan Wilson (Oxford: Basil Blackwell, 1970), pp. 1-17, 78-111, 131-71, and 240-68.

35 Wilson, Knowledge and Totality, chapter 3.

36 Adorno, Scientific Experiences of a European Scholar in America, op.

cit., p. 353; Sociology and Empirical Research, in 'The Positivist Dispute in German Sociology', translated by Glyn Adey and David Frisby (London: Heinemann, 1976), pp. 68-86.

37 Thomas Kuhn, 'The Structure of Scientific Revolutions', 2nd edition, enlarged (Chicago: University of Chicago Press, 1970), 1st edition published 1962, for the distinction between normal and revolutionary science. On Kuhn's dispute with Popper, see my 'The American Ideology', pp. 75-100. On the 'deep nature' of large-scale social change, see Wittgenstein, 'Remarks on the Foundations of Mathematics', p. 57, no. 4. Note the agreement between Wittgenstein and Marx on this matter.

38 See G.K. Helleiner (ed.), 'A World Divided' (Cambridge: Cambridge University Press, 1976), where the issue of Third World solidarity against incorporation into the 'international economy', particularly for countries lacking a key resource needed by the advanced societies, is discussed.

39 H.T. Wilson, Notes on the Achievement of Communicative Behaviour and Related Difficulties, forthcoming in 'Dialectical Anthropology' (1983).

40 See Wilson, 'The American Ideology', pp. 68-71 on the 'political' dilemma of science in the advanced societies. Also Joseph Haberer, 'Politics and the Community of Science' (NY: Van Nostrand Reinhold, 1969).

41 Paul Diesing, 'Reason in Society' (Urbana, Illinois: University of Illinois Press, 1962), particularly pp. 1-13 and passim pp. 14-64.

42 I discuss this in The Significance of 'Instrumental Reason' for the Critical Theory of Society, (unpublished paper).

43 Wilson, Knowledge and Totality, chapter 4, sections on the difference between 'sharing' and empathic 'identification'.

44 Karl Marx, 'Early Texts', translated and edited by David McClellan (Oxford: Basil Blackwell, 1962). For interpretation, Alfred Schmidt, 'The Concept of Nature in Marx' (London: New Left Books, 1971); and Wilson, Knowledge and Totality, chapter 3.

45 Marx, 'Early Texts'; Schmidt, op. cit.

46 It is interesting here to note that different outcomes and unique or peculiar conditions, far from disputing the claim of social determination, effectively underwrite it.

47 See the relevant excerpts from Vico and Collingwood in Chapter 2, notes 43 and 47.

48 Wittgenstein, 'Tractatus Logico-Philosophicus', especially nos 6.4-7.

49 'Concrete Totality' is discussed by Karel Kosik, in his 'Dialectics of the Concrete' (Dordrecht, Holland: D. Reidel, 1976).

50 See my Knowledge and Totality, chapter 1. and the conclusion to chapter 2, where I distinguish Kosik not only from deductivists in the philosophy of science, but from 'realists' as well.

51 Ibid., chapter 3, next to last section on Bauman's conception of society as 'second nature', as discussed in 'Towards a Critical Sociology' (London: Routledge & Kegan Paul, 1976). For critical analysis see H.T. Wilson, The Poverty of Sociology, 'Philosophy of the Social Sciences', vol. 8 (1978),pp. 187-204.

52 On the distinction between ends and means, Max Horkheimer, 'The Eclipse of Reason' (NY: Seabury, 1973). Compare to Diesing, op. cit. Also see Jameson, op. cit.; and Wilson, The Significance of 'Instrumental Reason' for the Critical Theory of Society. In my opinion, however, Max Weber's analysis of both the ends/means and value/fact distinctions in 'Methodology of the Social Sciences' and elsewhere remains unsurpassed.

53 See Wilson, 'The American Ideology', pp. 4-6; Knowledge and Totality, preface and chapter 5.

54 Gabriel Tarde, particularly 'Laws of Imitation' (Gloucester, Mass.: Peter Smith, 1962), originally published by Henry Holt & Company in 1903, translated by Elsie Clews Parsons and introduced by Franklin H. Giddings.

55 See Chapter 2, notes 33-9 relevant to Tarde; and Barnett, op. cit.,
    pp. 2-3, 7-10 and 16.
56 Berkeley: University of California Press, 1944. See especially
    Kroeber's discussion of growth and its absence in various areas of
    scientific knowledge. Also see Alfred Kroeber and Clyde Kluckhohn,
    'Culture: An Inventory of Meanings' (NY: Vintage, 1965).
57 See Jameson, op. cit.; Theodor Adorno, Spengler After the Decline,
    and Cultural Criticism and Society, both in 'Prisms' (London: Neville
    Spearman, 1967), pp. 53-72 and 19-34; Max Horkheimer and Theodor
    Adorno, 'The Dialectic of Enlightenment' (NY: Herder ' Herder, 1972);
    Alfred Weber, 'Farewell to European History'; and Wilson, conclusion to
    The Significance of 'Instrumental Reason' for the Critical Theory of
    Society, op. cit., on 'culture' and 'capitalism' as interdependent analy-
    tic concepts in nineteenth- and twentieth century German intellectual
    history. It is important to contrast three basic conceptions of 'culture'
    in modern Western civilization: (1) culture as 'superstructure'; (2)
    culture as basic core of shared values; and (3) culture as sub-system.
    In the first case it is the labour theory of value to which Marx, no
    less than Ricardo, subscribed, which sees culture as a produced effect
    of capitalist surplus. In the second, we revert to a more anthropologi-
    cal notion - what remains after all points of difference have been
    accounted for in a people. In the third we address a 'system' concept
    of culture which sees it as a sub-system of society. My understand-
    ing, needless to say, favours (2), which is to say that for me one of
    the more problematic properties of Marxian thinking is precisely his
    loyalty to the first understanding from political economy. See particu-
    larly Alfred Kroeber and Clyde Kluckhohn, 'Culture: an Inventory of
    Meanings' (NY: Vintage, 1965).
58 See Wittgenstein's Bemerkungen über Frazers 'The Golden Bough',
    edited with a note by Rush Rhees, 'Synthese', vol. 17 (1967), pp. 233-
    53 and M.O'C. Drury's remarks in 'The Danger of Words', pp. x-xi.
59 Marion Levy, 'Modernization: Latecomers and Survivors' (NY: Basic
    Books, 1972). Also see Thomas Schelling, On the Ecology of Micro-
    motives, 'The Public Interest' (Fall 1971), pp. 59-98; and Alastair
    Taylor, The Computer and the Liberal: Our Ecological Dilemma,
    'Queens Quarterly' (Autumn 1972), pp. 289-300.
60 This is important rather than specious when one remembers the solidar-
    istic and cohesive features of 'culture' (or *a* culture). Durkheim
    clearly underestimated the capacity of the collective conscience to re-
    constitute itself far beyond dependence upon the relatively slender
    reed of his new individualism. This individualism was both the central
    opponent and the last vestige of this conscience in the emerging order.
    See 'The Division of Labour in Society' and 'The American Ideology',
    pp. 181-99.
61 But see Blum, 'Theorizing', pp. 230-1.
62 H.T. Wilson, Reading Max Weber ..., op. cit. The fact that Weber
    lacks a theory of tradition is not incidental to the absence of a concern
    for (and theory of) social change *given industrial society* in his work.
63 John O'Neill makes this point several times in 'Sociology as a Skin
    Trade' (London: Heinemann, 1972), a collection of his theoretical and
    sociological essays published between 1964 and 1971. Also see his
    introduction to 'Modes of Individualism and Collectivism', edited by
    John O'Neill (London: Heinemann, 1973).
64 See note 21, this chapter.
65 John K. Roberts, Expressive Aspects of Technological Development,
    'Philosophy of the Social Sciences', vol. 1, no.3 (September 1971), pp.
    207-19.
66 See note 62, this chapter. This was why I believed Marx would be
    far less hostile to our problematic-innovation - than would Weber.
67 Weber, 'Methodology of the Social Sciences', passim; Weber, 'Theory of
    Social and Economic Organization' (Chicago: Free Press, 1947), pp. 92-
    3, 109-18, 158-71; Diesing, op. cit., pp. 1-64; Horkheimer, op. cit.

68   Sigmund Freud, 'Civilization and its Discontents' (Garden City, NY: Doubleday Anchor, 1958), originally published in 1938.
69   See particularly no. 190, 'The Philosophy of Right'. This is discussed in 'The American Ideology', pp. 178-9.
70   Here I would be encountering the way in which a radical doctrine, namely political economy, could reverse itself on the matter of its initial critique of landed and pre-bourgeois values standing against both technology and meritocracy once it had become established. Neither profit maximization nor capital accumulation (to the extent that they can be distinguished) would *necessarily* be benefited by 'autonomous' technology underwritten by capital investment once industrial capitalism had achieved *both* economic *and* political ascendancy.
71   David Hume, 'An Enquiry Concerning Human Understanding', in 'The English Philosophers from Bacon to Mill', edited by E.A. Burtt (NY: Modern Library, 1939), pp. 585-689. Compare to Karl Popper, 'Conjectures and Refutations' (London: Routledge & Kegan Paul, 1963), essays on rationality, science and the role of tradition; and Popper, 'Objective Knowledge' (London: Oxford University Press, 1972), pp. 1-105. Discussed in 'The American Ideology' at pp. 78-83.
72   Bourdieu, op. cit., pp. 96-158.
73   See Arendt, 'The Human Condition', particularly the chapter on Action, where she discusses how one must necessarily display himself if there is to be authentic talk about questions as to how life should be lived. On the critique of 'legal-rational' speech as 'anonymous', and straining toward anonymity as its ideal, Blum, 'Theorizing', passim.
74   Ellul, 'The Technological Society'; The Characterology of Technique; Wilson, The Sociology of Apocalypse, op. cit.
75   H.T. Wilson, Innovation: the Practical Uses of Theory, in 'Social Change, Innovation and Politics in East Asia', edited by Y.S. Yim, H.T. Wilson, and Richard W. Wilson (Hong Kong: Asian Research Institute, 1980), pp. 9-29.
76   Such a fulsome endorsement of Durkheimian 'positive' individualism seems quaint in light of the now-questionable assumptions regarding technology, progress, and continued affluence on which it, and books like Galbraith's, 'The New Industrial State' (Boston: Houghton Mifflin, 1967), were largely premised.
77   Thus the 'negative' consequences of 'feedback' as institutional learning in the advanced societies. See Harold Wilensky, 'Organizational Intelligence' (NY: Basic Books, 1967) on the Janus-faced nature of 'information'. Also H.T. Wilson, Rationality and Decision in Administrative Science, 'Canadian Journal of Political Science', vol. 6, no. 3 (June 1973), pp. 271-94, for a critique of certain notions of rational organization and rational decision in this (and allied) disciplines.
78   Wilson, 'The American Ideology', pp. 181-9.
79   Wilson, Innovation: the Practical Uses of Theory, op. cit.
80   This constitutes a major criticism of Ellul's thinking in 'The Technological Society' and Ideas of Technology, op. cit. Though Weber does take account of the organizational factor as something which is more than a mere technique to be subsumed under an incremental, rather than a holistic understanding, he fails to mobilize his analysis, but instead fetishizes 'organization' as inevitable bad possibility in a thoroughly rationalized society. See Wilson, The Sociology of Apocalypse ..., op. cit., for commentary; and Wilson, 'The American Ideology', chapters 6 and 7.

CHAPTER 4   THE RATIONALITY QUESTION

1   Karl Marx and Friedrich Engels, 'The German Ideology' in 'Marx-Engels Archiv', vol. I, p. 227. Also in English by Lawrence & Wishart (London, 1965).
2   H.T. Wilson, 'The American Ideology' (London: Routledge & Kegan Paul, 1977), pp. 4-6.

3 See particularly Arthur Koestler, 'The Act of Creation' (London: Pan, 1970); and Julian Jaynes, 'The Origin of the Bicameral Mind' (Princeton, NJ: Princeton University Press, 1976).
4 Karel Kosik, 'Dialectics of the Concrete' (Dordrecht: D. Reidel, 1976).
5 H.T. Wilson, Knowledge and Totality, chapter 5.
6 Ibid. See A.R. Manser, The End of Philosophy: Marx and Wittgenstein, inaugural lecture, Southampton University, 1973.
7 Paul Zweig, Naipaul's Losers, 'Harpers' (January 1980), p. 69. Also see Patrick Marnham's Ahmed and the Gamekeepers in this same issue, pp. 58-67; and Marnham, 'Fantastic Invasion' (London: Jonathan Cape, 1980).
8 H.T. Wilson, Notes on the Achievement of Communicative Behaviour and Related Difficulties, 'Dialectical Anthropology' (forthcoming).
9 H.T. Wilson, Reading Max Weber: the Limits of Sociology, 'Sociology', vol. 10, no. 2 (May 1976), pp. 297-315; Frederic Jameson, The Vanishing Mediator: Narrative Structure in Max Weber, 'New German Critique', vol. 1 (1973), pp. 52-89; and A.J. Greimas, The Interaction of Semiotic Constraints, 'Yale French Studies', no. 41 (Spring 1968), pp. 86-105.
10 Hannah Arendt, 'The Human Condition' (Chicago: University of Chicago Press, 1958); and Weber, 'Theory of Social and Economic Organization' (Chicago: Free Press, 1947), pp. 111-18.
11 Wilson, Reading Max Weber, op. cit., pp. 310-11; and Karl Mannheim, 'Man and Society in an Age of Reconstruction' (London: Routledge & Kegan Paul, 1940), pp. 49-60.
12 Weber, 'Theory of Social and Economic Organization', pp. 87-115.
13 Ibid., p. 117.
14 Ibid., p. 186; and Karl Loewith, Weber's Interpretation of the Bourgeois-Capitalistic World in terms of the Guiding Principle of Rationalization, in 'Max Weber', edited by Dennis Wrong (Englewood Cliffs, NJ: Prentice Hall, 1970), pp. 101-22.
15 H.T. Wilson, The Significance of 'Instrumental Rationality' for the Critical Theory of Society (unpublished paper).
16 Wilson, 'The American Ideology', pp. 122-70. See Herbert Marcuse, Industrialization and Capitalism in the Work of Max Weber, in 'Negations' (Boston: Beacon Press, 1968), pp. 201-26. Also, note Loewith's description of the objectives of Weber's social science at op. cit., pp. 102-3, citing Weber, 'Methodology of the Social Sciences', p. 72.
17 Jameson, op. cit., p. 63.
18 Greimas, op. cit.
19 See the discussion of traditional action or behaviour in Weber in Nature, tradition and the primitive, this chapter.
20 Wilson, Reading Max Weber; and The Significance of 'Instrumental Rationality' for the Critical Theory of Society, op. cit.
21 Ibid. But Weber resists the significance of this fact for the meaning of 'rationality' as a 'tradition'. See Nature, tradition and the primitive, this chapter.
22 See Kosik, op. cit.; and Wilson, Knowledge and Totality, for a discussion of the difference between the concrete and abstract whole, and why the latter position is instrumental for the unimpeded operation of an empirical convention.
23 Weber, 'The Protestant Ethic and the Spirit of Capitalism' (NY: Scribners, 1952), pp. 180-3.
24 Marcuse, Industrialization and Capitalism in the Work of Max Weber, op. cit.
25 See Weber, 'Theory of Social and Economic Organization', pp. 328-9, 358-92.
26 Weber, 'From Max Weber', edited by Hans Gerth and C. Wright Mills (NY: Oxford University Press, 1946), pp. 77-128 at p. 128.
27 See H.T. Wilson, Max Weber's Pessimism, 'International Journal of Contemporary Sociology', vol. 8 (April 1971), pp. 183-8.
28 See Arendt's discussion of the 'hierarchy' of activities in 'The Human Condition'.

29   Giambatista Vico, 'The New Science', paragraphs 332-3.
30   See particularly Robin Horton, African Traditional Thought and Western
     Science, in 'Rationality', edited by Bryan Wilson (Oxford: Basil Black-
     well, 1970), pp. 131-71.
31   H.T. Wilson, The Meaning and Significance of 'Empirical Method' for
     the Critical Theory of Society, op. cit.;   and Anti-Method as a
     Counterstructure in Social Research Operations ..., op. cit.
32   As an example, see Pierre Bourdieu, 'Outline of a Theory of Practice'
     (Cambridge: Cambridge University Press, 1977).   Compare to H. Bar-
     nett, 'Innovation: the Basis of Cultural Change' (NY: McGraw Hill,
     1953).
33   Wilson, Notes on the Achievement of Communicative Behaviour and Re-
     lated Difficulties, 'Dialectical Anthropology' (forthcoming).
34   Patrick Marnham, Ahmed and the Gamekeepers, op. cit.;   Marnham,
     'Fantastic Invasion';   William Tucker, Is Nature too Good for Us?,
     'Harpers' (March 1982), pp. 27-35.
35   See Clarence Glacken, Man Against Nature: An Outmoded Concept, in
     'The Environmental Crisis', edited by Harold Helfrich (New Haven:
     Yale University Press, 1970), pp. 127-42.
36   The infinitely elastic character of human need given the fact that it was
     a product of human *consciousness* as well as 'instinct' was pointed out
     by Hegel, who anticipated capitalism's thoroughgoing dependence upon
     its unending expansion in 'The Philosophy of Right', translated with
     notes by T.M. Knox (London: Oxford University Press, 1967), no.
     190.   The reference to Weber is in Science as a Vocation, in 'From
     Max Weber', pp. 138-9.
37   Emile Durkheim, 'The Division of Labour in Society' (NY: Macmillan,
     1952), particularly his conclusion and the preface to the 2nd edition,
     A Note on Occupational Groups.   Also, Wilson, 'The American Ideol-
     ogy', pp. 186-9.   On the 'Third Estate', J.K. Bluntschli, 'The Theory
     of the State' (Oxford: Clarendon Press, 1892).
38   Wilson, Reading Max Weber, op. cit.;   The Significance of 'Instrumental
     Rationality' for the Critical Theory of Society, op. cit.
39   On the real difference being between things the organism learns with
     ease and things it learns with difficulty, see Lionel Tiger and Robin
     Fox, 'The Imperial Animal' (NY: Basic Books, 1973).   Also see
     Michael T. Ghiselin, The Individual in the Darwinian Revolution, 'New
     Literary History', vol. 3 (1971-2), pp. 113-34.
40   George Spencer Brown, 'Laws of Form' (London: George Allen & Unwin,
     1969), p. 126, note on 'ex-planation'.
41   Here I have in mind Wittgenstein's final statement (7.) in 'Tractatus
     Logico-Philosophicus' which says: 'What we cannot speak about we must
     pass over in silence.'   See Wilson, Knowledge and Totality, chapter 5.
42   H.T. Wilson, Innovation: the Practical Uses of Theory, in 'Social
     Change, Innovation and Politics in East Asia', edited by Y.S. Yim,
     H.T. Wilson, and R.W. Wilson (Hong Kong: Asian Research Service,
     1980), pp. 9-29.   Note my claim regarding the notion of 'organized
     environment' as it takes shape in *both* laboratory experimentation and
     R & D in Science, Technology and Innovation, op. cit.
43   Andre Delbecq, A.H. Vandeven, and D.H. Gustavson, 'Group Tech-
     niques for Program Planning: A Guide to Nominal Group and Delphi
     Processes' (Glenview, Illinois: Scott, Foresman, 1975).
44   See Charles Perrow's framework for analysing stability and change in
     large organizations in A Framework for the Comparative Analysis of
     Organizations, 'American Sociological Review', vol. 32 (1967), pp. 194-
     208.
45   Compare Donald Schon, 'Technology and Change' (NY: Delta Books,
     1968) to the 'classic' study by S.C. Gilfillan, 'The Sociology of Inven-
     tion' (Cambridge, Mass.: MIT Press, 1935), particularly his '38 social
     principles of invention' and the appended bibliographies at pp. 164-75.
     Also see the current references cited in Wilson, Innovation: the Practi-
     cal Uses of Theory, op. cit.

46 Wilson, 'The American Ideology', pp. 171-99.
47 See particularly the work of Edwin Mansfield on innovation and techno-
    logical change *given* economic objectives.   Both 'Industrial Research
    and Technological Innovation' (NY: W.W. Norton, 1964) and 'The Econo-
    mics of Technological Change' (NY: W.W. Norton, 1968) provide highly
    useful frameworks and have recently been updated.   Also see David
    Noble, 'America by Design' (NY: Oxford University Press, 1977).
48 Durkheim, op. cit.   The excerpt is from 'Man and Society in an Age
    of Reconstruction' (London: Routledge & Kegan Paul, 1940), p. 58.
49 Paul Diesing, 'Reason and Society' (Urbana, Illinois: University of
    Illinois Press, 1962).   But see particularly H. Barnett, 'Innovation:
    The Basis of Cultural Change', pp. 3, 7-9, 16.
50 M.O'C. Drury, 'The Danger of Words' (London: Routledge & Kegan
    Paul, 1973), using as his point of departure Wittgenstein's remark on
    'progress' which is also a starting point for this study.
51 Weber, Science as a Vocation, in 'From Max Weber', pp. 137-40, 155-6.
52 Wittgenstein, 'Tractatus Logico-Philosophicus', 5.631;   5.632;   5.633;
    5.6331.
53 See: Alfred Schutz, The Problem of Rationality in the Social World, in
    'Collected Papers II' (The Hague: Martinus Nijhoff, 1962);   Harold
    Garfinkel, The Rational Properties of Scientific and Commonsense
    Activities, in 'Studies in Ethnomethodology' (Englewood Cliffs, NJ:
    Prentice Hall, 1967);   and H.T. Wilson, Rationality and Decision in
    Administrative Science, 'Canadian Journal of Political Science', vol. 6,
    no. 3 (June 1973), pp. 271-94.   Also see Karl Mannheim, 'Man and
    Society in an Age of Reconstruction', p. 58.
54 Wilson, 'The American Ideology', pp. 200-30, 231-2, 241-8.
55 Wilson, Reading Max Weber, op. cit., pp. 310-11.
56 See generally Mannheim, op. cit., pp. 49-60 on those who benefit sub-
    stantially ('own goals') with increases in functional rationalization, as
    well as the discussion about an alleged equipoise realized in early capi-
    talistic societies between entrepreneurs and 'unattached intellectuals'.
    Compare to Weber, 'Theory of Social and Economic Organization' and
    'From Max Weber' on leadership and the 'chief'.   John Galbraith, in
    'The New Industrial State' (Boston: Houghton Mifflin, 1967), attempts
    to respond to this with his 'dispersion of power' thesis resulting in a
    'techno-structure' of group problem-solvers in the large corporations.
57 This was a major basis of difference on the matter of innovation
    between Gabriel Tarde, 'Laws of Imitation' (Gloucester: Peter Smith,
    1962) and Emile Durkheim, 'The Division of Labour in Society'.   I
    argue that the division of labour ought mainly to be seen as an obstacle
    to real innovation in Innovation: the Practical Uses of Theory, op. cit.
58 For the institutional ramifications of this position given the priority of
    economic considerations, see L.A. Boland, An Institutional Theory of
    Economic Technology and Change, 'Philosophy of the Social Sciences',
    vol. 1, no. 3 (1971), pp. 253-8.
59 The 'division of labour' operating in R & D contexts as a whole linking
    basic research to various applications and to 'development' per se is
    highly relevant here.   See Wilson, Science, Technology and Innovation,
    op. cit.   This is not to argue that ideas are socially (culturally) and
    historically unmediated.   See the discussion at notes 70-2, this chapter,
    for analysis in the light of theoretical materialism.
60 Donald Schon, 'Technology and Change', based to a considerable extent
    on Schon, 'The Displacement of Concepts' (London: Tavistock, 1963).
61 Karl Popper, 'The Open Society and its Enemies', 2 vols (London: Rout-
    ledge & Kegan Paul, 1945), introductory section of Volume 1 on Hera-
    clitus as the 'founding father' of historicism.   Recall Adorno's critique
    of Hegel's 'Heraclitean' transfiguration in 'Negative Dialectics', p. 5.
62 Schon, 'Technology and Change', pp. 3-41, covering his discussion and
    relatively moot distinction between invention and innovation.   In both
    cases, he argues for the 'non-rational view'.
63 Ibid., and Schon, 'The Displacement of Concepts'.

64 See J.O. Wisdom, The Need for Corroboration, 'Technology and Culture', vol. 7 (1966), pp. 367-70, a defence of Popper and the intellectualist approach generally.
65 Compare Schon, 'The Displacement of Concepts' to Mary Hesse, 'Models and Analogies in Science' (Indianapolis: Notre Dame University Press, 1966).
66 Jonathan Bennett, 'Rationality: An Essay Towards Analysis' (London: Routledge & Kegan Paul, 1964), pp. 93-101.
67 Henry George, 'Progress and Poverty (NY, 1926) on the 'seamy' side of progress. Also John Goldthorpe, On the Recrudescence of Historicism and the Future of Futurology, paper presented to the World Congress of Sociology, Varna, Bulgaria, June 1970.
68 Wittgenstein, following Schopenhauer in 'The World as Will and Representation', thus overcomes the subject/object distinction from inside it. Limit is the point beyond which human knowledge can go no further *into* 'the world'.
69 Karl Marx, 'Early Texts', translated and edited by David McClellan (Oxford: Basil Blackwell, 1971).   See Wilson, Knowledge and Totality, chapter 3, Man, Science and Society: the Concept of 'Nature'.
70 See A.V. Miller, 'Hegel's Philosophy of Nature' (Oxford: Basil Blackwell, 1970);   and Alfred Schmidt, 'The Concept of Nature in Marx' (London: New Left Books, 1971).
71 See Kosik, op. cit., pp. 21-2, discussion of Gonseth.
72 Marx, 'Early Texts', pp. 153-5, 169.
73 Marx and Engels, 'The German Ideology' (London: Lawrence & Wishart, 1965).   Also see Wilson, 'The American Ideology', pp. 11-14.
74 I try to deal with this as a feature of all such scientism, whether committed to a 'unified science' concept or a 'distant model' notion such as that propounded by Karl Popper, in Science, Critique and Criticism: The 'Open Society' Revisited, in 'On Critical Theory', edited by John O'Neill (NY: Seabury Press, 1976), pp. 205-30.   Also see 'The American Ideology', pp. 51-74, 101-21.   The idea of nature as a 'world' without man has received a sustained lease on life in the idea of game reserves, sanctuaries, and wilderness areas to be preserved against human intrusion.   See Marnham, op. cit., and William Tucker, Is Nature Too Good for Us?, 'Harpers' (March 1982), pp. 27-35.
75 On the distinction between agency and causation, G.H. Von Wright, 'Explanation and Understanding' (Ithaca, NY: Cornell University Press, 1972), II;   and 'Causality and Determinism' (NY: Columbia University Press, 1974).   On science as a cultural artifact and product, A.L. Kroeber, 'Configurations of Culture Growth' (Berkeley, California: University of California Press, 1944).   On the social sciences in their relation to the natural sciences, Wilson, Knowledge and Totality, chapter 4 and the conclusion to chapter 3.
76 Wilson, Science, Critique and Criticism ..., op. cit.
77 Marx and Engels, 'The German Ideology', generally.
78 See Nicolas Gier, Wittgenstein and Forms of Life, 'Philosophy of the Social Sciences', vol. 10, no. 3 (September, 1980), pp. 241-58.
79 Alan Blum, 'Theorizing' (London: Heinemann, 1974), pp. 230-1.
80 Weber, 'Theory of Social and Economic Organization', pp. 111-12.
81 Ibid., pp. 109-10.
82 Ibid., p. 116.   Compare to his discussion of 'traditional authority' at pp. 341-50.
83 Ibid., p. 116.
84 Greimas, op. cit.
85 Wilson, The Significance of 'Instrumental Rationality' for the Critical Theory of Society, op. cit.
86 Weber, 'Theory of Social and Economic Organization', pp. 101-4.
87 New York, 1953.   Compare to L. and S. Rudolph, 'The Modernity of Tradition' (Chicago: University of Chicago Press, 1967), especially the introduction and part one.
88 On the scheme of contrarieties and contradictories, see Jameson,

op. cit., and Greimas, op. cit.   Weber's self-limitation here fails to
catch the irony of the difference between the phenomenon and its description.   It is Weber's understanding of what is at stake in a description that leads him to state that 'complex' phenomena cannot be
described.   Of course they (and 'simple' phenomena) can!

89 David Goddard, The Concept of Primitive Society, 'Social Research',
    vol. 32, no. 3 (Autumn 1965), pp. 256-76.   Also, Stanley Diamond,
    The Search for the Primitive, in 'Man's Image in Medicine and Anthro-
    pology', edited by Iago Galdston (NY: International Universities
    Press, 1963), pp. 62-115; and 'The Idea of Primitive Man', edited by
    Stanley Diamond (NY: Columbia University Press, 1963), especially
    the introduction and the essay by Goldstein, pp. 1-19.

90 Sigmund Freud, 'Civilization and its Discontents' (Garden City, NY:
    Doubleday Anchor, 1958), originally published in 1938.

91 Talcott Parsons, 'The Evolution of Societies' (Englewood Cliffs, NJ:
    Prentice Hall, 1966);   Parsons, Evolutionary Universals, 'American
    Sociological Review' (June 1964).

92 Max Weber, 'Methodology of the Social Sciences' (Chicago: Free Press,
    1949), pp. 33-6 at p. 34.

93 A similar point of view informs Karl Popper's view of man as the
    supreme problem-solver at the top of the evolutionary ladder, with
    science his supreme accomplishment.   See Popper, 'Objective Know-
    ledge' (London: Oxford University Press, 1972); and Wilson, 'The
    American Ideology', pp. 84-6, 101-3.   Also see Goldthorpe, op. cit.

94 Durkheim, op. cit.

95 Goddard, op. cit., pp. 260-1.

96 See Wilson, Science, Technology and Innovation, op. cit.

97 Thus the problem of the stranger becoming the 'insider' and the norm
    rather than the exception, discussed in Wilson, 'The American Ideol-
    ogy', pp. 185-8.   Also, the idea that the 'primary' group becomes
    secondary in all but name.

98 See particularly Robin Horton, African Traditional Thought and West-
    ern Science, in 'Rationality', edited by Bryan Wilson (Oxford: Basil
    Blackwell, 1970), pp. 131-71.

99 See note 1, this chapter.   Peter Winch, 'The Idea of a Social Science'
    (London: Routledge & Kegan Paul, 1958);   and The Idea of a Social
    Science and Understanding a Primitive Society, both in 'Rationality',
    pp. 1-17, 78-111.   Compare to Ludwig Wittgenstein, Bemerkungen
    über Frazers 'Golden Bough', edited with a note by Rush Rhees,
    'Synthese', vol. 17 (1967), pp. 233-53.

100 Bourdieu, op. cit.   See Allan Berger, Structural and Eclectic Revi-
    sions of Marxist Strategy: A Cultural Materialist Critique, 'Current
    Anthropology', vol. 17, no. 2 (June 1976), pp. 290-6;   Comments, pp.
    296-301;   and Reply, pp. 301-5;   and Judith Ennew, The Material of
    Reproduction: Anthropological Views on Historical Materialism and Kin-
    ship (review essay), 'Economy and Society', vol. 8, no. 1 (February
    1979), pp. 99-124.

CHAPTER 5 CULTURE: INSTITUTIONS AND IDEOLOGIES

1 Max Weber, 'The Protestant Ethic and the Spirit of Capitalism' (NY:
   Scribners, 1952);   'Theory of Social and Economic Organization'
   (Chicago: Free Press, 1947);   'From Max Weber' (NY: Oxford
   Press, 1946);   'Methodology of the Social Sciences' (Chicago: Free
   Press, 1949);   and 'Law in Economy and Society' (Cambridge, Mass.:
   Harvard University Press, 1954).   For commentary, H.T. Wilson,
   'Reading Max Weber: the Limits of Sociology, 'Sociology', vol. 10,
   no. 2 (May 1976), pp. 297-315.

2 Ludwig Wittgenstein, Remarks on Frazer's 'Golden Bough', 'The Human
   World', vol. 3 (1971), pp. 18-41, published originally in German in
   'Synthese', vol. 17 (1967), pp. 233-53.

3 Ibid., p. 30.
4 Ibid. See Richard H. Bell, Wittgenstein and Descriptive Theology, and Understanding the Fire Festivals, both in 'Religious Studies', vol. 5 (1969), pp. 1-18 and vol. 14 (1978), pp. 113-24 respectively.
5 Donald Schon, 'The Displacement of Concepts' (London: Tavistock, 1963); Gabriel Tarde, 'Laws of Imitation' (Gloucester: Peter Smith, 1962), originally published in 1903; H. Barnett, 'Innovation: the Basis of Cultural Change' (NY: McGraw Hill, 1953); H.T. Wilson, Innovation: the Practical Uses of Theory, in 'Social Change, Innovation and Politics in East Asia', edited by Y.S. Yim, H.T. Wilson, and R.W. Wilson (Hong Kong: Asian Research Institute, 1980), pp. 9-29.
6 Wittgenstein, op. cit., p. 30.
7 Ibid., p. 35.
8 See William Leiss, 'The Domination of Nature' (Boston: Beacon Press, 1974).
9 Emile Durkheim, 'The Division of Labour in Society' (NY: Macmillan, 1952).
10 John Galbraith, 'The New Industrial State' (Boston: Houghton Mifflin, 1967); H.T. Wilson, The Dismal Science of Organization Reconsidered, 'Canadian Public Administration', vol. 14, no. 1 (Spring 1971), pp. 82-99.
11 H.T. Wilson, 'The American Ideology' (London: Routledge & Kegan Paul, 1977), chapters 7, 8 and 9; Charles Perrow, 'Complex Organizations' (NY: Scott Foresman, 1972), chapter 1, Why Bureaucracy?, pp. 1-60. Also see H.T. Wilson, Technocracy and Late Capitalist Society: Reflections on the Problem of Rationality and Social Organization, in 'The State, Class, and the Recession', edited by Stewart Clegg et al. (London: Croom Helm, 1983), pp. 152-238.
12 See chapter 2, and Wilson, 'The American Ideology', chapter 9.
13 Donald Schon, 'Technology and Change' (NY: Delat Books, 1967), pp. 1-3. Compare to Schon, 'Beyond the Stable State' (NY: Norton, 1971), pp. 80-115. One could make a strong case for a *greater* likelihood of a fusion between the event and its recognition in early capitalist development than today.
14 Wilson, Innovation: the Practical Uses of Theory, op. cit. Also Boland, op. cit., on the crucial distinction between innovations in production *processes* and in the goods and services they 'produce'.
15 This distinction is employed in the concluding section of this chapter. See especially Ludwig Wittgenstein, 'Philosophical Investigations' (NY: Macmillan, 1953), nos 19, 23, 174, 226, 241; and the excellent interpretative essay by Nicolas Gier, Wittgenstein and Forms of Life, 'Philosophy of the Social Sciences', vol. 10, no. 3 (September 1980), pp. 241-58.
16 S.C. Gilfillan, 'The Sociology of Invention. An Essay in the Social Causes, Ways and Effects of Technic Invention' (Cambridge, Mass.: MIT Press, 1935). Compare to David Noble, 'America by Design' (NY: Oxford University Press, 1977), who dates large-scale R & D in certain industries from the turn of the century or the First World War.
17 Schon, 'Technology and Change', pp. 1-41.
18 Gilfillan, op. cit., pp. 157-8.
19 Compare this emphasis on *economic* dislocation to Barnett, op. cit., pp. 291-410, where he discusses 'acceptance and rejection'.
20 See the broad definitions formulated by the Science Council of Canada in the following: Report no. 15, October 1971; Special Study no. 22, December 1971; Special Study no. 23, October 1972.
21 H.T. Wilson, Science, Technology and Innovation: the Role of Commonsense Capacities, 'Methodology and Science', vol. 15, no. 3 (1982), pp. 167-200.
22 Jane Jacobs, 'The Economy of Cities' (NY: Random House, 1969); Wilson, Innovation: the Practical Uses of Theory, op. cit.
23 H.T. Wilson, Attitudes toward Science: Canadian and American Scientists, 'International Journal of Comparative Sociology', vol. 18, nos 1

and 2 (March/June 1977), pp. 154-75, reprinted in 'Cross National Perspectives: United States and Canada', edited by Robert Presthus (Leiden: E.I. Brill, 1977). Also see Wilson, Science, Technology and Innovation, op. cit.

24 Schon, 'Technology and Change', p. 1. None of this, of course, is to say that invention no longer exists. On the contrary. It is rather our understanding of what the term means today, in contrast to its meaning a century ago, that I am addressing here. My point is made unambiguously when we consider the differing notion of invention held by historians on the one hand and scientists, technologists, and engineers on the other. This difference is evident in the answers given to the following questions by the first and second groups respectively.

	Historians	Scientists, technologists, engineers
Who invents?	an individual	a group or sub-organizational unit
What is an invention?	an artifact	a product or process
How is it developed?	capital from banks	organizationally, by ownership or purchase
How dependent is it on science?	not directly dependent	often very dependent
Where do inventions take place?	home or private laboratory	R & D sub-units of large organizations
How relevant is patent protection for the inventor?	very relevant, however weak	far less relevant, given employee status

A final point relates to the assumption, made by the standard (Schumpeter) model, that invention leads to innovation, and on into diffusion and therefore underwrites economic growth and more invention, etc. as a consequence. This may not hold for certain industries or certain countries, where custom rather than mass-production industry underscores the country's satellite status relative to others for whom the standard model may be more appropriate, though even in this case too linear-sequential unless time-bound and industry-specific. My argument, even in this instance, however, is that such a model ignores the feedback effect of invention, etc. on subsequent invention given capital (and social) sunk costs. See Wilson, Science, Technology and Innovation, op. cit. Also see Joseph Schumpeter, 'Business Cycles - A Theoretical, Historical and Statistical Analysis of the Capitalist Process' (NY: McGraw Hill, 1939); and R.T. Naylor, 'The History of Canadian Business', 2 vols (Toronto: Lorimer, 1975).

25 Schon, 'Beyond the Stable State', pp. 80-115. Galbraith made a similar appeal to the 'educational and scientific estate' four years earlier in 'The New Industrial State' (Boston: Houghton Mifflin, 1967).

26 Schon, 'Technology and Change', p. xiii. Compare to Durkheim's optimistic assessment of the 'enfeeblement' of the collective conscience in 'The Division of Labour in Society', pp. 364-5.

27 Karl Mannheim, 'Man and Society in an Age of Reconstruction' (London: Routledge & Kegan Paul, 1940), pp. 49-60 at p. 58.

28 In 'Technology and Change', Schon lists the three industrial revolutions in note 1, chapter 1, p. 233. Note the parallel between the 'stable state' straw man and the earlier argument against the 'rational' view of innovation in 'Technology and Change'.

29 See 'A World Divided', edited by G.K. Helleiner (Cambridge: Cambridge University Press, 1976).

30 Schumpeter, op. cit.: Gilfillan, op. cit.; William F. Ogburn, 'Social

Change' (Boston: Huebsch, 1922), and 'Culture and Social Change'
(Chicago: University of Chicago, 1964), particularly nos 1, 2, 5, 6,
11, 12, 23 and 25.   See Schon, 'Technology and Change', note 6,
chapter 1, p. 235.

31 Thus, Mannheim may well have been off the mark when he argued that
only those at the top of the process gain 'substantially' from 'increases
in functional rationalization'.   See Mannheim, op. cit., pp. 55-60 at
p. 58.

32 On managerial ideology: Victor Thompson, 'Modern Organization' (NY:
Alfred Knopf, 1961), chapter on Ideology;   Alvin Gouldner, 'Patterns
of Leadership' (NY, 1956);   and Charles Perrow, 'Complex Organizations', pp. 61-95.

33 Jacques Ellul, 'The Technological Society' (NY: Vintage, 1964);   Ellul,
Ideas of Technology, in 'The Technological Order', edited by Carl
Stover (Detroit: Wayne State University Press, 1963);   Ellul, 'The Tech-
nological System' (NY: Continuum Books, 1980).   For commentary,
H.T. Wilson, The Sociology of Apocalypse, 'Human Context', vol. 7,
no. 3 (Autumn 1975), pp. 474-94.

34 See the discussion under Limits of the Technical Bias in Chapter 2.
Also note Gilfillan's concern for the 'hurt-bearing impact' of *necessary*
inventions at op. cit., p. 158.

35 Ludwig Wittgenstein, 'Tractatus Logico-Philosophicus' (London: Routledge & Kegan Paul, 1961), 6.4321, 6.5, 6.51, 6.52.   See Chapter 1,
this study.   Also note how this vindicates Wittgenstein's observation,
cited at note 3, this chapter, as well as Ellul's point about the excess
of means over ends in 'The Technological Society', pp. 19-20, 29, 41-3,
59-79.

36 See H.T. Wilson, 'The American Ideology', chapters 2 and 6.

37 In this regard, see James Q. Wilson, Innovation in Organization: Notes
toward a Theory, in 'Approaches to Organizational Design', edited by
James Thompson (NY: John Wiley, 1966), pp. 194-218.

38 Abraham Edel, The Concept of Levels in Social Theory, in 'Symposium
on Sociological Theory', edited by Llewelyn Gross (NY: Macmillan, 1959),
pp. 167-93.

39 Orville Brim and Stanton Wheeler, 'Socialization after Childhood: Two
Essays' (NY: John Wiley, 1966);   John Findlay Scott, 'The Internalization of Norms' (Englewood Cliffs, NJ: Prentice Hall, 1973).

40 Jurgen Habermas, Aspects of the Rationality of Action, in 'Rationality
Today', edited by Theodore Geraets (Ottawa: University of Ottawa
Press, 1979), pp. 185-212.   The insufficiency of the dichotomy between
substantial and functional rationality in Mannheim, op. cit., is well
illustrated by Habermas's effort.

41 The impact of this at the organizational/social level of analysis must be
clear.   The dichotomy between the individual and society is shown to
be relevant mainly as a topic.

42 Galbraith, op. cit., chapters 5 and 6;   Schon, 'Beyond the Stable
State'.

43 Wilson, 'The American Ideology', chapter 6.   Thus the 'normal' rate of
importing new *commonsense* knowledge through employment is seen to be
insufficient.   R & D speaks to the need to do *more* than simply import
specialists into the organization from the 'outside'.

44 NY: Alfred Knopf, 1961.   Also see Victor Thompson, 'Bureaucracy and
Innovation' (University, Alabama: University of Alabama Press, 1968).

45 A useful schema is provided by Charles Perrow, A Framework for the
Comparative Analysis of Organizations, 'American Sociological Review',
vol. 32 (1967), pp. 194-208.   Also see Perrow, Organizational Analysis:
A Sociological View' (Belmont, California: Wadsworth Publishing Co.,
1970).

46 Max Weber, 'Methodology of the Social Sciences', pp. 33-6;   M.O'C.
Drury, 'The Danger of Words' (London: Routledge & Kegan Paul, 1973),
pp. ix-x.

47 See Wilson, Science, Technology and Innovation: the Role of Common-

sense Capacities, op. cit.   Again note how this correlates with Barnett's analysis of 'acceptance and rejection' at op. cit.
48 Michel Crozier, 'The Bureaucratic Phenomenon' (Chicago: University of
Chicago Press, 1964), pp. 299-300.
49 Victor Thompson, 'Modern Organization', chapter 2, Specialization.
Compare to H.T. Wilson, Technocracy and Late Capitalist Society. Reflections on the Problem of Rationality and Social Organization,
in 'The State, Class, and the Recession', edited by Stewart Clegg,
et al. (London: Croom Helm, 1983), pp. 152-238.
50 Perrow's discussion of the 'transformation of raw materials' by organizations would seem to apply as much to the employees as to inert
material.   See Perrow, 'Organizational Analysis', where he appears to
recognize this.   Also Wilson, Technocracy and Late Capitalist
Society, op. cit.
51 This more dynamic focus is probably needed to provide a supplement to
Habermas, Aspects of the Rationality of Action, op. cit.   The question
is always the *direction* from which pressure comes to rationalize activities and thoughts, and the element of reciprocity and interdependence
present or emerging.
52 This point is developed by Thomas Schelling, in On the Ecology of
Micromotives, 'The Public Interest', no. 25 (Fall 1971), pp. 59-98,
where he criticizes some of the incrementalist presumptions implicit in
social planning theories.
53 See Karl Loewith, Max Weber's Interpretation of the Bourgeois-Capitalistic World in terms of the Guiding Principle of Rationalization, in 'Max
Weber', edited by Dennis Wrong (Englewood Cliffs, NJ: Prentice Hall,
1970), pp. 101-22.   The statement is a somewhat modified version of
what appears in Weber, 'The Protestant Ethic and the Spirit of Capitalism', p. 182.
54 Compare this to the claims of Jurgen Habermas in 'Legitimation Crisis'
(Boston: Beacon Press, 1976).   It is important to see capital allocation
decisions by economic and political actors and organizations, both
singly and in the aggregate, as cultural versions of the phenomenon of
acceptance and rejection discussed with reference to 'non-Western'
cultures by Barnett and Bourdieu.   The issue then becomes the extent
to which these actors and organizations have come to monopolize technical invention, innovation, and diffusion, and perhaps even scientific
discovery itself, in their determination to influence, and ideally to
govern, the pace and character of R & D activities and technological
outcomes.   In this regard see Wilson, Attitudes toward Science, 'International Journal of Comparative Sociology', vol. 18, nos 1 and 2 (March-
June 1977), pp. 154-75; Innovation: the Practical Uses of Theory, op.
cit.; and Science, Technology and Innovation, op. cit.
55 Mannheim, op. cit., pp. 49-60; and Wilson, 'The American Ideology',
pp. 245-8.
56 Weber, 'Methodology of the Social Sciences', p. 34.
57 Loewith, op. cit.; Wilson, Reading Max Weber, op. cit.; Durkheim,
op. cit.
58 Edel, op. cit.   See the discussion of 'complexity' and 'differentiation'
as it relates to 'primitive society' in chapter IV.
59 Weber's ambiguity is to be discovered in his tendency to 'fall into' the
world of technical rationality to which sociology, thus Weber as sociologist, is subject.
60 Weber, 'Methodology of the Social Sciences', p. 35.   Compare Weber's
definition of technique to that of Ellul in 'The Technological Society'
forty years later.   Both are discussed in Wilson, The Sociology of
Apocalypse, op. cit.
61 Weber, 'Theory of Social and Economic Organization', pp. 324-9, 124-32.
62 Ibid., pp. 209-10.   See Wilson, Reading Max Weber, op. cit.   Compare to Thorstein Veblen's position in 'The Theory of Business Enterprise' (Boston: Huebsch, 1904) and 'The Engineers and the Price
System' (Boston: Huebsch, 1921).

63 See Anton Zijderveld, 'The Abstract Society' (Garden City, NY: Doubleday, 1970); and R.K. Crook, Modernization and Nostalgia: Notes on the Sociology of Pessimism, 'Queens Quarterly', vol. 73 (Winter 1965-6), pp. 269-84.

64 H.T. Wilson, The Significance of 'Instrumental Rationality' for the Critical Theory of Society (unpublished paper).

65 Loewith, op. cit.; Wilson, Reading Max Weber, op. cit.   See especially Weber, 'Methodology of the Social Sciences', p. 72 for his understanding of sociology as an 'empirical discipline'.

66 Barnett, op. cit.   See Herbert Marcuse, 'One Dimensional Man' (Boston: Beacon Press, 1964), for the most clearsighted formulation of this idea.

67 Wilson, 'The American Ideology', chapter 9.   This organization of innovation and its effects (no *real* exceptions - *vide* Perrow) is what Weber really means by rationalization and resulting world de-enchantment.   See Weber, 'From Max Weber', pp. 137-40.

68 Loewith, op. cit.

69 Though my approach is indebted to that of Frederic Jameson, in The Vanishing Mediator: Narrative Structure in Max Weber, 'New German Critique', vol. 1 (1973), pp. 52-89, it is somewhat different.   Jameson bases his analysis on the work of A.J. Greimas and F. Rastier, The Interaction of Semiotic Constraints, 'Yale French Studies', no. 41 (Spring 1968), pp. 86-105.   For mine, see H.T. Wilson, Reading Max Weber, op. cit.

70 Weber, 'Theory of Social and Economic Organization', pp. 87-123.

71 See ibid., pp. 24-6, where Talcott Parsons, the editor, discusses Weber on institutionalization and change.   Note how such an understanding of change fails to take account of the impact of these 'individual' acts on their recipients *in advanced industrial societies*!

72 On determinism in Weber, see Gabriel Kolko, A Critique of Max Weber's Philosophy of History, 'Ethics', vol. 70, no. 1 (October 1959), pp. 21-36; Reinhard Bendix, 'Max Weber, An Intellectual Portrait' (Garden City, NY: Doubleday, 1960); Talcott Parsons, 'The Structure of Social Action' (Chicago: Free Press, 1937), part II.

73 Shmuel Eisenstadt, 'Essays on Comparative Institutions' (NY: John Wiley, 1965).

74 Alan Blum, 'Theorizing' (London: Heinemann, 1974), pp. 230-1.

75 Ludwig Wittgenstein, Remarks on Frazer's 'Golden Bough', op. cit., p. 35.

76 Krishan Kumar, Revolution and Industrial Society, 'Sociology', vol. 10, no. 2 (May 1976), pp. 245-69; Wilson, Reading Max Weber, op. cit.

77 Weber, 'Theory of Social and Economic Organization', pp. 117-18, 92-3; 'Methodology of the Social Sciences', pp. 41-3, 89-112.

78 Weber, 'Theory of Social and Economic Organization', pp. 329-41, 363-92; Weber, 'Law in Economy and Society' (Cambridge, Mass: Harvard University Press, 1954).   On the *difference* between organised structures built up out of each of the two processes, see Helen Constas, Max Weber's Two Concepts of Bureaucracy, 'American Journal of Sociology', vol. 52 (1958), pp. 400-9

79 Jurgen Habermas, 'Legitimation Crisis'.

80 Weber, 'Theory of Social and Economic Organization', p. 152.   This was later to become a central element in the highly influential, though independently conceived, organization theory of Chester Barnard, 'The Functions of the Executive' (Cambridge, Mass.: Harvard University Press, 1938).

81 Ibid., p. 146.   To be sure, Weber's tendency to reify collectives as 'structures', and his consequent pessimism, clearly contradict this,

82 See Loewith, op. cit.; and Wilson, Reading Max Weber, op. cit.

83 Weber, 'Theory of Social and Economic Organization', pp. 124-32, 324-9. Weber, 'From Max Weber', pp. 77-81.

84 See Loewith's discussions of Weber's association of the unique with that which is most 'worthy of being known' in op. cit., pp. 100-1.

85 Parsons, op. cit., and Habermas, in Aspects of the Rationality of Action, op. cit., spend little time dealing with levels of routinization, preferring to focus on levels of rationality. The first notion favours institution and institutionalization, the second system and change. Victor Thompson thinks that charisma is simply a property of those without knowledge in 'Modern Organization', and Weber seems occasionally to agree with this. Crozier views charisma as discretion in 'The Bureaucratic Phenomenon'.

86 Wilson, Science, Technology and Innovation, op. cit. Wittgenstein addresses this distinction in Remarks on Frazer's 'Golden Bough', op. cit.

87 One ironic aspect of Weber's work is the way it displays both the fact and the consequences of what it means when only facts and what Veblen called 'matter of factness' have 'value' in and for a given culture as civilization. See Thorstein Veblen, The Place of Science in Modern Civilization, 'American Journal of Sociology', vol. 11 (1906), pp. 585-609.

88 Weber, 'Theory of Social and Economic Organization', pp. 115-16, 341-58.

89 Ibid., p. 116, discussing principled (*wertrational*) action.

90 Ibid., p. 117.

91 Thus the full consequences of a sociology based completely on bourgeois negative individualism. See note no. 50, discussing Weber's 'sociology of scarcity' based on economics as the paragon social science in Wilson, Reading Max Weber, op. cit.

92 Compare 'Theory of Social and Economic Organization', pp. 329-41 and 'From Max Weber', pp. 196-244, to the more legal-judicial and less bureaucratic approach to legalism and constitutionalism in 'Law and Economy and Society'.

93 Compare Weber's emphasis on rationalization and de-enchantment in 'The Protestant Ethic and the Spirit of Capitalism' and in 'From Max Weber', pp. 128-56 to Theodor Adorno, Society, in 'The Legacy of the German Refugee Intellectuals', edited by Robert Boyers (NY: Shocken Books, 1969), pp. 144-53.

94 The discussion of behaviour-cum-action is found at pp. 115-18, while that on authority types and bases of legitimacy is found at pp. 324-9. This may of course be accounted for by the way the book was put together after Weber's death, but it does nevertheless seem to follow from his view of the concrete individual and groups built up out of them.

95 Weber, 'Theory of Social and Economic Organization', pp. 358-63. Note how the four types of behaviour-cum-action translate into three types of authority with the fusion of value-rationality or principle and either charisma ('dysfunctional' principles) or legal rationality ('functional' principles).

96 Emile Durkheim, op. cit. Note also how the man-induced character of technical rationality correlates with change where the agent is the 'cause'. Compare to Von Wright's distinction between action and causality at op. cit.

97 See Corinne Gilb, 'Hidden Hierarchies' (NY: Harcourt Brace, 1966), particularly the last chapter, The Status Society.

98 Compare 'Theory of Social and Economic Organization', pp. 363-86 on 'the routinization of charisma' to pp. 386-92 'the transformation of charisma in an anti-authoritarian direction'.

99 On the difference between an ethics of responsibility and one of ultimate ends in politics, see Weber, 'From Max Weber', pp. 77-128 at pp. 117-28. On conferral and acceptance, see Barnard, op. cit., particularly his discussion of authority and communication.

100 On an understanding of 'objectivity' consonant with theoretical materialism, see Theodor Adorno, 'Negative Dialectics' (NY: Seabury Press, 1973); and H.T. Wilson, Knowledge and Totality.

101 See the sections of 'Philosophical Investigations' cited in note 15, plus the following: nos 25 and 415.

102 This is discussed in Nicolas Gier, op. cit.   See note 15.   Note that
     Wittgenstein treats *both* the first and second meanings of progress in
     Weber as 'developmental' hypotheses, rather than only the second like
     Weber.
103 Wittgenstein, 'Tractatus Logico-Philosophicus', 6.4-7, especially 6.421.
104 Gier, op. cit., p. 247.
105 Ibid., pp. 244-5.   See Norman Malcolm, 'Knowledge and Certainty:
     Essays and Lectures' (Englewood Cliffs, NJ: Prentice Hall, 1963).
106 Gier, op. cit., p. 248.   See Wittgenstein, 'On Colour' (Oxford:
     Blackwell, 1977).
107 See M.O'C. Drury, op. cit., particularly pp. 57-96 at pp. 60-72.
     Also note the parallel to Marx's discussion of sense-making and
     sensuous need discussed in Chapter 4.
108 Wittgenstein, Remarks on Frazer's 'Golden Bough', op. cit., pp. 31-3.
109 Ibid., pp. 30, 37.   Compare to Thorstein Veblen, The Place of Sci-
     ence in Modern Civilization, 'American Journal of Sociology', vol. 11,
     no. 5 (March 1906), pp. 585-609, who takes the same argument to
     radically different conclusions.
110 Ibid., p. 35.
111 Gier, op. cit., p. 250.   See Wittgenstein, 'Philosophical Investiga-
     tions', p. 223.
112 Wittgenstein, Remarks on Frazer's 'Golden Bough', op. cit., p. 35.
113 See Mary Midgely, 'Beast and Man: The Roots of Human Nature'
     (London: Methuen, 1979) for an excellent discussion of many of the
     issues raised here.

CHAPTER 6   SUMMARY AND CONCLUSIONS

1 M.O'C. Drury, 'The Danger of Words' (London: Routledge & Kegan
   Paul, 1973), p. ix.
2 Ludwig Wittgenstein, 'Tractatus Logico-Philosophicus', edited by
   D. Pears and B. McGuinness with the introduction to the first
   English translation of 1922 by Bertrand Russell (London: Routledge &
   Kegan Paul, 1961), 6.51.
3 See Hannah Arendt, 'The Human Condition' (Chicago: University of
   Chicago Press, 1958), particularly all references to society as an
   'artificial realm' of labourers and consumers.   For a critique, H.T.
   Wilson, 'The American Ideology' (London: Routledge & Kegan Paul,
   1977), pp. 171-81.
4 Wilson, 'The American Ideology', references to social sciences;
   Wilson, The Meaning and Significance of 'Empirical Method' for the
   Critical Theory of Society, 'Canadian Journal of Political and Social
   Theory', vol. 3, no. 3 (Fall 1979), pp. 57-68; Wilson, Anti-Method as
   a Counterstructure in Social Research Operations: Critique as subversion of Established Professional Practices, in 'Beyond Method: A Study
   of Organizational Research Strategies', edited by Gareth Morgan
   (Los Angeles: Sage Publications, 1983).
5 H.T. Wilson, Knowledge and Totality: A Critical Analysis of the
   Causal Principle in Science and Life, particularly chapters 3 and 4.
6 See M.O'C. Drury, op. cit., pp. 57-80.
7 C.K. Ogden and I.A. Richards, 'The Meaning of Meaning' (NY: Harcourt, Brace & World, 1946), originally published in 1922.
8 As argued by Donald Schon, in 'Displacement of Concepts' (London:
   Tavistock, 1963), and Mary Hesse, 'Models and Analogies in Science'
   (Indianapolis: Notre Dame University Press, 1966).
9 H.T. Wilson, Anti-Method as a Counterstructure ..., op. cit.; Functional Rationality and 'Sense of Function': the Case of an Ideological
   Distortion, 'International Yearbook of Organization Studies 1980',
   edited by David Dunkerly and Graeme Salaman (London: Routledge &
   Kegan Paul, 1981).
10 Wittgenstein, 'Tractatus Logico-Philosophicus', 6.54.

11 Cited in Paul Englemann, 'Letters from Ludwig Wittgenstein, with a Memoir' (Oxford: Basil Blackwell, 1967), pp. 143-4.
12 Wilson, Knowledge and Totality, passim.
13 See particularly Nicolas Gier, Wittgenstein and Forms of Life, 'Philosophy of the Social Sciences', vol. 10, no. 3 (September 1980), pp. 241-58.
14 Wittgenstein, Remarks on Frazer's 'Golden Bough', in 'The Human World', vol. 3 (1971), pp. 18-41, published originally in German in 'Synthese', vol. 17 (1967), pp. 233-53; Lecture on Ethics, 'Philosophical Review', vol. 74 (January 1965), pp. 3-12, and the appended discussion by Waismann and Rhees, pp. 12-26.
15 Wittgenstein, 'Tractatus Logico-Philosophicus', 6.342.
16 Wittgenstein, Remarks on Frazer's 'Golden Bough', p. 37.   On science v. magic, also see Paul Feyerabend, 'Against Method' (London: New Left Books, 1975).
17 See particularly Collingwood's conclusion to his 'The Idea of History' (NY: Galaxy, 1956).
18 Thus what 'makes an impression' on Frazer is really what remains beyond the reach of an explanation, even as we feel (form of life) *satisfied* by its (re) arrangement of what we already know.   Also, what remains of an enigma when we feel we have resolved it?   Do we feel that something is missing?   My contention here is that to the extent we do not, our form of life is historically problematic.   Also note Wittgenstein's refusal to embrace reason and rationality as problematics, following Schopenhauer in 'The World as Will and Representation'. Thus feelings are not 'inside', 'subjective', and 'irrational' as they are for Weber.   For Wittgenstein the rationality question is a non-starter. As for 'facts of life', these are the basis of descriptions which have the status of *opinions* rather than certainties for Wittgenstein.   See particularly 'On Certainty' (Oxford: Basil Blackwell, 1977).   Also see M.O'C. Drury's devastating criticism of J.C. Eccles in op. cit., pp. 57-96.
19 We may respond indignantly to such an accusation, but reflection compels us to admit its truth.   Emphasis on origins, however innocuous, tends to favour the idea of a beginning as the result of some sort of conscious decision or act.   Think of the way we construe the notion of the 'spontaneous': as something random, inchoate, incomprehensible given the kind of bias revealed by our commitment to rational mastery. What could happen to a 'festival' that we invented?   It could 'fail' to take root, or it could succeed.   But what would the latter outcome really tell us about the feasibility of invention vis à vis what we couldn't explain (or reach by explanatory means) as a way of bringing festivals into being?   Again, what do we lose when we 'make sense' of some religious or magical practice, gesture, or observance not 'familiar' to us?   See Wittgenstein, Remarks ..., op. cit., p. 30, about why an explanation is bound to be wrong *because it is satisfying*!   Also Norman Malcolm, 'Ludwig Wittgenstein: A Memoir', with a biographical sketch by G.H. Von Wright (London: Oxford, 1958), p. 47.
20 George Spencer-Brown, 'Laws of Form' (London: Allen & Unwin, 1969), p. 126.   The question here is whether *even if they were taken to be hypotheses* they could avoid being part of our form of life.   The parallel, of course, is to Weber's 'ideal types', which allegedly 'represent' hypothetically what they cannot 'really' capture in and through descriptions.
21 Wilson, 'The American Ideology', especially chapters 2, 5, and 9. Compare this proliferation to the one noted by Ellul regarding the excess of means over ends in 'The Technological Society'.
22 H. Barnett, 'Innovation: The Basis of Cultural Change' (NY: McGraw Hill, 1953), pp. 291-410, part IV Acceptance and Rejection.
23 Wittgenstein, Remarks ..., op. cit., pp. 29-30, where he shows how central our commitment to origins and *causality* is in our efforts to give 'good reasons' for such practices, as if they would then make

sense *if we were doing them in our 'own culture'.* Thus: 'where [a]
practice and [certain] views go together, the practice does not spring
from the view, but both of them are there.' Also, note pp. 30 and 31,
where reference is made to the expression of feelings as the non-instru-
mental 'reason' for such practices and observances, and how our patina
of rationality on these matters does not, after all, get around our own
need, in common with such 'primitives', to express needs and feelings
without any reference to an external end, goal or objective. 'Baptism
as washing. - There is a mistake only if magic is presented as science.'

24 Thus the idea of structurally decomposed theory in the form of 'hypotheses' which are either testable - verifiable (Ayer) or testable - falsifiable (Popper) is revealed for what it really is. See Karl Popper,
'Logic of Scientific Discovery' (London: Routledge & Kegan Paul, 1957).
On 'protocols' as a way of seeing such research practices in all sciences,
Felix Kaufmann, 'Methodology of the Social Sciences' (NY: Oxford University Press, 1944). On the social sciences in particular, H.T.
Wilson, The Meaning and Significance of 'Empirical Method' for the Critical Theory of Society, 'Canadian Journal of Political and Social Theory',
vol. 3, no. 3 (Fall 1979), pp. 57-68.

26 Wilson, Knowledge and Totality, chapter 5. See also Ludwig Wittgenstein, 'Lectures and Conversations on Aesthetics, Psychology and Religious Belief' (Berkeley: University of California Press, 1972), pp. 41-
52; and Sigmund Freud, 'Civilization and its Discontents' (Garden City,
NY: Doubleday Anchor, 1958).

27 On 'interestingness' as a criterion v. truth in theorizing, Murray
Davis, That's Interesting!, 'Philosophy of the Social Sciences', vol. 1
(1971). For a critique of psychoanalytic theory applied to Weber,
H.T. Wilson, Max Weber's Pessimism, 'International Journal of Contemporary Sociology', vol. 8 (April 1971), pp. 183-8.

28 Freud, 'Totem and Taboo' (London: Hogarth, 1934).

29 See Engelmann, op. cit., pp. 143-4, reference to 'saying' and 'gassing'
in the letter to Ficker. The crucial point here, of course, is that
such understanding *shows* that it knows that the thought-action distinction is false at its core.

30 Wittgenstein, 'Philosophical Investigations' (NY: Macmillan, 1953), no.
217.

31 Thus the real 'dead-end' in Weber's work is *the way* tradition is
allowed to survive as an alternative to the 'iron cage' of 'petrified'
rationality.

32 See Habermas, Aspects of the Rationality of Action, op. cit.: Edel,
op. cit.

BIBLIOGRAPHY

ADAMS, Brooks, 'The Law of Civilization and Decay' (NY: Vintage Books, 1955).

ADORNO, Theodor W., 'Prisms' (London: Neville Spearman, 1967).

ADORNO, Theodor W., Scientific experiences of a European scholar in America, in 'The Intellectual Migration: Europe and America, 1930-1960', edited by D. Fleming and B. Bailyn (Cambridge, Mass.: Belknap Press, 1968), pp. 338-70.

ADORNO, Theodor W., Society, in 'The Legacy of the German Refugee Intellectuals', edited by Robert Boyers (NY: Schocken Books, 1969), pp. 144-53.

ADORNO, Theodor W., 'Negative Dialectics' (NY: Seabury Press, 1973).

ADORNO et al., Theodor W., 'The Positivist Dispute in German Sociology', translated by Glyn Adey and David Frisby (London: Heinemann, 1976).

APEL, Karl-Otto, 'Towards a Transformation of Philosophy' (London: Routledge & Kegan Paul, 1980).

ARENDT, Hannah, 'The Human Condition' (Chicago: University of Chicago Press, 1958).

ARENDT Hannah, 'Between Past and Future' (NY: Viking Press, 1968).

ARON, Raymond, 'Eighteen Lectures on Industrial Society' (London: Weidenfeld & Nicolson, 1967).

ARON, Raymond, 'The Industrial Society: Three Essays on Ideology and Development' (NY: Frederick Praeger, 1967).

ARON, Raymond, 'Progress and Disillusion' (NY: Praeger, 1968).

AYRES, Clarence E., 'Toward a Reasonable Society' (Austin: University of Texas Press, 1961).

AYRES, Clarence E., 'The Theory of Economic Progress' (Kalamazoo: New Issues Press, 1978).

BAILLIE, John, 'The Belief in Progress' (London: Oxford University Press, 1951).

BANFIELD, Edwin, 'The Moral Basis of a Backward Society' (Chicago: Free Press, 1958).

BARNARD, Chester, 'The Functions of the Executive' (Cambridge, Mass.: Harvard University Press, 1938).

BARNETT, H., 'Innovation: The Basis of Cultural Change' (NY: McGraw Hill, 1953).

BARRETT, William, 'The Illusion of Technique, The Search for Meaning in a Technological Civilization' (Garden City, NY: Doubleday Anchor, 1979).

BAUMAN, Zygmunt, 'Towards a Critical Sociology' (London: Routledge & Kegan Paul, 1976).

BECKER, Carl L., 'The Heavenly City of the Eighteenth Century Philosophers' (New Haven: Yale University Press, 1932).

BELL, Richard H., Wittgenstein & descriptive theology, 'Religious Studies', vol. 5 (1969), pp. 1-18.

BELL, Richard.H., Understanding the fire festivals, 'Religious Studies', vol. 14 (1978), pp. 113-24.

BENDIX, Reinhard, 'Max Weber, An Intellectual Portrait' (Garden City, NY: Doubleday, 1960).

BENNETT, Jonathan, 'Rationality: An Essay.Towards Analysis' (London: Routledge & Kegan Paul, 1964).

BENNIS, Warren, and SLATER, Philip, 'The Temporary Society' (NY: Harper & Row, 1969).

BERGER, Allan, Structural and eclectic revisions of Marxist strategy: A cultural materialist critique, 'Current Anthropology', vol. 17, no. 2 (June 1976), pp. 290-6 (including 'comments' and 'reply').

BERGER, Peter, and PULLBERG, Stanley, Reification and the sociological critique of consciousness, 'History and Theory', vol. 4 (1965), pp. 196-211.

BIERSTEDT, Robert, Nominal and real definitions in sociological theory, in 'Symposium in Sociological Theory', edited by Llewelyn Gross (NY: Macmillan, 1959), pp. 121-44.

BIRNBAUM, Norman, 'The Crisis of Industrial Society' (NY: Oxford University Press, 1969).

BITTNER, Egon, The concept of organization, 'Social Research', vol. 32, no. 3 (Autumn 1965), pp. 239-55.

BLUM, Alan F., 'Theorizing' (London: Heinemann, 1974).

BLUM, Alan F., Criticalness and traditional prejudice, 'Canadian Journal of Sociology', vol. 2, no. 1 (1977), pp. 97-124.

BLUMENBERG, Hans, 'The Legitimacy of the Modern Age' (Cambridge, Mass.: MIT Press, 1983).

BLUMER, Herbert, 'Symbolic Interactionism' (Englewood Cliffs, NJ: Prentice Hall, 1969).

BLUNTSCHLI, J.K., 'The Theory of the State' (Oxford: Clarendon Press, 1892).

BOAS, George, 'The Limits of Reason' (NY: Harper, 1961).

BOLAND, L.A., An institutional theory of economic technology and change, 'Philosophy of the Social Sciences', vol. 1, no. 3 (1971), pp. 253-8.

BOSERUP, Ester, 'Population and Technological Change' (Chicago: University of Chicago Press, 1983).

BOURDIEU, Pierre, 'Outline of a Theory of Practice' (Cambridge: Cambridge University Press, 1977).

BRAUDEL, Fernand, 'Capitalism and Material Life, 1400-1800' (London: Weidenfeld & Nicolson, 1973).

BRIM, Orville, and WHEELER, Stanton, 'Socialization after Childhood: Two Essays' (NY: John Wiley, 1966).

BROWN, George Spencer, 'Laws of Form' (London: George Allen & Unwin, 1969).

BUNGE, Mario, 'Causality and Modern Science', 3rd revised edition (NY: Dover, 1979).

BURTT, E.A. (ed.), 'The English Philosophers from Bacon to Mill' (NY: Modern Library, 1939.

BURY, John B., 'The Idea of Progress' (NY: Macmillan, 1932).

CAHNMAN, Werner, Max Weber and the methodological controversy, in 'Sociology and History', edited by Werner Cahnman and Alan Boskoff (NY: Free Press, 1964), pp. 103-27.

COCH, Lester, and FRENCH, John R.P., Overcoming resistance to change, 'Human Relations', vol. 1 (1948), pp. 512-32.

COHEN, Jean, Max Weber and the dynamics of domination, 'Telos', no. 14 (Winter 1972), pp. 63-86.

COLLINGWOOD, R.G., 'Principles of Art' (London: Oxford University Press, 1937).

COLLINGWOOD, R.G., 'An Essay on Metaphysics' (London: Oxford University Press, 1940).

COLLINGWOOD, R.G., 'The Idea of Nature' (Oxford: Clarendon Press, 1945).

COLLINGWOOD, R.G., 'The Idea of History' (NY: Galaxy, 1956).

COLLINS, Randall, 'The Credential Society: A Historical Sociology of Education and Stratification' (NY: Academic Press, 1979).

CONSTAS, Helen, Max Weber's two concepts of bureaucracy, 'American Journal of Sociology', vol. 52 (1958), pp. 400-9.

CROOK, R.K., Modernization and nostalgia: notes on the sociology of pessimism, 'Queens Quarterly', vol. 73 (Winter 1965-6), pp. 269-84.

CROZIER, Michel, 'The Bureaucratic Phenomenon' (Chicago: University of Chicago Press, 1964).

CROZIER, Michel, 'The Stalled Society' (NY: Viking Press, 1973).
CUDDIHY, John Murray, 'The Ordeal of Civility' (NY: Basic Books, 1974).
CYERT, Richard, and MARCH, James, 'A Behavioural Theory of the Firm' (Englewood Cliffs, NJ: Prentice Hall, 1964).
DAVIS, Murray, That's interesting!, 'Philosophy of the Social Sciences', vol. 1, no. 4 (December 1971), pp. 309-44.
DELBECQ, Andre, VANDEVEN, A.H., and GUSTAVSON, D.H., 'Group Techniques for Programme Planning: A Guide to Nominal Group and Delphi Processes' (Glenview, Illinois: Scott, Foresman, 1975).
DELLA VOLPE, Galvano, 'Logic as a Positive Science' (London: New Left Books, 1980).
DIAMOND, Stanley (ed.), 'The Idea of Primitive Man' (NY: Columbia University Press, 1963).
DIAMOND, Stanley, The search for the primitive, in 'Man's Image in Medicine and Anthropology', edited by Iago Galdston (NY: International Universities Press, 1963), pp. 62-115.
DIESING, Paul, 'Reason in Society' (Urbana, Illinois: University of Illinois Press, 1962).
DREITZEL, H.P., Social science and the problem of rationality, 'Politics & Society', vol. 2, no. 2 (Winter 1972), pp. 165-82.
DRONBERGER, Ilse, 'The Political Thought of Max Weber' (NY: Appleton Century Crofts, 1971).
DRUCKER, Peter, 'The Age of Discontinuity' (NY: Harper & Row, 1968).
DRUCKER, Peter, 'Adventures of a Bystander' (NY: Harper & Row, 1973).
DRURY, M.O'C., 'The Danger of Words' (London: Routledge & Kegan Paul, 1973).
DURKHEIM, Emile, 'The Division of Labour in Society' (NY: Macmillan, 1952).
DURKHEIM, Emile, 'Professional Ethics and Civic Morals' (London: Routledge & Kegan Paul, 1957).
EDDINGTON, Arthur, 'The Philosophy of Physical Science' (Cambridge: Cambridge University Press, 1939).
EDELMAN, Murray, 'The Symbolic Uses of Politics' (Urbana, Illinois: University of Illinois Press, 1964).
EISENSTADT, Shmuel, 'Essays on Comparative Institutions' (NY: John Wiley, 1965).
EISENSTADT, Shmuel, 'The Protestant Ethic and Modernization: A Comparative View' (NY: John Wiley, 1968).
ELIAS, Norbert, 'The Civilizing Process' (NY: Urizen Press, 1978).
ELLUL, Jacques, Ideas of technology, in 'The Technological Order', edited by Carl Stover (Detroit: Wayne State University Press, 1963), pp. 10-37.
ELLUL, Jacques, 'The Technological Society' (NY: Alfred Knopf, 1964).
ELLUL, Jacques, 'The Technological System' (NY: Continuum, 1980).
ELSTER, Jon, 'Logic & Society: Contradictions and Possible Worlds' (Chichester: John Wiley, 1978).
ENGELMANN, Paul, 'Letters from Ludwig Wittgenstein, with a Memoir' (Oxford: Basil Blackwell, 1957).
ENNEW, Judith, The material of reproduction: anthropological views on historical materialism and kinship (review essay), 'Economy and Society', vol. 8, no. 1 (February 1979), pp. 99-124.
FALLDING, Harold, 'The Sociological Task' (Englewood Cliffs, NJ: Prentice Hall, 1968).
FALLDING, Harold, Only one sociology, 'British Journal of Sociology', vol. 23, no. 1 (March 1972), pp. 93-101.
FAUNCE, William, 'Problems of an Industrial Society' (NY: McGraw Hill, 1968).
FEYERABEND, Paul, 'Against Method' (London: New Left Books, 1975).
FLETCHER, Colin, 'The Person in the Sight of Sociology' (London: Routledge & Kegan Paul, 1975).
FOSTER, George M., 'Traditional Societies and Technological Change' (NY: Harper & Row, 1973).
FOUCAULT, Michel, 'The Birth of the Clinic' (NY: Pantheon, 1973).

FOUCAULT, Michel, 'Discipline & Punish' (NY: Random House, 1978).

FRANK, Andre Gunder, 'Capitalism and Underdevelopment in Latin America' (NY: Monthly Review Press, 1967).

FREIRE, Paolo, 'Pedagogy of the Oppressed' (NY: Herder & Herder, 1972).

FREIRE, Paolo, 'Education for Critical Consciousness' (NY: Seabury Press, 1973).

FREUD, Sigmund, 'Totem and Taboo' (London: Hogarth, 1934).

FREUD, Sigmund, 'Civilization and Its Discontents' (Garden City, NY: Doubleday Anchor, 1958).

GALBRAITH, John K., 'The New Industrial State' (Boston: Houghton Mifflin, 1967).

GARDNER, John, 'Self-Renewal: The Individual in the Innovative Society' (NY: Harpers, 1963).

GARFINKEL, Harold, 'Studies in Ethnomethodology' (Englewood Cliffs, NJ: Prentice Hall, 1967).

GEORGE, Henry, 'Progress & Poverty' (Garden City, NY: Doubleday, 1926).

GERAETS, Theodore (ed.), 'Rationality Today' (Ottawa: University of Ottawa Press, 1979).

GERMINO, Dante, Karl Popper's open society, 'Political Science Reviewer' (1979), pp. 21-61.

GHISELIN, Michael T., The individual in the Darwinian revolution, 'New Literary History', vol. 3 (1971-2), pp. 113-34.

GIDDENS, Anthony, Marx, Weber & the development of capitalism, 'Sociology', vol. 4 (1970), pp. 289-310.

GIDDENS, Anthony, 'The Class Structure of the Advanced Societies' (London: Hutchinson, 1973).

GIER, Nicolaus, Wittgenstein and forms of life, 'Philosophy of the Social Sciences', vol. 10, no. 3 (September 1980), pp. 241-58.

GILB, Corinne, 'Hidden Hierarchies' (NY: Harcourt Brace, 1966).

GILFILLAN, S.C., 'The Sociology of Invention' (Cambridge, Mass.: MIT Press, 1935).

GLACKEN, Clarence, 'Traces on the Rhodian Shore: Nature and Culture in Western Thought from Ancient Times to the End of the Eighteenth Century' (Berkeley, Cal.: University of California Press, 1967).

GLACKEN, Clarence, Man against nature: an outmoded concept, in 'The Environmental Crisis', edited by Harold Helfrich (New Haven: Yale University Press, 1970), pp. 127-42.

GODDARD, David, The concept of primitive society, 'Social Research', vol. 32, no. 3 (Autumn 1965), pp. 256-76.

GODELIER, Maurice, 'Rationality and Irrationality in Economics' (NY: New Left Books, 1972).

GOLDTHORPE, John, Theories of industrial society: on the recrudescence of historicism and the future of futurology, paper read at the World Congress of Sociology, Varna, Bulgaria, June 1970.

GOLDTHORPE, John, 'Sociology of the Third World' (NY: Cambridge University Press, 1975).

GOULD, Stephen Jay, 'The Mismeasure of Man' (NY: W.W. Norton, 1981).

GOULDNER, Alvin, Metaphysical pathos and the theory of bureaucracy, 'American Political Science Review', vol. 49 (1955), pp. 496-507.

GOULDNER, Alvin, Anti-Minotaur: the myth of a value-free sociology, in 'Sociology on Trial', edited by Maurice Stein and Arthur Vidich (Englewood Cliffs, NJ: Prentice Hall, 1963).

GOULDNER, Alvin, The sociologist as partisan: sociology and the welfare state, 'American Sociologist', vol. 3, no. 2 (May 1968), pp. 103-16.

GOULDNER, Alvin, 'For Sociology: Research & Critique in Sociology Today' (London: Allen Lane, 1973).

GOULDNER, Alvin, 'The Dialectic of Ideology and Technology' (NY: Seabury Press, 1976).

GOULET, Denis, 'The Cruel Choice' (NY: Athenaeum, 1971).

GREEN, Martin, 'The Von Richtofen Sisters' (NY: Basic Books, 1974).

GREEN, Peter, 'Tut, tut, tut, 'New York Review of Books' (11 October 1979), pp. 19-26, 31-2.

GREEN, Robert W. (ed.), 'Protestantism, Capitalism & Social Science: the Weber Thesis Controversy' (Lexington, Mass.: D.C. Heath, 1959).

GREIMAS, A.J., The interaction of semiotic constraints, 'Yale French Studies', no. 41 (Spring 1968), pp. 86-105.

HABERER, Joseph, 'Politics and the Community of Science' (NY: Van Nostrand Reinhold, 1969).

HABERMAS, Jurgen, Towards a theory of communicative competence, in 'Recent Sociology, No. 2', edited by H.P. Dreitzel (NY: Macmillan, 1970).

HABERMAS, Jurgen, 'Toward a Rational Society' (London: Heinemann, 1971).

HABERMAS, Jurgen, 'Legitimation Crisis' (Boston: Beacon Press, 1975).

HABERMAS, Jurgen, Aspects of the rationality of action, in 'Rationality Today', edited by Theodore Geraets '(Ottawa: University of Ottawa Press, 1979), pp. 185-212.

HABERMAS, Jurgen, 'Communication and the Evolution of Society' (Boston: Beacon Press, 1979).

HARRÉ, Rom, and MADDEN, E.H., 'Causal Powers' (Oxford: Basil Blackwell, 1975).

HARVEY, Donald, 'Limits to Capital' (Chicago: University of Chicago Press, 1983).

HAYEK, Frederick, 'The Counterrevolution of Science' (Chicago: Free Press, 1955).

HEGEL, G.W.F., 'The Science of Logic' (London: George Allen & Unwin, 1929).

HEGEL, G.W.F., 'The Phenomenology of Mind', translated with an Introduction and notes by J.B. Baillie (NY: Harper & Row, 1967).

HEGEL, G.W.F., 'The Philosophy of Right', translated with notes by T.M. Knox (London: Oxford University Press, 1967).

HELLEINER, G.K. (ed.), 'A World Divided' (Cambridge: Cambridge University Press, 1976).

HENDERSON, L.J., 'Pareto's General Sociology' (Cambridge, Mass.: Harvard University Press, 1935).

HENDERSON, L.J., 'The Fitness of the Environment' (Boston: Beacon Press, 1958).

HESSE, Mary, 'Models and Analogies in Science' (Indianapolis: University of Notre Dame Press, 1966).

HICKS, John, 'A Theory of Economic History' (Oxford: Clarendon Press, 1969).

HODSON, H.V., 'The Diseconomics of Growth' (London: Ballantine, 1972).

HOLM, Hans-Henrik, and RUDENG, Erik (eds), 'Social Science, For What?' (Oslo: Universitets Forlaget, 1980).

HORKHEIMER, Max, 'Critical Theory' (NY: Herder & Herder, 1972).

HORKHEIMER, Max, 'The Eclipse of Reason' (NY: Seabury Press, 1973).

HORKHEIMER, Max, and ADORNO, Theodor W., 'The Dialectic of Enlightenment' (NY: Herder & Herder, 1972).

HOROWITZ, I.L., 'Professing Sociology' (Chicago: Aldine Press, 1968).

HOROWITZ, I.L., The new fundamentalism, 'Transaction: Social Science & Modern Society', vol. 20, no. 1 (November/December 1982), pp. 40-7.

HORTON, Robin, The dehumanization of alienation and anomie, 'British Journal of Sociology', vol. 15 (1964), pp. 283-300.

ILCHMAN, Warren F., and UPHOFF, Norman Thomas, 'The Political Economy of Change' (Berkeley, Cal.: University of California Press, 1969).

ILLICH, Ivan, 'Gender' (NY: Pantheon, 1982).

JACOBS, Jane, 'The Economy of Cities' (NY: Random House, 1969).

JAMESON, Frederic, The vanishing mediator: narrative structure in Max Weber, 'New German Critique', vol. 1 (1973), pp. 52-89.

JANIK, Allan, and TOULMIN, Stephen, 'Wittgenstein's Vienna' (NY: Simon & Schuster, 1973).

JAY, Martin, The Frankfurt critique of Mannheim, 'Telos', no. 20 (Summer 1974), pp. 72-89.

JAYNES, Julian, 'The Origin of Consciousness in the Breakdown of the Bicameral Mind' (Princeton, NJ: Princeton University Press, 1976).

JOHNSTON, William, 'The Austrian Mind: An Intellectual and Social History, 1848-1938' (Berkeley, Cal.: University of California Press, 1972).

KAUFMANN, Felix, 'The Methodology of the Social Sciences' (NY: Oxford University Press, 1944).

KEYT, David, Wittgenstein's notion of an object, 'Philosophical Quarterly', vol. 13 (January 1963), pp. 13-25.

KLUCKHOHN, Clyde, 'Culture and Behaviour' (NY: Free Press, 1962).

KMICA, Jerzy, and NOWAK, Leszek, The rationality assumption in human sciences, 'Polish Sociological Bulletin', no. 1 (1970), pp. 43-70.

KNIGHT, Everett, 'The Objective Society' (NY: George Braziller, 1959).

KOESTLER, Arthur, 'The Act of Creation' (London: Hutchinson, 1969).

KOLKO, Gabriel, A critique of Max Weber's philosophy of history, 'Ethics', vol. 70, no. 1 (October 1959), pp. 21-36.

KOSIK, Karel, 'Dialectics of the Concrete' (Dordrecht: D. Reidel, 1976).

KOTARBINSKI, Tadeusz, 'Praxiology' (Oxford: Pergamon Press, 1965).

KROEBER, Alfred, 'Configurations of Culture Growth' (Berkeley, Cal.: University of California Press, 1944).

KROEBER, Alfred, and KLUCKHOHN, Clyde, 'Culture: An Inventory of Meanings' (NY: Vintage, 1965).

KUHN, Thomas, 'The Structure of Scientific Revolutions', 2nd edition (Chicago: University of Chicago Press, 1970).

KUMAR, Krishan, Revolution and industrial society, 'Sociology', vol. 10, no. 2 (May 1976), pp. 245-69.

KUMAR, Krishan, 'Prophecy and Progress' (Harmondsworth: Penguin, 1978).

LEISS, William, 'The Domination of Nature' (Boston: Beacon Press, 1974).

LERNER, Daniel, 'The Passing of Traditional Society' (Glencoe, Ill.: Free Press, 1958).

LEVI, Albert W., Wittgenstein as dialectician, 'Journal of Philosophy', vol. 61 (13 February 1964), pp. 127-39.

LEVY, Marion, 'Modernization: Latecomers and Survivors' (NY: Basic Books, 1972).

LINDBLOM, Charles, 'Politics and Markets' (NY: Basic Books, 1977).

LINDBLOM, Charles, and COHEN, David K,, 'Usable Knowledge, Social Science and Social Problem-Solving' (New Haven: Yale University Press, 1979).

LOEWITH, Karl, Weber's interpretation of the bourgeois-capitalistic world in terms of the guiding principle of rationalization, in 'Max Weber', edited by Dennis Wrong (Englewood Cliffs, NJ: Prentice Hall, 1970).

LOPEZ, Robert, 'The Commercial Revolutions of the Middle Ages, 950-1350' (NY: Cambridge University Press, 1976).

LYND, Robert S., 'Knowledge for What? The Place of Social Science in American Culture' (Princeton: Princeton University Press, 1939).

MCGUINNESS, B.F., The mysticism of the Tractatus, 'Philosophical Review', vol. 75 (July 1966), pp. 305-28.

MCHUGH, Peter, and BLUM, Alan, The social ascription of motives, 'American Sociological Review', vol. 36 (1971), pp. 98-109.

MCHUGH, Peter, RAFFEL, Stanley, FOSS, Daniel, and BLUM, Alan, 'On the Beginning of Social Inquiry' (London: Routledge & Kegan Paul, 1974).

MACKIE, J.L., 'The Cement of the Universe: A Study of Causation' (Oxford: Clarendon Press, 1974).

MADGE, Charles, 'Society in the Mind' (London: Faber & Faber, 1964).

MALCOLM, Norman, 'Ludwig Wittgenstein: A Memoir with a Biographical Sketch by G.H. Von Wright' (London: Oxford, 1958).

MALCOLM, Norman, 'Knowledge and Certainty: Essays and Lectures' (Englewood Cliffs, NJ: Prentice Hall, 1963).

MANNHEIM, Karl, 'Ideology and Utopia' (NY: Harcourt, Brace, 1936).

MANNHEIM, Karl, 'Man and Society in an Age of Reconstruction' (London: Routledge & Kegan Paul, 1940).

MANSER, A.R., The end of philosophy: Marx and Wittgenstein, inaugural lecture, Southampton University, 1973.

MANSFIELD, Edwin, Technical change and the rate of imitation, 'Econometrica', vol. 29 (1961), pp. 741-6.

MANSFIELD, Edwin, 'Industrial Research and Technological Innovation'
(NY: W.W. Norton, 1964).
MANSFIELD, Edwin, 'The Economics of Technological Change' (NY: W.W.
Norton, 1968).
MARCH, James, and SIMON, Herbert, 'Organizations' (NY: Wiley, 1958).
MARCUSE, Herbert, 'One Dimensional Man' (Boston: Beacon Press, 1964).
MARCUSE, Herbert, 'Negations' (Boston: Beacon Press, 1968).
MARCUSE, Herbert, 'Studies in Critical Philosophy' (Boston: Beacon
Press, 1973).
MARNHAM, Patrick, Ahmed and the gamekeepers, 'Harpers' (January 1980),
pp. 58-67.
MARNHAM, Patrick, 'Fantastic Invasion' (London: Jonathan Cape, 1980).
MARX, Karl, 'Capital', 3 vols (Moscow: Foreign Languages Publishing
House, 1961).
MARX, Karl, 'Early Texts', translated and edited by David McClellan
(Oxford: Basil Blackwell, 1962).
MARX, Karl, 'The Poverty of Philosophy' (NY: International Publishers,
1963).
MARX, Karl, 'Economic & Philosophical Manuscripts', edited by Dirk Struik
(NY: International Publishers, 1964).
MARX, Karl, 'The Grundrisse', complete English edition, edited and trans-
lated by Martin Nicolaus (Harmondsworth: Penguin, 1973).
MARX, Karl, and ENGELS, Friedrich, 'Marx & Engels: Basic Writings on
Politics & Philosophy', edited by Lewis Feuer (Garden City, NY: Double-
day Anchor, 1959).
MARX, Karl, and ENGELS, Friedrich, 'The German Ideology' (London:
Lawrence & Wishart, 1965).
MAYO, Elton, 'The Human Problems of an Industrial Civilization' (Cam-
bridge, Mass.: Harvard Business School, 1933).
MERTON, Robert, Durkheim's division of labour in society, 'American Jour-
nal of Sociology', vol. 40 (1934-5), pp. 319-28.
MERTON, Robert, 'Social Theory and Social Structure', 2nd edition (NY:
Macmillan, 1957).
MERTON, Robert, The role set, 'British Journal of Sociology', vol. 18
(1957), pp. 106-20.
MIDGELY, Mary, 'Beast and Man: The Roots of Human Nature' (London:
Methuen, 1979).
MILLER, A.V., 'Hegel's Philosophy of Nature' (Oxford: Basil Blackwell,
1970).
MILLS, C. Wright, 'The Sociological Imagination' (NY: Grove Press, 1959).
MONOD, Jacques, 'Chance & Necessity' (London: Collins, 1972).
MOORE, Barrington, The society nobody wants, in 'The Critical Spirit',
edited by Kurt Wolff and Barrington Moore (Boston: Beacon Press,
1967), pp. 401-18.
MOORE, Barrington, 'Reflections on the Causes of Human Misery' (Boston:
Beacon Press, 1973).
NAYLOR, R.T., 'The History of Canadian Business', 2 vols (Toronto:
Lorimer, 1975).
NIETZSCHE, Friedrich, 'Beyond Good and Evil' (London: Allen & Unwin,
1967).
NIETZSCHE, Friedrich, 'Thus Spake Zarathustra' (London: Allen & Unwin,
1967).
NISBET, Robert, 'History of the Idea of Progress' (NY: Basic Books, 1980).
NOBLE, David, 'America by Design: Science, Technology and the Rise of
Corporate Capitalism' (NY: Oxford University Press, 1977).
NOVAK, Michael, Why Latin America is poor, 'Atlantic' (March
1982), pp. 66-75.
OGBURN, William F., 'Social Change' (Boston: Huebsch, 1922).
OGBURN, William F., 'Culture and Social Change' (Chicago: University of
Chicago Press, 1964).
OGDEN, C.K., and RICHARDS, I.A., 'The Meaning of Meaning' (London:
Routledge & Kegan Paul, 1960).

O'NEILL, John, 'Sociology as a Skin Trade' (London: Heinemann, 1972).
O'NEILL, John (ed.), 'Modes of Individualism and Collectivism' (London: Heinemann, 1973).
O'NEILL, John, Defamilization and the feminization of law in early and late capitalism, 'International Journal of Law and Psychiatry', vol. 5, nos 3/4 (1982), pp. 255-69.
PARSONS, Talcott, The place of ultimate values in sociological theory, 'International Journal of Ethics', vol. 45 (1934-5), pp. 282-316.
PARSONS, Talcott, 'The Structure of Social Action' (Chicago: Free Press, 1937).
PARSONS, Talcott, 'The Social System' (Chicago: Free Press, 1951).
PARSONS, Talcott, Evolutionary universals, 'American Sociological Review', vol. 29, no. 3 (June 1964), pp. 339-57.
PARSONS, Talcott, 'The Evolution of Societies' (Englewood Cliffs, NJ: Prentice Hall, 1966).
PERROW, Charles, A framework for the comparative analysis of organizations, 'American Sociological Review', vol. 32 (1967), pp. 194-208.
PERROW, Charles, 'Organizational Analysis: A Sociological View' (Belmont, Cal.: Wadsworth, 1970).
PERROW, Charles, 'Complex Organizations' (NY: McGraw Hill, 1972).
PIAGET, Jean, 'Insights and Illusions of Philosophy' (London: Routledge & Kegan Paul, 1972).
PIPES, Daniel, The curse of oil wealth, 'Atlantic' (July 1982), pp. 19-20, 22-5.
PODGORECKI, Adam, 'Practical Social Sciences' (London: Routledge & Kegan Paul, 1975).
POLANYI, Karl, 'The Great Transformation' (NY: Oxford University Press, 1964).
POPPER, Karl, 'The Poverty of Historicism' (London: Routledge & Kegan Paul, 1957).
POPPER, Karl, 'The Logic of Scientific Discovery' (London: Routledge & Kegan Paul, 1959).
POPPER, Karl, 'Conjectures and Refutations' (London: Routledge & Kegan Paul, 1963).
POPPER, Karl, 'Objective Knowledge' (London: Oxford University Press, 1972).
POPPER, Karl, 'Unended Quest' (La Salle, Illinois: Open Court, 1976).
POPPER, Karl, and ECCLES, J.C., 'The Self and Its Brain' (Berlin and NY: Springer International, 1977).
RAFFEL, Stanley, 'Matters of Fact' (London: Routledge & Kegan Paul, 1979).
RAVETZ, J.R., 'Scientific Knowledge and Its Social Problems' (NY: Oxford University Press, 1973).
RAY, L.J., Critical theory and positivism: Popper and the Frankfurt School, 'Philosophy of the Social Sciences', vol. 9, no. 2 (June 1979), pp. 149-73.
RAY, L.J., Reply to Wilson, 'Philosophy of the Social Sciences', vol. 12, no. 4 (December 1982), pp. 415-18.
REX, John, 'Sociology and the Demystification of the Modern World' (London: Routledge & Kegan Paul, 1973).
ROBERTS, John K., Expressive aspects of technological development, 'Philosophy of the Social Sciences', vol. 1, no. 3 (September 1971), pp. 207-19.
ROSEN, Stanley, 'Nihilism' (New Haven: Yale University Press, 1969).
ROSEN, Stanley, 'G.W.F. Hegel: The Science of Wisdom' (New Haven: Yale University Press, 1974).
ROSENBERG, Nathan, 'Perspectives on Technology' (Cambridge: Cambridge University Press, 1976).
RUDOLPH, L., and RUDOLPH, S., 'The Modernity of Tradition' (Chicago: University of Chicago Press, 1967).
RULE, James B., 'Insight and Social Betterment' (NY: Oxford University Press, 1978).

RUNCIMAN, W.G., 'A Critique of Max Weber's Philosophy of Social Science' (Cambridge: Cambridge University Press, 1972).

SALOMON, Albert, 'The Tyranny of Progress: Reflections on the Origins of Sociology' (NY: Noonday Press, 1955).

SAMPSON, Ronald V., 'Progress in the Age of Reason' (London: Heinemann, 1956).

SCHELLING, Thomas, On the ecology of micromotives, 'The Public Interest', no. 25 (Fall 1971), pp. 59-98.

SCHLUCHTER, Wolfgang, 'The Rise of Western Rationalism: Max Weber's Developmental History', translated with an Introduction by Gunther Roth (Berkeley, Cal.: University of California Press, 1981).

SCHMIDT, Alfred, 'The Concept of Nature in Marx' (London: New Left Books, 1971).

SCHON, Donald, 'The Displacement of Concepts' (London: Tavistock, 1963).

SCHON, Donald, 'Technology and Change' (NY: Delta, 1967).

SCHON, Donald, 'The Stable State' (NY: W.W. Norton, 1973).

SCHOPENHAUER, Arthur, 'The World as Will and Representation', 2 vols (NY: Macmillan, 1968).

SCHORSKE, Carl E., 'Fin-De-Siecle Vienna: Politics and Culture' (NY: Random House Vintage, 1981).

SCHUMPETER, Joseph, 'The Theory of Economic Development' (Cambridge, Mass.: Harvard Economic Studies, 1934).

SCHUMPETER, Joseph, 'Business Cycles - A Theoretical, Historical, and Statistical Analysis of the Capitalist Process' (NY: McGraw Hill, 1939).

SCHUMPETER, Joseph, 'Capitalism, Socialism and Democracy' (NY: Harper & Row, 1942).

SCHUTZ, Alfred, 'Collected Papers', vols I-III (The Hague: Martinus Nijhoff, 1962, 1964, 1967).

SCHUTZ, Alfred, 'Phenomenology of the Social World' (Evanston, Illinois: Northwestern University Press, 1967).

SCIENCE COUNCIL OF CANADA, Report no. 15, October 1971.

SCIENCE COUNCIL OF CANADA, Special Study no. 22, December 1971.

SCIENCE COUNCIL OF CANADA, Special Study no. 23, October 1972.

SCOTT, John Findlay, 'The Internalization of Norms' (Englewood Cliffs, NJ: Prentice Hall, 1973).

SCOTT, Robert A., and SHORE, Arnold R., 'Why Sociology Does Not Apply' (NY: Elsevier, 1979).

SHEEHY, Gail, 'Passages' (NY: Knopf, 1976).

SHILS, Edward, Some remarks on 'The Theory of Social and Economic Organization', 'Economica' (February 1948), pp. 36-50.

SHILS, Edward, 'Tradition' (Chicago: University of Chicago Press, 1983).

SIMMEL, George, 'The Problems of the Philosophy of History', translated and edited by Guy Oakes (NY: Free Press, 1977).

SKLAIR, Leslie, 'The Sociology of Progress' (London: Paladin, 1971).

SMITH, Adam, 'The Theory of Moral Sentiments' (NY: Augustus Kelley, 1966).

SPENGLER, Oswald, 'The Decline of the West' (NY: Alfred Knopf, 1970).

SPRANGER, Edward, 'Lebensformen', translated by P.J. Pigors as 'Types of Men' (NY: Hafner, 1928).

STERN, Fritz, 'The Politics of Cultural Despair' (Berkeley, Cal.: University of California Press, 1961).

TARDE, Gabriel, 'La Logique sociale' (Paris: F. Alcan, 1895).

TARDE, Gabriel, 'L'Opposition universelle' (Paris: F. Alcan, 1897).

TARDE, Gabriel, 'Les Lois sociale' (Paris: F. Alcan, 1899).

TARDE, Gabriel, 'Laws of Imitation' (NY: Henry Holt, 1903).

TAYLOR, Alastair, The computer and the liberal: our ecological dilemma, 'Queens Quarterly' (Autumn 1972), pp. 289-300.

THOMPSON, James, 'Organizations in Action' (NY: McGraw Hill, 1968).

THOMPSON, Victor, 'Modern Organizations' (NY: Alfred Knopf, 1961).

THOMPSON, Victor, 'Bureaucracy and Innovation' (University, Alabama: University of Alabama Press, 1968).

TIGER, Lionel, and FOX, Robin, 'The Imperial Animal' (NY: Basic Books, 1973).

TOFFLER, Alvin, 'Future Shock' (NY: Ballantine Books, 1970).
TONNIES, Ferdinand, 'Community and Society' (NY: Harper & Row, 1963).
TUCKER, William, Is nature too good for us?, 'Harpers' (March 1972), pp. 27-35.
VEBLEN, Thorstein, 'The Theory of Business Enterprise' (Boston: Huebsch, 1904).
VEBLEN, Thorstein, The place of science in modern civilization, 'American Journal of Sociology', vol. 11 (1906), pp. 585-609.
VEBLEN, Thorstein, 'The Instinct of Workmanship' (Boston: Huebsch, 1914).
VEBLEN, Thorstein, 'The Engineers and the Price System' (Boston: Huebsch, 1921).
VICO, Giambattista, 'The New Science' (Ithaca, NY: Cornell University Press, 1970).
VON WRIGHT, G.H., 'Explanation and Understanding' (Ithaca, NY: Cornell University Press, 1972).
VON WRIGHT, G.H., 'Causality and Determinism' (NY: Columbia University Press, 1974).
WAGAR, W. Warren, 'Good Tidings' (Bloomington: Indiana University Press, 1972).
WALLACE, Anthony C.F., 'The Social Context of Innovation' (Princeton: Princeton University Press, 1982).
WALLERSTEIN, Immanuel, 'The Modern World System' (NY: Academic Press, 1974).
WALLERSTEIN, Immanuel, 'World Systems, 1600-1900' (NY: Academic Press, 1977).
WALLERSTEIN, Immanuel, 'The Capitalist World Economy: Essays' (NY: Cambridge University Press, 1979).
WEBER, Alfred, 'Farewell to European History' (London: Kegan Paul, Trench, Trubner, 1947).
WEBER, Max, 'From Max Weber: Essays in Sociology', edited by Hans Gerth and C. Wright Mills (NY: Oxford University Press, 1946).
WEBER, Max, 'Theory of Social and Economic Organization' (Chicago: Free Press, 1947).
WEBER, Max, 'Methodology of the Social Sciences', edited by E. Shils and H. Finch (Chicago: Free Press, 1949).
WEBER, Max, 'The Protestant Ethic and the Spirit of Capitalism' (NY: Scribners, 1952).
WEBER, Max, 'Law in Economy and Society' (Cambridge, Mass.: Harvard University Press, 1954).
WEBER, Max, 'The Sociology of Religion' (Boston: Beacon Press, 1964).
WENT, F.W., The size of man, 'American Scientist', vol. 56, no. 4 (Winter 1968), pp. 400-13.
WHITE, Lynn, 'Medieval Technology and Social Change' (London: Oxford University Press, 1964).
WHYTE, William H., 'The Organization Man' (Garden City, NY: Doubleday, 1956).
WILENSKY, Harold, 'Organizational Intelligence' (NY: Basic Books, 1967).
WILES, Peter, The necessity and impossibility of political economy, 'History and Theory', vol. 11 (1972), pp. 3-14.
WILSON, Bryan (ed.), 'Rationality' (Oxford: Basil Blackwell, 1970).
WILSON, James Q., Innovation in organization: notes toward a theory, in 'Approaches to Organizational Design', edited by James Thompson (NY: John Wiley, 1966), pp. 194-218.
WILSON, H.T., The dismal science of organization reconsidered, 'Canadian Public Administration', vol. 14, no. 1 (Spring 1971), pp. 82-99.
WILSON, H.T., Max Weber's pessimism, 'International Journal of Contemporary Sociology', vol. 8 (April 1971), pp. 183-8.
WILSON, H.T., Rationality and decision in administrative science, 'Canadian Journal of Political Science', vol. 6, no. 3 (June 1973), pp. 271-94.
WILSON, H.T., The sociology of apocalypse, 'Human Context', vol. 7, no. 3 (Autumn 1975), pp. 474-94.

WILSON, H.T., Reading Max Weber: the limits of sociology, 'Sociology', vol. 10, no. 2 (May 1976), pp. 297-315.

WILSON, H.T., Science, critique and criticism: the 'open society' revisited, in 'On Critical Theory', edited by John O'Neill (NY: Seabury Press, 1976), pp. 205-30.

WILSON, H.T., 'The American Ideology: Science, Technology and Organization as Modes of Rationality in Advanced Industrial Societies' (London: Routledge & Kegan Paul, 1977).

WILSON, H.T., Attitudes toward science: Canadian and American scientists, 'International Journal of Comparative Sociology', vol. 18, nos 1 and 2 (March/June 1977), pp. 154-75, reprinted in 'Cross National Perspectives: United States & Canada', edited by Robert Presthus (Leiden: E.I. Brill, 1977).

WILSON, H.T., The poverty of sociology: 'society' as concept and object in sociological theory, 'Philosophy of the Social Sciences', vol. 8, no. 1 (March 1978), pp. 187-204.

WILSON, H.T., The meaning and significance of 'empirical method' for the critical theory of society, 'Canadian Journal of Political and Social Theory', vol. 3, no. 3 (Fall 1979), pp. 57-68.

WILSON, H.T., Innovation: the practical uses of theory, in 'Social Change, Innovation & Politics in East Asia', edited by Y.S. Yim, H.T. Wilson and R.W. Wilson (Hong Kong: Asian Research Service, 1980), pp. 9-29.

WILSON, H.T., The problem of discretion in three languages, research document, Judiciary Project, University of Paris, Paris, France (March 1980).

WILSON, H.T., Functional rationality and 'sense of function': the case of an ideological distortion, in 'International Yearbook of Organization Studies - 1980', edited by David Dunkerly and Graeme Salaman (London: Routledge & Kegan Paul, 1981), pp. 37-61.

WILSON, H.T., Response to Ray I and II, 'Philosophy of the Social Sciences', vol. 11, no. 1 (March 1981), pp. 45-8, and vol. 13, no. 1 (March 1983), pp. 63-5.

WILSON, H.T., Value: on the possibility of a convergence between economic and non-economic decision-making, in 'Management Under Differing Value Systems', edited by G. Dlugos and K. Weiermair (Berlin & New York: Walter de Gruyter, 1981), pp. 37-71.

WILSON, H.T., Science, technology and innovation: the role of common-sense capacities, 'Methodology and Science', vol. 15, no. 3 (1982), pp. 167-200.

WILSON, H.T., Technocracy and late capitalist society: reflections on the problem of rationality and social organization, in 'The State, Class, and the Recession', edited by Steward Clegg, Geoff Dow and Paul Boreham (London: Croom Helm, 1983), pp. 152-238.

WILSON, H.T., Anti-method as a counter-structure in social research operations, in 'Beyond Method: A Study of Social Research Strategies', edited by Gareth Morgan (Los Angeles: Sage Publications, 1983), pp. 247-59.

WILSON, H.T., Technology and/or/as the future (review essay), 'Philosophy of the Social Sciences' (forthcoming).

WILSON, H.T., Elites, meritocracy and technocracy: some implications for representation and political leadership, to appear in 'Political Leadership in Canada', edited by Hector Massey (forthcoming).

WILSON, H.T., Notes on the achievement of communicative behaviour and related difficulties, 'Dialectical Anthropology' (forthcoming).

WILSON, H.T., 'Political Management: Redefining the Public Sphere' (Berlin & New York: Walter de Gruyter, 1984).

WILSON, H.T., Critical theory's critique of social science, 'History of European Ideas' (forthcoming).

WILSON, H.T., Capitalism, science and the possibility of political economy (unpublished paper).

WILSON, H.T., Knowledge and Totality: A Critical Analysis of the Causal Principle in Science and Life (unpublished manuscript).

WILSON, H.T., The significance of 'instrumental reason' for the critical
    theory of society (unpublished paper).
WINCH, Peter, Heuristic and empirical typologies, 'American Sociological
    Review', vol. 12 (February 1947), pp. 68-75.
WINCH, Peter, 'The Idea of a Social Science' (London: Routledge & Kegan
    Paul, 1958).
WISDOM, J.O., Criteria for causal determination and functional relationship,
    'Mind', vol. 54 (1945), pp. 323-41.
WISDOM, J.O., The need for corroboration, 'Technology and Culture',
    vol. 7 (1966), pp. 367-70.
WITTGENSTEIN, Ludwig, 'Philosophical Investigations' (NY: Macmillan,
    1953).
WITTGENSTEIN, Ludwig, 'Tractatus Logico-Philosophicus', new translation
    by D.F. Pears and B.F.McGuinness, incorporating Bertrand Russell's
    1921 introduction to the first English edition (London: Routledge & Kegan
    Paul, 1961).
WITTGENSTEIN, Ludwig, Lecture on ethics, 'Philosophical Review', vol. 74
    (January 1965), pp. 3-12, 12-26.
WITTGENSTEIN, Ludwig, 'Remarks on the Foundations of Mathematics'
    (Cambridge, Mass.: MIT Press, 1967).
WITTGENSTEIN, Ludwig, Remarks on Frazer's 'Golden Bough', 'The Human
    World', vol. 3 (1971), pp. 18-41, originally published in German in
    'Synthese', vol. 17 (1967), pp. 233-53.
WITTGENSTEIN, Ludwig, 'Lectures and Conversations on Aesthetics, Psy-
    chology & Religious Belief' (Berkeley, Cal.: University of California
    Press, 1972).
WITTGENSTEIN, Ludwig, 'On Certainty' (Oxford: Basil Blackwell, 1977).
WITTGENSTEIN, Ludwig, 'On Colour' (Oxford: Basil Blackwell, 1977).
WOLIN, Sheldon, 'Politics and Vision' (Boston: Little, Brown, 1960).
WRONG, Dennis, The over-socialized conception of man in modern sociology,
    'Psychoanalysis and the Psychoanalytic Review', vol. 49, no. 2 (Summer
    1962), pp. 53-69.
WRONG, Dennis (ed.), 'Max Weber' (Englewood Cliffs, NJ: Prentice Hall,
    1970).
YOUNG, Michael, 'The Rise of the Meritocracy, 1858-2033' (Harmondsworth:
    Penguin, 1958).
ZEMACH, Eddy, Wittgenstein's philosophy of the mystical, 'Review of Meta-
    physics', vol. 18 (1964-5), pp. 38-57.
ZIJDERVELD, Anton, 'The Abstract Society' (Garden City, NY: Doubleday,
    1970).
ZINKERNAGEL, Peter, 'Conditions for Description' (London: Routledge &
    Kegan Paul, 1962).
ZNANIECKI, Florian, 'The Social Role of the Man of Knowledge' (NY:
    Columbia University Press, 1940).
ZWEIG, Paul, Naipaul's losers, 'Harpers' (January 1980), pp. 69-72.

NAME INDEX

Adorno, T.W., 25, 200
Arendt, H., 23, 74, 109
Aristotle, 73-6

Bacon, F., 21, 45, 201-6
Barnett, H., 37, 55-60, 70, 98,
  106, 144, 147, 157, 164, 169, 189,
  201
Beattie, J.H.M., 89
Bell, D., 69
Bendix, R., 82
Benjamin, W., 200
Bennett, J., 132
Bierstedt, R., 15-17, 19
Blum, A.F., 138
Blumer, H., 20, 28-9
Bourdieu, P., 78-80, 89, 103, 144,
  157, 189, 191
Brown, G.S., 122, 210

Collingwood, R.G., 199
Crozier, M., 162-3

Diesing, P., 125
Drury, M.O'C., 126, 187
Durkheim, E., 40-4, 46-9, 51-2,
  56, 70, 77, 104, 106, 116, 121,
  125, 141, 143, 148-9, 161, 165-6,
  173-4, 178, 188-9, 193-4, 207

Eaton, R., 17
Eisenstadt, S., 171
Ellul, J., 61, 65, 70, 80, 84, 104,
  157
Engels, F., 32-3
Engelmann, P., 202

Fallding, H., 29
Feuerbach, L., 134
Fichte, J., 134
Ficker, L., 198
Frazer, J.G., 146-58, 180-2, 184,
  194, 199-201, 205, 207
Freud, S., 140, 141, 202-3

Galbraith, J.K., 150, 156, 160
Gardner, J., 7, 105
Gilfillan, S.C., 151-2, 154, 156, 194
Goddard, D., 140, 142, 193
Goldthorpe, J., 69, 133

Gonseth, F., 94
Greimas, A.J., 113, 139, 192

Habermas, J., 73, 172, 195
Hegel, G.W.F., 10, 22, 32, 102,
  134-5, 193
Henderson, L.J., 70
Heraclitus, 130, 132
Hesse, M., 31
Horton, R., 89, 144
Hume, P., 103

Illich, I., 215

Jameson, F., 112, 113, 193

Kahn, H., 69
Kant, I., 23, 31, 73, 107, 114
Kerr, C., 69
Koestler, A., 31
Kroeber, A., 99

Lerner, D., 139-40
Levy, M., 57, 99

Malcolm, N., 181
Mannheim, K., 31, 70, 110, 125,
  127-8, 155, 157, 163, 165, 193-5,
  208
Marcuse, H., 23, 74-5, 85, 115,
  195
Marx, K., 30-3, 67, 92, 97, 102,
  108, 134-5, 182-3, 193
Mayo, E., 46
Merton, R., 12

Nietzsche, F., 2, 99, 173
Novalis (pseudonym), 134

Ogburn, W.F., 156
Ogden, C.K., 197
O'Neill, J., 215

Parsons, T., 69, 113, 141, 201
Perrow, C., 73, 132
Plato, 74, 76
Popper, K., 10-13, 22, 24, 32, 45,
  59, 69, 130, 199, 201, 206

Richards, I.A., 197

SUBJECT INDEX

Archimedean point, 87

Bureaucracy, 23, 195; and innovation, 38, 39, 150, 151; and management, 38; and meritocracy, 150; and technocracy, 38; and the social sciences, 38

Capitalism: link between science, technology and, 206; multinational corporate, 65; solidification of, 161

Civilization: and culture, 36, 99; as a culture, 39, 103, 117, 123, 145, 189, 198, 200, 205, 207; relation to individualism, 85; role of innovation in, 5, 6

Common human pattern: and change and difference, 174, 205; emphasis upon needed today, 118; and 'other cultures', 120; as the proper 'sense' of things, 185, 200; and rationality and reason, 120; 'rationality', as suppression of, 173; as recipient of human actions, 179; repudiation of through explanations, 183

Concepts: dichotomization and, 107; what their formulation presupposes, 93; innovation as a case in point, 5, 19; and objects, 24-9, 188; and real and possible worlds, 20; and reduction to definitions, 18-20, 84; and speech and meaning, 21; universalistic character of, 4, 19, 20-4, 122, 187-8

Crisis: as danger and opportunity, 6, 187; and innovation and innovativeness, 7, 8, 128, 208; as a problem and the basis for its resolution, 45, 88, 126; and unanticipated consequences, 6

Culture: adaptation in its relation to, 101; as affirmed by the commitment to progress, 60-1; as an approach to innovation, 52-9, 98-9; as the basis of innovation, 98; and civilization, 36, 56, 62, 99, 103, 178; and familiarity and difference, 53-6; and formal connectedness versus explanation, 180-1; as a form of life for Wittgenstein, 180-5; and improvisation, 103; and industrial society as the 'unit of analysis', 53, 149; as a property of all collective forms, 63, 70; religious and magical practices in, 149

Definitions: as descriptions, 14, 16, 18; and dialectics, 34; nominal and real, 15-20, 28; operational, 14, 22, 28; as protocols, 16, 17; and reality, 163, 34

Description: and addressing, 8-11; as applied to innovation, 101; and the complexity of the world, 26; and definition, 9, 34; and dialectics, 34; and explanation, 8, 9; function of, 11; and what grounds it, 182-3; and knowledge, 28; limits of, relative to life, 89; and objects and objectivity, 25; the phenomenon of, 13, 117; and 'states of affairs', 13; technical phenomenon as, 65

Development, 6

Dialectics: and critical thought, 28, 97; and development hypotheses, 203; its duty relative to disciplined observation, 87; as glimpse and grasp, 94, 97; and Marx, 97, 134-5; and materialism, 25, 35, 97, 108, 134; as objective property of understanding, 78, 94, 97, 122-3, 134; and a partial reflexivity, 90; its resistance to detopicalization, 122, 123; as superior to reductionism, 81; as the vehicle for mobilizing dichotomies, 89, 100; and Weber, 83-5; and Wittgenstein, 30, 108

Dichotomies, 14, 26, 30, 88-97; their central role in Weber's sociology, 112-16; those central in 'our' culture, 93; what is common and what is historically specific about, 94, 95, 100; and concept formation, 107; empiricization of, 91, 92, 94, 97,

as the whole or the world, 135, 136

Objectivity: and dialectics, 25, 81, 137, 202; Marx's understanding of, 92, 137; its preference for a focus on the common human pattern, 180; 'rational domination' and, 169; as related to reduction, 80, 81; and science, 96, 137; and social science as a creature of society, 202, 205; sociology's commitment to a false standard of, 27, 28, 143, 144; and the subject-object distinction, 25; and value, 173; Weber and, 116, 169, 173

Observation function: and dichotomization, 96; and disciplined observation, 77, 80, 87, 132, 137, 140, 205; its empiricization, 101; as increasingly autonomous, 80; interdependence with theory and practice, 91, 107, 204; legitimate and illegitimate types of, 107; as 'natural' and indispensible, 87, 103; and nature, 135, 136; relation to technical bias, 6, 102, 106; and a technicized practice, 90, 199, 205; unhinged and disembodied, 6, 82, 87-92, 97, 100, 101, 106, 111, 112, 116, 118, 120, 132, 137, 143, 191, 194, 196-9, 201, 202, 204, 105, 208

Observer: in anthropology, 79; autonomy of, 80; and behaviour, 44-8; and disciplined observation, 137; and the empirical convention, 90, 132; hidebound to 'rationalistic bias', 148; as an object of theory, 77; in own versus other cultures, 89, 90, 194; and practice, 82, 83, 88; rationality as a category of, 143, 144; religion as an 'error' for, 147; as a role, 77, 78, 107; stranger and outsider as, 79, 84, 89; and tradition and practice, 76; Weber as, 116

Practice, 26, 72-88, 107, 201; and commonsense rationality and knowledge, 72, 73; impact of social science on, 45; lack of instrumentalism in religious forms of, 148, 201, 202; as an observer based category, 76, 79, 87, 93, 103; pre-technicized and technicized form of, 81, 105; and the relation between ethical talk and ethical action, 202, 203; in rela-

tion to ethics and politics, 73-6; in relation to improvisation, 72, 73; in relation to theory, 45, 73-6, 80, 90; as a response to anticipatable problems, 73; technicization of, 80-8, 190, 191, 206; as traditional behaviour, 72, 76; and values, 82, 83; versus *praxis*, 73

'Primitive' people: and the common human pattern, 121; and complexity and change, 142, 143; and the concept of the primitive, 140-3, 193; and the concept of progress, 141; our differences from, 184, 185, 201, 202; and differentiation and division of labour, 141, 142; Durkheim on, 141-3; and the familiar, 140-1; gift-giving among, 78; and institutionalization, 174, 185; as an observer's category, 140, 183, 207; parallels on the matter of innovation, 37; participation versus exclusion from a human world, 183; as the prehistory of man, 140, 141; relevance of distinctions between science, religion and magic and, 183, 200, 201; as the simplicity available to members, 143

Progress: and civilization, 1, 145; as a code word, 187; distinction among meanings of, 81-2; and the drive to clarity in Wittgenstein, 205; as a form of life, 1, 70, 145, 151, 166, 168, 204, 208; and history, 208; as ideology, 68, 199; and individualism, 165; and innovation, 1, 4, 51, 58, 98, 132; in the organizational field, 162, 163; and the rationalization process, 116, 162, 165, 166, 201; and technique and technology, 56-68, 60, 193, 206; and tradition, 140; Weber's 3 meanings of, 165-7, 171-3, 177, 178

Rationality, 107-44, 191-4; as an analytical category, 118; and the common human pattern, 120; and culture and civilization, 109, 119, 145, 148; and domination, 149; and ethnocentrism, 118, 119; functional and substantial, 125, 127, 155; and history in Weber, 84; and innovation, 116-33, 143-5, 193; instrumental notion of, 207, 208; and judgment, 127; modes of, 102; and nature, 92, 119; and the observer and the observation function, 110; as a

Technology: and capitalism, 102;
as dependent on capital allocation
decisions, 62, 86, 116; and
determinism, 86; as knowledge
and process, 33, 62, 66, 162;
its lack of objectivity, 33, 66,
102, 115; as phenomenon, 61,
65, 66; and progress, 56, 60;
and rationality, 57, 82, 92; and
science, 38, 85
Theory, 21, 26; its indispensability
to practice, 88, 89; and practice,
76-8, 80; as reflection, 54, 55,
203; reformulated as testable,
falsifiable hypotheses, 21, 24,
80, 137, 202; its structural
'decomposition', 21, 137, 202;
and the theorist, 112
Third World, 56, 59, 60-1, 72, 189,
190, 205; and adaptation, 101;
compared to medieval Europe as
the pre-modern 'unit of analysis',
65; compared to Western (Northern) economic development, 61-4;
development relations between
countries in, 64; example of gift
giving in, 78; industrial development of, and consequences, 63,
64, 102, 105; and innovation,
98, 99, 103; and 'nature' as a
'Northern' concept, 119; as
object of disciplined observation,
91; and tradition, 100

Tradition, 100, 137-40, 193, 194,
196; as a concept for the disciplined observer, 140, 207; as a
concept in the social sciences,
138-40; and culture and civilization, 36, 139; as the 'familiar',
143; and innovation, 5, 99-101;
and the non-rational and sentimental, 138, 139; oral and written, 21; rationalization versus
institutionalization and, 139; and
reason and the rational, 36, 138-
40; in its relation to practice,
75, 76, 140; for Weber, 99, 138-
40, 176

Whole, the, and the concrete and
abstract, 21, 22, 24, 30, 82
'World', the, 24, 25, 30, 197; and
dichotomies, 83; difference
between human and animal, 183,
184; and what exists, 9; and
what can be explained, 2; and
'facts of life', 16; and 'forms of
life', 183, 198; and life, 2, 3;
and the nameable and describable,
2, 15, 81, 182; observer's role
in reproduction of, 90; and the
sayable and unsayable, 2; and
states of affairs, 81, 198; and
the subject as a limit, 2, 3; and
the transvaluation of value, 2, 82
Worlds, 1, 2, 3, 10-12, 32